# HISTORY OF BANKING II

# HISTORY OF BANKING II

## 1844–1959

*Edited by* Duncan M. Ross

### VOLUME I

*Introduction*
*1844 and the Currency Controversy*

Routledge
Taylor & Francis Group
LONDON AND NEW YORK

First published 1998 by Pickering & Chatto (Publishers) Limited

Published 2016 by Routledge
2 Park Square, Milton Park, Abingdon, Oxon, OX14 4RN
605 Third Avenue, New York, NY 10017

*Routledge is an imprint of the Taylor & Francis Group, an informa business*



BRITISH LIBRARY CATALOGUING IN PUBLICATION DATA
History of Banking II, 1844 – 1959
1. Banks and banking – History – 19th century 2. Banks and banking – History – 20th century
I. Ross, Duncan M.
332.1'09

LIBRARY OF CONGRESS CATALOGING–IN–PUBLICATION DATA
History of Banking II, 1844 – 1959 / edited by Duncan M. Ross.
p. cm.
A collection of essays originally published between 1844 – 1959.
Includes bibliographical references and index.
Contents: v. 1. General introduction; 1844 and the currency controversy — v. 2. Competition and free banking — v. 3. Bank failures, commercial distress, and limited liability — v. 4. Banking statistics — v. 5. Banking principles — v. 6. Reserves and elasticity — v. 7. Clearing and deposits — v. 8. Banks and industry — v. 9. The emergence of the Federal Reserve System — v. 10. Central banking, interest rates, and monetary policy.
ISBN 1–85196–443–6 (set : alk. paper)
1. Banks and banking—History—19th century. 2. Banks and Banking—History—20th century. I. Ross, Duncan M., 1963– .
HG1571.H57 1998 98–9191
332. 1'09—dc21 CIP

*New material typeset by*
*Waveney Typesetters, Wymondham, Norfolk*

ISBN 978-1-13876-057-8 (hbk)

VOLUME I

# CONTENTS

## VOLUME II

# CONTENTS

## VOLUME III

# CONTENTS

## VOLUME IV

# CONTENTS

## VOLUME V

# CONTENTS

## VOLUME VI

# CONTENTS

## VOLUME VII

# CONTENTS

## VOLUME VIII

# CONTENTS

## VOLUME IX

# CONTENTS

## VOLUME X

# CONTENTS

# COPY TEXTS

The following extracts are reproduced in facsimile.

In order to fit texts comfortably to the pages of this edition, certain liberties have been taken with the format of the original: occasionally right-hand pages have become left-hand pages (and vice versa) and text from consecutive pages has been fitted onto a single page. Endnotes in this edition refer to Pickering & Chatto page and line numbers. Readers wishing to consult the passages in the original are referred to the headnotes which appear immediately before each text.

Texts are reproduced by kind permission and with the assistance of the University of London Library, the British Library Board, the British Library of Political and Economic Science, the UK Public Records Office, the London Library and the Library of Congress.

# INTRODUCTION

The chief aims of Sir Robert Peel's Bank Act of 1844 were to enshrine currency management in a set of rules, force the Bank of England to operate in a manner consistent with its position as a private banking institution, and establish an automatic relationship between the balance of payments position, the domestic economy and the money supply through the operation of the gold standard. The *Committee on the Working of the Monetary System* (Radcliffe Committee of 1959) had been established by the government two years earlier 'to enquire into the working of the monetary and credit system and to make recommendations'.[1] This was largely because the preceding decade had revealed that the Treasury and Bank of England had very little understanding of the ways in which their decisions and policies influenced the money supply or the state of the domestic economy, or how movements in the external balance of payments were transmitted to levels of internal demand and hence to the reserve position of the Bank itself. From a clearly articulated set of rules designed to simplify and systematise monetary operation, therefore, and one of the few occasions (at least until the advent of the Conservative governments of 1979–97) of which it could be said that theory rather than exigency clearly dictated policy in this sphere,[2] we see confusion, uncertainty and wholesale tinkering, part of which we may describe as demand management, in that it was assumed that these bodies had an obligation to make use of policy levers in order to meet their objectives, and some part of which we may less charitably refer to as ill-advised interference.

A number of issues and questions arise from this contrast. In the first place it is clear that it deals largely with what is now termed Central Banking, and so we are directed towards exploring the relationships between Central Banks, the operation of the banking system, and the domestic economy. Secondly, to the extent that the 1844 Act reflected the certainty of a particular school of economists, it disguised the ferocious debate which had preceded it, and which was to continue in the subsequent decades. Disagreement and uncertainty over the nature of the relationships being examined were, if anything, greater than in the twentieth century, by which time more of the fundamental principles of banking had been discovered. Thirdly, this contrast largely reflects the state of the debate in Britain. It is important to consider the extent to which these perspectives were shared by writers and commentators elsewhere, or whether differing institutional configurations were reflected in, or justified by, different theoretical or polemical positions. The fourth element of considerable importance in discussing the history and development of banking in this period is that from the mid-nineteenth to the mid-twentieth century, the nature of modern economies, and therefore of what banks were required to do – the very concept of what banking was – changed enormously.

## I: The Emergence of the 1844 Act

The monetary and banking history of Britain in the nineteenth century can be characterised as a recursive series of crises, reports and legislation. Furthermore, the same issues reappeared in each cycle of this process, and many of them, indeed, remain subject to debate at the end of the twentieth century.[3] The fundamental issue is whether banking is an industry like any other, and should therefore be governed by the principles of free entry and exit, competition and minimum state interference or whether, thanks to its vital importance as a guarantor of the circulation of money and credit, it should be protected, regulated and (at least partly) be provided with state monopolies and guarantees. Consideration of this dichotomy raises a number of further questions, however. In the first place, the sets of relationships between the money supply, the banking system and the price level – some of which can be settled by policy, others not – need to be clarified in order to make effective any monetary policy. Secondly, the question of whether and how monetary policy should be used as a tool to control domestic economic fluctuations with their consequent impact on the balance of payments and international reserves must be resolved at the same time as the question of note issue and convertibility. These were all considered at great length throughout the period under discussion, but while it is clear that significant advances in understanding have been made, it is much less clear that a widely accepted 'correct set' of principles for management of the monetary and banking system has emerged.

The first cycle of crisis and legislation in which we are interested happened in 1825–6. The boom of 1822–5 collapsed in a massive loss of confidence. The country banks were thought to have over-extended themselves, and both their depositors and note-holders demanded payment in either coin or Bank of England notes. The pressure on liquidity was short and intense; it spread to all financial institutions and was relieved only by the Bank of England's willingness to provide funds to the stricken discount houses and London bankers, thus averting the threat to the Bank's own notes. Collins has suggested that this crisis 'was to prove decisive in determining the course of banking developments in England'.[4] Crucially, it provided confirmation that the monetary institutions in that country – thanks to different legal and institutional environments, the Scottish and Irish banks were to a large extent insulated from the English – were capable of acting as a system, with its various components connected and integrated. Systemic crisis, therefore, rather than localised runs on individual banks, became the main threat to continued operation, and large and powerful houses could be affected by troubles in smaller banks. The response of the legislators was twofold; in the first place they looked to the Scottish and Irish systems and concluded that the greater stability was due in large measure to the existence of joint-stock banks. Secondly, they placed much of the blame for the loss of confidence in the circulating medium on the variety and complexity of the country banks' note issue. The Banking Co-Partnership Act of May 1826[5] therefore permitted the creation of Joint-Stock banks beyond a radius of sixty-five miles around London. This was an explicit attack on the monopoly position of the Bank of England, although the Bank's privileges were maintained within this region – the new banks' notes and bills were not payable within the metropolitan area, and they were forbidden from issuing short-dated and small denomination bills on their London agents. The verdict of Crick and Wadsworth on this Act is that 'It is doubtful whether this step, which represented so great a gain to the banking system as a whole, involved any comparable loss to the former holder of country-wide privilege.'[6] The Bank remained the dominant player in the financial markets, and this was underscored by a clause in the Act which gave it the explicit right to open branches, and therefore compete with other banks, in the provinces, while retaining its own monopoly in London.

In the subsequent decades, two parallel developments of the financial system need to be understood.[7] The first is the emergence and growth of the provincial joint-stock banks, who were able to raise larger amounts of share capital than the private banks which they gradually replaced. This larger share capital provided both a measure of stability and access to a larger pool of funds for lending and investing in their local economy. These institutions shared in and contributed to the general economic boom of the period, although some of their practices were far from what could be expected of prudent and soundly managed organisations, as the Secret Committee on Joint-Stock Banks of the 1830s noted. The second element of note in this period is the improving communications and the development of a more efficient inter-provincial network of agencies and discounting houses. Because the financial system was centred on intermediation of the London money markets, and because the Bank of England was the single largest institution in these markets, the Bank came to dominate the entire system through its holding of the largest reserves. The ease or difficulty of obtaining credit in the economy, therefore, was, by the late 1830s, fundamentally a question of the policy of the Bank of England.

This fact assumed considerable importance in the 1830s, since the question of whether the Bank of England should operate as simply another bank, or whether its special status should be recognised, began to emerge as a crucial bone of contention. The 1826 legislation created new conditions of competition, and joint stock banks proliferated in the 1830s. The response of the Bank of England to this was to expand credit liberally and ignore completely the rule of 1832, which was to tie the liabilities (deposits and notes) of the Bank to the level of bullion held.[8] This boom reached its peak in 1837, and in the second half of that year a number of the new banking companies collapsed. The enquiries of the Secret Committee had discovered not only that, 'an inattention to the sound principles on which banking operations should be conducted, is exhibited in several cases', but that the relationship between credit and circulation in the country was no longer governed by the principles of caution and prudence.[9] Reserves declined steeply in the period from 1833–7, while currency in circulation changed little and deposits rose slightly; such a position was in marked contrast to what would have happened had the 'natural' principles governing the operation of the currency been allowed to operate. Strict convertibility under the gold standard would have seen currency in circulation fall in line with the outflow of reserves. The campaign for reform which was to culminate in the 1844 Act began to coalesce around what became known as the 'Currency Principle', which held that

> It is universally admitted, by persons acquainted with monetary science, that paper money should be so regulated as to keep the medium of exchange, of which it may form a part, in the same state, with respect as to amount and to value, in which the medium of exchange would exist were the circulating portion of it purely metallic.[10]

In order to achieve this position, which had previously been held by, among others, David Ricardo, it became established that there must be a separation of the issuing and the banking business of the Bank of England, that the Bank directors must have no possibility of discretion in managing the currency, and that (though this was not strictly necessary, but a vital component of the bid to remove destabilising elements from the system) there should be a monopoly on note issue held by the Bank of England. These various elements of the Currency Position were held to ensure internal and external convertibility, restore the 'natural' relationship between specie and the circulating medium and remove much of the instability in the banking system which had been exhibited in the boom and bust cycles of the 1820s and 1830s, encouraged by the mismanagement of the Bank of England. They rested on the view that the only important relationship for understanding the economy was that between gold and the amount of currency. Any discretion in this relationship would be to interfere with the laws of nature, and only exacerbate the difficulties.[11] In this, the Currency position reflected the general attitude of most of its proponents in favour of Free Trade. Fetter notes that in the period between 1836 and 1841, Parliament had conducted five committee investigations into the operation of the banking system, and posed 16,000 questions to witnesses, whose replies filled more than 1,200 pages. At the end of this process, he suggests, three main strands of majority opinion had emerged. The first was that the creation of money was a function of government, the second (perhaps contradictory position) was that free trade, and therefore competition, should be the guiding principle in this area, as elsewhere, and the third was an opposition to discretion in the prosecution of economic policy.[12] Each of these principles was to be enshrined in the Bank Act of 1844.

The opponents of these positions came to be known as the 'Banking School'. It has often been pointed out that the positions held by both the Currency and the Banking schools of thought evolved over time, were certainly not consistent across all protagonists, and contained much in common with each other.[13] Neither, as has been noted above, were their positions necessarily internally consistent. But there were some real points of issue. The most crucial one was the banking school's insistence that the significant element in the process of monetary control was not note issue alone, as the currency school would have it, but the total of notes and deposits. This is a significant point of dispute since it underlines the uncertainty over what currency actually was (and is – these debates were to be repeated in the 1970s and 1980s as successive British governments attempted to find an appropriate measure of the money supply which would respond to official guidance in the manner expected) and how it could be controlled. Fundamentally, if there is disagreement over what is being managed, then agreement on how to do so is unlikely.

The Banking School, and in particular Thomas Tooke, argued vociferously that notes and deposits both represented purchasing power, and that, faced with either an internal or an external drain on specie, it is dangerous to require only notes to behave in the same manner as specie. The difference between the two camps can be seen in Tooke's and Torrens's analyses of the implications of an outflow of gold. For the Currency School, the amount of bank notes in circulation would vary in direct proportion to the amount of specie held by the banking system. As notes were returned for gold, private bankers and bill brokers would seek to maintain their reserve ratios in the face of falling cash positions and would therefore reduce the credits which they were willing to offer. Interest rates would rise and prices and economic activity would fall until the outflow of specie had been arrested. The crucial element in this sequence is that the Bank of England has no role in trying to maintain the level of economic activity – since currency (note issue) contracts, the economy must also contract, until equilibrium is restored.

This latter aspect was unacceptable to the Banking School, who argued that the Bank of England's proper role was to maintain the note circulation by discounting securities offered to them. This would maintain the level of purchasing power and confidence in the economy. If the drain continued, it should be halted by raising the rate of interest on the bills being discounted. It can be seen that the difference in these two approaches is essentially one of when and how the interest rate is raised. For the currency school, this would happen automatically as the circulation fell and it became more difficult to gain credit from the banking system. For the banking school, the timing and extent of the interest rate rise was a matter for the Bank of England's discretion. Torrens's criticism of this was withering; since there was a general commitment to maintain purchasing power in the economy, and to discount bills, it was extremely unlikely that small or incremental increases in the interest rate would have any effect on the presentation of bills – to establish any meaningful or credible threat of refusal, the interest rate hike would need to be significant. By the time such a position had been reached, however, the drain may have caused serious damage to the reserves of the entire system. The longer the delay from the early signs of a drain to the raising of the rate, the more drastic the rise would have to be. In the end, argued Torrens, 'the convertibility of the banknote is secured through a calamitous commercial revulsion',[14] which was in marked contrast to his own analysis of an automatic, earlier and therefore less severe contraction. The curency and banking schools, therefore, disagreed over what the proper criterion for corrective action should be (the definition of the money supply), and whether this corrective action should be triggered automatically or by discretion of the Bank of England. They did not disagree over the fundamental mechanism of the relationship between the money supply and commercial activity.[15]

Nevertheless, in this conflict can be seen two important theories of economic behaviour. The automatic nature of the Currency School's analysis is reminiscent of the price-specie-flow mechanism which had been elaborated by Hume. The view that prices had an important international component, and that domestic increases could only be sustained with the active agreement of the authorities via the use of discretion to avoid the automatic withdrawal of currency, and that a reduction of domestic prices was a means of correcting an unfavourable exchange, either external or between notes and specie, derived a theory of bank behaviour from a theory of prices.[16] On the other hand, the banking school's approach was based firmly on the belief that, so long as the banking system discounted bills which represented the legitimate needs of trade, then no harm could be done to the system. This position is the basis of the real bills doctrine, which contends that the money supply is demand determined, and that the price level and its rate of change are exogenous.

The importance of the real bills doctrine – and its longevity – can hardly be overstated, and many of the items in this collection pay homage to it. The fundamental position of the real bills doctrine is that, so long as credit is advanced on the basis of short term commercial bills, which will be liquidated in the normal process of trade, then there can never be an overissue of currency. The conception is that the money supply is geared to production and that output therefore generates the purchasing power necessary to consume it. The money supply will then be an indication of the level of output, and will rise and fall accordingly.[17] Physical security was all that was required to ensure an equilibrium relationship between the money supply and economic activity. Henry Thornton had provided a fatal critique of the doctrine in 1802, pointing out that (a) the same goods could be used as security for more than one bill, (b) this monetary expansion would result in a rise in the general price level, and that the two would thereafter feed on each other in an inflationary spiral, and (c) that so long as the differential between the loan rate of interest and the expected rate of profit on new investment was positive, the opportunities for profit would increase the amount of borrowing, and the volume of bills, the money supply and the price level would chase each other upwards indefinitely.[18] It is clear from this analysis that the fundamental error of the real bills doctrine was to assume that one nominal variable (the price level) could be used to control another (the money supply). The inevitable result is inflation.

Despite this fallacy, and Thornton's criticisms, the real bills doctrine survived in the controversy surrounding the 1844 Act. Tooke, John Fullarton and J. S. Mill – who were the leading lights of the banking school – all subscribed to the theory of reflux, which suggested that, so long as short term commercial bills were the normal means of supplying credit, then there could be no overissue of currency. The intuition here was that discretion over control of the money supply raised no fundamental difficulties since it was the needs of trade which determined the amount of currency in circulation, not the discounting policy of the banking system. It was argued strongly that neither the country banks nor the Bank of England could make notes stay out in circulation if they were not wanted or required for commercial transactions. Unneeded notes would therefore be returned to the banking system to pay off debts; the only regulation needed was the obligation of convertibility. The argument that overissue of notes is not possible was to have important implications in subsequent years, when the problem became one of dealing with the monetary effects of depression; the argument was transformed into one about the point at which, if at all, the Bank of England should cease to accept good quality bills presented to it for discount.

The Bank Act of 1844 (and the subsequent ones relating to Scotland and Ireland in 1845) enshrined a number of important theoretical principles relating to the operation of banking systems. It established a Bank of England with two separate functions – issuing and banking, and it set a fixed relationship between the amount of securities held in the Issue Department and the money supply. The exact purity of the currency system was never quite established, however.[19] The fiduciary issue based on government securities held by the Issue Department was set at £14m, and all additional notes required full specie backing. The amount of notes issued at any one time varied directly with the Issue Department's gold reserve, therefore, but since the Issue Department issued notes only to the Banking Department, which then entered into circulation in the normal course of banking business, the Banking Department could hold a reserve of its own and exercise some independent judgement relating to discounting policy. The Act therefore sought to, but did not fully, remove the question of discretion – and therefore of active monetary policy – from the Bank of England. In addition, it effectively established the monopoly of the Bank over note issue in England and Wales. In largely accepting the principles of the Currency School, it was assumed that the Act would restore much of the natural relationship between the price level, money supply and banking system, and therefore reduce the amplitude of the monetary fluctuations which had been so marked in the first half of the century.

## II: The Banking System After 1844

The success of the Act in achieving this aim was put to the test twice in the following thirteen years, with the commercial difficulties of 1847 and 1857. These two dislocations are important since they raised for re-examination a number of the issues discussed earlier – the separation of the banking from the issue department, the definition of the money supply, the power of the Bank of England as holder of the nation's reserve (and therefore its relationship with other banks), and the extent of monetary policy discretion to be allowed to the Bank – and effectively set the conditions of banking policy until 1914 and beyond.

The general trade and credit expansion of 1845 and 1846 resulted in two prosperous years, peaking in the spring and summer of 1847. The Banking Department, competing for banking business, allowed credit to rise significantly throughout these years by following a policy of undercutting the market interest rate for discounts, and running very low reserve ratios.[20] By April 1847, the expansion of credit had reached a point where drastic measures were necessary; they began to charge above the published rates on most bills, and at the same time made it clear that they would not be acting as a lender of last resort – an absolute ceiling was placed on the total of bills which they were willing to discount, regardless of their provenance or creditworthiness. The Bank's position was that credit rationing was preferable to very high rates of interest. The difficulty with credit rationing, however, is that it excludes all potential borrowers, not just those likely to inflict harm on the system. The market responded predictably and a serious financial panic ensued in late April and early May 1847, with interest rates on perfectly respectable bills reaching as high as 12 or 13 per cent.[21] The reserve position improved throughout the second half of May and into June. By the time the merchants of London presented their petition to Parliament calling for a relaxation of credit conditions and the resumption of note issue on the basis of silver bullion,[22] the worst appeared to have passed. A variety of events conspired to bring about a reverse in the late summer, however;

> a sudden and unexampled demand for foreign corn, produced by a failure in many descriptions of agricultural produce throughout the United Kingdom, coincided with the unprecedented extent of speculation produced by increased facilities of credit...to these causes may be added a contemporaneous rise of price in cotton; and with respect to Houses connected with the East and West India Trade, a sudden and extensive fall in the price of sugar, by which the value of their most readily available assets underwent great depreciation.[23]

In this situation, a number of discount companies and provincial banking companies failed, and panic in the money markets reached new heights; 'people thought they were in an iron cage, and could not get out of it: that Iron cage was the Act of 1844'.[24] This is true in the particular sense that it was not so much the reserve position, or the scarcity of credit which occasioned the panic in October 1847, but the knowledge that the Issue Department held a large reserve which could not be touched. The reserve of the Banking Department was indeed very low, but it had been lower in both 1837 and 1839.

Under severe public pressure, the Government relaxed the reserve conditions, and authorised the Bank to issue notes without limit. This was to take effect from 25 October, but the Bank began to discount freely on the previous Saturday (23rd), thus restoring confidence in the system. Provincial bankers, who had been hoarding notes and increasing their own reserves, allowed them to re-enter circulation. Although it was discounting freely, at no time did the Bank actually break the note issue limit which had been set in 1844, reinforcing the opinion that it was the perception of the unattainable reserve, rather than the stringency of the actual position which had been the real problem. By the end of October, notes were returning to the Bank, and the reserve position improved considerably in the following month. Dornbusch and Frenkel suggest that this is one of the defining elements of an internal convertibility crisis: 'Suspension of the act removed any conceivable basis for panic and therefore immediately restored a measure of financial stability.'[25]

The difficulties of 1857 followed a similar pattern. A period of expansion was followed by one of gradual tightening of monetary conditions; Bank Rate reached 5½ per cent in August of that year. The depression in America, however, quickly became translated into failures of merchants and banking houses in Glasgow, Liverpool and London. The contraction in credit and currency which this caused was worsened by other banks adding to their own reserves and hoarding bank notes. By the beginning of November 1857, many bill brokers were completely unable to provide discounts, and could obtain cash only on difficult terms from the Bank of England. The Treasury Letter authorising the issuance of bank notes beyond the limit set in the 1844 Act was published on 12 November 1857. In this instance, the Bank was forced to exceed the fiduciary limit by around 2 million pounds before confidence was fully restored.

In both of these instances, the debates in the Committee focussed primarily on the extent to which the commercial distress was caused by the operation of the Act. The Act itself was of only secondary interest; the committee of 1858 reported that the evidence presented to its predecessor by one year was 'interesting in the highest degree to all who make the scientific study of the most abstruse questions of political economy their pursuit', but that it was unwilling and unqualified to discuss the technical issues itself. In neither instance was the Act felt to be responsible for the commercial distress and dislocation which had resulted in its suspension, the real culprit being 'excess speculation and abuse of credit'.[26] In both cases, the suspension of the Act was defended as appropriate in the emergency conditions, but although the earlier committee had recommended the insertion of a relaxation clause, to allow the Bank of England to exceed the fiduciary issue when such crises hit, that of 1858 took a different position, and sanctioned the continuance of the Act of 1844 as it stood. In the latter report, it is possible to discern a shift in emphasis towards an acceptance of the institutional framework bequeathed by the Act, and it contains some severe criticism of those banks and merchant houses which had failed. It may be that this represents to some extent the difference between a crisis triggered by real factors (the harvest failure in 1847) and one brought on by monetary difficulties (the fall in the price of American railway stocks in 1857), but it is also clear that the debate had moved on.

There were a number of areas of controversy which exercised contemporaries in the period between the 1850s and the 1870s, all of which tended to shift discussion from the Central Bank to the wider banking system and the operation of local, country and joint-stock banking outside London. The first was essentially a matter of statistical estimation, and a number of attempts at measuring the size of the money supply were undertaken. This was essentially a matter of building up from Bank of England notes to include bills of exchange and deposits. By the time of Palgrave's investigation, he was able to state, with little fear of contradiction that bank notes were 'by far the least part of the circulating medium'.[27] A much later analyst, Michael Collins, has noted that the monetary sector expanded rapidly in Britain in the half century before 1880, and that 'most monetary growth came from the expansion of commercial bank deposits while notes declined'.[28] The implications of this shifting focus were felt in two, closely related, directions. In the first place, the 1850s and 1860s saw a reaction to the monopoly of the Bank of England, and the idea of free banking was actively pursued by a number of authors. The freedom of country banks to issue their own notes was held to be one of the key tenets of free trade, and one which was violated by the restrictions introduced in the Banking Acts. The example of the Scottish banks was often referred to, despite English commentators' general hostility towards the banking system north of the border in the mid-Victorian period,[29] and the argument was again couched in terms of a natural system (this time, of competition) versus an imposed – and therefore obviously inferior, and destined to be swept away – structure of monopoly. Jevons, however, inveighed against those who followed this line of argument: 'And I venture to take this auspicious expression, Free Trade, from those who use it wrongly and confuse the free manufacture of currency with free trade in capital, the true business of the banker'.[30] Those who opposed the free banking position often did so, not because they held that the privileges of the Bank of England were inviolate, but because they sought to concentrate all note issue in a State Bank. This position allowed those who criticised the Bank's monopoly to join forces with the opponents of multiple issue, and it provided an opportunity to carry forward previous criticism of the Bank's power in the money markets. Fetter notes, however, that the theoretical positions were never fully clarified; 'the controversy was fought to a standstill as it was absorbed in the larger controversy over the clarification of the unwritten responsibilities of the Bank of England'.

It was argued above that the crisis of the 1820s revealed the existence of a unified money market, subject to systemic rather than purely localised pressures. This had largely been achieved by the use of bills of exchange. The rise of the inland bill – and of the bill brokers who were such an important part of the system – is usually seen as part of the process of unification of markets across England.[31] By replacing the local reputation and creditworthiness of regional banks with their own ability to manage a national credit market – aided by the three or six months' grace contained in most bills – the brokers provided one of the most important instruments in the expansion of the Victorian economy. However, once better communications – and in particular the telegraph – allowed merchants and traders to complete their transactions in a few days, bills were no longer necessary, and accounts could be settled by cheque, thus transferring funds directly from one bank account to another. However, in a recent analysis, Alborn has suggested that, from the 1850s onwards, by shifting the core of their business from note issuing to deposit collecting, the banks were able to channel much larger sums into commercial activities. At the same time, by making use of the intermediation services of third party brokers, they were able to avoid many of the risks and inconveniences of doing so:

> By sending out for bill brokers to perform banking duties for them, joint-stock banks could offer their customers all the advantages of a more efficient system without appearing to be directly responsible for any temporary inconveniences it might produce. In turning ordinary loans into marketable securities, bill brokers offered banks a type of "near cash asset" that paid interest but could still be recalled to meet sudden demands – just as the banks themselves had created an

> attractive asset when they offered their depositors interest-bearing accounts that were payable on demand.[32]

This system worked because the brokers were able to operate on narrower margins than the banks. But, because the brokerage market was highly competitive, they relied heavily on being able to rediscount much of their bill holdings at the Bank of England. The problem, of course, for the bill brokers was that the 1844 Act had sought to ensure that the Bank of England was one of the largest competitors in this market. Furthermore, it was required to compete strenuously in order to maintain the note issue, on which no interest was paid. The inevitable result of this situation, suggests Alborn, was the commercial crises of 1847 (based on domestic bills), and 1857 (American bills). Further, as was revealed in 1866, when a major bill broker found itself short of liquidity, the Bank of England was not necessarily the best place to turn. The Bank, angered by the brokers' attempts in 1860 to establish their own reserve by holding 2 million pounds in Consols rather than place it on deposit, (a position which Gladstone as Chancellor of the Exchequer was unwilling to countenance) retaliated by keeping its discount rate at 7 per cent, thus forcing unsustainable losses and the eventual collapse of a number of banks as well as the brokerage house of Overend Gurney.[33]

The arguments in favour of free banking received a fillip from such disturbances. J. W. Gilbart, in particular, argued that the relationship between local banks and local industry had been broken by the concentration of financial power in London. This separation was extremely harmful, he suggested, and could not be restored until banks were once again accountable to their industrial localities, by means of note issues and individual reserves.[34] By this time, however, the national money and financial markets had been entrenched and the hankering of some writers for the land they had lost was no more than wishful thinking; how this system was to be managed had become the important issue. In response to the crisis of 1866, the Bank of England very strongly took the view that it was not to operate as a Lender of Last Resort. Thomson Hankey took exception to Bagehot's preachings in *The Economist* on the responsibility of the Bank of England, and sought to confirm the view that the Bank was no more than one of many operating and competing in the money markets.[35] Once again, however, this was no longer a sustainable position. By the time that Bagehot published *Lombard Street* in 1873, he was describing what most accepted, rather than arguing forcefully for the adoption of the principle:

> The only safe plan for the Bank is the brave plan, to lend in a panic on every kind of current sucurity, on every sort on which money is

> ordinarily and usually lent. This policy may not save the Bank, but if it do not, nothing will save it.[36]

Justification for a single banking reserve, and for the Bank of England to manage it lay not so much in this being an inevitable outcome of the forces of nature ( Bagehot's theoretical preferences, in line with those of his father-in-law and predecessor as editor of *The Economist*, James Wilson, had been free banking and multiple reserve holding) but that, this being what had transpired, to meddle with it would be too unsettling and dangerous. This pragmatic view can be seen as acceptance of the Bank of England's position as a central bank, with the role and responsibilities which this entails – a unified reserve, a measure of control over the money and bill markets, and a Lender of Last Resort function in times of need.

## III: Commercial Banking in the Second Half of the Nineteenth Century

The structure of the banking industry in Britain changed enormously in the period between the 1850s and WWI. Most obviously, the banks grew in size. Collins notes that between 1850 and 1913, both average liability size and the average number of branches per bank grew by thirty-two times.[37] Much of this growth was internal, reflecting the symbiosis between local banks and the economies they served, but most of it came about as a result of the merger movement which swept through the industry, peaking in the late 1880s and early 1890s. This had a number of roots; Alborn suggests that, having gained access to the London Clearing House in 1854, the joint stock banks set about the task of regulating flows of credit in the economy. First, they replaced their reliance on the broking houses with their own cheque-clearing activities. Given this power base, size became the crucial competitive issue in the financial system.[38] Cottrell agrees; the only available form of growth for many banks in the 1870s and 1880s 'was to develop from a local or regional institution to become a national institution'.[39] Extensive networks of branches required considerable capital investment; this could be justified by gathering deposits, but also contained the imperative to keep as much of the inter-regional remittance and banking business within the institution as possible. Collins has shown how the particular economies of scale associated with the increasing size of banks provided a powerful incentive to continued growth.[40] Once Lloyds and Midland had absorbed members of the London Clearing House in 1884 and 1891 respectively, others were forced to follow. Between 1870 and 1913, 331 banks disappeared in merger activity, and by 1920, the Big Five (Barclays, Midland, Lloyds, National Provincial and Westminster) accounted for eighty per cent of English bank deposits.[41]

The most obvious outcome of the merger wave was that banking was removed from its local roots. In the middle of the nineteenth century, banking had essentially been a localised activity, in which those who raised the capital, subscribed to the shares, conducted the business and borrowed the funds were very closely interlinked, and were often, indeed, the same individuals.[42] Cottrell refers to this as the 'country banking tradition' but suggests that much of this would have been lost by organic growth in the second half of the century anyway.[43] The decline was certainly hastened by the collapse of the City of Glasgow Bank in 1878, a disaster which finally revealed the dangers of unlimited liability, and which resulted in banks adopting much higher levels of liquidity throughout the 1880s.[44] Some provincial bank promoters in the boom of the 1860s – many of whom had eschewed the limited liability on offer since the company law changes of 1858–62, in the belief that it was important to stake their reputations and wealth in order to attract depositors – were shown to be over-extended in their localities; the collapse of the City of Glasgow was held up as a salutary lesson to those who suffered from over-commitment to their geographical or industrial constitutencies.[45] William Kennedy has suggested that, having had their fingers burnt playing with industrial lending, many banks chose to engage in mergers and direct their attention (and their depositors' funds) towards the international money and capital markets.[46]

The second, and closely related, major effect of the merger wave was the creation of a wholly new form of national, integrated business organization, which required administrative coordination and professional direction. The Institute of Bankers in Scotland was founded in 1875, and England and Wales followed four years later. Holmes and Green detail how a combination of the demands of running a large bank, the requirements of the 1879 Companies Act and its provision for published, audited accounts, and the need to recover from the spate of bad debts which had been experienced in the second half of the 1870s, combined to force a reappraisal of the administrative structure of Midland Bank.[47] New lines of responsibility and reporting were created, the Board became more professional and a more careful and systematic approach to the prosecution of banking business – including more formal appraisal of security and guarantees – was adopted. Increasing size and standardization of banking activities delivered by branches remote from head offices in London rather than by locally-managed institutions certainly changed the nature of the relationship between industrial borrowers and their customers. The nature of the relationship between industrial borrowers and their bankers was changed; although it is hard to sustain the accusation that the banks henceforth abandoned their clients.[48] The lesson that had been learned from the crash of the City of Glasgow was that extensive branch banking could only be made to work if there were effective controls over the actions of the directors and managers of the bank. George Rae's *Country Banker*, first published in 1885, while impressing the advantages of local knowledge and contacts secured over the long-term relationships established in the 'country banking tradition', also attempts to capture and codify the new forms of standardization and professionalization, both in the business of accepting deposits and making loans and in the running of the bank office.[49]

The third major effect of the growth of the large banking institutions at the end of the nineteenth century was to increase the level of tension between the banking system and the Bank of England. As the system of deposit banking expanded, and the private sector's share of national income continued to rise, it became clear that the Bank's ability to influence money market rates of interest, and therefore protect its own reserve, could no longer be exerted via cash balances held at the Bank of England.[50] Bank Rate became the preferred tool of policy.[51] The debate over reserves had two main waves. The first, which lasted essentially from the 1850s to the 1870s, was resolved, as discussed above, by general acceptance of the Bank of England holding a unified banking reserve. The confusion which existed between clearing balances and the reserves available to meet sudden crises persisted, however, and, throughout the subsequent decades, the clearing banks relied far too heavily on the Bank of England for the provision of cash. The situation was laid bare by the Barings crash in 1890, and Goschen set about reforming the Bank-banking relationships by urging the latter to hold substantially bigger cash reserves in a famous speech in 1891:

> its proposals three. First, commercial bankers should keep bigger cash reserves and should publish the details more frequently. Second, he aired the possibility of a fiduciary issue of one pound notes and ten shilling notes backed by silver, thereby to reduce the domestic circulation of gold and to concentrate more in the central reserve. Third, the gold partially backing the one pound notes would constitute a second gold reserve...that is, the fiduciary issue would be increased ...provided that the foreign exchanges were or seemed likely to become favourable.[52]

The real issues to be tackled here were the sets of relationships between the bankers' reserves and the reserves of the Bank of England, and between the reserves of the Bank of England and the fiduciary issue of currency. Elasticity was not to be achieved by these means, although the same criticisms continued to be made. Pownall, in 1914, noted both that 'the banking reserves of the country are inadequate to the necessities of the country and are too *small*' (original emphasis), and that a measure of elasticity, through the issuance of a temporary fiduciary issue in moments of crisis, would help to maintain confidence in both the internal and external value of sterling.[53]

## IV: American Banking: Elasticity, Reform and the Genesis of the Federal Reserve

American banking in the later nineteenth century was dominated by the same issues: the relationships between the money supply and the currency, as expressed through debates over the need for elasticity and the operation of the real bills doctrine. The arguments in the United States, as in Britain, essentially reflected disagreements over whether a Central Bank was necessary, and what one could be expected to do. As in Britain, the impetus for reform of the banking system was provided by a series of crises, most particularly those of 1873, 1893 and, especially, 1907.

The deficiencies of the National Banking System are well enough known – the pyramiding of credit in New York and the restrictions on the reserve ratios and consequently the money supply.[54] The crisis of 1873, in which loans fell by approximately 5 per cent and deposits by 15 per cent, was cushioned effectively by the ability and willingness of the New York banks to act cooperatively, pool reserves and issue clearing house loan certificates. The substitution of clearing house loan certificates for cash, and the cooperative approach to the banking difficulties meant that the withdrawal of funds from the banking system was not so severe as it might have been. These loan certificates were further used in 1893, and again in 1907.[55] Calomiris and Gorton have referred to the 'random withdrawal risk' of bank failures; that unexpected withdrawals by bank depositors are linked in some way to upheavals in the real economy. These panics are indications that there are insufficient reserves to go round and that an injection of cash is required. The difficulty, under the National Banking System, was that the government 'was unable to conduct open market operations to inject cash'.[56]

The rigid constraints under which the banking system had to operate had of course been recognised as causing difficulty immediately after the 1873 crisis, when William Richardson, Secretary of the Treasury, had urged that the National Banks should be allowed to use part of their reserves to boost liquidity, 'at seasons of the greatest pressure, under proper restrictions and regulations'.[57] Richardson also suggested that the National Banks should desist from offering interest on demand deposits, but that, under exceptional circumstances, interest rates in excess of the legal maximum of 7 per cent should be offered. A later Secretary, Leslie Shaw, did attempt to introduce some flexibility by using Central Banking techniques of moving government deposits around the banking system and relaxing the rules on the legal reserve against government deposits.[58] Such moves were, however, controversial.[59]

The link between the perceived need for elasticity of the currency and the earliest signs of central banking and the emergence of the federal reserve system is clear, but it was neither simple nor direct. Mints has noted that, despite a majority of opinion being in favour of the introduction of an elastic currency in the two decades after 1890, few authors were able to go further in their advocacy than to make some kind of equivalence between elasticity and reduced fluctuations in the price level.[60] Friedman and Schwartz have made the distinction between the valid notion of inelasticity, the lack of convertibility between currency and deposits, and the 'highly dubious' notion 'that the money stock should conform to the needs of trade'.[61] Taylor suggested that many of the claims for elasticity were somewhat overplayed in the literature, but that it would allow the money supply to move more in sympathy with commercial demands.[62] The elastic nature of the currency was to be provided by the banks' issuance of currency secured on commercial paper. This would ensure that the note issue better reflected the needs of trade, while at the same time would be self-liquidating. These views were beginning to coalesce around the notion of asset currencies, which had first been suggested by the Indianapolis Monetary Commission in 1897[63], and been revived by the American Bankers' Association in 1906.

The crisis of 1907, however, 'probably the most severe in American financial history',[64] provided both a distraction and an impetus for change. High levels of bank loans and very low reserves coupled with increasing speculative activity in the stock market meant that a number of small New York banks became over extended and a run ensued. Clearing was suspended for the Knickerbocker Trust Company on 2 October 1907. This was the signal for the run to extend to other banks and trust companies, and a general financial panic continued until the end of the year. The Aldrich Vreeland Act of 1908 afforded some relief to the beleaguered banks, by allowing Currency Associations to issue heavily taxed currency based on either commercial paper or long term bonds, while at the same time allowing some centralization of reserves and cooperation among banks to ward off any subsequent panics. Both elements of Calomiris and Hubbard's prescription for avoiding bank runs under the random withdrawal risk assumptions – liquidity and cooperation – were therefore provided by legislation, when the banking system itself was signally unable to do so. As a result of this crisis, the National Monetary Commission was created to explore the structure of the American banking system and consider what it could learn from others.

The National Monetary Commission absorbed much of banking reformers' energy for the next couple of years, but two ideas had gained clear acceptance by 1908. One was that a greater degree of cooperation in banking was required to reduce the regularity and severity of the crises. The other, as described above, was that some form of asset currency would afford the required levels of elasticity to allow the note issue to reflect more accurately the needs of trade.[65] By issuing notes secured on short-term bills of exchange or other forms of commercial assets, the argument ran, their self liquidating nature would remove the restrictions under which loans could only be made at the expense of other banking assets. It is clear that this proposal rests soundly on the real bills doctrine, and although almost all of the major figures in the banking reform movement subscribed to some form of it, there were basically two camps. On the one hand, there were those, such as H. Parker Willis, J. Laurence Laughlin and A. Barton Hepburn, who argued that liquidity and self regulation were intrinsic characteristics of the asset currency and that therefore such notes could not be issued in excess of commercial requirements, since those requirements would regulate the means of payment.[66] This is clearly the standard real-bills position, but there was another view, unwilling to accept the self-regulating nature of this proposal, which argued that liquidity was not necessarily intrinsic to commercial assets, and that some form of Central Banking organisation was necessary in order to provide both a market for these securities and to regulate flows of credit and investment. This was the position held by Sprague, Paul Warburg and A. Piatt Andrew.[67]

This latter position was important, since it provided the basis for the development of thinking about the shape of the new Central Bank which the reformers began to pursue with zeal. There were two important stages to this process. In the first of these, Warburg outlined four fundamental principles:

1. the centralization of banking reserves.
2. commercial paper could be used as a means of exchange between the central reserve and the constituent banks.
3. a fluidity of credit (elasticity of currency) could be established

through the creation and use of two-name commercial paper as the basis for the banking assets.

4. an intercity clearing house could be created to economize on cash remittances.[68]

These principles, argued Warburg, provided the basis for the establishment of a responsive currency, a unified reserve and a centralized monetary authority. The suggestion of Morawetz, however, that a divisional reserve bank could be created, was crucial in providing the means by which Warburg's plan could be made to work. The real bills doctrine was the heart of the Federal Reserve System. The twelve regional banks were established to provide liquidity by discounting short-term commercial notes for member institutions. The discount rate was therefore to be the principal policy tool of each of the Reserve Banks, although they were also empowered to undertake open market operations. The Federal Reserve's founders were keen to promote the operation of an acceptance market, since this would further enhance liquidity and help to channel funds towards commercial activity and away from speculative investments.[69] Indeed, open market policy was to become the key tool by which the Federal Reserve intervened in the economy. By the publication of its Annual Report for 1923, it had accepted the responsibility not only for pursuing a policy based on the real bills doctrine, but for managing the amount and availability of credit in the economy.[70] Central Bank confidence had spread across the Atlantic.

## V: Commercial Banks: Deposits and Lending

One of the difficulties which bankers on both sides of the Atlantic faced at the end of the nineteenth century was that the theory of the multiple expansion of deposits was so little understood. The way in which a fractional reserve banking system could create deposits, and disbelief of this fundamental mechanism, lay at the heart of many of the misunderstandings related to notions such as the law of reflux and the expansion of credit. The classic statement of this theory is contained in Phillips's work on *Bank Credit* , in which he challenges the traditional view, as stated in the standard banking textbooks, that, if a bank has loans amounting to 500 per cent of its deposits, then a £100 increase in deposits will result in a £500 rise in loans.[71] Phillips is able to show that, where there are many banks in a system, multiple expansion based on an increase in deposits occurs not because each bank expands its lending, but because the entire system does. The mechanism is that, as a bank's deposits rise, it must put some of these new deposits to the reserve, and is able to make loans on the rest. These loans are then used in the normal way – the borrower writes cheques and the recipients place these funds in their own banks, thus causing a further increase in the system's total of deposits. These banks, however, must place some of these funds on reserve before they can make any loans on the new deposits. And so on. So each individual bank, on receiving C new deposits, must transfer r to their reserves, and is able to lend (1–r)C. Multiple expansion is possible because the reserves, despite not being available to any individual bank, are not lost to the system; 'the banking system collectively multiplies deposits per dollar of new reserves while the small individual bank fractionalizes reserves per dollar of new deposits'.[72]

This theory is now well enough understood, and Phillips's work is rightly seen as the crucial breakthrough. Humphrey shows how earlier authors, including Torrens, Joplin and Marshall contributed to understanding of this basic phenomenon. The insight of Marshall, in particular, was crucial, since he provided the first algebraic explanation of the multiplier, and identified the importance of each individual bank's reserve ratio to the process.[73] Work subsequent to Phillips by Karel and Ficek included the cash ratio, which thus reduced the multiplier effect. Meade expanded on the basic intuition to create the concept of the money multiplier by relating the total money stock to the high powered monetary base. [74]

This crucial understanding – that the banking system, rather than individual banks, is responsible for any expansion in loans resulting from an increase in deposits, has enormously important implications for the lending activity of banks in a fractional reserve system, since it brings into sharper relief the need for those banks to provide adequate safeguards for their depositors. This is an element which is often forgotten in the rush to criticise banks for their supposed lack of entrepreneurial ability in seeking out lending opportunities.[75] In Britain, it is generally accepted that, after the amalgamation movement of the late nineteenth and early twentieth century, the deposit banks did not provide long-term investment capital to their industrial borrowers. Yet the simplistic assumption drawn from this is that in some way the banking system 'failed industry'.[76] In particular, the argument is that the stress on liquid assets, on short-term lending and the importance of security meant that banks were unable to foster and encourage the growth of new industrial enterprises along the lines of the German Great Banks.[77] Foxwell held up the German example as the one from which most could be learned; 'the financing of industry and trade should be the main business of banking...This is precisely what the German banks have done...a study of their methods is perhaps the best way by which we Englishmen can approach the subject'.[78]

The theoretical issue here is that, by being closely involved with their industrial clients – acting as both investor, banker and board member, the German banks did not suffer the high levels of information asymmetry which characterised the approach of the British banks once they withdrew from locally- based lending. This argument points to the institutional differences; British and German financial structures were radically different. The British system of intermediation was one in which the roles of commercial and investment banking, stock issuing, accepting and trading all developed in separate institutions. The universal banking system of Continental Europe, on the other hand, in which many of these functions were unified, had come about as a response to the inefficiency and poorly developed state of the financial and capital markets. The banks, it is assumed, would therefore be able to deliver better performance in terms of aiding industrial investment, providing mechanisms by which best practice techniques and technology could be adopted and ensuring that resources were not wasted in competition when opportunities for amalgamation or rationalization presented themselves. This was very much the rationale for the appointment of the Macmillan Committee on Finance and Industry in 1929.[79] But the evidence in support of this position is not convincing; Reisser and Tilly both note that German banks did very little for small manufacturers,[80] while Edwards and Ogilvie's assessment of the supposed better economic decision making resulting from superior information flows between the large banks and their industrial customers is that this is 'a misleading characterization of the German economy'.[81]

Nor does a comparison with American banking reveal a significantly superior institutional structure. Lamoreaux has recently shown how a system of banking displaying all the characteristics of the English 'country banking tradition' in industrialising New England responded to the development of its locality and the increasing demands for capital by adopting precisely the same strategies as those in Britain – amalgamation, professionalization and withdrawal from intimate connections between bank and industrial enterprise.[82] It is clear that, in the United States, commercial banks eschewed taking long term investment positions in industrial enterprises.[83] Brad De Long has shown, however, that this function was performed very effectively by a small number of powerful investment banks located in New York. He concludes that merchant bankers were able to make effective use of their unique combination of financial clout and privileged information to add significantly to the share value of those firms in which they were interested.[84] J.P. Morgan in particular, but other merchant banks such as Kuhn Loeb were able to extract significant value from their dealings with railroads, steel companies and other firms. The eventual price which they had to pay, however, was public outcry about a bankers' trust and the emergence of an insidious form of financial capitalism.[85]

## VI: Interest Rates and Monetary Policy

The conclusions reached in earlier sections of this introduction suggest that, by the inter war years, a series of principles of the relationships between banks and the monetary system, how they interacted and how they could be affected by the operation of Central Banks had been agreed. Some degree of understanding had certainly been reached, for example in terms of the expansion of deposits, and it is clear that commercial banks had come to understand the operation of their various reserve ratios, as well as come to terms with the difficulties posed by the conversion of repayable on demand deposits into semi-liquid forms of lending. At the heart of many of these relationships lay the general and fundamental understanding that interest rates could be used as a tool of economic adjustment. The inter war and immediate post-war years were to question this assumption, however.

An issue of the *American Economic Review* in 1925 contained two papers on opposing sides of this question. In the first, Commons held the conventional view that the Federal Reserve, by acting on the money market rates of interest through open market operations could and did exercise a stabilizing influence on the general price level. Gregory was less sanguine, however, and entertained a number of doubts about the ability of Central Banks to do very much other than interfere with the market mechanisms in a counter-productive fashion.[86] Wicksell, as early as 1907, had provided in English some elements of his cumulative process model in which he made the crucial distinction between the natural rate of interest and the real rate. If the prevailing interest rate was held lower than the natural rate, and therefore the prevailing marginal productivity of capital, this would result in a never ending upwards spiral of borrowing and prices. This of course mirrored the criticisms which Thornton had levelled at the real bills doctrine. The intuition, which Wicksell made clear, however, was that, in times of disequilibrium, the prevailing rate of interest could be moved closer to the natural rate, and that the general price levels could be adjusted by 'a proper manipulation of general bank rates, lowering them when prices are getting low, and raising them when prices are getting high'.[87]

Keynes, in the *Treatise on Money*, introduced further difficulties to the simple view, by focussing on the public's asset preferences. In this view, the decision to respond to particular price signals would depend, not simply on those signals, but on the particular preferences which individuals held for varying classes of financial assets. [88] The logical extension of this is that interest rates are neither a precise nor a reliable tool with which to adjust the general price level. Keynes of course greatly revised the *Treatise* and rejected much of it in construction of the *General Theory*, but the notion of asset preferences survived. Hawtrey provided detailed and trenchant criticism of the *Treatise*,[89] and stuck to the position that, since Bank Rate had proved an effective weapon of economic control since the 1844 Act, it was likely to remain so in the future. He did concede, however, that in the extreme circumstances of the 1930s, it was clear that the reduction of Bank Rate to its historic minimum of 2 per cent had done little to stimulate demand.[90]

Empirical testing of these relationships was undertaken by a group of researchers at Oxford in the 1930s. After interviewing a number of businessmen about the factors influencing the decision to undertake investment projects, they concluded that 'short term rates of interest do not directly affect investment either in stocks or fixed capital'.[91] This original survey was extended in the post war years, but the conclusions were simply confirmed.[92] In a similar study conducted in the United States, J. F. Ebersole was able to conclude that 'the interest rate is seldom considered as a factor in the entrepreneurial decisions of business'.[93] D. H. Robertson provided a defence of interest rates by noting that interest rates could be overriden by other factors, but the damage had been done.[94] It is not clear, of course, that many scholars held a straightforward instrumentalist view of the relationship between the interest rate and borrowing decisions. But, by the 1950s, such a view had been undermined both empirically and theoretically.

It is fitting that this introduction should close by referring to three important contributions. Sayers, in his concise analysis of central banking, noted that, despite the dangers and attendant difficulties, 'the essence of central banking is discretionary control of the monetary system'[95] This of course was one of the evils which the 1844 Act had sought to banish. Rules, suggested Sayers, lacked flexibility, were difficult to police, and would always be evaded. Discretion, and therefore trust of central bankers, was necessary to maintain a smoothly operating monetary system. Rosa's piece has an equally important, but similar message. It rests on the unreliability of the rate of interest as a moderator of investment demand, and provides the first theoretical case for credit rationing.[96] This was of course later extended to a theory of equilibrium credit rationing, which locates considerable discretion on the choice of loans to competing, but identical borrowers, in the commercial banking institution.[97] It is not perhaps surprising that the terms of appointment of the Radcliffe Committee in 1957 were explicit about the need to inform the authorities on the workings of the monetary and banking system.

## Notes

1 Parliamentary papers, 1959, Cmnd. 827.
2 P. Barret Whale, 'A Retrospective View of the Bank Charter Act of 1844', *Economica*, 1944.
3 For contemporary discussions of many of the issues raised in this introduction and the collection, see F. Capie and G. Wood (eds), *Monetary Economics in the 1980s: the Henry Thornton Lectures, Numbers 1–8* (Basingstoke, 1989) and K. Dowd, *Private Money; the Path to Monetary Stability* (London, 1988).
4 M. Collins, *Money and Banking in the UK: A History* (London, 1988), p. 16.
5 7 Geo. IV, c.46.
6 W. F. Crick and J. E. Wadsworth, *A Hundred Years of Joint-Stock Banking* (London, 1936), p.17.
7 Collins, *Money and Banking*, chapters 2 and 3.
8 See E. Wood, *English Theories of Central Bank Control, 1819–1858* (Cambridge, Mass., 1939), p. 111, fn. 9, for a fuller discussion of the 'Palmer Rule', named after Horsley Palmer.
9 *Report from the Secret Committee on Joint Stock Banks*, P.P. 1836, IX, pp. 415–18.
10 R. Torrens, *A Letter to the Right Honourable Viscount Melbourne on the Causes of the Recent Derangement in the Money Market and on Bank Reform.* (London, 1837), p. 29.
11 Wood, *English Theories of Central Banking Control*, chapter 10.
12 F. W. Fetter, *Development of British Monetary Orthodoxy, 1797 – 1875* (Cambridge, Mass., 1965), p.177.
13 Schumpeter has suggested that, apart from some technical elements relating to the Act of 1844 'there cannot have been much left to disagree about', J. Schumpeter, *History of Economic Analysis* (London, 1954), p.727.
14 R. Torrens, *An Inquiry into the Practical Working of the Proposed Arrangements for the Renewal of the Charter...* (London, 1844).
15 Wood, *English Theories of Central Banking Control*, p. 115.
16 Fetter, *Development*, p. 190.
17 The following is adapted from T. M. Humphrey 'The real bills doctrine', *Federal Reserve Bank of Richmond Economic Review* 68 (1982), pp. 3–13, reprinted in T. M. Humphrey, *Money, Banking and Inflation: Essays in the History of Monetary Thought* (Aldershot, 1993).

18 Henry Thornton, *An Enquiry into the Nature and Effects of the Paper Credit of Great Britain* (London, 1802).
19 See Collins, *Money and Banking*, p. 175.
20 Fetter, *Development*, pp. 203–4.
21 T. Tooke, *A History of Price and of the State of the Circulation from 1792 to 1856* (London, 1838–57), vol. IV, p. 305.
22 *The Petition of the Merchants, Bankers and traders of London Against the Bank Charter Act* (London, 1847).
23 *Report from the Secret Committee from the House of Lords Appointed to Inquire into Causes of Distress* (P.P. 1847–8, Cmnd. 565), p. iii.
24 Ibid., p.viii, quote from the evidence of Mr Lister.
25 R. Dornbusch and A. Frenkel, 'The Gold Standard and the Bank of England in the crisis of 1847' in M. Bordo and A. Schwartz (eds), *A Retrospective on the Classical Gold Standard, 1821–1931*' (Chicago, 1984), p. 256.
26 *Report from the Select Committee on the Bank Acts*, P.P. 1857–8, V. para 81, p.28.
27 R. H. I. Palgrave, 'Notes on banking in Great Britain and Ireland, Sweden, Denmark and Hamburg; with some remarks on the amount of bills in circulation , both inland and foreign, in Great Britain and Ireland; and the banking law of Sweden', *Journal of the Statistical Society*, XXXVI (1873), p. 151.
28 M. Collins, 'Long-term growth of the English banking sector and money stock, 1844–80', *Economic History Review*, XXXVI (1983), p. 390.
29 see M. Gaskin 'Anglo-Scottish banking conflicts, 1874–1881', *Economic History Review*, XII (1960), pp. 445–55 and R. Saville, *Bank of Scotland: A History, 1695–1995* (1996), pp. 364–7.
30 Statistical Society of London, *Journal*, XXIX (1867), p. 250, quoted in Fetter, *Monetary Orthodoxy*, p. 252.
31 The best account of the bill market, its rise and fall, is contained in S. Nishimura, *The Decline of Inland Bills of Exchange in the London Money Market 1855–1913* (Cambridge, 1971).
32 T. Alborn, *Conceiving Companies: Joint-Stock Politics in Victorian England* (forthcoming, 1998).
33 Cottrell stresses the inevitable nature of this crash as an outcome of the rapid expansion of the joint stock banking sector in the early 1860s. P. L. Cottrell, 'Finance and the germination of the British corporate economy' in P. L. Cottrell, A. Teichova and T. Yuzawa (eds), *Finance in the Age of the Corporate Economy* (Aldershot, 1997).
34 J. W. Gilbart, *The Logic of Banking: A Familiar Exposition of the Principles of Reasoning, and their Application to the Art and Science of Banking* (London, 1859).
35 T. Hankey, *The Principles of Banking, its Utility and Economy, with Remarks on the Working and Management of the Bank of England* (London, 1867).
36 W. Bagehot, *Lombard Street* (London, 1873), p. 199.
37 M. Collins, *Banks and Industrial Finance in Britain, 1800–1939* (Basingstoke, 1991), p. 37.

38 Alborn, *Conceiving Companies*, chapters 5–6.
39 Cottrell, 'Finance and germination', p. 31.
40 M. Collins, 'The growth of the firm in the domestic banking sector' in M.W. Kirby and M. Rose (eds), *Business Enterprise in Modern Britain* (London, 1994).
41 F. Capie and G. Rodrik-Bali, 'Concentration in British banking, 1820–1970', *Business History*, 24 (1982), pp. 280–92.
42 See M. Collins and P. Hudson, 'Provincial bank lending, Yorkshire and Merseyside, 1826–60', *Bulletin of Economic Research*, 31 (1979); L. Newton, 'Regional bank-industry relations during the mid-nineteenth century: links between bankers and manufacturing in Sheffield, c.1850–c.1885', *Business History*, 38 (1996).
43 Cottrell, 'Finance and germination', p. 21.
44 M. Collins, 'The banking crisis of 1878', *Economic History Review*, 42 (1989).
45 W. Newmarch, 'The failure of the City of Glasgow Bank and its lessons', *Fortnightly Review*, 30 (1878).
46 W. Kennedy, 'Institutional response to economic growth : capital markets in Britain to 1914' in L. Hannah (ed), *Management Strategy and Business Development: An Historical and Comparative Study* (London, 1975) .
47 A. Holmes and E. Green, *Midland; 150 Years of Banking Business* (London, 1986), pp. 64–7.
48 M. Best and J. Humphries, 'The City and Industrial Decline' in B. Elbaum and W. Lazonick (eds), *The Decline of the British Economy* (Oxford, 1986).
49 G. Rae, *The Country Banker: His Clients, Cares and Work. From an Experience of Forty Years* (London, 1885).
50 L. S. Pressnell, 'Gold reserves, banking reserves and the Baring crisis of 1890' in C. R. Whittlesey and J. S. G. Wilson (eds), *Essays in Money and Banking in Honour of R. S. Sayers* (Oxford, 1968).
51 G.J. Goschen, *The Theory of the Foreign Exchanges* (London, 1861). See also G. J. Goschen, 'Seven Per Cent', *Edinburgh Review*, 71 (1865), pp. 223–51.
52 Pressnell, 'Gold reserves', p. 209. G. J. Goschen, Speech to Leeds Incorporated Chamber of Commerce, 28 January 1891. *The Times*, 29 January 1891, p. 10.
53 G. H. Pownall *English Banking: Its Development and Some Practical Problems it has to Solve* (London, 1914), pp. 51–7.
54 An early discussion is provided in L. A. Rufener, *Money and Banking in the United States* (London, 1935), chapter 17.
55 A. D. Noyes, 'The Banks and the Panic of 1893' *Political Science Quarterly*, 9 (1894) heaps praise on these certificates.
56 C. W. Calomiris and G. Gorton, 'The origins of banking panics: models, facts and bank regulation' in R. G. Hubbard (ed.), *Financial Markets and Financial Crises* (Chicago, 1991).
57 William A. Richardson, *Annual Report on the State of the Finances* (United States 43rd Congress, December 1873), p. 18.

58 R. H. Timberlake, *The Origin of Central Banking in the United States* (Cambridge, Mass., 1978), pp. 175–85.

59 A. P. Andrew, 'The Treasury and the Banks under Secretary Shaw', *Quarterly Journal of Economics*, XXI (1907).

60 L. W. Mints, *A History of Banking Theory in Great Britain and the United States* (Chicago, 1945), p. 225.

61 M. Friedman and A. J. Schwartz , *A Monetary History of the United States, 1867–1960* (Princeton, 1963) pp. 168–9.

62 F. M. Taylor, 'Do we want an elastic currency', *Political Science Quarterly*, II (1896), pp. 133–57

63 *Report of the Monetary Commission of the Indianapolis Convention of Boards of Trade, Chambers of Commerce, Commercial Clubs and other Similar Bodies of the United States* (Indianapolis, 1900).

64 H. A. Krooss and P. A. Samuelson (eds), *Documentary History of Banking and Currency in the United States* (New York, 1969).

65 R. C. West, *Banking Reform and the Federal Reserve, 1863–1923* (Cornell, 1977).

66 J. L. Laughlin, 'The Aldrich-Vreeland Act', *Journal of Political Economy*, XVI (1908), pp. 489–513; *The Federal Reserve Act: Its Origins and Problems* (New York, 1933), chapter 1. H. Parker Willis, *The Federal Reserve* (New York, 1915); A. Barton Hepburn, 'Government Currency vs. Bank Currency' in *The Currency Problem and the Present Financial Situation* (New York, 1908).

67 O. Sprague, *Banking Reform in the United States* (Cambridge, Mass. 1913); A. Piatt Andrew, 'Criticisms of the note-issuing provisions of the Owen-Glass Bill', *Proceedings of the Academy of Political Science*, IV (1913–14); Paul M Warburg, 'A united reserve bank of the United States', *Proceedings of the Academy of Political Science*, I (1910–11), pp. 302–42.

68 P. M. Warburg, 'Principles that must underlie monetary reform in the United States', *Proceedings of the Academy of Political Science*, IV (1913–14) pp. 500–12.

69 D. C. Wheelock, *The Strategy and Consistency of Federal Reserve Monetary Policy, 1924–1933* (Cambridge, 1991), chapter 1.

70 Wheelock, *Strategy and Consistency*, pp. 16–17; Friedman and Schwartz, *Monetary History*, p. 251. *Tenth Annual Report of the Federal Reserve Board, Covering Operations For the Year 1923* (Washington, Government Printing Office, 1924), pp. 1–39.

71 Phillips cites particularly H. D. MacLeod, *Theory and Practice of Banking*; and H. White, *Money and Banking*. C. A. Phillips, *Bank Credit: A Study of the Principles and Factors Underlying Advances Made By Banks to Borrowers* (New York, 1924). Much of this section is based on the discussion in Humphrey, *Money, Banking and Inflation*, chapter 1.

72 Humphrey, *Money, Banking and Inflation*, p. 4.

73 A. Marshall, Evidence before the Royal Commission on Gold and Silver, 19 December 1887, Questions 9623–9651.

74 J. W. Angell and K. F. Ficek, 'The expansion of bank deposits', *Journal of Political Economy*, XLI (1933); J. E. Meade'The amount of money and the banking system', *Economic Journal*, 44 (1934), pp. 77–83.

75 Best and Humphries, 'The City'.

76 A good introduction to these issues is provided by Collins, *Banks and Industrial Finance* and by F. Capie and M. Collins, *Have the Banks Failed British Industry?* (London, 1992).

77 The following paragraphs follow the analysis presented in D. M. Ross, 'The Macmillan gap and the British credit market in the 1930s' in Cottrell, Teichova and Yuzawa (eds), *Finance in the Age of the Corporate Economy.*

78 H. S. Foxwell, 'The financing of industry and trade', *Economic Journal*, 27 (1919).

79 *Report of the Committee on Finance and Industry* (P.P. 1931, Cmnd 3897).

80 J. Reisser, *The German Great Banks and their Concentration in Connection with the Economic Development of Germany*, United States National Monetary Commission; 61st Congress, 2nd Session, Document no. 593. (Washington, Government Printing Office, 1911); R. Tilly, 'German banking 1850–1914: development assistance for the strong?', *Journal of European Economic History*, 15 (1986), pp. 113–52.

81 J. Edwards and S. Ogilvie, 'Universal banks and German industrialization: a reappraisal', *Economic History Review*, XLIX (1996), p. 444.

82 N. R. Lamoreaux, *Insider Lending: Banks, Personal Connections and Economic Development in Industrial New England* (New York, 1994).

83 Lamoreaux, *Insider Lending.* See also C. Calomiris, 'The costs of rejecting universal banking: American finance in the German mirror' in N. Lamoreaux and D. Raff (eds), *Coordination and Information. Historical perspectives on the Organization of Enterprise* (Chicago, 1995).

84 B. De Long, 'Did J. P. Morgan's men add value? An economists's perspective on financial capitalism' in P. Temin (ed.), *Inside the Business Enterprise. Historical Perspectives on the Use of Information* (Chicago, 1991).

85 Final report of the Pujo Committee; United States; House Report No. 1593; 62nd Congress, 3rd Session; February 28.

86 J. R. Commons, 'The stabilization of prices and business', *American Economic Review*, X, (1925), pp. 43–52; T. E. Gregory, 'What can Central Banks really do?', *American Economic Review*, X, (1925), pp. 53–9.

87 K. Wicksell, 'The influence of the rate of interest on prices', *Economic Journal*, XVII (1907), pp. 213–20.

88 Ibid.

89 R. G. Hawtrey, *The Art of Central Banking* (London, 1932), chapter 6. For a discussion of this, see D. E. Moggridge, *Maynard Keynes: An Economist's Biography* (London, 1992), pp. 485–8.

90 R. G. Hawtrey, *A Century of Bank Rate* (Longmans, Green and Co.: London, 1938), chapter IX.

91 J. E. Meade and P. W. S. Andrews, 'Summaries of replies to questions on effects of interest rates', *Oxford Economic Papers*, 1 (1938), p. 28.

92 H. F. Lydall, 'The impact of the credit squeeze on small and medium sized manufacturing firms', *Economic Journal*, 67 (1957), pp. 415–31.
93 J. F. Ebersole, 'The influence of interest rates upon entrepreneurial decisions in business: a case study', *Harvard Business Review*, XVIII (1939), p. 39.
94 D. H. Robertson, 'What has happened to the rate of interest', *Three Banks Review*, I (1949).
95 R. S. Sayers, *Central Banking After Bagehot* (Clarendon Press: Oxford, 1957), p. 1.
96 R. Rosa, 'Interest rates and the central bank' in *Money, Trade and Economic Growth: Essays in Honour of John H Williams* (Clarendon Press: Oxford, 1951).
97 J. Stiglitz and A. Weiss, 'Credit rationing in markets with asymmetric information', *American Economic Review*, 71 (1981), pp. 393–410.

# 1

## An enquiry into the currency principle, the connexion of the currency with prices and the expediency of a separation of issue from banking

T. Tooke, *An enquiry into the currency principle, the connexion of the currency with prices and the expediency of a separation of issue from banking*. (London, Brown, Green and Longmans, 1844).

Thomas Tooke was the leading protagonist on the side of the Banking School in the arguments around the 1844 Act. Author (with William Newmarch) of the monumental *History of Prices,* Tooke's output was all the more impressive for being a Governor of the Royal Exchange Corporation and Director and Chairman of the St. Katharine's Dock Company.

Tooke's work on the *History of Prices* was based on careful and empirical observation; he formed the view that the quantity of money in circulation was dependent on the level of transactions and prices, not the cause of them. The real bills doctrine is clearly embedded in this approach to the price-transactions relationship, and it is further elaborated in this pamphlet, written in 1844. Pivetti, in the *New Palgrave Dictionary of Economics* describes the *Inquiry into the Currency Principle* as Tooke's 'most representative and outstanding piece', while Schumpeter suggests that it is the work in which 'polemical ardor got the better of him and led him to abandon some of his best results'. It is certainly a robust challenge to the Currency School and contains the three crucial components of the Banking School's views; a criticism of the separation of notes and deposits for the purposes of setting reserve requirements, the real bills doctrine as represented by the law of reflux and the notion that the money supply was determined by the level of transactions, and the view that the monetary authorities did not have the power to determine the rate of interest. At the same time, however, wise banking policy – determined at the discretion of the Bank of England – was argued to be the main guarantor of banking stability and the maintenance of convertibility.

# PREFACE.

Some part of the following pages was written immediately after the appearance of the reports of the committee of the House of Commons on Banks of Issue, and the greater part has since been put together without any definite view to publication. The reason which has determined me in now publishing them is, that whether the views here presented be assented to or not, they are such, I think, as ought not to be wholly overlooked in the consideration of the measures which the government has announced its intention of proposing to Parliament in the course of the present session, with a view to placing the banking system of the United Kingdom on an improved and permanent footing.

Some of the points which I have endeavoured to establish may probably be thought not to be made out with sufficient fulness of explanation, and doubtless on several of the topics a more exhaustive process of proof and illustration might be required for the purpose of anticipating and answering objections. But such a process could not be comprised within a readable compass. It would require a book instead of a pamphlet.

The necessity for compression, which I feel to be thus imposed upon me, has prevented me from touching at all upon topics which are of importance and connected in some points of view with the subject here discussed, but to which justice could not be done in an incidental notice.

One of the great difficulties of dealing with the subject about to be discussed, as indeed in most cases of controversy, but in this more than in most others, arises from the use of the same words in different senses. Not to mention the mooted points, as to whether deposits, bankers' cheques, and bills of exchange should be considered as money or currency; because these involve rather definition and classification, according to the purposes for which they are supposed to be employed, than that loose and ambiguous use of terms to which I allude.

This consists in a shifting of the meaning of the term, when applied indiscriminately in the same argument to designate things and processes totally distinct.

It will be seen in the course of this discussion how much of the obscurity and perplexity and error, in which the objects of inquiry are involved, may be traced to the vague and ambiguous language commonly employed in treating of them: such for instance as "gold and silver," "the precious metals," and "bullion," used indiscriminately and synonymously with "money" and "currency;" the terms "money and currency" employed when "capital" is meant. "Issues of paper," meaning bank notes, for mere advances of capital where no bank notes pass; — the "value of money or currency," for the rate of interest or discount. "Abundance and cheapness, or scarcity and dearness of money," to signify a lower or a higher rate of interest, or a tendency to either. And

" expansion and contraction of the currency, or of the circulation," when undue extension of credit, and its consequent revulsion, would be the correct description of the facts of the case.

The instances in which confusion and inconsistency in reasoning may be traced to this loose and ambiguous use of language are innumerable; and if I could hope that by directing attention to the sources of error so pointed out, and thus induce more care and distinctness of phraseology, so as to render future discussions on the subject more intelligible, and consequently to narrow the grounds for difference of opinion, I should consider that my labour in this publication has not been thrown away, even although I should fail of gaining assent to the conclusions, or any part of them, which I have endeavoured to establish.

London, March, 1844.

# AN INQUIRY

INTO

# THE CURRENCY PRINCIPLE,

ETC. ETC.

---

## INTRODUCTION.

It was held by most writers of any authority on the subject of the Currency, till within the last few years, that the purposes of a mixed circulation of coin and paper were sufficiently answered, as long as the coin was perfect, and the paper constantly convertible into coin; and that the only evils to be guarded against by regulation, were those attending suspension of payment and insolvency of the banks, a large proportion of which blend an issue of promissory notes with their other business. This, in point of fact, is what is understood in general terms as the banking principle, and is that upon which our system of currency is constructed and conducted.

But a new canon of currency has of late been promulgated by persons of no mean authority. According to these authorities, it is not sufficient that the bank notes should be at all times strictly convertible into coin, and that the banks, whether issuing or not issuing, should be solvent; they consider that a purely metallic circulation (excepting only as regards the convenience and economy of paper), is the type of a perfect currency, and contend that the only sound principle of a mixed currency is that by which the bank notes in circulation should be made to conform to the gold, into which they are convertible, not only in value, but in amount; that is to say, that the bank notes being supposed to be a substitute, and the only substitute, for so much coin, should vary exactly in amount as the coin would have done if the Currency had been purely metallic; and that the test of good or bad management is not, as is considered under the mere banking principle, in the extent or proportion of reserve in treasure and in immediately-convertible securities held by the banks; but in the degree of correspondence between variations in the amount of bullion, and variations in the amount of bank notes in circulation. A regulation of the issue of bank notes, in conformity with this doctrine, is now understood to be designated as the Currency principle.

With a view to the application of this principle to practice, it has been suggested that either a national bank should be established under commissioners, whose duty and functions should be confined to the exchange of paper against gold, and of gold against paper, for all beyond a fixed amount of paper issued against securities; or that the Bank of England should be the sole source of issue, under the strictest rule of separation of the functions of issue from the merely banking department.

The arguments urged in favour of such separation have, as it should seem, made considerable impression on the public mind, and schemes founded upon this principle have been strongly pressed on the attention of government, on the ground not only of guarding against the danger of suspension and insolvencies, but of imparting more confidence and stability to credit and trade, and of securing greater steadiness in prices, and thus obviating or abating the alternations of feverish excitement, and the extreme of depression, which have prevailed under the existing system, and which are imputed to a neglect of the Currency principle.

The question whether the constant convertibility of the paper can, or cannot, be preserved and maintained under a prudent management, on the existing footing of a union of issue and banking, will be considered hereafter. But, waiving for the present all consideration of the question of security against suspension and insolvencies, it is desirable to examine the grounds on which it is contended that other evils, besides the danger of non-convertibility and insolvencies of banks of issue, arise out of the present system as compared with the currency-principle system, and that the test of good or bad management of the country banks of issue consists, not in the amount of their reserves in gold and available securities, compared with their liabilities, but in the conformity of the variations of their circulation to those of the circulation of the Bank of England; while the test of the management of the Bank of England is in the conformity of the variations in the amount of its circulation to those of the efflux or influx of the precious metals.

# CHAPTER I.

## STATEMENT OF THE CURRENCY PRINCIPLE.

The theory of the Currency principle numbers among its advocates many distinguished names. The fullest and most elaborate statements of it, however, are to be found in the publications of Mr. Norman, Mr. Loyd, and Colonel Torrens, and in the evidence of the two former gentlemen before the Committee of the House of Commons on Banks of Issue in 1840. I therefore avail myself mainly of their exposition of the doctrine, and their arguments in support of it, as affording the best grounds for an examination of the theory, and of the practice recommended as an application of it.

The following extract from Mr. Norman's evidence conveys a concise statement of the theory, and of the proposed application of it, as the only sound rule for the paper portion of the currency, namely bank notes, which he limits to those notes which are in the hands of the public: —

" I consider a metallic currency to be the most perfect currency, except so far as respects inconvenience in some respects, and cost. In every thing else a metallic currency is the most perfect, and should be looked upon as the type of all other currencies; and as from their superior convenience and greater cheapness, bank notes are introduced to supply the place of a certain portion of metallic currency, I think that bank notes should be so managed, that they should possess all the other attributes of a metallic currency, and among those attributes, I conceive the most important to be that they should increase and decrease in the same way that a metallic currency would increase and decrease. I do not think it is possible to improve upon a metallic currency, except in the two points of convenience and cheapness." *

Mr. Norman afterwards explained, that by convenience he meant the easier transfer, and by cheapness, the economy of using the less costly material; so that the paper, thus regulated, would be so far an improvement on a metallic currency.

The following are the chief † evils which present themselves, according to Mr. Norman's view, in our existing paper circulation, from its not conforming to such rule: —

1. A tendency to vary, both as to excess and deficiency, in an unnecessary degree, and at unsuitable periods.

2. A liability to discredit, both mercantile and political, in a large portion of it, if not the whole.

3. Temporary or permanent insolvency on the part of many of the issuers.

Mr. Loyd in his evidence gives the following view of the inconvenience, which he ascribes to the present system: —

*Q.* 2748. "Are there any other evils besides the danger of nonconvertibility that arise out of the present system?" *A.* "There can be no doubt about it; the state of the circulation has a very direct effect upon the state of credit, of confidence, of prices, and of banking; and if the state of the circulation be allowed to become an unnatural one, unnatural and pernicious effects will be produced upon all those. If your circulation is subject either to depreciation from excess of its amount, or to violent fluctuations of amount, then undoubtedly that will be followed by corresponding effects upon confidence, upon credit, upon prices, upon banking, and so forth. Those things are also affected

* G. W. Norman. Evidence. Committee on Banks of Issue. Question No. 1749.

† "Remarks on Currency and Banking," by G. W. Norman, 1838.

by other considerations. I do not see that it is possible to analyse the effects, and to attribute to each cause its respective share in producing those effects; all that can certainly be understood is, that if you regulate the paper circulation upon sound principles, you may be quite sure that you have then removed that portion of the evil effects which was attributable to the want of due regulation."

By an unnatural state of the circulation, and the want of due regulation, must be understood, in the sense in which Mr. Loyd uses the term, a non-conformity of the amount of bank notes to the amount of bullion.

---

## CHAP. II.

### MODE OF OPERATION OF A METALLIC CIRCULATION.

ADMITTING, for the sake of argument, that a metallic circulation is the type of a perfect currency, it should seem that those who confidently pronounce it to be so, labour under a most egregious misconception of what the working of it would be.

Upon the grounds which I have now to state, it will be evident that the operation of a perfectly metallic circulation would not be attended with the advantages which they contemplate; nor, on the other hand, with the disadvantages which might be apprehended, if it were to work as they seem to imagine it would.

According to the Currency principle, every export of the precious metals under a metallic circulation, would be attended with a contraction of the amount and value of the currency, causing a fall of prices, until the degree of contraction and consequent fall of prices should be such, as by inducing a diminished import and increased export of commodities, to cause a reflux of the metals and a restoration of prices to their proper level. So, on the other hand, an influx of the precious metals would raise prices, till they reached a level at which the converse of the process would take place. This oscillating process of a rise and fall of prices with every influx or efflux of the precious metals, independently of circumstances connected with the cost of production of commodities, and the ordinary rate of consumption, would be perplexing enough, and any thing but convenient to the commercial, or the manufacturing, or the agricultural community.

The advocates, however, of the doctrine contend that, although thus the oscillations might be more frequent, the scale of them would be more contracted, every divergence being more quickly checked. I firmly believe, however, that if every export and import of the precious metals were attended with the effects imputed to them by this theory, the inconvenience would be felt to be intolerable; and that some of what Mr. Norman calls economising expedients would be devised and applied as a remedy.

But the operation would not be that which the theory, as it is stated in the following passages, supposes: —

"It is universally admitted by persons acquainted with monetary science, that paper money should be so regulated as to keep the medium of exchange, of which it may form a part, in the same state, with respect to amount and to value, in which the medium of exchange would exist, were the circulating portion of it purely metallic. Now, it is self-evident, that if the circulation were purely metallic, an adverse exchange, causing an exportation of the metals to any given amount, would occasion a contraction of the circulating currency to the same amount; and that a favourable exchange, causing an importation of the metals to a given amount, would cause an expansion of the circulating currency to the same amount. If the currency of the metropolis consisted of gold, an adverse exchange, causing an exportation of gold to the amount of 1,000,000*l.*, would withdraw from circulation one million of sovereigns."—TORRENS. *Letter to Lord Melbourne, pp.* 29, 30.

"The amount of the import or export of the precious metals, is a pretty sure measure of what would have been the increase or decrease of the amount of a metallic currency."—S. J. LOYD. *Further Reflections on the Currency, page* 34.

And Mr. Norman, after explaining the manner in which the exchanges, as between two countries, A and B, may be rendered adverse to A, so as to cause an export of coin or bullion, goes on to say—

"The export of coin and bullion will cause general prices to fall in country A, and to rise in B, supposing the debt to B not to be sooner discharged, until it becomes more advantageous to export goods than money."—*Letter to C. Wood, Esq. M. P., p.* 17.

In these passages, and many more that might be cited, it is assumed that the precious metals, gold, and silver, and bullion, are synonymous with currency and money, and are convertible terms. And accordingly every export of the precious metals is not only considered, in the supposition of a metallic circulation, as a contraction of the currency of this country; but as so much added to the currency of the country to which it is exported. Such alteration in the relative quantity of the metals in the respective countries from which or to which they are transmitted being, according to this theory, an abstraction or addition of so much money; and prices, that is, the general prices of commodities, being considered as depending on the quantity of money, a corresponding rise or fall of them is assumed to be the consequence. In this view some very important considerations are overlooked.

Before entering upon them, however, I must premise, that throughout this discussion the value of gold in the commercial world is assumed to be constant, *i. e.* that the cost of production and the general demand are unvaried; also that the tariffs of foreign countries are *in statu quo*, so as to confine the consideration to the effects of an influx or efflux of bullion on the currencies of the respective countries, divested of any reference to disturbing causes, beyond those incidental to the course of trade and international banking.

There is, and must generally be, in a country like this or like France, a stock greater or less of gold and silver, beyond that which is in use as money or as plate, or which is in the mint, and in goldsmiths' and silversmiths' hands, in preparation for use as either. This surplus or floating stock may be considered as seeking a market, whether for internal purposes or for export; and, be the quantity greater or less, can it be said of it, if it is exported, that the amount is so much abstracted from the currency of the country, any more than if an equal value of tin or zinc, or lead or iron were exported?

Moreover, of that part of the stock existing in the shape of coin in this country it may be observed, that as the coinage is not subject to a seignorage, there may be, and frequently is, in that shape a considerable amount of the precious metals which may not be in the hands of the public, circulating as money, nor in the reserves of the different banks, the Bank of England excepted; but may, like the uncoined metals, be seeking a market at home or abroad. It may be in the coffers of the Bank of England; but held as bullion, being in the shape of coin equally convenient for every purpose, and more convenient for some purposes, in that form, besides that of serving for currency, than in uncoined gold, that is, in bars or ingots.

The idea of gold seeking a market, and not immediately finding one, may seem strange, and by the firm believers in the currency-principle doctrine may be set down as paradoxical and absurd.

Gold is an object in such universal demand, or in other words so universally marketable, that its being supposed to be kept on hand at all, under the uncertainty of finding a suitable market for it, appears to be inconceivable, or almost a contradiction in terms.

I am ready to admit that gold is a commodity in such general demand that it may always command a market, that it can always buy all other commodities; whereas, other commodities cannot always buy gold. The markets of the world are open to it as merchandise at less sacrifice upon an emergency, than would attend an export of any other article, which might in quantity or kind be beyond the usual demand in the country to which it is sent. So far there can be, I presume, no difference of opinion.

But there will be found to be no inconsiderable difference, if we distinguish as we ought to do, for the purpose whether of theory or practice, between gold considered as merchandise, *i. e.* as capital, and gold considered as currency circulating in the shape of coin among the public.

Mr. Senior, in one of his lectures on the value of money, observes, "The value of the precious metals as money must depend ultimately on their value as materials of jewellery and plate; since if they were not used as commodities, they could not circulate as money." And he makes a remark to the same effect in an article in the "Edinburgh Review" for July last, on Free trade and Retaliation. "The primary cause of the utility of gold is of course its use as the material of plate. The secondary cause is its use as money." Of the truth of these propositions there can be no doubt.

In a new and enlarged edition, just published, of that vast repertory of various and important information, "The Commercial Dictionary," Mr. M'Culloch, after weighing different authorities, gives the following estimate of the consumption of the precious metals for purposes distinct from their use as money:—

"According to this view of the matter, the present annual consumption in the arts will be—the United Kingdom 2,500,000*l.*; France, 1,000,000*l.*; Switzerland, 450,000*l.*; the rest of Europe, 1,600,000*l.*; in all, 5,550,000*l.* To which adding 500,000*l.* for the consumption of North America, the total consumption will be 6,050,000*l.*

"But a portion of the gold and silver annually made use of in the arts, is derived from the fusion of old plate, the burning of lace, picture frames, &c.

"Assuming that, as a medium, twenty per cent., or one-fifth part, of the precious metals annually made use of in the arts, is obtained from the fusion of old plate, we shall have, by deducting this proportion from the 6,050,000*l.* applied to the arts in Europe and America, 4,840,000*l.* as the total annual appropriation of the new gold and silver dug from the mines to such purposes, leaving about 4,400,000*l.* a year to be manufactured into coin, and exported to India," &c.

Mr. M'Culloch estimates the present annual produce of the precious metals from the American, European, and Russo-Asiatic mines, at 9,250,000*l.**

* Although the question of the total annual produce of gold and silver may not be considered as having any immediate bearing on the point now under discussion, it is a matter of such general interest, especially as relates to the vast increase of gold in Siberia and the Oural district of Russia, that I am induced to give Mr. M'Culloch's view of the quantities produced from the several sources which he specifies. After stating from the most recent authorities the quantities produced from the South American and Mexican mines, he goes on to observe—

"But in addition to the above quantity of 631 poods obtained from washings in Siberia in 1842, the silver obtained from the mines of Kolyvan yielded, in the course of the same year, 30 poods of gold,

As this country is not only a large consumer of the precious metals for purposes other than money, but is also an entrepôt for receiving from the mines,

while the washings and mines of the Oural mountains yielded no fewer than 310 poods; making the total produce 971 poods; equal to 35,030 lb. avoirdupois, or 42,571 lb. Troy, which, at 46*l.* 14*s.* 6*d.* per lb. is equivalent to 1,989,128*l.* 11*s.* — (*Supplement au Journal de l'Intérieur* for 1842, p. 16.)

It is necessary, however, to bear in mind that the Russian government imposes a duty, varying, according to circumstances, from 20 to 25 per cent., on the produce of the mines and washings; and there can be no doubt that the temptation to avoid so heavy a duty, and the peculation on the part of the agents for the Crown, must give rise to a great deal of smuggling. Perhaps, under such circumstances, we should not be far wrong if we estimated the metal of which no account is taken at ¼th part of the above; but taking it only at ⅕th part, we have a sum of no less than 2,386,000*l.* for the produce of the Russian gold mines and washings in 1842.

It may be supposed, perhaps, that it would be wrong to take the produce of the Russian washings and mines in 1842 as a fair criterion of their future produce, seeing that the produce of the washings in that year was not far from being twice as great as it had been in any previous year. But it is to be observed, that the produce in question has been progressively and rapidly augmenting during the 13 years ending with 1842; and it is stated in the official journal whence we have borrowed these details, that *selon toute probabilité, et à moins qu'on ne manque d'ouvriers, le chiffre de l'année* 1843 *offrira de nouveau sur celui de l'année dernière un excédant très-considérable.*[1]

" In addition to this vast quantity of gold, Russia produces a quantity of silver, which may, perhaps, be estimated, at an average, at about 1,300 poods a year, worth, at 5*s.* 2*d.* an ounce, 193,440*l.*

" We have seen no very recent accounts of the produce of the Saxon, Hungarian, and other European mines, on which it would be at all safe to place much reliance. We incline, however, to think that their produce may be safely estimated at about 750,000*l.* a year.

" Hence, supposing we are nearly right in these estimates, the total available produce of the American, European, and Russo-Asiatic mines will be, S. American and Mexican, 5,600,000*l.*; U. States, 100,000*l.*; European, 750,000*l.*; Russo-Asiatic, 2,600,000*l.*; making in all, 9,050,000*l.* And therefore, should these estimates be not very wide of the mark, it may be concluded, in opposition to the commonly received opinions on the subject, that the supply of the precious metals is at present but little inferior to what it amounted to when the American mines were most productive.

[1] We have since learned, as this article was going to press, that the produce of the Russian gold mines and washings in 1843 amounted to no less than 1342 poods! being equivalent, adding one fifth for the quantity not brought to account, to 3,298,962*l.* 11*s.* 1*d.* sterling; an increase which is altogether extraordinary, and will have the most powerful influence.

and distributing the greater portion of the quantity applicable to the consumption of other countries, the bullion trade, totally independently of supplying the currency, must of necessity be very considerable. In resorting to this entrepôt the metals can only be considered as merchandise in transit, seeking a market for consumption either in this country or abroad.

But beyond the stock which is requisite for this purpose, and which must always include more or less of surplus to meet occasional extra demand, there must be a very considerable amount of the precious metals applicable and applied as the most convenient mode of adjustment of international balances, being a commodity more generally in demand, and less liable to fluctuations in market value than any other. I will not venture, in the absence of any recognised grounds for computation, to hazard an estimate of the amount so required; but bearing in mind the immense extent of international transactions; and the vicissitudes of the seasons, and other circumstances affecting the relative imports and exports of food, and raw materials, and manufactures, besides the variations in the market value of national and private securities interchangeable, it cannot but be that the quantity of bullion required to be constantly available for the purpose must be very large; the principal deposits of it being in the Bank of England, the Bank of France, and the public banks of Hamburg and Amsterdam. These deposits may, moreover, in some of the public banks, be swelled by coins which have become superfluous in the circulation.

If, therefore, we take into account the magnitude of the stock necessarily imported, partly for the consumption of plate in this country, and partly for that abroad, and of the amount required as available funds for the adjustment of international balances, it may not be deemed an extravagant supposition that there might occasionally be under a perfectly metallic circulation fluctuations, within moderately short periods, to the extent of at least five or six millions sterling in the import and export of bullion, perfectly extrinsic of the amount or value of the coin circulating as money in the hands of the public, and perfectly without influence on the general prices of commodities, as equally without general prices having been a cause of such fluctuations.

It may be objected that the quantity of bullion which I have supposed to be in deposit among the principal public banks of the commercial world, applicable to the adjustment of international balances, should be looked upon as performing the functions of money, in restoring the level of the currencies, which the very fact of the necessity for the transmission of money from one country to another proves to have been disturbed. This objection is founded on the assumption that gold and silver are money or currency, and it is supposed that the transmissions of bullion for the purposes in question have a direct operation upon the amount of money or currency in actual circulation in the several countries. But in this objection the consideration is overlooked, that the coins only which enter into, that is, form part of the internal circulation of the country, can be designated as currency, while bullion can only be viewed in the light of capital.*

* With the exception of Mexican dollars, this being the form in which the produce of the silver mines of America is mainly distributed, and Imperials, the golden coin of Russia, being the form in which the extraordinarily large and increasing produce of the Asiatic provinces of that empire is adding to the general supply of the precious metals; and further excepting the gold coins of this country, which, being issued without any charge whatever for manufacture, are found to be for some purposes of export more convenient than bars or ingots: with these exceptions, the instances are rare in which, unless depreciated at home by compulsory paper money, the coins usually circulating as money are withdrawn to supply foreign payments of any magnitude.

The distinction between bullion, as merchandise or capital, and coins, as money or currency, may be exemplified in the case of coins which are subject to a seignorage, and in cases such as that of Hamburg, where the money current for all the ordinary expenditure of income consists chiefly of a variety of foreign coins, passing from hand to hand at a conventional value, while all mercantile payments are made by transfers of capital, deposited in the form of fine silver, and called bank-money.

In such a case as that of Hamburg there have been, and must often again be, very great fluctuations in the amount of silver in the bank, and consequently of bank-money, without any obviously corresponding variations in the amount of money in circulation for current purposes of expenditure by the community, or any variation as arising from that cause in the general prices of their commodities. And if a seignorage were imposed on the gold coin of this country on correct principles (that is, accompanied by a limitation of tender, and by a power on the part of the holders to demand gold bullion at 3*l.* 17*s.* 10½*d.* per ounce), there might be, and there would be, supposing a purely metallic circulation, occasionally very considerable variation in the amount of bullion in the coffers of the national bank, or in the hands of dealers in bullion, without necessarily in the slightest degree affecting the amount of the currency actually in circulation, in the ordinary daily transactions arising out of the expenditure of individuals composing the public, and without variation in general prices.

The views, of which an outline has here been sketched, distinguishing bullion as a commodity, constituting the readiest means of international transfers of capital, from the currency employed for internal purposes, will be rendered more clear when I come to point out, as I shall presently endeavour to do, an important distinction between that part of the circulating medium which is employed in the transfer and distribution of capital, from that which is employed in the expenditure of incomes, that is, in the retail trade of the country. And I do not now enter more fully into detail as to what I conceive would be the working of a purely metallic circulation, because that question does not form the main ground of the present inquiry, which is as to the sufficiency of the arguments adduced in accordance with the theory of the currency principle, in favour of an entire separation of the functions of banks of issue from those of ordinary banking.

In the doctrine which it is my purpose here to examine, the perfection of a metallic circulation is assumed to be beyond question; while the imperfection of our present system of paper credit, quite apart from the danger of inconvertibility, is pointed out and enlarged upon, by reference to the degree in which it is asserted to depart from this assumed model of perfection,—a model of whose properties and mode of operation the most erroneous notions seem to be entertained by those who set it up.*

* In the text I have taken what may be called the mercantile view of the question of international temporary movements of the precious metals, the general value of them being assumed to be constant; and this view I am persuaded is the correct one, for the purpose either of practical application, or of intelligible explanation of the actual course of commercial affairs. As to the more general and abstruse question of the laws which determine the more permanent distribution of those metals among the nations of the earth, constituting the level of the currencies of different countries, as exhibited in their general prices, and in wages especially, valued in gold and silver, it would require, in order to have justice done to it, a more scientific exposition, embracing a much wider range of reasoning and of facts than would comport with the scope or purpose of my present argument.

# CHAP. III.

## MISTAKEN VIEW BY THE CURRENCY THEORY OF THE WORKING OF THE EXISTING SYSTEM.

If sufficient grounds have here been adduced to give rise to, at least, a suspicion that the propounders of the currency theory are unaware, or rather are under a total misconception, of what would be the working of a purely metallic circulation, we are inevitably led to suspect, or rather I should say to conclude, that they may and do labour under a misconception fully as great, not only as to what would be the working of a mixed circulation of coin and bank notes, administered according to the currency principle, that is, so as to conform to what they suppose would be the working of a metallic circulation, but as to what the working of it actually has been and is under the existing banking system.

The misconception which, as it should seem, they labour under, may be referred mainly to the view which they take of bank notes, as being essentially distinct in all their attributes and functions from each and every other of the component parts of the circulating medium, and as coming exclusively along with coin under the designation of *money*.

Bank notes, accordingly, they call paper money, and ascribing, as they do, a direct influence to the quantity of money on the state of trade, of confidence, and credit, and on prices, they attach great importance to the fact of any increase or diminution of bank notes in circulation, more especially as regards a conformity, or non-conformity, of such increase or diminution to variations in the amount of bullion. As therefore they conceive that it is in the power of the banks of issue so to regulate the amount of their notes in circulation, as to conform to variations in the amount of bullion, or, as it is more commonly termed, to regulate their issues, by the exchanges (inasmuch as attention to the exchanges will serve to indicate whether gold is coming in or going out, or likely to come in or go out), they consider the conformity or discrepancy between the fluctuations in the amount of bank notes in circulation and the amount of bullion in the coffers of the Bank of England, as the test or criterion of the good or bad management of the banks.

On occasions of marked discrepancy, the persons who espouse the currency principle, and are, at the same time, favourable to the Bank of England, charge the country banks with counteracting, by their inattention to the exchanges in regulating their issues, all attempts of the Bank of England to restrain the general circulation within due bounds; while the country banks, both private and joint-stock, maintain, through their organs, that it is not in their power to determine what shall be the amount of their notes in the hands of the public. And not content with thus repelling the charge made upon them, they retort it upon the Bank of England, which, according to them, has the controul of the whole circulation, and expands or contracts the amount according as suits its own purpose.

It appears to me that neither of these parties is right in charging the other; and, moreover, that those persons who, on the part of the public, judging only by the criterion set up by the currency theory, namely, by the conformity of variations in the amount of bank notes to variations in the amount of bullion, charge the present system with causing irregularity in the circulation, and with all the evils which flow from bad regulation, are equally far from a right judgment.

I am quite convinced, and will endeavour to show, that the amount of bank notes in circulation, that is, out of the walls of the issuing banks, and in the hands of the public, furnishes no criterion of good or bad management by the banks of issue, and is not an efficient cause operating upon trade and confidence and credit, and upon prices; and that, excepting the greater inconvenience attending the insolvency of an issuing than of a non-issuing bank, there is no difference between the two descriptions of banks as regards their influence on the value of the currency.

I cannot help thinking that there is a lurking impression among the doctrinaires of the currency theory, arising mainly from their use of the term "issue of paper money," which leads them to confound bank notes strictly convertible into coin, with a compulsory and inconvertible paper currency. It is true, no doubt, that they are aware that the liability to payment on demand in gold will eventually check any excess of issue in the one, and will thus distinguish it from the other. But it seems to me equally true, judging by all their expressions and the whole course of their arguments, that they are misled by a false analogy, and that although they admit in general terms that there must be a check to the power of issue by its being brought to the test of convertibility, they are of opinion that there is a power in each individual bank of issue, and in the banks of issue collectively, to operate at any given time in adding directly to the amount of bank notes in circulation, and in withdrawing them from it. The presumption that the advocates of the currency principle are under the influence of this mistaken analogy will be strengthened when we come to the consideration of the effects on trade, credit, and prices, which they ascribe to the influence of the quantity of money, meaning bank notes and coin. In the meantime it may be proper to bestow some remarks on the reasoning by which it is proposed to be proved that bank notes differ in all essential properties, as regards the performance of the functions of money, from all other forms of paper credit employed in the business of interchange.

---

## CHAP. IV.

### DISTINCTIVE PROPERTIES ASCRIBED TO BANK NOTES.

Mr. Norman, after noticing what he calls the contrivances usually resorted to for the purpose of either dispensing with the use of money altogether, or of diminishing the quantity of it, which is absolutely required for the adjustment of existing transactions, observes, —

> " On these contrivances one general remark may be made, as it affords a ready and practical, if not a strictly scientific distinction between such substitutes for money, and that which, as I conceive, really constitutes money, viz. coin and bank notes. If bank notes are withdrawn from circulation, their place must necessarily be supplied by an equal amount of coin; but the abolition of any, or of all of the contrivances for dispensing with the use of money, will not necessitate the introduction in their place of an equal amount of coin or bank notes."—*Letter to C. Wood, Esq., p.* 34.

In dealing with this proposition, let us try it by putting the case in the strongest way, and suppose that the Bank of England has the power, and is disposed to withdraw all its notes from circulation; or, in order to obviate the objection, that in such case other banks might supply the vacuum, let us suppose that all promissory notes, payable on demand, were suppressed by act of parliament. Would Mr. Norman contend, that the whole amount must of necessity be replaced by coin? Most assuredly such would not be the effect.

A moment's consideration must be sufficient to satisfy any one that it would only be the smaller denomination of notes, which, if suppressed, would require to be replaced by coin ; the whole of the 1*l.* notes which still circulate in Ireland and Scotland, would require to be so replaced, and the greater part of the 5*l.* notes, and a small part of the 10*l.* notes, in the United Kingdom.

All the larger amounts might be, and most probably would be, supplied by cheques and bills of exchange and settlements.

The employment of the higher denominations of Bank of England notes is chiefly for the following purposes : —

1. Collection of the public revenue, and the payment of it into the Exchequer.

2. Payments on sales and mortgages of landed and other fixed property. Till lately the rule in transactions of this nature, was almost uniformly that the payment, on conveyance of the deeds, should be made in bank notes. But there has of late been a tendency to relax this rule, and cheques are now not unfrequently received in payment on such occasions.

3. Dividends and rents received by persons who do not employ bankers.

4. Payments for debts in cases in which the debtor has not a banker, or in which he would not be trusted so far as to have his cheque received in satisfaction of the claim.

5. Payments into Court in litigated claims.

6. Reserves held by bankers, and especially those

of the west end of the town, and by the joint-stock banks in the city who are not admitted to the clearing-house.

7. Settlements at the clearing-house.

Now these are peculiar purposes, most or all of which might be answered by other means than bank notes, and most assuredly not by supplying their place by coin.

1. The public revenue is, in an increasing number of instances, paid into the Exchequer by drafts on the Bank of England.

2. Payments for landed and fixed property are in an increasing number of instances paid by cheques.

3. Dividends to persons not keeping bankers, might be retained by them in the shape of warrants.

4. and 5. Involve so small an amount, as not materially to affect the question.

6. The circulation of Bank of England notes among bankers, whether between the Bank of England and the west-end bankers, and the city joint stock bankers, and the circulation of country bank notes, in settlements among each other, are mere conventional transfers of capital, which, with

7. The clearings among the bankers of the city of London, might all be effected either by Exchequer bills, as in the case of the banks of Edinburgh, or by cheques on the Bank of England.

The country bank notes above the lowest denominations, (which are in use in the retail trade, and in the payment of wages,) are mostly employed in the provision markets, and in cattle and horse fairs, purposes for which, as I shall proceed to show, bills of exchange were formerly, and might be again very extensively employed.

# CHAP. V.

## DEPOSITS AND CHEQUES.

AMONG the contrivances which the currency theory allows to be the means of dispensing with the use of money, although it will not admit that they perfectly perform the functions of money, are deposits or lodgements in banks, subject to certain stipulations of repayment. In the examination by the Committees on Banks of Issue in 1840, there seems to have been a great waste of time and temper in the discussion of the question, whether deposits should be considered as currency, and as performing the functions of money.

There is an obvious objection to speaking of deposits in general terms as performing the functions of money, inasmuch as deposits are of different descriptions as to the conditions of repayment attaching to them. But supposing the deposits to be strictly payable on demand, there is still an apparent impropriety in ascribing to them *quâ* deposits a direct agency or activity.

It sounds oddly, to say the least of it, to speak of deposits or lodgements of money as being active. The activity, if any, is in the payment by cheques founded upon the deposits. It is not the deposits, but the transfers of them; or, in other words, the cheques that constitute the actual instruments of interchange, and effect payments concurrently with bank notes. They perform the functions of money not only as perfectly as bank notes, but in the description of transactions to which they are applicable, they are more convenient than bank notes.

They obviate the trouble of paying fractional parts of the sum in coin; they, in many cases, supersede the use of stamped receipts, inasmuch as the books of the bankers serve as evidence of the payment. They obviate the risk of robbery or fire, which attends the possession of bank notes by persons not having the accommodation of strong and fire-proof safes. The cheque books of the drawers serve also to preserve a counterpart of all the particulars of the payment, and so assist in tracing error or irregularity, if there be any, in the payment or in the entry of it. And the use of crossed cheques, as far as regards the London bankers who resort to the clearing-house, admits of the drawers of such cheques adjusting their receipts and payments between the opening of business and half-past three or four o'clock, so as that their banker shall have only the balance to pay, or receive, or set off. Some or all of these advantages, with possibly others, which may exist and may have escaped my observation, are sufficient to account for the great and increasing tendency to the employment of cheques in preference to bank notes in the pecuniary transactions of the metropolis and of the metropolitan district.* Independently of the greater convenience which is found to attach to the use of cheques instead of bank notes, by persons who are in the habit of employing bankers, the employment of bankers by persons, whether traders or not, of the middle classes (the upper classes of course, all, or nearly all, employ bankers), is daily gaining ground, and this is an additional cause of the displacement of bank notes by cheques.

There is every reason to believe that a much larger

* In illustration of the tendency to a preference of the use of cheques over bank notes in mercantile transactions in London, it may here be observed, that if a merchant in the course of his business receives Bank of England notes of 100*l.* or upwards, and has on the same day to pay away a sum or sums exactly equal to the notes, he will in most cases make his payment by a cheque or cheques, and put the bank notes into his banker's, to be placed to his credit against his drafts.

amount of payments in the metropolitan districts is effected by drafts on bankers than by bank notes. And the circumstance that deposits payable on demand are the foundations on which drafts are passed, such drafts effecting more payments than bank notes, seems to be the ground on which the late Mr. Page in his evidence (and Mr. Hume in his examinations, his views being identical with those of Mr. Page) contended that deposits are currency and more active in making payments than bank notes.

*Qu.* 770. (Mr. Hume.) "As you have stated that circulation and deposits are both currency, which of the two do you consider to be most active in making payments?"

*An.* "Deposits beyond all question."

I do not, as I have before had occasion to observe, concur in the propriety of applying the term currency to deposits, because, although such of them as are payable on demand may and do serve for payments by the means of transfer, it is the transfers or cheques, and not the deposits, which, in point of fact, constitute the instruments of exchange. But whether deposits payable on demand, or only the drafts against them, are to be considered as currency, is immaterial to this part of my argument, which is to show that, as instruments of exchange, cheques, or the deposits on which these are founded, answer the purposes of money, as conveniently in nearly all instances as bank notes, and more conveniently in most cases*; and that therefore whatever influence may be ascribed to bank notes, whether on prices, or on the rate of interest, or on the state of trade, cannot be denied to cheques or to their substratum, deposits payable on demand.

* There is a great saving of coin in paying by drafts instead of bank notes. In payments by bank notes all fractional parts of 5*l.* must be paid by coin. Upon the very numerous payments in the Kingdom (Ireland and Scotland, where 1*l.* notes still circulate, excepted) the saving of coin thus effected must amount to a considerable sum.

# CHAP. VI.

## BILLS OF EXCHANGE.

THAT transactions to a very large amount are adjusted by bills of exchange has long been known and admitted in general terms; but the vastness of the amount was not brought distinctly under the notice of the public till the appearance of a pamphlet by the late Mr. Leatham, an eminent banker at Wakefield. According to a computation, which he seems to have made with great care, founded upon official returns of bill stamps issued, the following are the results:—

RETURN OF BILL STAMPS, FOR 1832 TO 1839 INCLUSIVE.

| | Bills created in Great Britain and Ireland, founded on returns of Bill Stamps issued from the Stamp Office. | Average amount in circulation, at one time in each year. |
|---|---|---|
| | £ | £ |
| 1832 | 356,153,409 | 89,038,352 |
| 1833 | 383,659,585 | 95,914,896 |
| 1834 | 379,155,052 | 94,788,763 |
| 1835 | 405,403,051 | 101,350,762 |
| 1836 | 485,943,473 | 121,485,868 |
| 1837 | 455,084,445 | 113,771,111 |
| 1838 | 465,504,041 | 116,376,010 |
| 1839 | 528,493,842 | 132,123,460 |

Mr. Leatham gives the process by which, upon the data furnished by the returns of stamps, he arrives at these results; and I am disposed to think that they are as near an approximation to the truth as the nature of the materials admits of arriving at. And some corroboration of the vastness of the amounts is afforded by a reference to the adjustments at the clearing house in London, which in the year 1839 amounted to 954,401,600*l.*, making an average amount of payments of upwards of 3,000,000*l.* of bills of exchange and cheques daily effected through the medium of little more than 200,000*l.* of bank notes.

As illustrative of the position for which Mr. Leatham contends, and conclusively, as I think, that bills of exchange perform the functions of money, he observes,—

"For a great number of years, it had been the custom of merchants to pay the clothiers in small bills of 10*l.*, 15*l.*, 20*l.*, and so up to 100*l.*, drawn at two months after date on London bankers. I have always considered this the best part of our paper currency, ranking next to gold; the bills existing only for limited periods, and acquiring increased security as they pass from hand to hand by endorsement. From the unreasonably high stamp laid on small bills in 1815, the merchants have ceased to pay in bills, but pay notes instead, requiring 2*d.* in the pound for cash from the receiver; and I find the revenue has much decreased in consequence in this class of stamps."—pp. 44, 45.

Mr. Lewis Loyd, when examined by the House of Lords' Committee on the Resumption of Cash Payments in 1819, gave the following evidence:—

*Qu.* 9. At the time when you began business in Manchester, in 1792, were there any country banks which issued notes in that town, or in any other part of Lancashire?

None, I believe.

10. Have there never been, at any time, country banks issuing notes in Lancashire?

None within my recollection. I began to reside in Manchester in 1789. There had been, before that period, notes issued there about the year 1787 or 1788; I think by a bank which failed. I believe that was the only attempt ever made in Lancashire till lately, except that there was lately, and is now, an attempt made to issue them at Blackburn.

11. How has the circulation of Lancashire been carried on since the period to which you refer?

Wholly in Bank of England notes and bills of exchange.

12. Is the proportion of Bank of England notes very considerable as compared with bills of exchange?

About one-tenth, I think, in Bank of England notes, and nine-tenths, at least, in bills of exchange. These bills of exchange circulate from hand to hand, till they are covered with endorsements.

13. Is any inconvenience felt from this mode of circulation by bills of exchange?

None whatever.

14. Has the circulation of Bank of England notes increased or decreased of late years in proportion to bills of exchange?

I think the proportion of bank notes has increased.

15. To what do you attribute that increase?

Partly to the great increase of the stamp duties. It is within my knowledge, from the transactions of my own house, that the supplies of provisions, which are drawn from the neighbouring counties, used to be paid for in small bills of exchange, mostly of 10*l*. or lower; but now the persons going to the neighbouring localities for supplies of provisions take with them bank notes and bank post bills, stating that the stamp is too serious an object to them to be paid on such small sums. There is scarcely a day when I do not send 2000*l*. in bank post bills for that purpose to Manchester, which we hardly ever used to do before the last addition to the stamp duty.

16. Were these bills of exchange drawn for specific loans previous to their employment, or were they bills resulting from antecedent transactions?

Those who purchased provisions used to go to fairs and markets with bills ready drawn in their favour, very often for specific sums, as for the round sum of 10*l*., just as they now take 10*l*. in Bank of England notes and bank post bills. There was this peculiar circumstance attending them, that the bills were usually drawn at two months' date, and were considered as cash payment; they were bills, drawn on London by country bankers, and remitted to London as suited the convenience of the parties who received them. Now, in consequence of having bank post bills and Bank of England notes, the persons who receive the bills make an allowance to those who pay them of two months' interest.

My answer applies to the supply of the town with provisions. Nearly all the other transactions of Manchester, except the payment of labourers, are still carried on in bills of exchange, and the payment of labourers is mostly made in 1*l.* Bank of England notes.

If by an alteration in an opposite direction, the stamp duty on bills of exchange were reduced or abolished, while that on promissory notes on demand remained the same, and still more, if it were raised, there would be a considerable change in practice, by making the smaller payments among dealers in bills of exchange as a substitute for bank notes.

In a work by the late Mr. Henry Thornton *, which attracted considerable attention at the time, and which formed the subject of an article by Mr. Horner, in the first Number of the Edinburgh Review in 1802, there is a distinct and full description of the manner in which bills of exchange performed in his time the function of money; a description which is strictly applicable at the present day. He observes with reference to bills of exchange, —

"They not only spare the use of ready money, they also occupy its place in many cases. Let us imagine a farmer in the country to discharge a debt of 10*l.* to his neighbouring grocer, by giving to him a bill for that sum, drawn on his corn-factor in London, for grain sold in the metropolis; and the grocer to transmit the bill, he having previously endorsed it to a neighbouring sugar baker, in the discharge of a like debt, and the sugar baker to send it, when again endorsed, to a West India merchant in an out-port, and the West India merchant to deliver it to his country banker, who also endorses it, and sends it into further circulation. The bill, in this case, will have effected five payments, exactly as if it were a 10*l.* note payable to bearer on demand. It will, however, have circulated in consequence chiefly of the confidence placed by each receiver of it in the last endorser, his own correspondent in trade; whereas the circulation of a bank

* "An Inquiry into the Nature and Effects of the Paper Credit of Great Britain."

note is rather owing to the circumstance of the name of the issuer being so well known as to give to it an universal credit. A multitude of bills pass between trader and trader in the country in the manner which has been described; and they evidently form, in the strictest sense, a part of the circulating medium of the kingdom.

"Bills, since they circulate chiefly among the trading world, come little under the observation of the public. The amount of bills in existence may yet, perhaps, be at all times greater than the amount of all the bank notes of every kind, and of all the circulating guineas. Liverpool and Manchester effect the whole of their larger mercantile payments, not by country bank notes, of which none are issued by the banks of those places, but by bills at one or two months' date, drawn on London. The bills annually drawn by the banks of each of those towns amount to many millions."

The late Sir Francis Baring, writing at a still earlier period (1797), and of a state of things within his immediate experience, refers, in the following passage, to the practice prevalent among country bankers, of issuing notes payable after date or after sight,—

"In the beginning of the year 1793, and of the present year, 1797, the banks of Newcastle stopped payment, while those of Exeter and of the West of England stood their ground. The partners in the banks at Newcastle were far more opulent, but their private fortunes being invested could not be realised in time to answer a run on their banks. Their notes allowed interest to commence some months after date, and were then payable on demand; by which means they had not an hour to prepare for their discharge. The banks of Exeter issued notes payable twenty days after sight with interest, to commence from the date of the note, and to cease on the day of acceptance. There can be no doubt that the practice of the banks at Newcastle is more lucrative, whilst it must for ever be more liable to a return of what has happened. The twenty days received at Exeter furnishes ample time to communicate with London, and receive every degree of assistance which may be required." *

* "Observations on the Bank of England, and on the Paper Circulation of the Country," p. 17.

If, according to the currency theory, the circumstance that written promises to pay being after date or sight, and to order, and therefore requiring an endorsement, are disqualified from being considered as performing the functions of money, on what ground is it that bank post bills, which are after sight and to order, have been always included in the returns of the circulation of the Bank of England? They are by their form strictly bills of exchange, being not only after sight and to order, but commonly used for transmission by post; and if these are considered to be part of the circulation, on what ground are the bills of the Bank of Ireland, and of the chartered Banks of Scotland, and of such banks throughout the United Kingdom as are of undoubted credit, not included in the return of the country circulation? This applies indeed only to short-dated bills of the most unquestioned credit; longer-dated bills, of more doubtful security, seem to have been alone in the view of those persons who assert the exclusive title of bank notes to be considered as money. Bills of this description, that is long-dated bills, are sometimes not used for purposes of circulation,—they are simply written evidence of a debt which is discharged at maturity, without passing into third hands. I will not stop now to enter into the distinction between long and short-dated bills in the comparison with bank notes, and between bills drawn by bankers, and bills by merchants or dealers on dealers. It is a sufficient negative of the main proposition on which the currency theory rests, to have shown that short-dated bills of exchange are substitutes not only for coin, but for bank notes.

If, as a last resort in the argument, it be said that bills of exchange require the intervention of bank notes for the ultimate payment, the answer is, that this is a mere fiction, for that in fact the adjustment takes place by settlement, and that a small amount of bank notes for the balance effects the liquidation, which might equally be effected by drafts on the Bank of England; or, as is done in Scotland, by exchequer bills. An alteration in the stamp duties has, as stated by Mr. Lewis Loyd and Mr. Leatham, operated against the employment of the smaller bills of exchange instead of bank notes. If the case were reversed, the stamps lowered on bills and raised on notes, we should see an immense increase in the former, and a great diminution in the latter,—in other words, bank notes would be withdrawn, and bills of exchange supply their place.

It is hardly perhaps necessary to advert to the latter part of the proposition quoted at page 20., viz., that the abolition of any or of all the contrivances for dispensing with the use of money, will not necessitate the introduction in their place of an equal amount of coin or bank notes. There surely can be little doubt but that the abolition of such contrivances would necessitate the substitute of an equal amount of bank notes or coin.

Sufficient grounds have, as I venture to think, been stated for establishing the claim in behalf of cheques on bankers, and of bills of exchange, to be considered as performing, concurrently with bank notes, the functions of money for the purposes for which they are respectively used.

If the propounders of the currency theory would confine their distinction in favour of bank notes to the lowest denominations, namely, the 1*l.* notes wholly, and the 5*l.* and 10*l.* notes partially, it might, as I have already observed, be conceded; but then what becomes of the dogma or the axiom of Mr. Norman and Mr. Loyd, on which the currency theory is made to rest?—and what becomes of the inferences which they have drawn as to the management of banks, from a view exclusively to the whole of the circulation, large notes as well as small? In truth, their tests of good and bad management, and their views of the purposes and properties of the whole of the circulating medium and of its component parts, are essentially defective and erroneous. They draw distinctions which are not real or substantial, as, for instance, of the higher denomination of bank notes compared with bills of exchange and cheques; while they totally overlook and confound the distinctive character of the instruments of interchange which are used in the distribution and expenditure of incomes, as compared with that of the instruments which are used in the distribution and employment of capital.

---

## CHAP. VII.

### DISTINCTION OF CIRCULATION AS BETWEEN DEALER AND DEALER, AND BETWEEN DEALER AND CONSUMER.

It is of the greatest importance to a clear view of the working of the present system that the distinctive characters of the instruments of interchange should be observed and defined. Dr. Adam Smith has noticed the distinction, and has accordingly, in his views of the operation of paper money, steered clear of the confusion between currency and capital which pervades and disfigures nearly all modern reasonings on the subject.

" The circulation of every country," Dr. Smith observes, " may be considered as divided into two " different branches — the circulation of the dealers " with one another, and the circulation between the " dealers and the consumers. Though the same pieces

" of money, whether paper or metal, may be em-
" ployed, sometimes in the one circulation and some-
" times in the other, yet as both are constantly
" going on at the same time, each requires a certain
" stock of money of one kind or another to carry it
" on. The value of the goods circulated between the
" different dealers with one another never can exceed
" the value of those circulated between the dealers
" and the consumers, whatever is bought by the
" dealers being ultimately destined to be sold to the
" consumers. Paper money may be so regulated as
" either to confine itself very much to the circulation
" between the different dealers, or to extend itself
" likewise to a great part of that between the dealers
" and the consumers. When no bank notes are cir-
" culated under ten pounds value, as in London,
" paper money confines itself very much to the circu-
" lation between the dealers. When a ten pound
" bank note comes into the hands of a consumer he
" is generally obliged to change it at the first shop
" where he has occasion to purchase five shillings'
" worth of goods, so that it often returns into the
" hands of a dealer before the consumer has spent a
" fortieth part of the money."*

There can be no doubt that the distinction here made is substantially correct. Bearing in mind this distinction, the reason is obvious why, as far as relates to the interchange between dealers and consumers (including the payment of wages, which constitute the principal means of the consumers), coin, and the smaller denomination of notes serving as coin, are essential to such interchange, and why, consequently, if those smaller notes are withdrawn, their place must be supplied by coin; but not so as regards the interchange between dealers and dealers. Bank notes are

* "Wealth of Nations," M'Culloch's Edition, pp. 141, 142.

not only not essential to that interchange, but it must be manifest to any one having even a slight knowledge only of the manner in which such interchange is conducted, that, in point of fact, bank notes are rarely used in the larger dealings of sales and purchases.

The great bulk of the wholesale trade of the country is carried on and adjusted by settlements or sets-off of debts and credits, the written evidences of which are in bills of exchange (including in that term all promissory notes payable to order after date), while current payments for what are called cash sales are mostly discharged by cheques; the ultimate balance only, arising out of the vast mass of such transactions, requiring liquidation in a comparatively small amount of bank notes. The principal exceptions to this, I apprehend, are in the provision trade, and in the sheep and cattle and horse fairs, in which the payments are mostly made in coin and bank notes; but there can be no question that for amounts of 10*l.* and upwards, bills of exchange might be, as they formerly were, and, but for the increased stamp duty, would be, substituted.

Of the fact that, with the exception of these, and perhaps of some few other wholesale trades in which no credit is given, there is little or no intervention of bank notes in purchases or sales among wholesale dealers, no doubt can be entertained. And I have now to state the explanation, which I am not aware of having met with among the various lucubrations on the subject of the currency which it has been my lot to see, of the reason why, with the exceptions I have pointed out, such sales and purchases are effected without actual payment in money, which, by the currency theory, is defined to be coin or bank notes.

The reason is, that all the transactions between dealers and dealers, by which are to be understood all sales from the producer or importer, through all the stages of intermediate processes of manufacture or otherwise to the retail dealer or the exporting merchant, are resolvable into movements or transfers of capital. Now transfers of capital do not necessarily suppose, nor do actually as a matter of fact entail, in the great majority of transactions, a passing of money, that is, bank notes or coin — I mean bodily, and not by fiction — at the time of transfer. All the movements of capital may be, and the great majority are, effected by the operations of banking and credit without the intervention of actual payment in coin or bank notes, that is, actual, visible, and tangible bank notes, not supposititious bank notes, issued with one hand and received back by the other, or, more properly speaking, entered on one side of the ledger with a counter-entry on the other. And there is the further important consideration, that the total amount of the transactions between dealers and dealers must, in the last resort, be determined and limited by the amount of those between dealers and consumers.

The business of bankers, setting aside the issue of promissory notes on demand, may be divided into two branches, corresponding with the distinction pointed out by Dr. Smith of the transactions between dealers and dealers, and between dealers and consumers. One branch of the banker's business is to collect capital from those who have not immediate employment for it, and to distribute or transfer it to those who have. The other branch is to receive deposits of the incomes of their customers, and to pay out the amount, as it is wanted for expenditure, by the latter in the objects of their consumption. The former may be considered as the business behind the counter, and the latter before or over the counter: the former being a circulation of capital, the latter of currency.

The distinction or separation in reasoning of that

branch of banking which relates to the concentration of capital on the one hand and the distribution of it on the other, from that branch which is employed in administering the circulation for local purposes of the district, is so important in its bearing on the question of regulating the circulation by the foreign exchanges, and on that of the connection between the currency and prices, that the fullest elucidation of the practical operation of that distinction may naturally be required. I have, therefore, as the best method of elucidating this point, drawn largely on the examinations by the Committee on Banks of Issue in 1841; and if it be objected that more than enough of the evidence is here adduced for the purpose, seeing that the point is so clear when simply stated, my answer to the objector is, that simple and clear as the distinction may appear to him, so imbued were the members of the Committee who took a prominent part in the examination, with the tenets of the currency theory, as to have remained apparently (judging at least by the reiteration of their questions to the same effect) unconvinced of the powerlessness of the banks of issue to influence directly the amount of the circulation. And even to this day, with all the light of subsequent experience, it should seem, judging by speeches and publications, and the declamations against excessive paper issues, which still appear occasionally on the subject, that the dogma of the power of banks of issue to create paper money *ad libitum* prevails to nearly as great an extent as ever.

# CHAP. VIII.

## REGULATION OF THE CIRCULATION BY THE FOREIGN EXCHANGES.

All the country bankers examined concur in stating that they have not the power by loans or discounts beyond the ordinary transactions of the neighbourhood to extend or contract the local circulation or to influence prices. They could, indeed, refuse to issue their own notes in answering the demands of their depositors, but such refusal must be accompanied by offering Bank of England notes or coin, and thus the local circulation would be equally filled up; they may curtail or call in their advances and so diminish their engagements, and eventually render a smaller amount of circulation necessary; but the immediate demands for notes for local purposes must still be satisfied.

It appears by that evidence, that their circulation is devoted and confined to local purposes, chiefly in small amounts, for the retail trade; and in the rural districts, in advances to farmers for the purchase of stock and seed, and to cattle dealers and provision merchants: but that when called upon to make advances by way of loan or discount on a larger scale, it is always by a draft or order upon London, or upon such of their correspondents in other towns as happen to suit the borrowers — such loans or discounts being invariably made out of capital, or, in other words, out of the general resources of the bank.

Among the country bankers of England I have selected the evidence of Mr. Stuckey, the head of the admirably conducted banks of Somersetshire under his firm, because there is no one more conversant, both theoretically and practically, than he is with the subject of banking. By his position formerly he was in intimate communication with Lord Liverpool and Mr. Huskisson. He was examined by the Bullion Committee in 1819. He was an adherent to the principles of the late Mr. Ricardo; and he expressed opinions of the desirableness of having the circulation of bank notes regulated by a view to the foreign exchanges.* But what is the result of his very large experience as a banker?

477. (*Chairman.*) Do you conceive that, generally speaking, there is an insuperable difficulty in country banks exercising such a controul over their own issues, as to reduce them to some extent during a period of adverse foreign exchange?

*I really do not see how that is to be done.*

* The regulation of issues by the foreign exchanges is an expression which, like all the rest of the language of the currency theory, conveys no clear description of the actual process. One would suppose that the directors of the Bank of England, who profess to regulate their issues by the foreign exchanges, attend to the variations in the quotations, and according as these indicate an adverse or a favourable tendency, regulate their issues, or rather their advances, accordingly. No such thing. It is only by the influx or efflux of bullion that they are guided, and very properly so. It is impossible for any but Exchange-jobbers to judge of the quotations, allowing for agios, and dates, and distances. And the idea that country-bankers could judge of them! The evidence of Mr. Palmer before the Committee on the Bank Charter in 1832, is decisive on this point:—

122. "How do you regulate your issues according to the foreign exchanges?—By the notes being returned for gold or silver for export."

123. "Do you regulate them from the returns you have of what the foreign exchanges are, or from the action which takes place upon the Bank?—The action which takes place upon the Bank."

125. "Do you not sometimes anticipate the actual action upon the Bank, by the demand for gold, when you see there is a tendency in the foreign exchanges to produce that action?—No; we wait for the actual demand."

It is clear that in point of fact the directors are and can be guided only by the state of their treasure; and that, instead of the expression of "regulating the circulation by the foreign exchanges," the terms descriptive of the actual process should be, "regulating the securities by the efflux or influx of bullion."

478. Then what is the practical effect of the regard to foreign exchanges, which you think all country bankers ought to pay?

The practical effect is to make them more cautious and circumspect in the management of their money transactions; but I should not state, that in the agricultural districts, the circulation would be altered by the foreign exchanges.

479. Do you conceive, that although the country bankers ought to pay regard to the state of the foreign exchanges, it is not in their power to bring that regard into practical effect by reducing the amount of their issues during the period of adverse exchange?

*I do not see how it could be done.*

480. Will then the regard which you recommend they should pay to the foreign exchanges produce any practical effect whatever upon their issues?

Yes, it would produce effect in the management of their monied concerns.

481. What practical effect would it produce on their *issues?*

*Very little;* my own opinion is, that country issues have very little to do with exchanges.

482. Would the regard which you recommend to the foreign exchanges produce any effect upon their issues?

*Very little;* it would produce some effect upon the management of their monied concerns.

483. (*Sir T. Fremantle.*) Upon their liabilities?

Yes.

484. *But comparatively little on their issues?*

*Yes:* particularly in the agricultural parts of the country.

485. Upon what do you think the issues of the country bankers depend?

More on the state of agriculture than any thing else. When the landed interest is in a comfortable state, I consider the issues to be increased.

491. (*Sir T. Fremantle.*) The advance which you make to the agriculturists is an advance of capital, whether it is paid to them in your own notes, or Bank of England notes or gold?

Yes; the advance is generally made to agriculturists in our own notes.

492. But if the state of the country is such as not to require an increase of your own issues, you are quite sure that those notes will come back to you in the course of a short time?

Exactly.

493. Therefore the advance that you make in that case *is an advance of capital, and not an advance of mere issue?*

*Exactly; it is made out of our resources.*

501. (*Chairman.*) Will you state how you are affected by foreign exchanges?

I think the London banker is affected by them, therefore I am affected; I naturally know that if my deposits are withdrawn, and any demand is made upon me, I must sell my securities; therefore I look to the foreign exchanges in order to ascertain how the money market is, that I may know what securities I shall dispose of.

524. (*Chairman.*) Suppose the case of an adverse foreign exchange, when, according to your own opinion, the paper circulation of the country ought to be reduced, would you, on a depositor asking for the payment of a deposit in notes, be at all guided by the circumstance of the foreign exchanges, as to whether you paid that deposit in Bank of England notes, or in your own local notes?

*I admit that I should not be guided by the foreign exchanges,* but I should be guided by knowing where the deposit money was to go to.

525. (*Sir T. Fremantle.*) You have stated that when you have observed gold going out of the country, and money becoming tight in London, you have been in the habit of issuing directions to your different branches, to be more circumspect in the advances they make; has the effect of that been practically to diminish the amount of your notes in circulation in those districts?

*I do not think it has; I am not aware that it has.*

526. What has the effect been?

To make them *more cautious in their advances,* keeping our resources more within our own command; instead of discounting a bill, which we should discount under some circumstances, we have refused it; and instead of advancing

1000*l.* or 2000*l.*, we have desired the person to take 500*l.*; therefore we keep our banking capital and banking resources more under our own command.

527. But are you prepared to say that the circulation of your own notes has not been affected by that course of conduct?

*I am not aware that it has.*

527. Supposing, for instance, it should ultimately be thought that it is desirable that the country circulation should have a general conformity to the state of the foreign exchanges, do you conceive that this could be in any way effected by the country bankers?

*I do not at present know how it could be accomplished;* and I may take the liberty of going further in that question, and saying that it appears to me that the country issues, as conducted in the west of England, have very little or nothing to do with the foreign exchanges.

538. Do you conceive then that the only circulation which ought to have reference to the foreign exchanges is that of the Bank of England?

I do conceive that it is the only thing which ought to have reference to them, being the circulation of London, and London being the spot where the foreign exchanges are generally effected.

539. (*Mr. Grote.*) Do you mean to state that you think the circulation of the Bank of England ought to be made to vary in conformity with the foreign exchanges, but that the circulation of the country banks ought not to be affected by the foreign exchanges?

No, I do not go so far as that; my opinion is that the country circulation does not affect the foreign exchanges, because it is a different kind of circulation; the foreign exchanges are, we all know, affected in various ways, but I do not think they are affected by the country circulation, and I have looked attentively at that question.

The evidence of Mr. Gilbart, of the London and Westminster Bank, of Mr. Hobhouse, of a bank at Bath, and of Mr. Rodwell, of a bank at Ipswich, is full of information as to the circumstances which influence and limit the country circulation without the possibility of reference to the exchanges. But as these gentlemen do not profess ever to have entertained an opinion of its being desirable, if it were practicable, to regulate the country circulation by the foreign exchanges, I have preferred a reference to Mr. Stuckey's evidence, he having entertained and professed an opinion that it was desirable, but had made the discovery, confirmed by long experience on a very extensive scale, of its utter impracticability.

Mr. Gurney was examined on this point by the Committee on the Bank Charter in 1832. I have before had occasion to notice his evidence at some length*, and will now only refer to the concluding part of it:—

Does it not follow from what you have said, that an over-issue of notes of country bankers cannot easily be effected?

*My belief is that it cannot be effected by any act of the country bankers.*

As far as this point is concerned, it might perhaps be deemed to be sufficiently proved by the evidence already adduced. But not the evidence only on this point is confirmed, but also much additional light is thrown on the distinction between capital and currency, by a view of the Scotch system of banking. The examinations of some of the managers of the Scotch banks by the Committee in 1841, are accordingly well worthy of attention as illustrative of that distinction.

* "History of Prices," vol. iii. p. 193.

# CHAP. IX.

## SCOTCH BANKING. REGULATION BY FOREIGN EXCHANGES, AND DISTINCTION BETWEEN CAPITAL AND CURRENCY.

THE evidence of Mr. Alexander Blair, treasurer and manager of the Bank of Scotland, which is the oldest of the chartered banks, having been established in 1695, and which appears to be conducted with great ability and prudence, is full of valuable information as to the machinery and working of the Scotch system of banking.

He mentions a curious fact relating to the mode in which the balances resulting from the exchanges twice a week among the banks are adjusted by the means of exchequer bills which, to the amount of 450,000*l.*, they hold for that express purpose. Here we have exchequer bills answering all the purposes that Bank of England notes at the clearing house in London do.

Mr. Blair also states that seven millions in amount of notes is found to be requisite in order to keep up an *average* circulation of three millions,— a very curious fact, as it appears that the stamp duty is paid upon the whole stock, whether in the hands of the public or within the walls of the banks, and that the whole amount is out in circulation for a few days at two seasons of the year.

It is stated, moreover, upon the same authority, that the total amount of deposits which, in 1826, was computed to be about twenty-one millions, had in 1841 reached to about twenty-seven millions.

It is a remarkable circumstance that, while there has been a great extension of banking capital, and of banking accommodation, and of banking competition, in Scotland since 1826, the amount of the aggregate circulation has considerably diminished. What a commentary upon the received doctrine of the power of banks to increase their issues of paper money as suits their interests or convenience; and that it is the effect of the competition of banks of issue to create a vast mass of worthless paper.

Mr. Blair gave the following statement of the increase of banking accommodation in Scotland: —

"There are about 380 bank offices in Scotland, of which 348 are branches. The population may be stated at 2,500,000; thus there is one bank for every 6600 individuals.

"There were in 1825, 167 offices, of which 133 were branch banks. The population being then 2,200,000, there was one bank to every 13,170 individuals.

"The amount of notes exchanged per annum by the banks of Scotland is believed to be not under 100,000,000*l.* delivered, and 100,000,000*l.* received. The Bank of Scotland alone delivers 10,000,000*l.*, and receives in exchange as much."

But the immediate purpose of my reference to the evidence of Mr. Blair and other managers of the Scotch banks, is to show that they do not and cannot regulate their *circulation* by the foreign exchanges; and that, when they make advances, it is out of their capital or that of their depositors, without any direct influence on their circulation; that they attend to the conduct of the Bank of England in regulating their *advances*, which, however, have no immediate influence on their *circulation*.

Mr. Blair was asked by the chairman, —

Do you conceive that the amount of notes in circulation should be regulated in any way with reference to the state of the foreign exchanges? — I conceive that the loans and discounts of banks should be regulated with reference to the state of the foreign exchanges, *but I would not consider it necessary to regulate the circulation by the foreign exchanges.*

1879. (*Mr. Grote.*) Then, is it your opinion that, at the same time when the Bank of England is contracting its circulation, for the purpose of correcting an unfavourable exchange, the provincial banks should proceed in the same track, and contract their circulation also?

I think that they should consider the action of the Bank of England, at that time, with reference to their general rules of discount. *I would beg to leave the circulation out of the question;* I would say that the banks should look to the amount of their loans and discounts under such circumstances; and, at the same time, I would say, that the Bank (of England) should keep a large reserve, to be determined by their past experience and observation, for which, to the extent it is held for public account, they should receive compensation.

1880. Then, is it your opinion, that at a period when the exchanges are unfavourable, and the Bank of England are contracting their circulation, the provincial banks ought to be more cautious in granting loans and discounts than they were before?

Certainly.

1881. (*Sir J. R. Reid.*) Does your bank act upon that principle?

It does.

The examinations, however, of Mr. Kennedy, manager of the Ayrshire Bank, and of Mr. Anderson, of the Glasgow Union Banking Company, went more particularly to the question of the distinction between capital and currency; and their evidence is calculated to throw great light on this point.

Mr. Kennedy is asked:—

2092. (*Mr. Grote.*) You stated that the causes affecting the quantity of your notes which were out in circulation at any time, were, in your opinion, independent of the action of the foreign exchanges?

I did.

2093. But you also stated that at the time when the foreign exchanges were unfavourable, and when there was a pressure upon the money market, you thought it imperative, as a measure of prudence, to realise some of your reserves and to call in funds from Edinburgh or London?

Yes, that is an accurate representation.

2094. Then do you not think that that act of yours, in bringing into your country funds realised in Edinburgh or London is, in point of fact, tantamount to your acquiring for yourself a certain portion of the London currency or the Edinburgh currency, inasmuch as the local increase of your currency is not at that moment tantamount to the increase of the aggregate currency of the country?

But we do not bring into our country the Edinburgh or London money. The diminution of our reserves takes place in this way: parties have payments to make in Edinburgh or London or other places, and we draw upon our reserves there to meet those payments, *but we do not bring down gold or Bank of England* notes from the London market in order to pay them away in our country.

2095. Though you may not actually bring down gold or Bank of England notes, is not the effect of your diminishing the amount of your reserve in Edinburgh and London, and increasing by that means the advances to certain local borrowers, *tantamount to bringing down so much of the Edinburgh or London currency into your locality?*

*I cannot see that I bring any currency down;* it is merely a payment made in London, or in Edinburgh, from one party to another.

2096. Will you describe in what way your reserves are usually kept?

In easy negociable securities, such as exchequer bills and short-dated bills of exchange, money lying in our banker's hands in London, and in other parties' hands in London, and money lying in our agents' hands in Edinburgh and Glasgow, and other places.

2097. Suppose you sell so many thousand exchequer bills either in London or in Edinburgh, of course the proceeds of those exchequer bills are placed to the credit of your agent, whether your Edinburgh agent or your London agent?

Yes.

2098. In that case, when you direct those funds to be paid out, *you do in point of fact dispose of an equal amount of London currency or of Edinburgh currency* for the purposes of your bank?

Yes.

2099. Then, in point of fact, do you not consider that you are enabled by means of *that portion of the London currency or the Edinburgh currency* of which you thus acquire the disposal, to obtain a certain increase of the amount of notes in your own district, and does not that, in point of fact, occasion a certain *diminution in the London or the Edinburgh currency* which may be set against the increase of your own local issues at the time?

But when I give a draft upon the London agent I do not in consequence of the increased sum that I have put at his command give out notes for it. I give a draft upon London payable to some party in London; the money is paid over in London, so that I do not make an issue upon that.

2100. But *the quantity of currency* which is available to other parties in London or Edinburgh is diminished by that portion which you draw for your own use?

*I do not see how it diminishes the quantity of currency in London: it merely transfers it from one party to another.*

2101. If you were not to employ that portion of *the London currency which you acquire* by realising your exchequer bills, that portion would be at the disposal of some other person in London for the purpose of granting accommodation to London borrowers?

*But I do not take it out of London; it is still in the hands of some party in London.*

2102. But if by means of that operation you are enabled to extend your accommodation to your local borrowers, you do make it serviceable to the wants of your district, and is it not tantamount, in point of fact, to a transfer of so much capital from employment in London to employment in Ayrshire: is not that the general effect of the operation?

That may be the effect of it; *but it has no effect in diminishing the amount of the currency in the London market.* I do not bring out of London any currency; I merely take the currency from one party in London, and give it to another.

2103. Do not you bring down from London to Ayrshire a certain portion of capital which was before in London?

I do not see that.

2104. If the effect of this transaction be to enable you to supply the wants of borrowers in Ayrshire, which otherwise you could not supply, surely that does amount to a transfer of so much of your banking capital from London to the country?

It is rather more the payment of a debt due by some parties in Ayrshire to some parties in London.

Mr. Kennedy is right: the operation is the mere transfer of a debt. The Ayrshire bank is creditor of a bank in London to the amount of 1000*l.*, and passes its draft on London for that sum; the person or firm that takes and pays for the draft of the Ayrshire bank has a payment to make to his correspondent in London. The transactions balance each other. The ultimate balances, as between Scotland and England, must be adjusted by an increase or diminution of the funds possessed in England by the Scotch banks; and in some cases, although not frequent, nor to any considerable amount, there may be a transmission of Bank of England notes or coin.

Notwithstanding the clearness of this evidence, the following questions put by the Committee, as to the distinction between capital and currency, in the subsequent examination of Mr. Anderson, manager of the Glasgow Union Banking Company, will show the little impression produced by it on the examiners: —

2323. (*Chairman.*) Do you at all attempt to regulate your circulation by the state of the foreign exchange?

*Not the circulation;* we regulate our business by the state of the foreign exchanges, but we consider that the circulation does not require any regulation; *our advances and loans we regulate, but not the circulation of our notes.*

2324. Do you conceive that the circulation is sufficiently regulated by your simply answering the demands of your customers?

I think so.

2335. Do you conceive that the consequence of restraining your loans and advances is to produce any effect upon the amount of your circulation?

*No immediate effect upon the amount of our circulation.*

2336. Does it eventually?

The circulation is eventually affected by the languor that follows a pressure; when wages are low and people are out of employment, there is less money circulating among them, and our circulation is diminished, but the immediate effect of a pressure *is not to diminish the circulation.*

2337. Does then any diminution of the circulation which takes place *arise from a less demand on the part of the public, and not as the result of any greater caution on the part of the bank?*

*Exactly.*

2338. (*Mr. Grote.*) But the effects you have described imply an increased demand on the part of the public at such periods for your circulation?

It is an increased demand for money *, but not for circulation.

2339. When those demands are made, in what manner do you supply them; is it not by an increase of your own notes?

In most cases an increased demand comes upon us in the shape of orders upon London, or orders upon Manchester or Liverpool; the pressure upon us is chiefly from the South, and an extra demand from London, Liverpool, and Manchester we feel as the first indication of pressure; it is not from our own immediate districts.

2340. (*Chairman.*) Do you mean that your customers have demands upon them, which it is necessary for them to discharge in Manchester, London, and other places?

Yes, that is to a considerable extent the case.

2341. (*Mr. Grote.*) In what manner do you enable your customers to make those payments which you have to make in Liverpool, or London, or Manchester?

By giving them orders upon our agents and correspondents in those places.

2342. You direct a certain portion of the funds which you have in London, or Liverpool, or Manchester to be applied to that purpose?

We do.

2343. Then, in point of fact, you make those advances

* It is quite clear that by *money* the witness means capital, as distinguished from circulation.

not out of your own local currency, but out *of a certain portion of the London currency* upon which you have a demand?

*No; I think that does not precisely describe the operation. It is our capital;* it is capital which we have collected in Scotland, and placed in London for that purpose; *it is not London currency* lent to Scotland, *but it is capital* belonging to Scotland that has been placed in London, and is now applied to the purposes for which it is wanted.

2344. But if you direct payment to be made in London, this payment must be made by means of the notes of the Bank of England, which alone circulate in London?

Of course.*

2348. When increased demands are made upon you by your customers in Glasgow, do you not answer those demands by means of your own local notes, and not by orders upon London?

Certainly; our circulation from Tuesday to Friday, and from Friday to Tuesday again, is increased upon this occasion; but *we do not reckon that circulation,* because we know that it is immediately to return upon us, and that it is an advance, not of circulation, but of capital; it becomes at the next exchange-day *an advance of our capital.*

2349. You feel satisfied that the increase of notes which you might make at that period would immediately come back upon you in the exchange, and that you would be required to pay them by orders on London?

Yes; or by exchequer bills in Edinburgh.

2361. Do you not, by means of this increased amount of advances in the extraordinary periods to which the questions have alluded, add to the means of purchasing goods possessed by the persons who borrow from you?

Yes, we do.

2362. And is not that practically tantamount to *so much increase of circulation* in the local districts in which your loans take place?

*I think not of circulation; I think it is capital;* because

* The question and answer are both wrong. The former assumes that the payment *must* be made in Bank of England notes, and the latter acquiesces in the supposed *necessity:* they *may* be paid, and most commonly *are,* by set-off at the clearing-house.

the notes we pay out are not retained for days or weeks to make the purchases, they are paid immediately to some other bank, and come back to us upon the exchange, and *they become an advance of capital* by us to the party, to enable him to make his purchases.*

2363. But although ultimately it comes to be an advance out of your capital, yet for a certain time it is an advance made by means of your circulation only, without the aid of your capital?

For two or three days it is.

2364. For a certain time, longer or shorter, as the case may be?

It cannot, I think, be longer than till the next exchange-day with regard to those extra advances.

2365. (*Mr. Gisborne.*) Practically, has it more effect *in giving power of purchasing* goods in London, than if you gave them a draft upon your banker in London?

*No; I think not.*

2366. (*Mr. Grote.*) But during the period which elapses between the time of your making the advance originally in your own notes, and the time when you give the order on London, in consequence of the notes coming back to you during that interval, whether it be long or whether it be short, must there not be an increase of the circulation of the country generally?

I think that brings us back to the question which has been so much discussed here, viz. whether deposits form a part of the circulation. *Those notes which we pay out do not remain out;* they must be paid back either to us or to some other bank, in the shape of deposits, till they are to be used, and *they do not increase the permanent circulation of the country,* unless for a day or two, scarcely for even a day.

2367. (*Sir James Graham.*) What proportion of the people of Scotland receiving notes employ bankers?

A very large proportion of the people of Scotland employ bankers; we have been enquiring into that since we came together. One of the gentlemen here, who is at the head of

* It is impossible to place in a clearer light the distinction between capital and circulation, as applied to purchases between dealers and dealers.

a bank with a large number of country branches, informs me, that the number of creditors of his bank is 20,000. In our case I have a return since I came to town, making the number in our bank 15,770; and one of the gentlemen who is here, and who is at the head of a bank without branches, says that he has 7000 people holding his obligations.

2368. (*Mr. Grote.*) Deposit accounts?

Yes; deposit accounts, or current accounts bearing interest.

2369. (*Sir James Graham.*) Inasmuch as every payment into a bank, whether in the shape of a deposit, or to the credit of a current account, bears interest day by day, and inasmuch as no commission is charged upon operations on an account, and inasmuch as a great proportion of the people receiving money in Scotland employ bankers, does it not follow that every payment made in local notes finds its way almost immediately within the space of twenty-four hours into the hands of some banker?

I think it does.

2370. (*Mr. Grote.*) Would not the consequence of that proposition be, if followed out, that there should be no notes whatever in the hands of the public, but that all the notes issued by each bank should be in fact in the hands of other banks?

That is the effect. There are three millions of notes out, which is a very small amount; *people must have a certain amount of money in their pockets and boxes at home, and shop-keepers must keep a certain amount of money in their tills,* the daily receipts of their business; *and manufacturers must keep notes to pay people's wages, and so on;* but that altogether forms but a small proportion compared to the circulation of England. Our three millions in Scotland amount to about 1*l.* a head of the whole population; in England, although you have a gold circulation for every thing below 5*l.*, your paper circulation amounts to 2*l.* a head. I am taking about fifteen millions for the population, and thirty millions for the currency.

The distinction between currency and capital, which is so clearly shown by these remarkably intelligent witnesses, is not a mere matter of classification or of verbal criticism. The confounding of one with the other is a prolific source of fallacy in reasoning, and of error in practical application, in questions relating to the management or regulation of banks.

Of this a striking instance was exhibited in the reasons adduced by the advocates of the currency theory, in justification of the advances made by the Bank of England in 1835, against the deposits on the West India loan. The justification proceeded on the ground that, but for those advances, *the currency would have been unduly contracted.* What the notion could be of undue contraction of the currency, that is, of an inconvenient want of bank notes in the hands of the public or of the bankers, as long as any amount might be obtained by discount at 4 per cent., passes all reasonable comprehension. The truth is, that it was wholly a question of disposable capital; and was it possible to imagine that there could be any danger of an insufficiency of it, at a time when the disposal of it was so recklessly going forward in credits to America? While as regards the circulation or currency, there is every reason to believe, on a view of the state of things at that time, that the amount would have been neither more nor less than it was, whether the advances had been made or withheld.

---

## CHAP. X.

### CHARGES AGAINST THE MANAGEMENT OF THE BANK OF ENGLAND.

THE foregoing extracts from the examinations of the country bankers give the evidence of witnesses who, while explaining the working of the country bank system, offer no opinion, adverse or otherwise, as to the management of the Bank of England. But there are witnesses before that Committee who, while giving very elaborate evidence, comprising highly interesting details, serving to exhibit what, from their regularity, may be deemed to be laws determining the variations of the country circulation, change the whole course of their reasoning when they give their opinion upon the conduct of the Bank of England.

They charge that institution with being the main cause, by undue expansion and subsequent contraction of *its issues*, of causing the alternations of excitement and depression which have characterised the commercial state of this country of late years. And a whole host of writers, some as partisans of the joint stock banks, others unconnected with any banks, are loud in their declamations against what appears in their eyes the monster monopoly of the Bank of England; contending, as they do, that whereas the country banks of issue are limited as to any power of adding to the circulation, no limitation exists to the power of the Bank of England to make any addition to its issues, which a view to the interests of its proprietors may dictate; that it can purchase exchequer bills and other government securities and bullion, and discount bills, and make advances to any amount that may suit its convenience, against issues of its notes; and that if then the exchanges become adverse, and its bullion goes out, it puts on the screw, to the great derangement of all commercial operations.

The evidence of Mr. Hobhouse and Mr. Gilbart furnishes striking instances of the mode of reasoning by which it is attempted to be shown that, while the country banks are perfectly powerless in any attempt to regulate their issues, the Bank of England is all powerful, and can enlarge and contract its circulation at pleasure, subject only to an ultimate limitation by the exhaustion of its treasure.

*H. W. Hobhouse, Esq.*

158. (*Mr. Gisborne.*) Can you state any marked distinction between the Bank of England and country bankers as issuers?

I think the banks in the country are banks of issue to a very small amount compared with the Bank of England. The Bank of England deals with nothing *but its own currency; it is always buying and selling circulation,* if I may use the expression; *it issues circulation against gold,* which I consider to be a very unwholesome thing, whether London or the country wants the circulation or not. Then, again, they lend their notes for circulation in the country, which a country banker never does; he would lose his credit if he did that: he could never hold up his head afterwards, *if he attempted to put out his circulation as the Bank of England does;* then the Bank of England are buying and selling securities, *and acting upon the circulation,* whereas the country bankers are entirely passive, and that is the great distinction which I should draw: they carry on the business of issuing to an infinitely smaller extent than the Bank of England, and therefore that is not a fair measure to judge them by.

159. (*Mr. Hume.*) Are the Committee to understand that you object to the Bank of England issuing notes for gold?

If there is no actual demand for purposes of circulation, *it increases the circulation when it is not wanted.* If a person were to come to my bank and put a quantity of gold into my bank and ask me to issue notes against it, I would not do it, for I could not make them stay out unless they were wanted; they would come back; therefore, as I say, I could not conduct my business in the same way as the Bank of England does. If a person brought gold to me I should have to pay coin for it.

160. (*Mr. Grote.*) And the person who brings to you bullion might go and get that coined at the Mint?

Yes, but if there is no demand for circulation he does not do it; but in the case of the Bank of England he puts it in for a temporary purpose, and *out come the bank notes;* it may be a very wholesome thing for the Bank of England to have that power, but I could not do it. I know that the notes would return upon me immediately; *in short, I have no power over the circulation.*

*J. W. Gilbart, Esq.*

1015. (*Chairman.*) What are the other tests by which you ascertain whether the issue of bank notes was or was not required?

Besides the rate of interest, I consider the amount of money in circulation, as far as regards the Bank of England, as a test.

1016. Will you explain that answer more fully?

An increase in the circulation of the Bank of England, I conceive, differs from an increase in the circulation of the country banks, because the increase of the circulation of the country banks is drawn out by the state of trade in their respective districts. The country bankers having no power to purchase stock, or exchequer bills, or bullion, with their notes, an increase of circulation by them is indicative of an increase of trade in their districts; either that there is a greater briskness of trade, and a greater quantity of commodities bought and sold, or else, from some other circumstance, there is an advance in the price of those commodities, and, therefore, I do not consider that any positive increase in the amount of the circulation of the country banks is any absolute proof of excess of issue; if that were the case, it would appear that the circulation of Ireland, which was very much larger in December, is a proof of an excessive issue of notes in that country, whereas the fact is, that a larger number of notes at the end of the year are drawn out by the produce of the harvest being brought to market. But an increase of *the Bank of England circulation* arising *from an issue of its notes against bullion*, or against purchase of government securities, would be an increase not required by trade, and would necessarily reduce the rate of interest and lead to speculation in trade, and investments in foreign securities.

1017. Do you mean, then, that any increase of issue of bank notes against bullion, or by the purchase of securities, is, in your opinion, an excess of issue?

I must again guard myself; I am very averse to universal propositions, because I believe there are no universal propositions in the science of political economy; that they are all subject to exceptions, and may be modified by circumstances. But taking it as a general rule, and, referring to experience, *I think that an issue of notes against a lodgement of bullion will be usually found to be an excess of issue.*

From the tenour of these answers it might be inferred that every purchase of securities or of bullion by the Bank of England is made in bank notes which remain out and add to the amount of the circulation; and if they do not remain out, how can they be said to add to the circulation? As to the buying and selling of securities, this, the Bank, having a large capital and deposits, might do if it were not a bank of issue. But, say Mr. Hobhouse and Mr. Gilbart, the country banks, if they buy securities, cannot pay for them in their notes, the demand for these being limited; they must therefore pay for them in an order on London. But what is that order? It enables the holder of it to get gold for it, if he has occasion for or can make use of the gold. And what does the Bank of England do, more or less, when it makes advances by loan or discount, or buys securities? The seller of the securities or the borrower may claim bank notes or gold as he might claim Bank of England notes or gold from any other bank of issue. But he may not, and in most cases does not, want the bank notes or gold. He may require only the power of passing a cheque against the amount, which he pays into his banker. And, in point of fact, unless there is a demand for gold, the great bulk of the transactions of the Bank of England, whether in the purchase or sale of securities or of bullion, is accompanied with as little effect upon the amount of bank notes in the hands of the public as are the transactions of the country banks of issue.

The most extraordinary part of the charge against the Bank of England is, that *it issues its notes* in excess by its purchases of bullion. In the first place, there is no more reason for supposing that bank notes of necessity actually pass out of the Bank for purchases of bullion than for purchases of securities; but, in the next place, the Bank cannot help purchasing gold.

The gold comes into the Bank sometimes from the internal circulation, and in that case it is paid in as a matter of course; sometimes it comes in as bullion from abroad in the shape of sovereigns which had been previously exported, there being no seignorage; and in such case also it is quite obvious that the Bank must be passive in receiving them and in paying for them either in notes or in a book credit. But take the case of uncoined gold. If the Bank objected to buy it, it might be taken to the Mint by the importer, and when coined paid into the Bank. Mr. Hobhouse says that it would not be taken of necessity to the Mint, because there might be no want of it in the circulation. This would be true if it could only find vent in the circulation as currency, meaning for retail purposes, those being the only purposes for which coins circulate. But the importer requires the use of it as capital, and if the Bank will not buy it as bullion he must submit to the delay of having it coined, so that he might pay it into the Bank, and thus by a small sacrifice of interest get the command of his capital. The Bank, therefore, in buying the bullion at *3l. 17s. 9d.* per ounce spares the importers this round-about process. It is, moreover, to be observed, that the Bank is by its constitution a dealer in bullion, and if it were not, some other establishment would be.

So inconsistent, indeed, are the charges against the Bank of England with reference to its supposed management of the circulation, that while the country bankers are charging it with issuing its notes in excess by purchases of bullion, the partisans of the currency principle, that is, of a metallic variation, consider it to be an imputation upon the present system or upon the management, that an import of bullion is not attended with a corresponding increase in the circulation.

## CHAP. XI.

### THE BANK OF ENGLAND HAS NOT THE POWER TO ADD TO THE CIRCULATION.

FROM the description which has been given (at p. 21.) of the employment of bank notes when issued and circulating out of the walls of the Bank, it must be evident that the uses of them are such, the purposes for which they are wanted so defined and limited, that in no case could the Bank, by its own volition, add one hundred thousand pounds, perhaps not one hundred pounds to the amount already in circulation among the public. I do not mean that the Bank might not enter into some spontaneous operation which should be of such a nature as to require notes to pass out of its hands without being returned on the same or the following day in the shape of deposits or of a demand for bullion. The nature of the transaction might be such as to require a lodgement of the bank notes in the exchequer or in the hands of agents or of bankers for a few days. What I do mean to say is, that the notes would, in such case, inevitably return to the Bank as deposits, or, what comes to the same thing, be idle in the tills of the bankers, without having performed any of the functions of money in the transactions of purchase or of payment, distinct from that to which they had been specifically applied. I quoted on a former occasion* an opinion of Mr. Gurney's delivered in 1833, that while the transactions of London are abundantly supplied with notes, the effect of an additional 5,000,000*l.* would be, that it would remain inoperative or rather idle in the tills of the bankers.

* History of Prices, vol. iii. p. 156.

In the evidence before the Committee of 1840 on Banks of Issue, the question of the power of the Bank to increase the circulation is raised in a form which admits of a further illustration of the negative of the existence of such power. It is to be borne in mind that the following questions and answers involve a reference to the effect of the supposed operation of the Bank of England on prices, as well as on the amount of the circulation and on the rate of interest. My immediate object in the quotation is to show that the Bank could not add by the operation to the amount of its outstanding notes in circulation.

The following questions by Sir Robert Peel, and answers by Mr. Page, had been preceded by a question which assumed the Bank to have 20,000,000*l*. of notes in circulation, and 10,000,000*l*. of coin in its coffers.

*Qu.* 832. Supposing the 20,000,000*l*. of notes issued upon the discount of bills of exchange or advances to government remained the same, and that the Bank were suddenly to throw 5,000,000 of sovereigns into *active circulation*, as advances upon landed securities, would there be no effect produced upon the currency of the country?

Yes, if they remained out there would be an effect on prices; but they would soon come back. There would in that case, in the first instance, be no alteration in the total quantity of money as administered by the Bank of England, but the Bank would do just what a private banker does—he would employ the money he has in deposit in the purchase of securities without increasing his liabilities; but that state of things would never last; because *either those sovereigns would be wanted in the circulation or they would not; they most certainly would not; because before that time they were never called for, and, not being wanted in the circulation, they would return to the Bank to increase the deposits*, and then the Bank would be precisely in the situation I have mentioned before; they would increase their securities and increase their liabilities.

833. They would return to the Bank because they would

have depreciated the currency; but would not they affect prices while they remained out?

They would not remain out for any length of time.

If Mr. Page had confined himself to that part of his answer which I have marked with italics he would have been correct. The sovereigns, not being wanted in the circulation, would return to the Bank to increase the deposits ; and then, if the following question, instead of " 833. They would return to the Bank " because they would have depreciated the currency ; " but would they not affect prices while they remained " out?" which assumes that they would have entered into the circulation as currency — if instead of this erroneous assumption, the question had been *why* or in what sense the sovereigns would not be wanted and would return to the Bank, the proper answer would have been, that the circulation of sovereigns is wanted chiefly, if not exclusively, for purposes of income, including wages, and of expenditure, and not as instruments for transfers of capital. It is in the retail trade between dealer and consumer that coins are principally used. Now, as it does not appear why any additional demand in the retail trade should be caused by this forced issue of sovereigns by the way of loan on mortgage, they would, in all probability, as being most inconvenient instruments for a mere advance of capital, return to the Bank as deposits.

By the supposition it is a forced operation of the Bank. In effecting its purpose of making advances to that extent on mortgage, it would have to displace the existing capital (because the hypothesis assumes that things were in a sound and quiescent state, in other words, *in equilibrio*, there being no new circumstances to induce fresh borrowers on that description of securities at the existing rate of interest) which had been previously advanced and was absorbed in mortgages. This could not be effected without a great reduction in the rate of interest on that description of securities by way of a sufficient inducement to fresh borrowers, or to the existing mortgagees to pay off their loan and to borrow from the Bank at the reduced rate.

The mortgagees being unexpectedly, and to them inconveniently, paid off, would of course seek other investments; but these they would not readily find, unless by offers of capital at a still lower rate of interest. This would only remove the difficulty of finding employment for the capital by a single step, or rather merely shift it; for whatever securities were purchased by the capitalists whose mortgages had been paid off and transferred to the Bank, would set afloat just so much capital as would be produced by the transfer of those securities.

The result would not be materially varied if the supposed advances made by the Bank on mortgage were to parties who were buying land speculatively or otherwise. There would, of course, while the operation was in progress, be a temporary rise in the number of years' purchase of landed property. In this case the sellers of the land would probably, after paying off incumbrances, seek investment for the remainder of the amount in securities at home or abroad, and would, in the first instance, with the mortgagees who were paid off, deposit the sovereigns so received at their banker's. In either or both cases, the deposits in the Bank of England or other banks would be increased. The deposits so accumulated would, by the operation of a greatly reduced rate of interest, gradually find employment as capital at home or abroad, without necessarily having in the mean time produced the slightest effect in increasing the amount of the circulation or depreciating the currency, as by the question was supposed, in any other sense at least than in reducing the rate of interest.

I have been the rather induced to remark upon the opinion of Sir Robert Peel, as conveyed by his question No. 832., because it should seem that the examinations of the Committee on Banks of Issue, of which he was a member and in which he took part, had not shaken his belief that it was in the power of the Bank, by an attempt at a forced issue, to increase the amount of the circulation either in gold or bank notes, and so to depreciate the currency. On the last day of the session of 1842, Sir Robert Peel, after remarking on the tendency of the improvements effected by his tariff to mitigate the existing distress, concluded with saying, —

"I admit that there are modes by which a temporary prosperity might be created. I might create a temporary prosperity by the issue of 1*l.* notes, and by encouraging the Bank to make large issues of paper; but such a prosperity would be wholly delusive. It is much wiser, in my opinion, to abstain from the application of the stimulus." *

The effect of the issue of five millions being in 1*l.* notes instead of sovereigns would be so far, and only so far different, that although they would not, provided they were issued on securities, form an addition to the amount of the circulation, there might be such a preference on the part of the public for 1*l.* notes over sovereigns, that gold coin would go back to the Bank instead of the small notes.

It would appear from the conclusion of the speech just quoted, and from his examination of Mr. Page, that Sir Robert Peel is of opinion that a forced issue of sovereigns or of 1*l.* notes would be *most* efficacious, but that large issues of paper generally by the Bank

* Hansard, 12th August, 1842.

under encouragement from government, would in *the next degree* be effectual, and serve as a *stimulus* in creating a temporary prosperity.

Now, whatever may be the ultimate permanent effects of a fall in the rate of interest on the prosperity of the country, it is quite clear that temporary prosperity is not the necessary or immediate consequence of a greatly reduced rate. At the time when Sir Robert Peel made the remark which I have quoted, namely, in August, 1842, the rate of interest had fallen below what it had been for several years before, and most assuredly nothing like a return of prosperity, however short-lived, had yet manifested itself. He cannot, therefore, any longer have supposed, whatever may have been his impression when examining Mr. Page two years before, the rate of interest being then still comparatively high, that mere advances on securities, that is, loans or discounts by the Bank (always assuming that the securities are unexceptionable) could have the desired effect. How he would have proposed the extra issue to be made, with the view of creating temporary prosperity, does not appear.

The object of tracing thus far the operation, hypothetically suggested by Sir Robert Peel, is to show that the Bank of England cannot, any more than the country banks, at its pleasure, or for the purpose of employing productively, that is, in securities, a larger than usual proportion of its deposits or of its bullion, cause an enlargement of the circulation; and that the usual phraseology, by which the Bank of England and the country banks are said to enlarge their circulation as a voluntary act, is incorrect, so far as implying a power which they do not possess of directly adding to the amount of bank notes remaining out in circulation, passing from hand to hand among the public, and performing the functions of money in daily transactions.

It is possible that, coincidently with this operation of the Bank in a sudden forced advance of 5,000,000*l.* on mortgage, there might be circumstances in progress, such as an extension of trade and a rise of prices, or a state of discredit of country bank paper, which might absorb a part of the extra sum issued by the Bank ; in which case a part only of that extra sum would return to the Bank, some of it as deposits, and some of it to be exchanged for notes, the gold not being wanted for internal purposes. But, under the circumstances here supposed, an increased amount of bank notes would, but for this operation of the Bank, have been called forth, either by depositors or by discounts, or by an influx of bullion.

The conclusion from the view here presented is, that neither the country banks nor the Bank of England have a *direct* power (their advances being on securities, and the paper convertible) of enlarging their circulation ; and that the inference, from the mere fact of an increase or diminution of the amount of bank notes in circulation, as being an indication of a designed enlargement or contraction of issue by the Bank of England to the extent of the difference, proceeds on a false analogy by neglecting a consideration of the distinction between issues used synonymously with advances " on securities," and issues of government bank notes or assignats. It is only the latter description of circulation of bank notes which admits of being increased in amount at the will of the issuers.

# CHAP. XII.

## ON THE CONNECTION BETWEEN THE AMOUNT OF THE CURRENCY AND THE PRICES OF COMMODITIES.

A GREAT part of the examination of witnesses by the Committee of the House of Commons on Banks of Issue in 1840 was directed to the eliciting of opinions as to the terms by which the various kinds of instruments of exchange should be designated and classified. The witnesses were severally called upon to define the sense in which they used the terms "money, currency, and circulation," and to say whether they included deposits in the Bank and bills of exchange under any or all these terms.

The importance which was attached to the attempt at settling those definitions seems to have arisen from an opinion which prevailed evidently among the members of the Committee *, that, by arriving at a conclusion as to what part of the various forms of paper credit should be considered exclusively as money or

* From the tenour of the questions which were put to me and other witnesses by Mr. Hume, it might be inferred that he was of opinion that bank notes and deposits, as they conferred *a power of purchase*, were operative as a cause of variations of prices. And it is possible that such was *then* his opinion; but, not long before, he seems to have entertained a very different view. In the debate on Sir W. Clay's motion for a committee on Joint Stock Banks, May 12. 1836, Mr. Hume said, "With regard to the amount of paper issues, I think I could show that it would be impossible to issue too much paper money, if it were made convertible into gold in every part of the kingdom on demand. Indeed, I believe that great delusion exists in the country with regard to the effect on prices of the currency. My opinion is, that the quantity of money depends on the rise of prices; and that the rise of prices does not depend on the quantity of money. I hold the prevailing doctrine to be extremely erroneous on this point. The currency doctors I know differ from me; but there has never been a fair opportunity of demonstrating the truth of my propositions."

currency, conferring *a power of purchase*, some criterion or test might be found of the influence of one of the principal elements upon which not only the state of trade and credit, but also general prices depend; it being assumed that commodities, although liable in each particular instance to be influenced by circumstances affecting the supply and demand, are more or less under a direct influence from variations in the quantity of money or currency. And the same assumption of a direct agency of the quantity of money, according to the assumed definition of it, on prices, will be found to be either expressed or implied in the vast majority of the numberless publications to which the currency question has given rise. *

An increase or diminution of the amount of bank notes is evidently considered, not only by the professed adherents of the doctrine of the currency principle, but by a large proportion of the public who take an interest in the subject, to be analogous, in the effects on markets, to alterations in the quantity of a government compulsory paper; or, in other words, they consider that prices in such cases are under a direct influence from, and affected in the same manner by, variations in the amount of bank notes in circulation, which they designate indiscriminately as paper money.

This erroneous impression arises from a neglect of the consideration of the difference in the manner and purpose of the issue. I have not met with an instance in the inquiry by the committees, or in the numerous publications which have appeared on the subject of the currency, of any attention having been paid to this particular point. Indeed, the context in all of them seems to assume that there is no difference, and that therefore any attempt at explanation would be a work of supererogation. Thus,

* See Appendix (A).

Mr. Porter who, in the chapter on Currency, in his highly valuable work "On the Progress of the Nation," attributes to the amount of the circulation great influence on prices, contents himself with observing, "*It is not necessary to explain*, at any length, *in what manner* excessive issues of currency tend to raise the general prices of goods."* Now an explanation, however brief, of this point was exactly the thing wanted. And I cannot help thinking, that if he had suffered himself to pause and reflect upon it, he could hardly have failed to modify the opinion he has there expressed of the influence of the amount of the currency on prices, and he would possibly have been led to distrust the correctness of the view presented by the table which he has inserted in illustration of his opinion of that connection.

A moment's consideration will serve to show the importance of the distinction to which I have here alluded.

When a government issues paper money, inconvertible and compulsorily current, it is usually in payment for—

1. The personal expenditure of the Sovereign or the governing power.
2. Public Works and Buildings.
3. Salaries of Civil Servants.
4. Maintenance of Military and Naval Establishments.

It is quite clear that paper created and so paid away by the Government, not being returnable to the issuer, will constitute a fresh source of demand, and must be forced into and permeate all the channels of circulation. Accordingly, every fresh issue, beyond the point at which former issues had settled in a certain rise of prices and of wages, and a fall of the

* Progress of the Nation, vol. ii. p. 225.

exchanges, is soon followed by a further rise of commodities and wages, and a fall of the exchanges; the depreciation being in the ratio of the forcibly increased amount of the issues.*

It will hence appear that the difference between paper money so issued and bank notes such as those of this country consists, not only in the limit prescribed by their convertibility to the amount of them, but in the mode of issue. The latter are issued to those only who, being entitled to demand gold, desire to have notes in preference; and it depends upon the particular purposes for which the notes are employed, whether a greater or less quantity is required. The quantity, therefore, is an effect, and not a cause of demand. A compulsory government paper, on the other hand, while it is in the course of augmentation,

* Discredit is not an essential element in variations of the value of an inconvertible paper, nor is depreciation always a necessary consequence of inconvertibility. The notes of the Bank of England, and of the private banks of this country, were, for two years after the restriction, of the same value as if they had been convertible, and never experienced any discredit. There were great fluctuations in the credit of the paper money of the United States of America during the war of independence, and also in the case of the French assignats, arising from fluctuating opinions as to the chances of redemption; and both descriptions became ultimately valueless by excess, when all prospect of redemption had ceased. But the Russian government paper, although, during the progress of its depreciation, by successively increasing issues, no certain or probable prospect of redemption had been held out, seems never to have suffered any discredit; and the variations of the exchanges, beyond those produced by the mere excess of the paper, were such only as are incidental to variations in the state of trade. The effect of increased issues so made was exactly analogous to a progressive deterioration of the coin. The depreciation of the paper reached 75 per cent. At this point it stopped, and the government, by requiring payments for customs and other taxes to be made in the proportion of four paper rubles to one silver ruble, virtually established a degradation of the standard in that proportion, just as if the standard in this country had been reduced to five shillings for the sovereign. After continuing for some years at this rate of depreciation, the value of the paper was raised to 3 rs. 60 cs. for the silver ruble; and in 1838 a silver currency was re-established at the standard which existed previous to the degradation, provision being made for contracts that had been entered into *specifically* in bank notes, as contradistinguished from contracts in silver money.

acts directly as an originating cause on prices and incomes, constituting a fresh source of demand in money, depreciated in value as compared with gold, but of the same nominal value as before.

In a convertible state of the currency, given the actual and contingent supply of commodities, the greater or less demand will depend, not upon the total quantity of money in circulation, but upon the quantity of money constituting the revenues, valued in gold, of the different orders of the state under the head of rents, profits, salaries, and wages, destined for current expenditure.

Dr. Adam Smith, in the passage which I have before quoted from him (at p. 34.) observes: " The value of " the goods circulated between the different dealers " never can exceed the value of those circulated be- " tween the dealers and the consumers; whatever is " bought by the dealers being ultimately destined to be " sold to the consumers." Assuredly, then, the prices at which the commodities have gone into consumption, the result of them constituting the return for the capital expended in the production, may be considered with greater propriety than any other description as general prices.

The cost of production will determine whether and to what extent the supply will be continued, but the extent of the effectual demand, in a given state of the supply, will be measured by the prices which the consumers may be able and willing to pay. Now, the power of purchase by the consumers depends upon their incomes; and the measure of the extent and of the exercise of such power is, as has just been observed, in that portion of their revenues which is destined for expenditure in objects of immediate consumption.

Of the revenues or incomes of the community devoted to immediate expenditure, by far the largest proportion consists of wages, from those of the skilled artizan, who gets his 5*l.* a week or upwards, to those of the day labourers and common workmen, whose earnings with their families are from 20*s.* to 7*s.* a week. Any increase, accordingly, of incomes, of which wages constitute the largest part, will raise general prices, and a fall of wages will depress them, supposing no alteration in the cost of production, or in the actual and contingent supply.

If prices of one or more articles of consumption fall from diminished demand, and continue for any length of time below the cost of production, the supplies will fall off until, in consequence of the diminution of supply, the price rises, so as again to cover the cost. Or if the cost of production is raised by permanent causes, the means of the consumers being limited if the article is not a necessary of life, and if the supply fall off so as to raise the price, there will be a permanent falling off of the demand, and less of the article will be produced and consumed. But, given the cost of production, and, barring the effect of vicissitudes of the seasons, and other casualties affecting the supply, the quantity consumed, at certain prices, which is the test of effectual demand, will, as I have said, depend upon that portion of the incomes of the different orders of the community which may be destined for expenditure in immediate objects of consumption.

As an instance of the false practical conclusions to which the currency theory leads, in the view taken of the distinction between bills of exchange and bank notes, and in overlooking, as it does, the distinguishing features of credit, and capital, and currency, and between wholesale and retail dealings, I have to cite the following passage from Mr. Norman's Letter to Charles Wood, Esq. (page 43.) proposing to show, according to his view, the usual effect of bills of exchange on price: —

" A buys cotton of B at 10 per cent. in advance " on the previous price, payable at three months, and " gives his acceptance for the amount. At the close " of this period, or after one or more renewals, the bill " must be paid out of the currency in existence; and if " there is not enough money to sustain such a price, a " fall in prices must ensue, and B will suffer from his " bargain. But further, if the advanced price has " become general, a stimulus will be given to the " importation of cotton, a check to its exportation, or " to that of articles manufactured from it, and the final " result will probably be a fall below the original price, " commensurate with or perhaps greater than the " original rise. This imaginary case may be taken as " a fair representation of *the usual effect* of bills of " exchange on price."

The bills of exchange are here supposed to have an effect on price, that is, to be a cause of price; whereas *the very reverse is the fact.* The bills of exchange, so far from being a cause, are the effect of price. *The prospect of advantage supplies the motive, and the credit of the buyer constitutes the power of purchase,* while the bill of exchange is a mere written evidence or acknowledgment of the debt, accompanied with a promise to pay the amount at some definite period. If A, the buyer at the advanced price, has not under-estimated the supply, or over-estimated the consumption, the manufacturer must give the advanced price, and, by his acceptance or cheque, enable A to discharge his acceptance at the time of its becoming due, with a profit, or, by the supposition, without loss. But if A has been mistaken in his view of the supply, actual and contingent, compared with the rate of consumption, the price will fall, and he will suffer from his bargain; and if he trades upon a large proportion of borrowed capital and the loss be heavy, he will fail.

So much of the results, in the alternative of the

two suppositions, is clear enough according to the ordinary course of business. But, according to Mr. Norman's view, if I understand it rightly, the price would fall, not because the buyer had been mistaken in his view of facts and in his reasoning as to the supply relatively to the rate of consumption, but *because there was not enough money to sustain the advanced price.*

Mr. Norman does not attempt to show that the quantity of money requisite to sustain the advanced price of cotton in the case supposed is necessarily dependent on the aggregate of coin and bank notes, which he considers as the currency in existence in the country, and out of which he states that the bill given by the buyer of the cotton must be paid. He seems not to be aware that the quantity of money applicable to the purchase of cotton and cotton goods from the raw material in the hands of the grower, to the finished article in the hands of the consumers, is dependent upon that portion of the money incomes of the consumers at home and abroad, which they are able and willing to expend in the satisfaction of their wants for cotton clothing and the other uses of cotton goods. All sales and purchases from those of raw cotton in the hands of the planters, till the finished goods find their way into the hands of the consumers, must in the aggregate reach that amount, and cannot but by miscalculation of employers of capital and labour, in the distribution and the manufacture through the intermediate stages, exceed that amount, whatever may be the multiplication of bills arising out of the intermediate transactions.

The principle of limitation, therefore, to the maintenance of an advanced price of any particular article, in consequence of actual or apprehended deficiency of supply, *is not the quantity of money in existence in the country*, but *the quantity of money in the hands or pockets of the consumers destined for expenditure in that article.* And the eventual fall of price will not be from deficiency of the quantity of currency in the country to sustain the advance, as supposed in the foregoing passage, but from the inability or unwillingness of the consumer to pay the advanced price, and from a restoration, actual or expected, of the usual or a greater supply.

But then follows a passage which shows that in that which I have just quoted, the effect ascribed to bills of exchange on prices is supposed to arise from the circumstance, not of their creation, but of their changing hands by indorsements: " A large propor-" tion of bills are drawn and paid which *have no effect* " *on the currency whatever.* Thus let A sell coffee to B " at three months, and at a fair current price, draw for " the amount, and keep the bill in his portfolio until " due; it is clear that the result will be the same as if " he had given a simple credit for the same period. " The economy in the use of money will commence " when he makes a payment to C by means of an " indorsement, and will be repeated as often as the bill, " by a repetition of this process, changes hands. Thus " even purchases on credit, at advanced prices, against " which bills are drawn, *may be made without any new* " *creation of money*, and without the necessity of em-" ploying an economising expedient."

The *advance in the* price paid for cotton in the first of the hypothetical cases stated, and *the fair price* at which the coffee is in the second case supposed to have been sold, should seem upon the face of the statements to be essential conditions of the cases; but the two concluding sentences are calculated to remove that impression, and to lead to the inference that the prices paid have nothing to do with the question, how far bills of exchange do or do not answer the purposes of money *in a supposed effect on prices.*

The cases only prove what I have before endeavoured to show, that purchases and sales between dealers and dealers may be, and are in a great majority of cases, transacted through the medium of credit, of which bills of exchange are the written evidence; the successive indorsements adding to the credit of the original names on the bills, and serving the purpose of so many transfers of capital. And I have only referred to the cases stated by Mr. Norman as bearing on the question of the connection of the currency with prices, in order to point out the grave error of his doctrine, in ascribing to bills of exchange an effect *on* prices, instead of viewing them as an effect *of* prices.

The same error, being no less than that *of substituting cause for effect*, is observable in a still greater degree (because more importance is attached to it) in the influence ascribed by the currency theory to the amount of the circulation, that is, of bank notes, on prices. It is an error which perverts the reasoning, and distorts the view of facts, in every attempt to apply the theory of the currency principle to the actual course of commercial affairs.

---

## CHAP. XIII.

### ON THE CONNECTION BETWEEN THE RATE OF INTEREST AND PRICES.

On the Stock Exchange, and in the Money Market, the term money is used synonymously with capital. Abundance and cheapness of money mean abundance of capital seeking employment, and a low rate of interest as the consequence; as, on the other hand, scarcity of money, and tightness of the money market, mean comparative scarcity of disposable capital, and a consequent advance in the rate of interest. And when confined to operations on the stock exchange or in the money market, the terms so applied being technical and perfectly understood among the parties using them, lead to no inconvenience either in practice or in reasoning. But, in all general reasonings on the subject of the currency, and in the application of them to proposed regulations of banking, the ambiguity of the term value of money or of the currency, when employed indiscriminately as it is, to signify both value in exchange for commodities, and value in use of capital, is a constant source of confusion: accordingly, in many of the writings on the subject, and in much of the evidence given before the Banking Committee, abundant instances may be found in which parties using the terms appear to have their minds floating between the two meanings, and to come in consequence to any thing but clear conclusions.

I will not here stop to point out the fallacious inferences to which, on the general subject, this ambiguous use of the terms necessarily leads. My immediate purpose is to remark upon it only as relates to the inquiry how far the abundance or scarcity of money, in the language of the money market, or in more correct and less mistakeable terms, a low or high rate of interest, is calculated to exercise a direct influence on the prices of commodities. The commonly received opinion is, that a low rate of interest is calculated to raise prices, and a high rate to depress them. Mr. Gilbart in an article in the Westminster Review for January, 1841, thus explains the effects which he ascribes to the abundance or scarcity of money in the stock exchange and money market use of the term, meaning capital:—"Speculators and "merchants have always some peculiar reason for "dealing in one commodity rather than another; but "the facility of obtaining the *money* (*i. e.* the use of "capital) is the moving cause of the speculation, and "the price of each commodity will advance according "to the quantity of money brought to bear on that "particular market." So far from its being true that the facility of obtaining money (always understood on sufficient securities) *is the moving cause* of speculation in commodities, Mr. Gilbart would find it difficult to point out a single instance where the mere facility of borrowing on sufficient security has been the moving cause of any considerable speculation in commodities.

It may be worth while, by way of exhibiting the mode in which advances by the Bank of England, unattended with an increase of the circulation, may be supposed, according to the doctrine which is here under examination, to act upon the prices of commodities, to refer to the following further extract from Mr. Gilbart's review:—

"Again, suppose the circulation is at its proper "amount, and the Bank should purchase a million of "exchequer bills, the notes *thus put in circulation* not "finding immediate employment might be returned to "the Bank, and be lodged on deposit. *Here there* "*would be no increase in the circulation, but an increase* "*of a million in the deposits. A power of purchase to* "*the extent of a million sterling* would have been "created by the Bank, and the efforts of the depositors, "to make the most advantageous investments, would "have the effect of advancing the prices of commo- "dities, and of stimulating a spirit of speculation; and "should the Bank consider this increase in the deposits "a sufficient reason for adding another million to the "circulation, this additional million might also come "back, and be added to the deposits; *thus a power of*

" *purchase to the extent of two millions* would be created, " and a spirit of speculation would be still further pro- " moted, without any addition in the monthly returns " to the amount of the circulation."

This might be taken for a caricature of the notion of the *power of purchase*, which seemed to be so prevalent in the minds of some of the members of the Committee. A power of purchase might thus doubtless be created; but why should it be directed to the purchase of commodities if there was nothing in the state of supply, relatively to the rate of consumption, to afford the prospect of gain on the necessary eventual resale? The truth is, that the power of purchase by persons having capital and credit is much beyond any thing that those who are unacquainted practically with speculative markets have any idea of.* The error is in supposing the *disposition* or *will* to be co-extensive with the power. The limit to the motive for the exercise of the power is in the prospect of resale with a profit.

Mr. Bosanquet, in a tract entitled, " Metallic, Paper, and Credit Currency," containing much valuable information and ingenious reasoning on those topics, whilst agreeing with me † as to the absence of any direct influence of the amount of the currency on

* See Appendix (B).

† " I perfectly agree with Mr. Tooke that, whatever may be the increase or diminution in the amount of money, bills of exchange, or deposits, *as long as the increase or diminution shall have taken place strictly according to the wants of the community*, variation in quantity is in no way chargeable with variation in the prices of commodities. Prices may rise beyond their just level (inevitably to fall again from want of demand), and the currency may increase in quantity in proportion; or prices may be depressed from the state of markets at home or abroad below their ordinary level, trade may become stagnant, goods may want purchasers (inevitably to rise again from increase of demand), and the quantity of currency may decrease in proportion; but the amount of currency will neither be the cause of the state of prices, nor will it in any way affect the value of money." If, instead of the lines which I have marked with italics, be introduced the clause *as long as the paper is convertible*, I perfectly assent to that exposition of my views.

prices, attaches great importance to the influence which he ascribes to the rate of interest on the prices of commodities. At the time, however, when he wrote, which is more than two years ago (and the same remark applies to Mr. Gilbart), the rate of interest was not so low as it has since been, and it may perhaps be considered hardly fair to make use of recent experience in commenting upon opinions delivered under such different circumstances.

It is not, however, as judging by the event that I have to remark upon Mr. Gilbart's and Mr. Bosanquet's opinions on this point. My reason for referring to them is, that they state, in a manner more positive and detailed than I have met with in other writers, what they conceive to be the mode of operation of variations in the rate of interest on prices of commodities.

Mr. Bosanquet observes (p. 73.): —

" Were the rate of interest reduced as low as 1 per " cent., capital borrowed would be placed nearly on a " par with capital possessed."

That a capital borrowed at that, or even a lower rate, should be considered nearly on a par with capital *possessed*, is a proposition so strange as hardly to warrant serious notice, were it not advanced by a writer so intelligent, and, on some points of the subject, so well informed. Has he overlooked the circumstance, or does he consider it of little consequence, that there must, by the supposition, be a condition of repayment? He goes on, however, to say: —

" The demand for issues of money" (loans of capital?), " or the means of procuring capital, would, " in such cases, be limited merely by the amount of " available security to be produced, and the effect " would be, the rise in price of all those commodities " which can in any way be turned to account so as to " produce profit."

There seems to be a strange misapprehension involved in this mode of accounting for the effect here ascribed to the low rate of interest. We must suppose that this reduced rate is general, but that good security is required; because, if credit is given indiscriminately, without reasonable security for repayment, there is no recklessness of adventure that would not be entered into. Suppose, then, that the reduced rate is general, and the loans for such length of time as to admit of being extensively acted upon by the different dealers in commodities. The effect would be precisely the reverse of that which the author would anticipate.

A general reduction in the rate of interest is equivalent to or rather constitutes a diminution of the cost of production. This is more especially and very obviously a necessary effect where much fixed capital is employed, as in the case of manufactures, but it likewise operates in all cases where an outlay of capital is required, according to the length of time ordinarily occupied in bringing the commodities, whether raw produce or finished goods, to market; the diminished cost of production hence arising would, by the competition of the producers, inevitably cause a fall of prices of all the articles into the cost of which the interest of money entered as an ingredient. And the presumption accordingly is, that the very reduced rate of interest which has prevailed within the last two years must have operated as one of the contributing causes of the great reduction of prices of some of our most important manufactures which has occurred coincidently with reduction in the rate of interest.

It is probable, however, that Mr. Bosanquet, in his theory of high prices as a consequence of a low rate of interest, may be under the influence of the same opinion as that of Mr. Gilbart and many others — that a facility of borrowing at a low rate of interest not only confers the power of purchasing, but affords the inducement — applies *the stimulus* to speculation in commodities. If by facility of borrowing be meant a laxity of regard to security for repayment on the part of the lender, there is every probability that money so borrowed will be hazardously, if not recklessly employed; and whether in the purchase of shares, or of foreign securities, or of merchandize, or in any other mode of adventure or enterprise, or in mere personal expenditure, is a matter of chance, depending on the disposition and views of the borrower; such borrowers are not *stimulated* to purchase commodities speculatively, merely because they can borrow on low terms; they are but too happy if they can borrow at all. But to suppose that persons entitled to credit are likely to be induced — *stimulated* is the favourite term — by the mere circumstance of a low rate of interest to enter into speculations in commodities (using the term speculation in its obnoxious sense), argues a want of knowledge of the motives which lead to such speculations. These are seldom if ever entered into with borrowed capital, except with a view to so great an advance of price, and to be realized within so moderate a space of time, as to render the rate of interest or discount a matter of comparatively trifling consideration.

In truth, the importance attached to speculations in commodities, whether as connected with bank notes, or with the rate of interest, or with expansions and contractions of the Currency, in whatever sense these terms are used, is greatly exaggerated. As long as vicissitudes of the seasons are among the ordinances of Providence, and as long as political and fiscal obstructions to the freedom of commercial intercourse are among the errors of legislation, aggravating all other causes of fluctuation, and among these the sliding-scale of our Corn Laws in a pre-eminent degree, there will, in any state of the Currency, be speculation, which, in its obnoxious sense, implies an exaggerated view of a deficiency of supply, and of the probable effect of it on prices.

Not only in the view which Mr. Bosanquet takes of the effect of variations in the rate of interest on prices, but in the influence which he ascribes to those variations on the state of trade and of credit, I differ from him most widely. Agreeing with him as I do in his argument against some of the prominent assumptions involved in the currency theory, nothing, in my opinion, can exceed the inconsistency of reasoning, and the unfounded supposition of facts, upon which he grounds his belief (p. 108.), that in the attempts on the part of the Bank to rectify the exchanges, a variation is sometimes effected in prices of from 25 to 50 per cent. He, in this instance, takes for gospel the assertion in the report of the Manchester Chamber of Commerce, published at the close of 1839, that the revulsion of credit and of prices in 1837 had entailed a diminution in the value of commodities to that extent. And with the framers of the report he ascribes that revulsion of credit and fall of prices to the measures of the Bank of England, in discountenancing the paper of the American houses, and in raising the rate of discount.

As to the revulsion of credit, it was a necessary effect of the previous undue and extravagant extension of it. But what I have to remark upon is the assumption that the raising of the Bank rate of discount, in 1836, to 4½ per cent., and ultimately to 5 per cent., had a considerable influence in depressing prices. Now if this advance in the Bank rate of discount were to be considered as the main cause, or even a materially contributing cause, of the fall in the prices of commodities at that time, how was it that an advance in the rate of discount by the Bank of England in 1839 to 6 per cent. had not any such depressing effect? There was a great feeling of uneasiness, and even of alarm, through the summer and autumn of 1839, and yet not the slightest depressing effect from these combined circumstances was felt in the prices of produce. Circulars of brokers and merchants are usually published at the close of the past and the commencement of the coming year; and in some of those of the 1st of January, 1840, it was stated as a matter of wonder, that though the value of money (meaning the rate of interest) had advanced 50 per cent., that is, from 4 to 6 per cent., the markets for produce had been so well maintained.*

There was, moreover, during the whole period of pressure on the money market (by which is meant an advanced and unusually high rate of interest), a remarkable absence of commercial failures of any magnitude; whereas the progressive fall in the rate of interest from the commencement of 1840 to the close of 1842, when it reached its lowest point, was accompanied by a marked fall in most of the leading articles of consumption (the greatest depression of prices coinciding with the lowest rate of interest, viz. 1½ per cent.), and by numerous failures, among which were mercantile and banking firms of considerable importance. A fall in the rate of interest between 1818 and the close of 1822, was accompanied by a still greater fall in the prices of commodities; and instances without end could be multiplied to the same effect. It is not easy, indeed, to imagine evidence of facts more decisive, than those which can be adduced of the negative of the direct influence ascribed to a low rate of interest in raising the prices of commodities, and *vice versâ*. The theory is not only not true, but the reverse of the truth.

* Appendix C.

The rise of prices in 1835-6 was mainly the consequence of an extraordinary demand, arising from a spirit of speculation which had its origin in America, and to which an infatuated confidence of the houses here in that trade, ministered by unbounded credits. A collapse of credit, as the ultimate result of such a previous inflation of it, is so obviously an inevitable necessity, as to supersede any call for explanation.

But, in truth, both the currency theory, and the money market theory, that is, on the one hand, the theory which connects prices with bank notes, and, on the other hand, the theory which connects them with the rate of interest, are equally in error.

The phenomena of the great fluctuations of prices which they attempt, in the face of all facts and of all correct reasoning, to account for by the supposed influence of bank notes, or of the rate of interest, are those of credit, too easily and extensively given in the first instance, and withdrawn of necessity in the end with more or less violence, according to the previous greater or less undue extension. The alternations of excessive extension of credit under the influence of exaggerated opinion, with the subsequent more or less violent contraction, are, by the convenient ambiguity and laxity of the phraseology which is in use in discussions on this subject, more, perhaps, than on any other, termed *expansions and contractions of the currency or of the circulation.*

Nothing, indeed, can be more convenient in argument than this ambiguous phraseology as a ground, whether of attack or defence of the management of the Bank of England, or of the country banks, or of the present system of banking generally (with a view to the substitution of some other system), in order to prove, according to the sense in which the term currency is used, that the mismanagement of one or other of these is the cause of all the mischief of which the public thinks itself entitled to complain.

There is one further remark before dismissing the question of the connection of the currency with prices which it occurs to me to make, and that is, that with the same laxity of language as is observable in all discussions on this topic, the term prices is often applied indiscriminately to commodities and to securities. Now it must be quite obvious, that these two descriptions of objects of purchase are acted upon by a low rate of interest in an exactly opposite direction. A low rate of interest is almost synonymous with a high price of securities; while, as I have shown, its necessary tendency is to reduce the prices of commodities by diminishing the cost of production. And in point of fact, the phenomena of the last three years have exhibited a rise in the prices of the public funds, and of shares and of securities generally, and a fall in the markets for commodities.

---

## CHAP. XIV.

### DISTINCTION BETWEEN ISSUING AND NON-ISSUING BANKS.

We have thus seen, that neither the amount of the circulation (bank notes) nor the rate of interest or discount, to the extent to which it has hitherto varied, can be considered as exercising a direct influence on the prices of commodities, but that the greater part, if not the whole of the fluctuations of prices which are over and above those that are necessarily incidental to the nature of the commodities, are attributable to the expansion and contraction of credit, under the influence of the opinion of dealers or speculators, more or less exaggerated, of the prospect of markets.

Credit, in its most simple expression, is the confidence which, well or ill-founded, leads a person to entrust another with a certain amount of capital, in money, or in goods computed at a value in money agreed upon, and in each case payable at the expiration of a fixed term. In the case where the capital is lent in money, that is, whether in bank notes, or in a cash credit, or in an order upon a correspondent, an addition for the use of the capital of so much upon every 100*l.* is made to the amount to be repaid. In the case of goods the value of which is agreed in terms of money, constituting a sale, the sum stipulated to be repaid includes a consideration for the use of the capital and for the risk, till the expiration of the period fixed for payment. Written obligations of payment at fixed dates mostly accompany these credits, and the obligations or promissory notes after date being transferable, form the means by which the lenders, if they have occasion for the use of their capital, in the shape whether of money or goods, before the expiration of the term of the bills they hold, are mostly enabled to borrow or to buy on lower terms, by having their own credit strengthened by the names on the bills in addition to their own. A great proportion of the vast transactions of the country among wholesale dealers are carried on by credit, simple and direct for the most part in its origin, however ramified and complicated in some of its subsequent processes.

It is quite clear that credit as between dealers and dealers (including in this term, merchants, manufacturers, and farmers), however liable to occasional abuse, does not admit of being regulated by any legislative interference. But it is charged against our banking system, on its present footing, that it is, if not an originating, a very powerfully aggravating cause of the violent variations of credit to which the commerce of the country is occasionally exposed. And to some extent the charge must be admitted. There is no doubt that banks, whether private or joint stock, may, if imprudently conducted, minister to an undue extension of credit for the purpose of speculations, whether in commodities, or in over-trading in exports or imports, or in building or in mining operations, and that they have so ministered not unfrequently, and in some cases to an extent ruinous to themselves, and without ultimate benefit to the parties to whose views their resources were made subservient, is unfortunately but too true.

According to the general opinion founded on the prevalence of the theory of the currency principle, it is to banks of issue mainly, if not exclusively, that the charge here stated is made to apply. And the House of Commons appears to have been under a full persuasion to this effect, when it appointed a Committee of Inquiry into the subject of banking, having named for its object Banks of Issue. The question which I now therefore propose to examine, is to what extent this opinion may be considered to be well founded.

It is, I conceive, impossible, upon a view of the evidence before the committee in 1841, on the part of the country banks, of which I have given extracts, to resist the force of the conclusion that the amount of notes which can circulate in a given district is strictly determined and limited by the wants of the neighbourhood, so that it is not in the power of any one or more of the banks, or of all of them together, to add to the total amount of notes in the hands of the public within that district; nor, unless by substituting

Bank of England notes or coin, *directly** to diminish the amount of local notes. If this be true, and that it is so rests, as it seems to me, upon facts and reasoning so clear as not to leave room for the shadow of a doubt, what becomes of the distinction set up by the currency theory, between issuing and non-issuing banks in the power of the former as compared with the latter, to influence and disturb the amount of the circulation?

The following passages in Mr. Norman's letter to Mr. C. Wood present an elaborate view of the supposed difference of the inducement and power of banks in a purely metallic circulation (being the same as non-issuing banks) to make advances, and thereby influence prices, as compared with banks that have the power of creating, as it is termed, paper money in aid of their other business.

"It is plain that it *would never be the interest of any body to issue metallic money in excess,* because the coin can never exchange for a greater amount of commodities than the metal of which it is formed has cost, plus the seignorage, if a seignorage be taken, *it yields therefore, in ordinary circumstances, no profit.* With bank notes the case is widely different; they yield a very considerable profit, and it is the interest of their issuers *to keep in circulation as large an amount as possible.* Hence one source of the danger of *an over-issue.* Another is

* I use the term "directly," because after a period in which there has been a pressure on the money market, and the banks generally have curtailed their advances, a state of languor (as Mr. Anderson in his evidence, p. 50., observed) is apt to supervene, and to be attended with diminished transactions, and a consequent reduction of the amount of bank notes. So, on the other hand, after a period in which a low rate of interest and revived confidence and extended credit have been in operation for some time, the consequent increase of transactions would probably require to be followed by an increased amount of bank notes in the hands of the public. I say probably, not necessarily, because in 1835, notwithstanding the unbounded confidence and extension of credit which then prevailed, there was no extension, and, if any thing, a reduction of the amount of notes in circulation. In every case they are a consequence, and not a cause.

found in the bodies from which they emanate. In this country the banks of England and Ireland, joint stock and private banks, are not merely *creators*, but also bankers in the proper sense of the term, *dealers in money*, and in this capacity they are exposed to a strong *temptation* to avail themselves of their privilege as issuers in aid of the other branch of their business. When the prices of goods rise, or when there is a struggle in progress against an impending fall of prices, the customers of a banker usually call upon him for increased assistance which it is difficult for him to refuse, while if at the same time interest rises the prospect of enlarging his profit is an additional inducement for him to enlarge his advances, *and to aid his banking resources by an augmentation of his circulation.* Now a rise in prices frequently precedes an unfavourable state of the exchanges, and a struggle against a fall of prices and an advance in the rate of interest, are its ordinary concomitants. Thus we see that the first stages of an export of treasure are generally characterised by circumstances which tend to cause an augmentation of bank notes, while with a metallic currency they would necessarily be accompanied by a reduction in the circulation, as in that case all the coin exported would be taken from it. It appears, then, that with a mixed currency, like that which exists in this country, the tendency of things when the exchanges are unfavourable, is exactly contrary to what would occur had we only coin. During a favourable exchange it is equally so. Further, with a metallic currency *the gold imported would be added to the circulation*, while at present in such a state of things prices fall, and the rate of interest being usually low, loans are redeemed, advances are paid off, and the paper circulation is thus kept down. The experience of the last few years furnishes us abundance of facts confirmatory of this theoretic view of the subject." *

The passages in this extract marked with italics appear to me to involve ambiguity of meaning in the terms and fallacy in the reasoning. The proposition involved in the very first sentence is untenable. It undoubtedly might be occasionally the interest,

* See also "Reflections, &c." by S. J. Loyd, p. 45. &c.

real or fancied, of bankers dealing only in metallic money, to issue it in excess. Supposing all the deposits received by a banker to be in coin, might it not be his business then, as now, in consideration of his care and trouble in keeping the cash and answering the depositors' drafts, to employ so much of the deposits as by experience he computes may not be immediately wanted by the depositors, in loans and discounts. How then can it be said that the issue of metallic money in ordinary circumstances yields no profit? And can it with truth be maintained that he cannot issue it in excess? Is he not, just as much as the issuing banker, exposed to the importunity of customers, whom it may be impolitic to refuse, for loans or discounts, or to be tempted by a high interest? and may he not be induced to encroach so much upon his deposits, as to leave him, under not improbable circumstances, unable to meet the demands of his depositors? Would not this be issuing metallic money in excess? In what respect, indeed, would the case of a banker in a perfectly metallic circulation differ from that of a London banker at the present day? He is not a creator of money, he cannot avail himself of his privilege as an issuer in aid of his other business, and yet there have been lamentable instances of London bankers issuing money in excess.

But, says the theory, it is the interest of issuers of notes to keep in circulation as large an amount as possible; granted: but have they the power as well as the inclination to add to the amount of their notes in the hands of the public at any given time, and thus "to aid their banking resources by an augmentation of their circulation?" The supposition of their having the power, implies, as I have before observed, a lurking impression of similarity in the *issue* between a convertible and an inconvertible paper. The issuer of inconvertible paper has the power up to the limit of utter worthlessness; while there are, as has been incontrovertibly shewn, narrow and impassable limits, totally independent of the foreign exchanges, to the power of issue of a strictly convertible paper. Admitting, although with qualification, as matters of fact "that a rise in prices frequently precedes an unfavourable state of the exchanges, and that a struggle against a fall of prices and an advance in the rate of interest are its ordinary concomitants, and that the first stages of an export of treasure are generally characterised by circumstances which tend to cause an augmentation of bank notes." I am not only not prepared to admit "that with a metallic currency they would necessarily be accompanied by a reduction in the circulation, as in that case all the coin exported would be taken from it;" but I have no hesitation in stating it as my opinion, that in the early stages of a rise of prices, and for a limited time there would, with a metallic currency, be an increase in the circulation of coin notwithstanding an incipient export of bullion*; such export of bullion not being necessarily or probably "so much coin taken from it;" nor during a favourable exchange "with a metallic currency would the gold imported be added to the circulation" any more than it is now. And I utterly deny that "the experience of the last few years furnishes abundance of facts *confirmatory* of the theoretic view of the subject as set forth in the foregoing extracts." I admit some of the facts, but no part of the hypothetical contrast, upon which the theory is founded.

In corroboration of my views on this point I avail myself of the authority of a very accomplished writer,

* If asked whence the increase of coin could come, the answer is, from the reserves of the bankers; who, if they could not answer all the demands upon them by depositors, must stop payment.

who unites with the practical experience of a banker a rare power of philosophical and scientific exposition: I mean the author of an Essay on Value, On the Formation of Opinions, &c. In a tract entitled "A Defence of Joint Stock Banks and Country Issues," he observes, p. 85. :—

"If the country banks have erred at all, it has not been in their conduct as banks of issue, but in their conduct as banks for discounts and loans; a matter altogether different and distinct, with which the legislature has no more to do than with rash speculations in corn or cotton, or improvident shipments to China or Australia.

"These two things are often confounded, and many of the evils which have been attributed to mismanagement of the circulation, to improper and excessive expansions and contractions, have in reality proceeded from improper discounts and loans, — transactions which would take place under any system whatever, and the evils of which can be remedied only by a progress in intelligence. On this distinction, indeed, being properly understood and kept in view, will depend, in a great measure, the wisdom of any decision which may be come to relative to the great question of a single Bank, or a multiplicity of Banks of issue.

"No one would be mad enough to attempt to interfere in any way with the management of establishments for borrowing and lending money, and yet it is not too much to say, that in that character banks are of far greater importance to the community than the other; that they produce far more extensive consequences by the regulation of their loans than they can produce by any fluctuations which they have the power of effecting as banks of issue, so long as their paper is convertible. Whatever arrangements consequently are adopted in regard to the currency, the principal sources of good and evil in the system of banking will continue.

"Supposing country issues to be suppressed, and no paper but that of one single issuer to be allowed, the banks would still be at liberty to make any loans they might think proper. All the effects, whether good or bad, produced on the commerce of the country by banking institutions would remain, except those which are specifically occasioned by local paper. Banks properly conducted would then be of the highest service to commerce as they are now, while banks improperly conducted, making immoderate and unwarrantable advances for improvident undertakings, and risking their money on hazardous or worthless securities, would bring great evils both on themselves and on the community, just like any other mercantile establishments in the hands of bad managers.

"It is necessary, therefore, in order to arrive at sound conclusions on the questions before us, not to mix up the benefits and evils of the trade of borrowing and lending capital, with the specific effects of issuing promissory notes.

"If we would form a proper judgment of the competency of any banks of issue whatever, to perform their functions, we must endeavour to attain definite views of the peculiar advantages and disadvantages of that sort of currency which they circulate.

"What then are the specific effects of a paper currency? What are the resulting advantages and disadvantages to the community, and what are the institutions best adapted to secure and properly distribute the one, and to avoid the other?

"A few brief hints in answer to these questions are all that can be here offered to the reader.

"Every one must see on reflection that there are two advantages resulting from what may be termed a credit-note currency such as ours — the convenience arising from its form and the saving of capital.

"The former advantage would be as effectually attained if every note were the representative of an actual quantity of gold in deposit; or, in other words, if notes were not issued to a greater amount than the coin or bullion lodged in the bank which issued them. For the sake of distinctness in the present discussion, let these be called bullion-notes.

"The latter advantage, viz. the saving of capital, depends on notes being issued to a greater amount than the bullion held in deposit, and it is important to remark that it is the *sole peculiar advantage* necessarily attending such a currency."

And yet seeing so clearly as he does this distinction between the business of loans and discounts and that of issue in the case of the country bankers, he seems to lose sight of the distinction when he refers to the effects of the management of the Bank of England. He says, p. 62., when comparing the character and position of the Bank of England with country banks, " The former, in order to put out an additional amount of paper, has merely to purchase securities to that amount, while the latter have no direct means whatever of effecting an expansion." Now I have shown, as I trust satisfactorily, that the Bank of England has no more *direct* power in this respect than the country banks.

The only plausible argument that I have met with for a distinction between issuing and non-issuing banks, in their tendency to issue *money* in excess (meaning, if translated into correct language, " to make advances of capital in excess"), is, that in the competition, either of new Banks of Issue, to get a portion of the existing circulation, or of established banks to get an increased share at the expense of neighbouring banks, they are induced, with a view of getting out their notes, to make advances to an undue extent and upon insufficient securities. This, I think, may be admitted as true to some extent; and to this extent there may be sufficient ground for making whatever regulations should be thought advisable to guard against malversation of banks generally, more stringent as against Banks of Issue. But the distinction, to the extent which I have here admitted, does not affect the question of the currency principle.

According to that principle, Banks of Issue have the power of issuing paper money *ad libitum* up to the check of convertibility, in giving accommodation to their customers, beyond the ordinary resources of their banking business. Now, so far from this being the case, namely, that the power of issue has come in aid of their resources, the truth is, that in all the flagrant cases of mismanagement of banks, the resources of the business, that is, the deposits and the capital of the shareholders or partners, have been brought in aid of the efforts to get a share of the existing circulation, not to add to it, for that was impossible. But it is doubtful, to say the least of it, whether, in point of fact, the more striking instances of excessive advances were in any degree owing to their being the means of getting into circulation an additional amount of notes.

In the case of the Northern and Central Bank, which was a striking instance of a recklessly managed establishment, their liabilities were said to exceed 1,600,000*l.*, while their circulation was somewhat under 300,000*l.* Now the presumption is, that although their advances were beyond all doubt in great excess, their issues, meaning their notes which remained out, were not excessive; that is, did not exceed the necessities of the circulation; or, in other words, the amount that would have been in circulation, if, for instance, Bank of England notes only had circulated there. A strong ground for presumption to this effect is, that the whole amount of the notes of the Northern and Central Bank, when withdrawn by their discredit, appear to have been replaced by an equal amount of Bank of England notes. It was on the 1st of December, 1836, that the Bank of England came to a determination to assist the Northern and Central Bank, and a part of the arrangement was to take up the circulation of the latter. Now the circulation of the Bank of England stood thus: —

| | 29th Nov. 1836. | 3d Jan. 1837. |
|---|---|---|
| London - | £13,556,000 | £13,023,000 |
| Country - | 3,733,000 | 4,074,000 |
| | £17,289,000 | £17,097,000 |

And I would ask whether presumptive proof can be stronger than that this excess of the country issues of the Bank of England, at the precise time of its intervention for the Northern and Central Bank, was a necessary substitute for the withdrawn notes of the latter ?

There is, moreover, this important consideration arising out of the view here presented, and that is, that whereas the propounders of the currency theory have stated it as an anomaly of the existing system, that the country circulation has occasionally been extended (and this has been particularly remarked by them in regard to the very time here mentioned) when the Bank of England has contracted its circulation, and so far counteracted the efforts of the Bank of England to redress the exchanges; here was an increase of the *country issues* of the Bank of England (not distinguished as such in the Gazette returns) of 340,000*l.*, while the London circulation was reduced by upwards of 500,000*l.* !

It is not, therefore, the *issues* (notes) of the Northern and Central Bank that were in excess, but their *advances* that were greatly so. And this, I have no doubt, would be found to be the case, if inquired into, of every issuing bank that has failed. If the issues (notes) of a Bank, however small the amount, prove to be beyond the power of the issuers to pay on demand, they are virtually in excess as soon as, on being tested by that criterion, they are found to fail in the performance of the condition on which they were issued, and which gave them their value. But as long as they continue in credit, however undeserved, and in circulation, under the impression of their being strictly convertible, the amount cannot be excessive. The *quality* may, unsuspected by the holders, be bad, when the *quantity* may not be more than sufficient to answer the purposes of convenience for which alone there is a call for any circulation or currency whatever.

In treating of Banks of Issue, as contradistinguished from non-issuing Banks, it is material to bear in mind a distinction between Joint-Stock and Private Banks of Issue, which is, that in the case of Joint-Stock Banks there has not, to the best of my recollection, been a single instance of a failure of any importance which has extended to the non-payment of the notes in circulation.

My impression is, that in most, if not in all instances, the notes of Joint-Stock Banks in the hands of the public have been paid without delay, and at all events that they have been ultimately discharged. Delay or hesitation applying only in the first instance to the depositors, while the loss has ultimately fallen, as it ought to do, upon the shareholders. In the instances of private issuing Banks that have failed, the case has so far been different that the holders of notes and the depositors have equally been sufferers. But although the failures of private Banks of Issue have (as well as those of Joint-Stock Banks) been within the last two or three years lamentably frequent, the collective amount of their notes in the hands of the public has been very inconsiderable, not to say insignificant. So inconsiderable, as assuredly not of itself to be allowed to weigh in any degree worth mentioning among the reasons for the great change which has been proposed in the footing of our paper circulation by the propounders of the currency principle, that is, of superseding all other sources by a single Bank of Issue.

I am ready to admit that the failure of a private issuing Bank on the grounds here stated, namely, that the holders of notes come in only *pari passu* with depositors, is a greater evil than the failure of non-issuing Banks, or than the failure of issuing Joint-Stock Banks.

But admitting, as I do, that this is an evil attending private Banks of Issue as compared with non-issuing Banks, or with issuing Joint-Stock Banks, it is an evil of infinitely less importance now than when country bank notes under 5*l.* were in circulation throughout the United Kingdom. They are now confined to Scotland and Ireland. The difference is immeasurably great as relates to the suffering or hardship attending the suspension of payments of the notes of a local bank, between notes of 1*l.* and notes of 5*l.* and upwards. Where the smaller notes, that is, of 1*l.*, are issued, they circulate among the working classes of the population. Consequently, whenever banks issuing 1*l.* notes failed, the loss fell heavily on those classes among whom the artisans and better class of operatives received their wages in that form. That I have not been unmindful of the evil attending the issue of this description of notes, as connected with the risk of failure of the issuing banks, may be seen by the following extract from a Tract of mine, entitled, "Considerations on the State of the Currency," published in January, 1826.

"Whatever may be determined upon as to the expediency of providing additional security for the general circulation of the country banks, there is one part of that circulation which ought not upon any footing, or with any modification, to be any longer tolerated. I mean the notes under 5*l.* These are in every point of view a most objectionable medium of exchange. Leaving out of the question the consideration of fluctuations in the value of the currency, some protection of the lower classes against the severe losses to which they have so often been exposed, as the holders of small notes, when the banks issuing them have failed, is imperatively called for. It is quite idle to say that the lower classes have the option of refusing to take the country notes, practically in the great majority of instances, they have not and cannot have any such option. But if there is any object more important than another, for which the government of every state has been invested with the privilege of coining money, it is that of protecting the lower classes of society, who are little competent in this particular to protect themselves, from the risk of loss in receiving their stipulated wages or other payments. And this function of the sovereignty of issuing coin, which, under the strongest sanctions, certifies to every member of the community the weight and fineness of the money, when he may be entitled to receive it, justly guarded against the interference of private individuals by the severest penalties. But by a strange inconsistency, while such care is manifested to secure the community from being imposed upon by metallic money of less than standard value, every adventurer who chooses to follow the trade of a banker is allowed to issue a spurious paper money, which having neither intrinsic value nor any adequate security for eventual convertibility, is in too many instances neither more nor less than a fraud, a fraud of which the most numerous and helpless classes and those who can least bear the loss are most commonly the victims." — *Consideration on the State of the Currency*, 1826, p. 127, 128.

At the time when these remarks were written, the amount of the circulation of one pound notes in England and Wales had been computed at upwards of five millions. The evil, therefore, of the suspension of so many issuing banks as had then recently failed was one of great magnitude, which fully justified, or rather demanded, the interference of the government and the legislature to provide a remedy, and this was most effectually done by the suppression of that objectionable class of notes. At present the entire circulation of notes of 5*l.* and upwards, issued by private banks in England and Wales, hardly exceeds in amount what was the circulation of 1*l.* notes alone prior to 1826. And however to be regretted that the holders of private country banker's notes, being now of the denomination of 5*l.* and upwards, should occasionally be exposed to loss by failure of the issuers, it will hardly be contended that their case is so important and so clearly distinct from the case of depositors, and other sufferers by the failure of Banks, as to justify, with the view of protecting them, an alteration of the whole system of issue in the Kingdom.

But as it appears that whatever the relative merits may in other respects be, as between private and Joint-Stock Banks of Issue, the circulation of the latter is much more secure, a mode of gradually substituting the issues of them for those of private Banks with the least inconvenience to the public, and without injury to existing interests, would be simply that of not granting licenses for the issue of notes to any private Banks which are not already in possession of the privilege. The notes of Joint-Stock Banks and of the Branches of the Bank of England would thus by degrees supersede those of the private Banks, and so remove one source of inconvenience from the present system.

I have noticed at some length this point, namely, the insecurity of the notes of private Banks, because it has been brought in as a make weight among the arguments in favour of a single Bank of Issue. On the grounds which have here been stated, I hold it to be utterly insignificant in that view.

I shall therefore proceed to make the few further remarks which occur to me on the currency principle, in its application to our Banking system, leaving out of the question, or leaving as a point for separate discussion by those who deem it of sufficient importance, the liability to insolvency of private Banks of Issue.

# CHAP. XV.

## REVIEW OF THE CURRENCY PRINCIPLE IN ITS APPLICATION TO OUR BANKING SYSTEM.

If the views which have thus far been unfolded are admitted to be correct, it can hardly fail of being seen as a fair deduction from them, that the whole of the ground on which the theory of the Currency principle proceeds is unsound. The error of supposing that, if the currency were purely metallic, every export or import of bullion would be so much taken from or added to the quantity of money in circulation, is so obvious, so palpable, as to make it a matter of surprise that such a notion should ever have been entertained. And must it not, as an inevitable consequence, follow that it is equally an error to suppose that the paper money, if administered upon the footing proposed by the currency doctrine, of a single source of issue, having a fixed amount on securities, and beyond that, exchanging only paper against gold, and *vice versâ*, would vary in amount and value in the hands of the public, with variations in the quantity of bullion exported or imported, or in the quantity of bullion in the coffers of the Bank?

I would not misrepresent the doctrine; but instances innumerable might be adduced from the writings, and from the examination by the Committee on Banks of Issue, of the advocates of that doctrine, that it goes to the full extent here stated; tabular statements being exhibited of the discrepancies between bullion in the Bank and notes out of it, with a view to prove, according to the occasion, sometimes against the country banks, and sometimes against the Bank of England, the charge of mismanagement. One source of their error is their imagining that, in their supposed Bank of exclusive Issue, the notes paid for gold exported must necessarily be taken from out of those circulating among the public, and that the gold imported would be taken to the Bank in exchange for bank notes, which would go into the hands of the public ; and they hold it to be the opprobrium of the present system, that this is not now the case. It must, however be clear, if I have made myself at all intelligible, that in neither case would it necessarily or generally be the case, or rather, it would be rarely so, under a single bank of issue; and, except under extraordinary circumstances, the amount of notes in the hands of the public would be nearly, if not quite, the same under one system as under the other.

It may be asked, and the question is a very natural one for those who are impressed with the notion that bank notes are operative by their amount, and who are not aware of the distinction between currency and capital, how it is that the Bank of England, or the banks collectively, if they cannot contract the circulation, (as I maintain that they cannot by any *direct* operation,) nor operate through that medium on the prices of commodities, are to be supposed to have the power of influencing the exchanges ? The answer is, that it is only by a forcible action on their securities that they can influence the exchanges, so as to arrest a drain, or to resist an excessive influx. By a forcible action on securities is meant a great advance in the rate of interest on the one hand, or a great reduction of it on the other. And the rationale of such operation on the rate of interest is, that it renders *disposable capital* in the one case scarce, and in the other abundant ; forcing it *from* foreign countries in the former, and *to* them in the latter case. The effect of the *pumping in* or *forcing out* of bullion by this means is infallible ; and the only practical question is of the moral, or commercial, or political considerations, which may interfere with the full exertion of the power.

A forcible operation by the Bank on its securities, in either direction, will not, of necessity, as I have shown, be attended with an immediate or direct effect on the prices of commodities. The effect, if any, can be only indirect, through the medium of credit, and dependent on the previous state of the market.

I have before had occasion to notice, in referring to the examinations of the country bankers, the confounding of currency with capital, which was observable in the questions put by some of the members of the Committee. That confusion, being traceable to the deep-seated impression which they seem to have been under, that the amount of bank notes in the hands of the public was the main point for consideration, as having a direct and an important influence on prices, and on credit, and on trade, instead of being as it is, — a mere effect or indication of the circumstances which call out and maintain that amount. The same wedded attachment to the doctrine of the Currency principle which looks to bank notes, and to bank notes only, as the *primum mobile* in our monetary system, may account for the little research which the Committee made into the causes and effects of variations in the rate of interest, and for the strange misconception which pervaded the questions relating to that point, of those of its members who took a leading part in the examinations. They seem from first to last to have looked upon variations in the rate of interest as of importance only, inasmuch as those variations might be supposed to affect the amount of the circulation.

In point of fact, the liability to variation, greater or less, in the rate of interest, constitutes in the next degree only to the preservation of the convertibility of the paper, the most important consideration in the question whether the present system, with some amendment, should be continued, or some one or other of the numerous schemes for a government or national bank should be substituted for it. Mr. Bosanquet, in his publication, to which I have alluded, entertains such exaggerated views of the disastrous effects on the commerce of the country, of a considerable advance in the rate of interest, which he seems to consider as an alteration of the value of the currency, that in his scheme for a bank or banks of issue, he would prescribe a compulsory maximum and minimum of the rate, variable between six and four per cent., according to certain rules which he lays down with reference to the exchanges: and rather than allow a forcible operation on the rate of interest, in order to stop a drain on the treasure of the Bank, he would resort first to a temporary issue of 1*l.* notes, and if that should prove insufficient, suspend the convertibility of the paper! How any well-informed person, not of the Birmingham school, could seriously propose to have cash payments suspended, rather than that the mercantile community should be subjected to some inconvenience from an advance in the rate of interest, and what he chooses to consider as a necessary consequence, a fall of prices, is to me matter of unutterable surprise. It may serve as a proof of the exaggerated views entertained in some quarters of the effects of a forcible operation on the rate of interest, and it forms a contrast to the little attention paid to that point, not only by the committee on Banks of Issue, but by the propounders of the various schemes for a government or national bank.

Now, without attaching such exaggerated importance as Mr. Bosanquet and Mr. Gilbart, and some others who oppose the currency principle do, to the effects of great variations in the rate of interest, I am inclined to think, that excepting the convertibility of the paper and the solvency of banks, which are and ought to be within the province of the legislature most carefully to preserve, the main difference between one system of banking and another, is the greater or less liability to abrupt changes in the rate of interest, and in the state of commercial credit incidental to one as compared with the other; and a careful consideration of the various plans which have been submitted to the public for carrying out the currency principle, has led to a confirmation of the opinion which I have before expressed, that under a complete separation of the functions of issue and banking, the transitions would be more abrupt and violent than under the existing system; unless, and upon this, in my opinion, the question hinges, the deposit or banking department were bound to hold a much larger reserve than seems to be contemplated by any of the plans which I have seen.

The difference between the two systems cannot be placed in a more striking point of view than in the following passages of a printed letter which Colonel Torrens addressed to me on occasion of the opinions which I had expressed on the subject in a former work.

"The difference," Colonel Torrens says, "between us is this, you contend that the proposed separation of the business of the bank into two distinct departments would check over-trading in the department of issue, but would not check over-trading in the department of deposit; while I maintain, on the contrary, that the proposed separation would check over-trading in both departments. The manner in which the separation would have this two-fold effect will be seen by the following example.

"Let us assume that the bank holds 18,000,000*l.* of securities and 9,000,000*l.* of bullion, against 18,000,000*l.* of outstanding notes and 9,000,000*l.* of deposits, and let an adverse exchange require that the depositors should draw out their deposits in bullion to the amount of 3,000,000*l.*

" In this case, if the business of issue were mixed up with that of deposit, the drawing out of the 3,000,000*l.* of deposits in bullion would have no other effect than that of reducing both deposits and bullion by the amount of 3,000,000*l.*, while the amount of the circulation and of the securities, and the power of the bank, as its securities fell due, to continue the discount business to the same extent as before, would suffer no diminution. But let the department of issue be wholly separated from that of deposit, and the result would be widely different.

" As soon as the separation was effected the deposit department holding 9,000,000*l.* of deposits with 9,000,000*l.* of securities would be obliged to sell some part of its securities, say one-third, in order to be prepared to meet the demands of its depositors. The state of the two departments would then stand thus :—

*Circulating Department.*

| | |
|---|---|
| Circulation - - - | £18,000,000 |
| Securities - - - | 9,000,000 |
| Bullion - - - - | 9,000,000 |

*Deposit Department.*

| | |
|---|---|
| Deposits - - - - | £9,000,000 |
| Securities - - - | 6,000,000 |
| Reserve in bank notes - - | 3,000,000 |

" This being the previous state of things, the demand of the depositors for 3,000,000*l.*, in gold would produce the following changes. The 3,000,000*l.* of bank notes held by the deposit department as reserve would be drawn out by the depositors and paid into the circulating department in exchange for gold, while the directors of the deposit department, in order to recover a reserve equal to one-third of their deposits would be obliged to sell 2,000,000*l.* out of the 6,000,000*l.* held in securities. The results would be, that in the circulating department the bullion would be reduced from 9,000,000*l.* to 6,000,000*l.*, and the circulation from 18,000,000*l.* to 15,000,000*l.*, and that in the deposit department the deposits would be reduced from 9,000,000*l.* to 6,000,000*l.*, the securities from 6,000,000*l.*, to 4,000,000*l.*, and the reserve from 3,000,000*l.* to 2,000,000*l.* It is self-evident that the effect of these changes would be not only a contraction of the circulation but a limitation to the power to over-trade in discount and loans."

I am willing to admit this statement as exhibiting in substance the difference between us. According to my view, as there may be variations of international payments, in other words, of a balance of trade, without any grounds for inference of alterations in the value of the currencies of the countries from which or to which such balance may be due, the presumption is, that an occasional efflux of four or five or six millions would be followed at no distant period by a fully equal reflux. Such was the case in 1828-29 and 1831-32, when the treasure of the Bank having been reduced by five or six millions was replenished without the slightest operation of the Bank on the amount of its securities, or its rate of interest. And such efflux and reflux might again take place under a continuance of the present system, provided that the Bank habitually held a large reserve, without any disturbance of the money-market, and without any influence on the amount of bank notes in the hands of the public. Now, under a system of separation, and in the position of the two departments in the case supposed by Colonel Torrens, what would be the operation of a demand for export to the extent of three millions of gold? In all probability, this demand would almost exclusively fall upon the deposit department.

This being the case, the Directors would not have a moment to lose upon the first manifestation of such demand, without taking measures for retaining or restoring the proportion of their reserve. They must sell securities, or allow the existing ones, if short-dated, to run off, and they must inexorably shut their doors to all applications for advances or discounts. This would, as Colonel Torrens justly observes, operate as a limitation of the power to over-trade in discount and loans. Most effectual, indeed, would it be, and under certain circumstances of the trade, it would operate with a degree of violence on the state of credit of which, as it appears to me, Colonel Torrens has no adequate idea. This is not to be wondered at in a writer not practically conversant with trade or banking; but that other advocates for the measure of separation, who number among them merchants and bankers, should be so unaware of it as they seem to be, does indeed surprise me. Before two or three millions of bank notes could be forcibly abstracted from the amount in circulation among the public, the pressure upon the reserves of the London bankers must be extreme. They would, of course, to the utmost extent practicable, call in their loans, and resolutely refuse further accommodation.*

Although there is no modern experience of such a state of things, if any merchant, banker, or money-dealer were to have the case laid distinctly before them, could any of them for a moment have a doubt as to the extremity of pressure which it would cause? I am most intimately persuaded that it would be within the mark to suppose that a rate of discount (assuming that the doors of the Bank and the ears of the Directors were inexorably closed against all applications) of 20 per cent. and upwards would, in many cases, be submitted to, and sacrifices of goods, if any

* It is to be regretted that the Committee on Banks of Issue in 1840, instead of expending so much time upon mere controversial points of definition, and confusing themselves and the witnesses by the ambiguous terms in which the questions were conveyed, did not see fit to examine some both of the West End and City Bankers and the money-dealers, as to such of the details of their business as, without any disclosure of their particular transactions, might have served to explain for what purposes bank notes are used, and how far it would be in the power of the Bank of England to operate directly upon the amount of the circulation.

large proportion were held on credit, would be made at a still greater loss. And, after all, it might be a question, whether even this effort of the Bank on its securities would be effectual in restoring its reserve *in sufficient time* to meet the exigency. This would depend entirely upon the character of its deposits. If these were strictly payable on demand, while the circumstances determining the efflux were strong and urgent, the payment of 3,000,000*l*. accompanied by forced sales of securities might prove insufficient in point of time to arrest the demand; and in this case, while the circulating department would still have 6,000,000*l*. of bullion, the deposit department would have no alternative but to stop payment. A most absurd, however disastrous a state of things. But it would be too disastrous, and too absurd to be allowed to take its course. If such a crisis were to happen, as most probably it would at the time when the dividends on the public funds became due, the Government would be imperatively called upon to interfere and prevent so ridiculous, however lamentable, a catastrophe. And the only interference that could meet the emergency would be to authorise a temporary transfer of coin from the issuing to the banking department.

The truth is, that no bank of mere deposit could undertake the Government business, involving an annual receipt and expenditure of 50,000,000*l*., subject to deficiency of the revenue at one time, and to overflow at another, with so small a reserve as 3,000,000*l*., whatever its other business might be; and it is difficult to conceive how it could, without the profit of the circulation, afford the much larger amount which would be requisite. But this is a point which it is foreign to my purpose to discuss. What I have to observe is, that supposing the violent effort of the Bank, on its securities, to be effectual, there cannot be a doubt that the violence of the effort would have been attended with inconvenience to the public. And all this inconvenience may have been purely gratuitous, as a sacrifice to the currency principle; because the utmost demand for gold might have been satisfied by an export of 3,000,000*l.* or 4,000,000*l.* which, under a system of union of issuing and banking, would have been attended, as in the instances of 1828-29, and 1831-32, with no inconvenience whatever.

But it may be asked; and here is the point; supposing that the demand for export of bullion be such that not three or four millions, but nine or ten millions will be required to satisfy it. What then becomes of a plan of quiescence? My answer is, that I would not be accountable for a plan of quiescence upon an amount of treasure in the Bank not exceeding nine millions at the outset of a drain. It was an error of the Bank in 1839, to have been perfectly quiescent until a loss of treasure from 9,336,000*l.* to 5,119,000*l.* had taken place. And the only effort then made was an advance of the rate of interest, step by step, to 6 per cent., and a reduction of the date of the bills admissible for discount from ninety days to sixty days; the limitation of days being of much more importance than the increase of the rate.

This effort was altogether inadequate; a difference in the rate of discount of 2 per cent. per annum, is a trifling consideration on bills having at the utmost sixty days to run; and accordingly, the Bank did not only not succeed by these measures in reducing its securities, but, as was inevitable as long as the door for discounts was left open, actually increased them. So that with advances on deficiency bills, the securities instead of being diminished, were actually increased by three or four millions during the greatest pressure of the drain. Still, with the aid of the credits on Paris, the drain was surmounted; and although this last resource was any thing but creditable, yet, inasmuch as the crisis was thus got over, merit may be claimed in behalf of the system for having come through with little, if any, suffering or inconvenience, commercial or financial. The markets for produce were perfectly undisturbed, there were no mercantile, or manufacturing, or banking failures of any note, and there was no great fall in the prices of public securities; so that the actual inconvenience proved to be in effect very unimportant. This exemption from suffering or material inconvenience, in surmounting the drain was, as some may think, and I among them, dearly purchased: but so it was.

Now, how would the case have stood, if the separation had existed in 1839?

Taking the actual situation of the Bank in January, 1839, and on the supposition of a separation of the functions, allotting twelve millions of securities (instead of nine millions, an amount obviously too low) to the circulating department, the two branches would have stood as follows:—*

*Circulating Department.*

| | | Securities. | Bullion. |
|---|---|---|---|
| Notes, public - | £18,201,000 | | |
| Banking department | 3,135,000 | | |
| | 21,336,000 | 12,000,000 | 9,336,000 |

* This is assumed as the position of the Bank of England in January, 1839, in a paper communicated to me by Mr. Pennington, and inserted in my "History of Prices," vol. iii. p. 279. 283., since reprinted in Mr. Pennington's Letter to Kirkman Finlay, Esq., in 1840, p. 97. As I consider Mr. Pennington's knowledge of the principles and working of the currency to be both profound and accurate, and as my views of the effects of a separation of issue from banking correspond with those which he has stated in the paper here alluded to, I am induced again to insert it, and accordingly refer the reader to it in the Appendix (D), with the addition of some remarks made by him on the letter addressed to me by Colonel Torrens.

*Banking Department.*

| | | | Securities. | Bank Notes. |
|---|---|---|---|---|
| Deposits - | - | £10,315,000 | | |
| Rest - | - | 2,500,000 | 9,680,000 | 3,135,000 |

Upon the occurrence of the demand for gold (which would naturally be, and was in point of fact made, by depositors in the banking department), and which was to the extent of a little more than a million between January and March, it may be taken for granted that the directors would see reason to sell or to allow the running off of securities to the same extent, and if they at the same time shut their doors against discounts and advances on deficiency bills, their liabilities would be reduced to the same extent. The notes would be taken from the banking to the circulating department in exchange for gold, and leave the amount of the circulation in the hands of the public without any alteration. And this process might by supposition have continued till the remaining bank notes were transferred from the banking to the issuing department, without producing the slightest effect on the amount of the circulation in the hands of the public.

A forcible reduction, however, of the securities to the extent supposed, would doubtless have abated the force of the drain, and might possibly have overcome it; but seeing the combination of circumstances which led to that drain, it may fairly be doubted whether the effort here assumed would have been sufficient to arrest it. My strong conviction is, that it would not have been sufficient, if even it had been practicable; but I doubt whether it would have been practicable. Notwithstanding the endeavours of the directors, when their attention had been fully roused to the importance of taking measures of precaution, and notwithstanding a rise in the rate of discount and a limitation of the date of bills admissible, the securities not only were not reduced by three millions, as I have supposed they would be under a separation, but were actually increased by three millions, partly by advances on deficiency bills. Now between a withdrawal from employment of disposable capital to the extent of three millions, and an actual advance to the same amount, is a difference of six millions. Such a reduction, suddenly effected, in the amount of available capital in the hands of the public, could not fail to be attended with very important and highly inconvenient effects. The state of credit would necessarily be deranged, as would be the markets into which credit entered largely.

But great as might be the inconvenience, it ought to be submitted to rather than that the Bank should fail in its engagements.

What I wish to impress by this view is, that by the separation, the banking department would not have time to judge of the nature and probable extent of the drain, but must take forcible measures for self-preservation upon the first manifestation of it. And with only such a proportion of treasure, that is, of bank notes and coin, as has hitherto been supposed necessary to allot to it, the chances are, that under such circumstances as occurred in 1839, (as also, indeed, in 1835 and 1836,) the measures to be taken to arrest a drain, however prompt and forcible, might not be effectual in sufficient time to prevent a suspension of payment by the banking department; while, by the time gained under a system of union, and the aid to the treasure of the deposit department by gold obtained from the circulating department, the pressure might be greatly diminished, and eventually got over, without any inconvenience to the public.

But then again comes the question, What is the

security that the pressure would be eventually got over, and the convertibility of the paper preserved?

I have on this point only to refer to the opinions which I have on former occasions expressed, and which all the additional light since thrown upon the subject by the mass of information contained in the Reports of the Committees on Banks of Issue, and by the currency pamphlets, and, above all, by recent experience, has tended to confirm and strengthen.

In a work published in the spring of 1838 *, I took occasion to observe, "that as far as the eventful "experience of the last fourteen years, viz. since 1824, "can serve as a guide for judgment, there appear to "be good grounds for believing that not less than "10,000,000*l.* can ever be considered as a safe position "of the treasure of the Bank of England, seeing the "sudden calls to which it is liable." And two years later, in February 1840, I ventured to suggest the following plan as that according to which, as it appeared to me, the circulation might be conducted with the greatest convenience to the public, and with the least danger to the convertibility of the paper:—

"The plan which I would propose is, that when "the tide of the metals sets fully in again, the Bank "rate of discount should be kept so steadily above "the market rate, as progressively to reduce the "securities through that channel, without increasing "them by other investments. The effect of this "would be to ensure a replenishment of their coffers "to ten millions; and with the purpose of endeavour-"ing to preserve that amount *on an average*, it would "not be expedient on the part of the Bank to take "any *active* measures for the increase of its securities. "It is not improbable, judging by the strength and "fulness of the tide with which the metals have

* "History of Prices," vol. ii. p. 330.

" flowed in on some former occasions, *that the* " *amount might thus reach fifteen millions,* beyond " which, according to analogy from former expe- " rience, it is not likely that it would go. The " probability is, that in the fluctuations to which our " trade, particularly that in corn, is liable, the ex- " changes would take an adverse turn; bullion would " flow out, the market rate of interest would rise to " the Bank rate, and then it would be that the ad- " vantage of the large stock of bullion would be felt; " because to the extent of five millions the foreign " exchanges or internal demand might be allowed to " operate upon the stock of bullion, without the " necessity on the part of the Bank to counteract that " demand by any active measures in raising its rate " of discount or selling its public securities. The " quantity of money in such case in actual circulation " would not be reduced, excepting in a small propor- " tion only, to the reduction of the amount of bullion, " because the withdrawal of deposits would, under " the slight pressure on the money market which " would attend a rise in the market rate of discount " to the Bank rate, restore to the circulation an " amount of Bank notes nearly equivalent to that " which had been in circulation against the bullion " taken out. In the majority of cases of the vari- " ations in the value of our currency relative to the " currencies of other countries, whether originating " on this side or the other, the balance of payments " would in all probability be satisfied by the export " of that amount of bullion. If the drain, however, " on the coffers of the Bank should, after a reduction " to ten millions, continue so as to give reason to " apprehend the existence of more extensive and " deeper seated causes of demand for the metals, " measures might be taken for its counteraction, " without producing alarm and disturbance of the

" money market on the one hand, or endangering an " extreme and unsafe degree of reduction of the Bank " treasure on the other.

" A latitude for variation between fifteen millions " and five millions would afford a much greater ex- " emption from shocks on the money market than a " variation, as it has recently been, between ten " millions and nothing.

" That the Bank might, by a regulation of its " securities, maintain a high average amount of " bullion, such as has here been suggested of fully " ten millions, cannot admit of any reasonable doubt. " And I believe that such a regulation would be " more easily practicable than either that of main- " taining the securities even, or of preserving the " bullion in any given proportion to the liabilities. " The money market would be less liable to be dis- " turbed than under either of the two latter alter- " natives. The utmost alteration of the rate of dis- " count to which the Bank might have occasion to " resort would probably not exceed 1 per cent.; and " the occasions for an alteration even to that extent " would probably be rare. A system like this would " be less restrictive, that is, the principle of limita- " tion would operate less rigidly under such a regu- " lation of the bullion, consistently with a blending, " as at present, of the issue and deposit departments " in the Bank of England, than by their total separa- " tion."*

After the lapse of four years since the passage here quoted was written, I see nothing to alter in this recommendation. The treasure has reached the maximum which I had contemplated; and this circumstance will render more practicable any scheme of regulation which should have for its object the

* "History of Prices," vol. iii. p. 187.

maintenance of a high average amount of treasure. The main objection or difficulty in the way of maintaining so large an average amount of treasure as ten millions, is in its unproductiveness, and its consequent drawback from the profits of the Bank: but against this consideration must be set the greater security of its position; and, after all, the amount is not larger than any prudent banker would deem it right to hold against liabilities so large and so fluctuating as those of the Bank of England.

In addition to this objection, which naturally has great weight, I took occasion in the same work, p. 198., from which the foregoing passage has been extracted, to state another, which, although in my opinion of no real weight, is so specious and popular that the remarks which I then made upon it may be worth here repeating.

" One among other reasons that might and pro- " bably would be urged against any scheme involving " so large a reserve of bullion as has here been sug- " gested, rests on the supposition that the attracting of " the extra amount must be preceded by, and attended " with, an undue and unnatural contraction of the " currency, the effect of which would be, a depression " of prices to an unnecessary extent.

" This is a consideration with a view to the public, " which, coinciding as the reasoning does with the " objection on the score of profit, to a large reserve, it " is probable weighed with the Bank directors in their " efforts to stop the influx, and to get rid of what " they seem to have considered the excess, of bullion, " in the spring of 1838. With reference to the influx " at that time, Mr. Norman, in the tract before " quoted, observed, —

" It is probable that an increase will be found in the treasure of the Bank, between its lowest amount last spring and the highest just previous to the next turn of the exchanges, of from seven to eight millions. Now such an influx of treasure is unnatural, and could never occur with a metallic circulation. Its effects, greater or less in proportion to the error, will be accompanied in the first instance by a depression of prices, unnecessary in extent and continued too long, and finally by a reaction, which will occasion an equally unnecessary and faulty excess on the other." p. 91.

" Why such an influx of treasure could never occur " with a metallic circulation, or why it should be con- " sidered as unnatural, does not very clearly appear. " With our very extended foreign trade, which is " habitually conducted on the footing of a large pro- " portion of our exports being on long credits, while " our imports are mostly paid for at short dates, and " with our present restrictions on the corn trade, " there might be, as there have been, on the one " hand, large sudden payments abroad requiring a " considerable export of bullion before any excess of " merchandise exported could bring returns; and, " on the other hand, when the demand for corn and " for other imports, including foreign securities, " ceased or abated, the returns for an excess of " former exports would be coming forward, and " bullion must in that case form, for want of other " means, a large part of such returns. Such was the " case in 1815–16, in 1820–22, and, excepting as " regards corn, such was the case with the influx of " bullion in 1826, and in the early part of 1838. *If " the ports should be shut against the importation of " corn for the next two or three years, and, at the " same time, from salutary distrust or other causes, " there should be a diminished demand for foreign " securities, there is likely to be a strong tendency to " an influx of the metals* *, and it is not easy to

* The tendency to an influx of the metals from these causes has been so strong, that the bullion in the Bank has exceeded the utmost amount that I had in contemplation as within reasonable probability, being now

" understand why it should not be equally strong " with a purely metallic variation. The Bank of " England may doubtless, as in 1836 and 1838, by a " competition for the investment of its deposits, " create a renewed demand for foreign securities, and " so stop the influx of bullion; but so the deposit " department likewise might do if its functions were " separated from the issuing department.

" But it is to the supposed unnatural depression of " prices, ascribed as an effect of the contraction of the " circulation which is assumed to lead to the influx " of the metals, that my remark is directed. This " hypothesis rests upon the currency theory of prices, " which supposes that the contraction of the cir- " culation, in such a case as that alluded to, reduces " prices, and that the reduced prices force an influx " of the metals; whereas the contraction, or rather " the diminution of the circulation, is in such cases " the consequence of a fall of prices from causes " arising from the state of trade, and peculiar circum- " stances affecting the supply and cost of production " on the one hand, and consumption on the other. " As to an increased value of the precious metals, " which might be supposed to be the consequence of " retaining permanently an addition of fully five mil- " lions as a reserve in the coffers of the Bank, it would, " according to any received grounds of computation, " amount to so very minute a per centage, as to have " no *perceptible* influence, and may, therefore, safely " be neglected."

The views which have here been presented for consideration, lead to the conclusion that a union of the business of banking with that of issue, when conducted by well regulated banks, is calculated to be

about 16,000,000*l*. But of this amount there is reason to suppose that about 1,000,000*l*. may be the consequence of the light gold taken out of circulation and replaced by notes.

much more convenient to the public than a separation of those functions.

Mr. Norman and Mr. Loyd have, very wisely as I think, refrained from committing themselves to any specific plan for carrying their views of the separation of functions into effect. Other writers who have espoused the same views have not been so cautious; and numerous, therefore, have been the schemes which have been proposed for establishing a single source of issue, and, for the most part, a government bank. It is not my purpose to enter into a detailed examination of any of them; but I cannot help remarking that, among those which have come under my notice, the greater part are crude and undigested, while some of them are so fanciful as to border on the burlesque. I have seen none in which the supposed advantages of the plans sketched out are not greatly exaggerated; while the inconveniences attending so great a change are underrated in the same degree, and in all of them the arguments urged in favour of the proposed alteration proceed upon a complete misconception of the nature of the machinery, and the working of the present system, which they seek to displace.

## SUMMARY OF CONCLUSIONS.

The conclusions which I have thus endeavoured to establish are, —

1. That if a purely metallic currency existed in a country situated as this is, transmissions of the precious metals might and would take place occasionally between this and other countries to a considerable amount (five or six millions *at least*), without affecting the amount or value of the currency of the country from which or to which the transmissions were made; and without being a cause or a consequence of alteration in general prices.

2. That consequently the doctrine by which it is maintained that every export or import of bullion in a metallic circulation must entail a corresponding diminution of, or addition to, the quantity of money in circulation, and thus cause a fall or rise of general prices, is essentially incorrect and unsound.

3. That the distinction set up by the currency theory between bank notes and other forms of paper credit, is not founded in any essential difference, except in so far as relates to the lowest denomination of notes, which are required in the transactions between dealers and consumers; that is, in the retail trade, and in the payment of wages.

4. That bills of exchange might, but for the obstacle of stamp duties, be extensively substituted in all transactions of purchase and sale between dealers and dealers for bank notes of 10*l.* and upwards, and that, in point of fact, they were extensively so used until a disproportioned duty was laid upon the smaller bills.

5. That cheques perform the functions of money as conveniently, in most respects, as bank notes, and more conveniently in many respects.

6. That bank notes of the higher denominations are used for peculiar purposes, chiefly in settlements, such as the clearing house, and in sales of landed and fixed property, as regards Bank of England notes; and in the provision markets and cattle fairs, as regards the country circulation; purposes for which substitutes might easily be found if bank notes were suppressed, by bills of exchange, and as regards the settlements among bankers, by exchequer bills, and by what have recently been termed economical expedients.

7. That the amount of bank notes in the hands of the public is determined by the purposes for which they are required, in circulating the capital, and in distributing the revenues of the different orders of the community, valued in gold.

8. That it is not in the power of Banks of Issue, including the Bank of England, to make any direct addition to the amount of notes circulating in their respective districts, however disposed they may be to do so. In the competition of Banks of Issue to get out their notes, there may be an extension of the circulation of some one or more of them in a large district, but it can only be by displacing the notes of rival banks.

9. That neither is it in the power of Banks of Issue *directly* to diminish the total amount of the circulation; particular banks may withhold loans and discounts, and may refuse any longer to issue their own notes; but their notes so withdrawn will be replaced by the notes of other banks, or by other expedients calculated to answer the same purpose.

10. That it is consequently an error to suppose that, however well informed the country bankers might be of the state of the foreign exchanges, and disposed to follow those indications, they would be able to regulate their circulation in conformity with such views. And that it is equally an error to suppose that the Bank of England can exercise a *direct* power over the exchanges, through the medium of its circulation.

11. That neither the country banks nor the Bank of England have it in their power to make additional issues of their paper come in aid of their banking resources. All advances by way of loan or discount, when the circulation is already full, can only be made by Banks of Issue in the same way as by non-issuing banks, out of their own capital, or that of their depositors.

12. That the prices of commodities do not depend upon the quantity of money indicated by the amount of bank notes, nor upon the amount of the whole of the circulating medium; but that, on the contrary, the

amount of the circulating medium is the consequence of prices.

13. That it is the quantity of money, constituting the revenues of the different orders of the State, under the head of rents, profits, salaries, and wages, destined for current expenditure, that alone forms the limiting principle of the aggregate of money prices, the only prices that can properly come under the designation of general prices. As the cost of production is the limiting principle of supply, so the aggregate of money incomes devoted to expenditure for consumption is the determining and limiting principle of demand.

14. That a reduced rate of interest has no necessary tendency to raise the prices of commodities. On the contrary, it is a cause of diminished cost of production, and consequently of cheapness.

15. That it is only through the rate of interest and the state of credit, that the Bank of England can exercise a direct influence on the foreign exchanges.

16. That the greater or less liability to variation in the rate of interest constitutes, in the next degree only to the preservation of the convertibility of the paper and the solvency of banks, the most important consideration in the regulation of our banking system.

17. That a total separation of the business of issue from that of banking is calculated to produce greater and more abrupt transitions in the rate of interest, and in the state of credit, than the present system of union of the departments.

# POSTSCRIPT.

THERE has recently been a good deal of animation in the markets for colonial produce, attended with a rise in the prices of several articles. And this improvement, and the speculative feeling with which, as usual on such occasions it is accompanied, have been, according to the prevailing doctrine which enters into all the reasonings of brokers in their circulars, and into the accounts furnished to the newspapers, ascribed to *the abundance of money.* Now I would, in the first place, ask those who assign this as the cause of the recent advance of prices to point out a single article in respect of which there are not, in the opinion of persons most conversant with the market, sufficient grounds, by reference to the actual and contingent supply compared with the rate of consumption, to justify a rise of price. A rise, be it observed, from a lower point of depression, in the case of several of the articles, than had ever been known, and in some cases below the lowest cost of production.

During the great and long continued fall, the dealers both wholesale and retail, and the manufacturers, having been repeatedly disappointed, by finding the price give way after they had got into stock, became disposed to run off their existing stocks before they re-embarked in fresh purchases. From the extensive prevalence of this disposition, there has been, in some of the leading articles of merchandise, a great reduction of stocks, both of raw produce and of finished goods, in the hands of dealers, and manufacturers, and shopkeepers; at the same time, the unprecedentedly low prices had extended the consumption both at home and abroad. Attention being at length drawn to this state of things, and confidence being acquired that prices had seen their lowest, a general disposition has naturally arisen to get into stock. Now it must be clear that, if a disposition among dealers and manufacturers to get out of stock is attended, as it is known to be, with dull and declining markets, a disposition to replenish their stocks when greatly reduced cannot fail of having an opposite effect. And as they erred in too confident an anticipation of a further fall of prices, they are liable to err in the opposite direction.

That some rise of prices, under such circumstances, is a necessary result, must be obvious. The degree of the rise must be matter of opinion, in the exercise of which there must be much latitude for miscalculation, till it be brought to the test of facts, viz. the supply and the consumption; the demand by consumers being the ultimate limit to the returns to be received by the wholesale purchasers, whether manufacturers, dealers, or speculators.

If, therefore, there be, as there can be no doubt that there is, in every instance of the recent rise of prices, a sufficient, or, at least, a plausible, reason for it on the plain mercantile ground of supply compared with consumption, why call in the aid of abundance of money, meaning the low rate of interest, as a cause originating or even contributing? And why, if the low rate of interest is the present *stimulus* to purchases, did it not *stimulate* dealers and speculators a twelvemonth ago, when the rate of interest was as low as it is now, or only six months ago, when there was not a trace of a speculative tendency in the markets for commodities? or why, above all, did it not operate in deterring the dealers and manufacturers from getting out of stock, and in thus arresting the decline of prices which (with the exception of those of corn) took place nearly, *pari passu*, with the fall in the rate of interest, or as it would in the modern use of the word be called, the increasing abundance of money from 1840 to the summer of 1843?

I have just now before me some of the circulars of the most considerable brokers in the markets for colonial produce; for it is in these that the recent advance of prices has given occasion to the supposition that what is called the abundance of money has been the cause of the rise. And it is not a little amusing to observe, that while the writers of the circulars think it incumbent upon them, according to the prevailing fashion, to ascribe considerable influence to the abundance of money, the information which they convey, respecting each of the articles that has been the subject of advance, is quite decisive in proving that the recent rise of prices has nothing to do with the low rate of interest, but is in each instance *amply justified upon the simple and obvious ground of a diminution of supply and an increase of the consumption.*

So striking and whimsical is this exhibition of the prevalence of what may be called *currency pedantry*, that although a detailed reference to actual or comparative prices, and the state of markets, formed no part of my plan in this publication, I am induced to give the following brief view of them, as showing how little they bear out the opinion expressed in the circulars, that it is the abundance of unemployed capital that has led to the investments in commodities.

In a circular dated 2d March, 1844, full of just and accurate information of the position of the markets for transatlantic produce, the details relative to that position are prefaced by the following remarks: —

"A very large amount of capital, both here and on the Continent, has been employed in the purchase of goods, and almost every article in the Colonial market has already felt the influence of it. *These operations have not altogether been influenced by any calculation of supply and demand, but were entered into from a conviction that the lowest point of depression had been reached, and that the abundance of unemployed money and the improved condition of trade were at length about to cause a general advance in prices.* This effect has been partially attained; during the past fortnight an increased value of from ten to fifteen per cent. has been realised upon coffee, sugar, rice, and many minor articles, and more animation has been witnessed in Mincing Lane than has existed for the last ten years.

"It cannot be denied that a decided movement has commenced, and that, from many circumstances, it bears the probability of further extension. The great commercial difficulties under which nations have laboured have been mainly surmounted;—the financial condition of Great Britain has been materially improved,—money is still very abundant, and the Bank coffers are full of bullion. All public funds have increased in value, and investments in railway securities (from their magnitude a most important item) have become less eligible, owing to their advanced price. *It was therefore almost an inevitable consequence, that articles of foreign merchandise which bore so depressed a value should attract money to them; and if the operations are confined within reasonable bounds, they seem legitimate enough, but it will become important to keep a watchful eye on the money market.*"

In former times, and in plain mercantile language, the expression of the first sentence would have been simply, that large purchases had been made, and that prices had risen in consequence — a very natural consequence. But the passage following, which I have marked with italics, exemplifies, in a pre-eminent degree, the tendency to introduce the money market, *à tort et à travers*, into the markets for commodities. If the operations alluded to were not altogether influenced by a calculation of supply and demand, all that could be said of them would be, that they were very silly ones. But it will be seen by the showing of this very circular, that they were very wise ones, proceeding as they are proved to have done, upon a very sound and rational view of supply and demand. Before entering upon the proofs to that effect, I would merely call attention to the last sentence of the above extract, remarking, however, upon it only, that instead of recommending to the operators in the markets for commodities to keep a watchful eye on the money market, the sounder recommendation would be to shut their eyes altogether to it, but to be wide awake to all circumstances affecting the actual and probable supply on the one hand, and the consumption, whether at home or abroad, on the other.

The articles alluded to in the circular as having experienced the most decided improvement are, sugar, coffee, and rice, and the following are the statements respecting these descriptions of produce: —

"*Sugar.*—There has been a very steady demand for British Plantation sugar throughout the month, and the West India market continuing very barely supplied, especially with good and fine qualities, and the arrivals of East India and Mauritius being very moderate, prices have advanced 1*s.* @ 2*s.*, the greatest rise being on the lower descriptions. An additional reason for this improvement is the large increase of the deliveries for the first two months of this year, which not only exceed the same period both of 1842 and 1843, but are in excess of the imports to this date, by nearly 13,000 tons, thus producing a large decrease of stock; to this circumstance may also be added a general belief that the crop in Jamaica will be deficient. The supplies near at hand are not large, prices consequently, are likely to be well maintained, particularly as consumption is evidently so largely on the increase.

"The Imports of ***East*** and ***West India*** and ***Mauritius*** into Great Britain amounted to 19,000 tons, against 26,500 in 1843, and 19,900 in 1842; the deliveries to 30,800 tons, against 26,800 in 1843, and 21,000 in 1842; and the stock to 29,800 tons, against 39,500 in 1843, and 28,800 in 1842."

And the demand for foreign sugars, independent of short stocks relatively to the exports, was increased by a prevailing impression of the chance of a reduction of duty.

" *Coffee.*—The business in the home market has been very large, the trade having bought extensively. The imports have fallen off, and the consumption has again increased, and as there cannot be any arrivals of importance for some time, there is a probability of still further advance in price, as the rise in the value of foreign descriptions suitable for the home trade will prevent their being brought into competition. Nearly 13,000 bags of *Ceylon* have changed hands, at 65*s.* @ 68*s.* 6*d.*, which is an advance of 2*s.* @ 3*s.* since the first ultimo. In foreign *East India* sorts 3,000 bags of *Java* have been sold at 36*s.* @ 53s.; from 3,000 @ 4,000 bags *Padang* at 26*s.* @ 32*s.*; and 1,500 bales *Mocha*, at 68*s.* @ 75*s.*

" A very important speculation has taken place in all descriptions of foreign coffee. It commenced in Holland, and has been extended to London, Hamburgh and Antwerp, and will doubtless spread throughout Europe. Statements of an extensive operation were privately put forth in certain quarters as early as the month of November last, and measures were silently prepared which have since been effectually accomplished. Upwards of 300,000 bags (19,000 tons) have been sold here and on the Continent, and an advance of 3*s.* @ 5*s.* has been realized in this market. These large transactions appeared rather unexpectedly, for although the stocks at the end of the year were less than it was calculated they would be, coffee had been so long subjected to neglect, that it was not a favourite article."

Could there be a better ground for a rise of price than that the stocks were less than had been calculated, and that the article had been long neglected? There seems, likewise, to have been an idea prevalent that some alteration of the duty might take place.

" *Rice.*—In common with many articles of extensive general consumption, rice of late has attracted attention as an object for investment, and large transactions accordingly have resulted therefrom, causing an advance in prices of 1*s.* @ 1*s.* 6*d.* ℔ cwt. The quotations for *Bengal* being now 12*s.* @

12*s.* 6*d.* ℔ cwt., and *Java* 9*s.* @ 12*s.* No less than 50,000 bags have changed hands in the course of the month, and the market still presents a buoyant aspect. The imports for the first two months amount to 11,300 bags, against 27,200 for the corresponding period in 1843, and the stock stands at 107,000 bags, against 139,600."

The speculation in cotton, and the rapid rise in the price of that article, took place some months ago, when reports of a deficiency of the crop of 1843 began to gain ground. That the crop has been a deficient one is on all hands now admitted; but as the advance of price had some weeks since reached the utmost height, which, as the result of the conflict of opinions and interests, the deficiency of the crop, combined with a view to the rate of consumption, seemed to warrant, this article has not participated in the animation which is described as prevailing in the markets for several other articles of transatlantic produce.

It would weary the reader to go on with a statement respecting other articles which had risen in price. Suffice it to say that there is not one, as to which it is not proved, that, upon the principle of supply and demand, there has been clearly a ground for some advance, and in no one does the rise of price hitherto appear to have been unreasonable.

While Indigo, of which the crop is reported to be unusually large, has of late experienced a fall of upwards of 20 per cent.

At the same time, several important articles, such, among others, as those of Baltic produce, are in a perfectly quiescent state.

I will only further give an extract from another price current, dated 5th March, 1844, for the purpose of a remark which I shall have to make upon it.

We confess it was always matter of surprise to us to see coffee so long and so fearfully depressed, not being like many things which are deteriorated by keeping; this, on the contrary, improves. *The abundance of money having at length caused the attention of capitalists to be turned to goods,* coffee has been one of the favoured articles; *the speculation commenced abroad,* but its influence was soon communicated to our market, causing, as before noticed, a rapid and great advance. The bulk of the transactions here have comprised Brazil and St. Domingo. The impression of many is that prices will be forced up still higher; and this is more likely to be the case, if, as is stated, the small merchants and shopkeepers abroad are entirely bare of stock.

Here, again, we have the money market gratuitously brought in. It was not the abundance of money that directed the attention of the *capitalists* (as it is becoming the fashion to call wealthy merchants), but the low price and long previous neglect of the article. But what I have principally to remark upon is, the observation in the above extract, — that the small merchants and shopkeepers abroad had become bare of stock. This process of getting out of stock by the dealers commonly accompanies, and is both cause and effect of declining prices when supplies have increased or consumption fallen off for some length of time, beyond the expectation of the dealers; till stocks have diminished, and consumption has increased, when attention is drawn to them, and a re-action is the consequence.

The best informed merchants and dealers are commonly the first to have their attention so drawn; and, as in the case of the large coffee speculation, which has had its origin in Holland, the parties to it having the most extensive correspondence on the Continent, were the best calculated and most likely to obtain information, and to act successfully upon it, respecting an article, the supplies of which are derived from many sources, and the stocks and consumers of which are spread over the whole civilised world.

They have thus anticipated the smaller merchants and dealers, as is mentioned in the circular. It is not their abundance of capital that directed their attention, for of capital they have long had abundance, but their attention being habitually engaged in the article, they must have been collecting information respecting it for some time, till they became assured that the consumption at the existing prices, which were below the cost of production, was rapidly gaining ground upon the supply; and when they became so assured, they acted upon that view, as they would equally have done, whether the interest of money had been 2 per cent. or 5 per cent. The only difference that this makes is, that, in a small degree, they may be induced to realise by re-sale at a lower price than if the cost had been somewhat raised by the charge of higher interest.

I have been induced to notice this point at some length, because I am convinced that opinions like those contained in the extracts which I have quoted are calculated to mislead, by inducing, in those to whom they are an authority, a reliance upon a supposed general cause, which has no existence, to the neglect of the more correct rule of reasoning and acting, according to the best information as to the actual and contingent supply and the rate of consumption. It cannot be too often repeated, that abundance of money in the hands of capitalists is in itself a cause of cheapness, while abundance of money in the hands of consumers is a cause of dearness.

There is one other remark suggested by the accounts in the Circulars, of the animation which prevails in Mincing Lane, and that is, that the speculation which has attracted most attention, namely, that in coffee has had its rise in Holland, and has extended in its effects to other towns on the Continent, as well as to this country; the prices abroad, however, being full as high as *here*, or, if anything, higher. And I understand that, in the case of nearly all the articles which have recently experienced a considerable advance in this country, the advance on the Continent of Europe is in fully the same, if not in a greater proportion. And, generally speaking, prices on the Continent, I mean of articles of consumption of its population, are fully as high in proportion as they are here, bating corn and such other articles as are subject to high or prohibitory duties in this country. Now, according to the currency theory, prices abroad ought to be depressed, and at a much lower range than they are here, seeing the large quantity of the precious metals which has been abstracted from them to form the accumulation of bullion now existing in the coffers of the Bank of England.

The present state of facts, therefore, may be considered as adding, if any addition were wanting, to the arguments which have in the foregoing pages been adduced to show the unsoundness of that theory.

# APPENDIX.

---

## (A.) Page 68.

FROM a wish not to encumber the argument as stated in the text, to which this is a note, I then abstained from noticing a prepossession or prejudice (besides that of the assumed analogy of a compulsory government paper), which, in the popular view, leads irresistibly to the persuasion, that the quantity of money, according to whatever may be the supposed test of the quantity, must have a direct influence on the prices of commodities. The prepossession or prejudice to which I allude, has its rise in the following very specious reasoning.

The prices of commodities depend upon supply and demand; now, *given* the supply, prices depend upon the demand. But money is the instrument of demand; therefore, any increase of money must be an increase of demand, and must consequently raise prices; and as bank notes are by the definition money, an increase of bank notes must increase the demand for, and raise the prices of commodities.

The following passage of the late Mr. James Mill's Essay on Political Economy (3d ed. p. 131.) is calculated to countenance this, which, as expressed in these general terms, I cannot but consider as an erroneous view: —

" It is not difficult to perceive that it is the total amount of " the money in any country, which determines what portion " of that quantity shall exchange for a certain portion of the " goods or commodities of that country.

" If we suppose that all the goods of this country are on one " side, all the money on the other, and that they are exchanged " at once against one another, it is obvious that one tenth, or " one hundredth, or any other part of the goods, will exchange " against one tenth or any other part of the whole of the money " and that this tenth &c., will be a great quantity or small " exactly in proportion as the whole quantity of the money of " the country is great or small. If this were the state of the " facts, therefore, it is evident that the value would depend " wholly upon the quantity of it. It will appear that the " case is precisely the same in the actual state of the facts."

Mr. Senior, in one of his lectures on the value of money, and in the article of the Edinburgh Review, which I have before referred to, has commented on the above passage in Mr. Mill's essay, and pointed out the fallacy of it, in overlooking the consideration, that it is the cost of production of the precious metals, and not their quantity, which constitutes their value, and determines the prices of commodities with reference to the cost of production of the latter measured in metallic value.

Mr. Mill, however, in a subsequent passage, page 167, illustrates his view by a hypothetical case. "Suppose," he says, "the market to be a very narrow one, of bread solely on "the one side and money on the other. Suppose that the or-"dinary state of the market is one hundred loaves on the one "side, and one hundred shillings on the other, the price of bread "accordingly a shilling a loaf. Suppose, in these circumstances, "that the quantity of loaves is increased to two hundred, while "the money remains the same; it is obvious that the price of "the bread must fall one half, or to sixpence per loaf."

It should seem from this last passage that Mr. Mill had so far qualified, or perhaps, more strictly speaking, lost sight of the view conveyed by the former passage, as to confine the supposition of the quantity of money affecting prices, to that which was in the pockets or hands of the consumers, going to market to supply their immediate wants. And to this limited extent it may be admitted that the quantity of money has an influence on prices. But, so limited, this proposition has nothing in common with the doctrine of the currency theory, which ascribes an influence to the quantity of money indicated by the amount of bank notes in circulation, or by the whole of the circulating medium.

(B.) Page 79.

The expression in the text respecting the power of purchase by persons having capital and credit may require some explanation, which I have here accordingly to give, accompanied by an illustration of my meaning by reference to actual occurrences. What I mean to say is, that a person having the reputation of capital enough for his regular business, and enjoying good credit in his trade, if he takes a sanguine view of the prospect of a rise of price of the article in which he deals, and is favoured by circumstances in the outset and progress of his speculation, may effect purchases to an extent perfectly enormous compared with his capital. The conditions requisite are that the market should be a large one, and the article susceptible of great fluctuation of price, from political or physical causes; and, in fact, it is only articles of this description that are the subject of speculations sufficiently extensive to attract notice. I propose to exemplify this by what occurred in the Tea trade in 1839, when the disturbances in China broke out; and by the speculation in the Corn trade between 1838 and 1842.

Among the earliest speculations for an advance in the price of Tea, in consequence of our dispute with China in 1839, were several retail grocers and tea dealers. There was a general disposition among the trade to get into stock, that is, to lay in at once a quantity which would meet the probable demand from their customers for several months to come. Some, however, among them, more sanguine and adventurous than the rest, availed themselves of their credit with the importers and wholesale dealers for purchasing quantities much beyond the estimated demand in their own business. As the purchases were made in the first instance ostensibly, and perhaps really, for the legitimate purposes, and within the limits of their regular business, the parties were enabled to buy without the condition of any deposit; whereas speculators, known to be such, are required to pay 2*l.* per chest, to cover any probable difference of price which might arise before the expiration of the prompt, which, for this article, is three months. *Without, therefore, the outlay of a single farthing of actual capital or currency in any shape,* they made purchases to a considerable extent; and, with the profit realised on the resale of a part of these purchases, they were enabled to pay the deposit on further quantities when required, as was the case when the extent of the purchases attracted attention.

In this way, the speculation went on at advancing prices (100 per cent. and upwards), till nearly the expiration of the prompt: and if at that time circumstances had been such as to justify the apprehension, which at one time prevailed, that all future supplies would be cut off, the prices might have still further advanced, and, at any rate, not have retrograded. In this case, the speculators might have realised by sales, if not all the profit they had anticipated, a very handsome sum, upon which they might have been enabled to extend their business greatly, or to retire from it altogether, with a reputation for great sagacity in thus making their fortune. But instead of this favourable result, it so happened that two or three cargoes of Tea which had been transhipped were admitted, contrary to expectation, to entry on their arrival here, and it was found that further indirect shipments were in progress. Thus the supply was increased beyond the calculation of the speculators; and, at the same time, the consumption had been diminished by the high price. There was, consequently, a violent reaction on the market: the speculators were unable to sell without such a sacrifice as disabled them from fulfilling their engagements, and several of them consequently failed. Among these, one was mentioned who, having a capital not exceeding 1200*l.*, which was locked up in his business, had contrived to buy 4000 chests, value above 80,000*l.*, the loss upon which was about 16,000*l.*

The other example which I have to give is that of the operation on the corn market between 1838 and 1842. There was an instance of a person who, when he entered on his extensive speculations, was, as it appeared by the subsequent examination of his affairs, possessed of a capital not exceeding 5000*l.*, but, being successful in the outset, and favoured by circumstances in the progress of his operations, he contrived to make purchases to such an extent, that when he stopped payment his engagements were found to amount to between 500,000*l.* and 600,000*l.* Other instances might be cited of parties without any capital at all, who, by dint of mere credit, were enabled, while the aspect of the market favoured their views, to make purchases to a very great extent.

And be it observed, that these speculations involving enormous purchases, on little or no capital, were carried on in 1839 and 1840, when the money market was in its most contracted state; or when, according to modern phraseology, there was the greatest scarcity of money.

## (C.) Page 84.

It is not easy to imagine a view less reconcilable with a correct appreciation of the state of things as regards prices, in connection with the state of the circulation in 1839, than is contained in the following question and answer in the examination of Mr. Norman by the Committee on Banks of Issue, the material fact being admitted, *that prices were firmly maintained at that time, notwithstanding an advance in the rate of interest to* 6 *per cent.*: —

" 1926. *Chairman.*—Were not, generally, the prices of " commodities in 1839 maintained during that period *by*

" *those issues of the Bank,* in defiance of their rule? *Ans.* I " believe that prices were very firmly maintained during " 1839; but I believe also that the restrictive measures of " the Bank *had an effect upon prices; because* I am confident " that the exportation of the precious metals was by no " means equal to the demand for extra-foreign payment; and " in explanation I would say that I apprehend the foreign " payment for corn from the autumn of 1838 to have been " fully ten millions sterling, and I cannot trace an export- " ation exceeding about six or seven millions."

The version in the answer of Mr. Palmer to the question, subjoined, conveys, as it strikes me, the correct view:—

" 1473. *Chairman.*—If more stringent measures for the " purpose of reducing the accommodation to the commerce " of this country had been taken (in 1839), would not prices " necessarily have come down, and exports thus have been " increased for the purpose of meeting the foreign payment? " *Ans.* I think it is very doubtful, from the extent and power " of capital in this country, and the diminished stocks of " goods then in the possession of the merchants, whether " that result could have been attained."

## (D.) Page 112.

*Paper communicated by Mr. Pennington.*

"It has been proposed that the business of the Bank shall " be separated into two distinct departments, one to be " called the circulation department, the other the deposit de- " partment; that the circulating department shall hold a " fixed and unvarying amount of securities, and that its func- " tions shall be confined solely to the exchange of gold for " notes, and of notes for gold; and that the deposit depart- " ment shall manage the funds intrusted to it on the ordinary " principles which are observed by the London bankers, and " independently of the promissory note department.

"It may be worth while to inquire, what would be the " probable operation of such a plan.

"In carrying it into execution, I apprehend, it would be " proper, in the first instance, to assign to the deposit depart- " ment such a proportion of the securities, and of the bullion, " in possession of the Bank, as would, together, be equal to " the amount of the deposits. Thus, if the Bank held eighteen " millions of securities, and nine millions of bullion, against " eighteen millions of outstanding notes, and nine millions of " deposits, it would probably be deemed expedient to assign

" to the deposit department six millions of securities, and " three millions of bullion, and to retain in the circulating " department six millions of bullion, and twelve millions of " securities.

" If such a separation were made, it is obvious, that as the " exchange of gold for notes, or of notes for gold, between " the two branches, *would not affect the amount of bank paper* " *in the hands of the public,* and as such interchange might " take place frequently, and to a great extent, *the increase or* " *diminution of outstanding notes would form no certain criterion* " *of the amount of paper circulating out of doors,* unless it " were, at the same time, known what amount of notes was " held by the department of deposit.

" Disregarding, for the present, any objection which it " may be supposed would arise from this consideration, let " us at once proceed to inquire what effect would be produced " by a demand upon the Bank for bullion.

" The action and condition of the deposit department will " be more distinctly perceived, if we suppose that, under cir- " cumstances above stated, the whole of the three millions of " bullion are exchanged, on its first establishment, for three " millions of notes. The position of the two departments " would then be as follows: —

| " *Circulating Department.* | | *Deposit Department.* | |
|---|---|---|---|
| " Outstanding notes - | £21,000,000 | Deposits - - | £9,000,000 |
| " Securities - - - | £12,000,000 | Securities - - | £6,000,000 |
| " Bullion - - - | 9,000,000 | Bank notes - - | 3,000,000 |

" This being the position of the two departments, let us " suppose that an adverse foreign exchange has created a " demand upon the Bank for bullion for exportation. Now, " such a demand for bullion may be satisfied, either by a " reduction of the notes in the hands of the public, or by a " reduction of the deposits at the Bank. If the former, then " the separation of the business of the Bank into two depart- " ments will have answered the purpose expected from it; if " the latter, then, in so far as relates to the increase or dimi- " nution of Bank notes in the hands of the public, by the " action of the foreign exchange, no satisfactory result will " have been produced. In the latter case, no advantage in " the regulation of the circulation will have resulted from the " separation.

" It may, perhaps, be said, that if the business of banking " were separated from that of circulation, and conducted in " the manner and upon the principles which are adopted by

" the private bankers of the metropolis, a diminution of de-
" posits would be immediately followed by the sale or realiza-
" tion of a corresponding amount of securities, and thus the
" amount of bank notes, in the external circulation, would
" be reduced to an extent commensurate with the delivery of
" bullion.

"But such a sale or realization of securities, in similar
" circumstances, may be effected under the present system of
" management. Whether the existing system be continued,
" or the business of the Bank be separated into two depart-
" ments, the sale or realization of securities must depend on
" the views and the discretion of the directors of the Bank.
" The only difference between the two cases is this; that the
" counteracting effect occasioned by paying out bank notes to
" the depositors would be limited to three millions: upon the
" present system it may be carried to a much greater extent.

" It may be observed, moreover, that if the demand for
" bullion for exportation should exceed three millions, and if
" that demand should fall on the deposit department, that
" department would be reduced to the necessity, *either of*
" *forcibly realizing a portion of its securities, or of stopping*
" *payment at a time when the circulating department was*
" *abundantly provided with specie.*

" It may be desirable to apply the foregoing principles and
" observations to the actual position of the Bank, at certain
" periods, within the last four years.

" In January 1834 the liabilities and assets were as fol-
" lows:

| | | | |
|---|---|---|---|
| " Circulation - - | £18,236,000 | Securities - - | £23,596,000 |
| " Deposits - - | 13,101,000 | Bullion - - | 9,948,000 |
| " Rest - - - | 2,207,000 | | |
| | £33,544,000 | | £33,544,000 |

" If, at that time, it had been determined to divide the
" business of the Bank into two departments, it would
" probably have been deemed expedient to assign 12,000,000*l.*
" of the securities to the circulating department, as a fixed
" amount which was at no future time to be exceeded. The
" remaining securities would, of course, go to the bank-
" ing department. The outstanding notes, amounting to
" 18,236,000*l.*, would then have for their basis 12,000,000*l.*
" of securities, and 6,236,000*l.* of bullion. But, as the de-
" posit department would probably prefer notes to gold, on
" account of the greater convenience of the former, the posi-
" tion of the two departments would have been as follows:—

| CIRCULATING DEPARTMENT. | | | | BANKING DEPARTMENT. | | | |
|---|---|---|---|---|---|---|---|
| | Circulation. | Securities. | Bullion. | | Deposits. | Securities. | Bank Notes. |
| Notes in the hands of the public - - | 18,236 | | | Deposits - - | 13,101 | — | — |
| Notes in the banking department - - | 3,712 | | | Rest - - | 2,207 | 11,596 | 3,712 |
| | 21,948 | 12,000 | 9,948 | | 15,308 | | |

The following would have been the position of two branches at the under-mentioned periods:

| | • | Circulation. | Securities. | Bullion. | | | Deposits. | Securities. | Bank Notes. |
|---|---|---|---|---|---|---|---|---|---|
| 1834:<br>Dec. Notes: Public - - -<br>Banking department - | 18,304<br>416 | 18,720 | 12,000 | 6,720 | Deposits<br>Rest - | 12,256<br>2,532 | 15,778 | 14,362 | 416 |
| 1835:<br>July. Notes: Public - - -<br>Banking department - | 18,283<br>nil. | 18,283 | 12,000 | 6,283 | Deposits<br>Rest - | 11,561<br>2,644 | 14,205 | 14,244 | nil. |
| 1836:<br>Jan. Notes: Public - - -<br>Banking department - | 17,262<br>1,814 | 19,076 | 12,000 | 7,076 | Deposits<br>Rest - | 19,169<br>2,599 | 21,768 | 19,954 | 1,814 |
| Aug. Notes: Public - - -<br>Banking department - | 18,061<br>264 | 18,325 | 12,000 | 6,325 | Deposits<br>Rest - | 14,796<br>2,813 | 17,609 | 17,345 | 264 |
| 1838:<br>Jan. Notes: Public - - -<br>Banking department - | 17,900<br>2,995 | 20,895 | 12,000 | 8,895 | Deposits<br>Rest - | 10,992<br>2,609 | 13,601 | 10,606 | 2,995 |
| 1839:<br>Jan. Notes: Public - - -<br>Banking department - | 18,201<br>3,135 | 21,336 | 12,000 | 9,336 | Deposits<br>Rest - | 10,315<br>2,500 | 12,815 | 9,680 | 3,135 |
| July. Notes: Public - - -<br>Banking department - | 18,049<br>nil. | 18,049 | 12,000 | 3,785 | Deposits<br>Rest - | 7,955<br>2,686 | 10,641 | 12,905 | nil. |

"It will be seen, by the foregoing statement, that if the "business of the Bank had been separated into two depart- "ments in January 1834, and if the rule, which we have "supposed to have been at that time established, had, since, "been inflexibly adhered to, the paper issues of the circu- "lating department in July last (1839) would have been "less by 2,364,000*l.* than their actual amount at that period, "and the cash of the deposit department would have been "wholly exhausted. In July 1835 and July 1839 the secu- "rities held by the deposit department would have exceeded "the aggregate amount of the rest and the deposits. This "excess of securities over deposits this department could not "have held, unless the circulating department had transgressed "the prescribed rule to an extent equal to the amount of that "excess.

"In order to prevent the exhaustion of its cash, the bank- "ing department would, no doubt, have endeavoured to "withdraw bank notes from the hands of the public, by dis- "posing of a large amount of its securities. A rigid adherence "to the rule by the directors of the circulating department, "and a due regard to its safety by the managers of the bank- "ing branch, would have rendered the amount of the securities "in possession of the latter, in July last, less by three or four "millions than it appears actually to have been; or, which "comes to the same thing, the amount of bank notes in the "hands of the public at that time would have been three or "four millions less than it appears to have actually been. "*The consequence would have been, a very severe pressure on* "*the money market.*

"Hitherto, we have supposed the business of the Bank to "be separated into two distinct departments, and a formal "apportionment of debts and assets to have been made. Now "without such a formal separation and apportionment, pre- "cisely the same action upon the currency would result from "the strict observance of the following rule; namely, that "the Bank shall not, upon any occasion, issue bank notes be- "yond a certain amount (that amount we have supposed to "be 12,000,000*l.*), except upon the deposit of bullion. If "this rule had been adopted in January 1839, and afterwards "rigidly adhered to, *a great reduction of the securities held* "*by the Bank would have been necessary, in order to avoid* "*a suspension of the payment of its deposits.* It is probable, "indeed, that such a reduction of the securities would have "arrested the drain of treasure at an early period of the year. "If, however, the drain had continued, notwithstanding the

" reduction, it would have been necessary, in July last (1839), " to have carried the reduction to the extent of three or four " millions below the amount which the Bank actually held at " that period.

" Whether a formal separation of the Bank into two depart- " ments take place, or the rule last mentioned be adopted, it " may be expected that *the public will be exposed to very " great alternations of comparative ease and difficulty in the " operations of the money market.*

" It may here be proper to observe, that the difference be- " tween the rule above mentioned and that explained by " Mr. Horsley Palmer and Mr. Norman in their evidence is " this;— that, while the former rule would preclude the " Bank from issuing notes in the payment of deposits to a " greater extent than is equal, in amount, to the difference " between the amount of notes at any time outstanding and " 12,000,000*l.*, plus the amount of bullion in possession of the " Bank, the latter would allow the Bank to substitute notes " for deposits to an unlimited extent. The former rule would " be the same in its operation as a division of the Bank into " two departments. The sole effect of the latter would be, " the increase or diminution of the aggregate amount of the " notes and deposits of the Bank with the increase or dimi- " nution of its bullion.

" There is one point connected with the proposed division " of the Bank into two departments to which I have not " adverted, but which it may be material to notice. It has " been suggested, that, in order to increase the disposable " funds of the banking department, it would be desirable " that a certain portion of the capital of the Bank, now lent " to the state, should be made available for banking pur- " poses. By this I apprehend it is meant, that a portion of " the 3 per cent. stock in which the original capital of the " Bank is invested shall be sold, and the proceeds of the " sale invested in other securities, and in commercial loans " and discounts, at the pleasure and discretion of the Bank.

" Of this suggestion it may be observed, that it is a pro- " posal to withdraw a certain amount of funds from the use " and employment of one class of persons, in order that it " may be transferred by the Bank to the use and employment " of another class of persons. By this process no new funds " would be created in the money market. The change " would be merely the transfer of funds already existing " from one kind of investment to another. The operation " would be the same as that of an individual stockholder

" who sells his stock in order to employ the money arising " from the sale in commercial discounts. The operation " of the individual stockholder would, in its consequences, " be comparatively of little importance; but if five millions " of the original capital of the Bank were sold, as has been " proposed, and the proceeds of the sale mixed up with and " employed in the same manner as the deposits at the Bank, " although no greater reserve of bank notes in the banking " department, in consequence of this accession of funds, " would be necessary, yet the varying employment of funds " of such magnitude, during alternate periods of commercial " excitement and depression, might produce a prodigious " effect upon the general circulation. At one time the " additional fund might be employed in commercial loans " and discounts; at another time a great part of it might be " withdrawn from the public, and held by the Bank, in bank " notes and specie; thus creating an alternate abundance " and scarcity of money in the hands of the public, at the " pleasure of the Bank."

Thus far was communicated to me in the paper by Mr. Pennington, and I have now to add the following extract from his letter to Mr. K. Finlay: —

" If it should be determined to adopt the proposed plan of " separation, the most difficult, and by far the most im- " portant, point for consideration, would be, to determine " the fixed amount of securities to be held by the department " of issue. If that point were once properly settled, the " principal object of the plan might be attained, without a " formal division into two departments of the business of the " Bank. Such a separation would be desirable only as it " might afford a better security than could be otherwise " obtained, that the fixed amount of securities would, at no " future time, nor upon any occasion, however urgent, be " exceeded.

" In the supposed case above stated, namely, that previous " to the separation, the Bank is in possession of 18,000,000*l.* " of securities, and 9,000,000*l.* of treasure, against 18,000,000*l.* " of outstanding notes, and 9,000,000*l.* of deposits, I have " assumed the fixed amount of securities, to be held by the " department of issue, to be 12,000,000*l.* If that were the " amount fixed, the outstanding notes must, according to the " prescribed rule, be 21,000,000*l.*, of which, as 18,000,000*l.* " are supposed to be in the hands of the public, 3,000,000*l.* " must necessarily be placed at the disposal of the banking " department.

" In a letter to Mr. Tooke, lately published, Colonel " Torrens has assumed, for the purpose of illustration, the " same supposed case, and has fixed the amount of securities " to be held by the circulating department, at 9,000,000*l.* " In so fixing the amount, he places (under the circumstances " supposed) the banking department precisely in the situ- " ation, the possibility of which is contemplated by Mr. " Tooke, that is, that of being without either notes or gold " wherewith to pay any immediate demands of the de- " positors, and of being obliged, in order to obtain the " requisite means, to force on the money market the sale of " a portion of its securities. He supposes that, for this " purpose, a sale of 3,000,000*l.* of securities would be neces- " sary, and that, consequently, the 18,000,000*l.* previously " in the hands of the public, would be reduced to 15,000,000*l.*

" Notwithstanding this pressure on the money market, we " are to suppose that an adverse exchange has produced a " demand upon the Bank for gold to the extent of 3,000,000*l.* " Colonel Torrens then says, ' The 3,000,000*l.* bank notes, " held by the deposit department as reserve, would be drawn " out by the depositors, and paid into the circulating depart- " ment in exchange for gold; while the directors of the " deposit department, in order to recover a reserve equal " to one-third of their deposits, would be obliged to sell " 2,000,000*l.* of the 6,000,000*l.* held in securities. The " results would be, that in the circulating department, the " bullion would be reduced from 9,000,000*l.* to 6,000,000*l.*, " and the circulation from 18,000,000*l.* to 15,000,000*l.*; and " that in the deposit department, the deposits would be re- " duced from 9,000,000*l.* to 6,000,000*l.*; the securities from " 6,000,000*l.* to 4,000,000*l.*; and the reserve from 3,000,000*l.* " to 2,000,000*l.* It is self-evident that the effect would be, " not only a contraction of the circulation, but a limitation " of the power to overtrade in discounts and loans.'

" To reduce the amount of bank notes in the hands of the " public from 18,000,000*l.* to 13,000,000*l.*, *would,* indeed, " *effectually prevent overtrading in discounts and loans.*

" Although so extreme a case as that put by Colonel " Torrens is not likely to occur, yet if it were to occur, all " the consequences which he has described would ensue, " without a separation of debts and assets, from a strict " observance of the rule described in the paper communicated " to Mr. Tooke, namely, that the Bank shall not, upon any " occasion, issue notes beyond a certain fixed amount, except " upon receiving into its possession a corresponding amount

" of gold. A division of the business of the Bank into two " departments, or a strict observance of the rule, without the " division, would produce the same results.

" There is one material circumstance, however, which " renders it doubtful whether a separation of functions in the " way proposed, would be the most effectual means of ob-" taining the requisite security for the due observance of the " rule.

" Hitherto it has been the practice of the Bank of England " to cancel all notes brought in for payment, — never to " re-issue them. Now, although an adherence to this practice " would not occasion any insuperable difficulty in carrying " out the proposed arrangement, yet it would render it " necessary that the banking department should generally " keep on hand a very large amount of gold, or of notes " signed, and ready for delivery. To hold a very large " amount of notes signed and completely executed, might be " deemed hazardous or inconvenient. If, in order to avoid " that risk and inconvenience, the banking department were " to keep on hand the cancelled notes, and require from the " department of issue new notes for the old ones, at such " times, and to such an extent, as suited its occasional wants " and convenience, the department of issue would be virtually " a depository for the banking department, and, through the " banking department, a depository, to a greater or less " extent, for others. Arrangements might, no doubt, be " made, and a system of checks contrived, that would prevent " any violation of the principle of the plan; *but the requisite " machinery would be a matter of considerable nicety, of which " the operation and the object would not easily be perceived and " understood by the public.*"

THE END.

# 2

# An enquiry into the practical working of the proposed arrangements for the renewal of the charter of the Bank of England and the regulation of the currency. With a refutation of the fallacies advanced by Mr. Tooke

R. Torrens, *An enquiry into the practical working of the proposed arrangements for the renewal of the charter of the Bank of England and the regulation of the currency. With a refutation of the fallacies advanced by Mr. Tooke* (London, Smith Elder and Co., 1844).

Torrens, as one of the leading lights of the Currency School, is generally credited with firing the first shots in the controversy which was to culminate in Sir Robert Peel's Act. This was done in his *Letter to Viscount Melbourne* (1837) in which he suggested – following Ricardo's earlier proposals – that the Bank of England should be divided into a Banking and an Issue Department, and in which he stated the general currency principle that notes and coin should be made to behave as if they were a purely metallic currency. Torrens pursued a number of careers; professional soldier, newspaper proprietor and Member of Parliament. He was also a founder member of the Political Economy club, and the architect of the colonization of New South Wales.

The view contained in this work, that convertibility alone would not protect the value of the currency, was a shift from the pro-real bills and anti-bullionist views which had been expressed in his *Essays on Money and Paper Currency* (1812). Torrens sent a copy of this pamphlet to Sir Robert Peel in 1844 and asked for office in the government. Although this was not granted, he did later receive a Civil List pension of £200 per annum for his services to Political Economy.

# AN INQUIRY,

*&c.*

---

THE effect of intellectual divisions of employment in augmenting knowledge is analogous to that of mechanical divisions of employment in increasing wealth. These analogous advantages are accompanied by analogous drawbacks. In either case independence is diminished as power is enlarged. The mechanical divisions of employment compel us to receive the greater part of our physical enjoyments from the hands of others; the intellectual divisions of employment constrain us to receive the greater portion of our opinions from the thoughts of others. The chemist adopts the Newtonian theory on the authority of the mathematician; the mathematician receives the discoveries of Davy and Faraday without repeating the experiments through which they were realized. On intricate questions, requiring long and patient investigation, the opinions even of the most enlightened classes, will have their origin, in a majority of cases, not in knowledge, but in faith. Hence, principles are received upon trust, doctrines become creeds, authority is implicitly followed, and blind leaders are enabled to assume the guidance of the blind.

Mr. Tooke was one of the earliest advocates of the enlightened views regarding currency and banking, which were developed by Ricardo, Huskisson, and Horner; which are embodied in the celebrated Report of the Bullion Committee; and which were carried into practical effect by the Act of 1819, for the resumption of cash payments. His deserved reputation imparts to his opinions an influence independent of their intrinsic worth, and causes him to be regarded as an authority by those who have not leisure or inclination to investigate for themselves the somewhat uninviting principles of monetary science. On this account it appears desirable that the errors which pervade his recent publication on the Currency Principle should be made manifest to the public, and on this account, therefore, I venture to undertake the task.

It appears to me, that in his recent publication* Mr. Tooke has presented some finished specimens of the errors and misconceptions which he attributes to his opponents; that he is "under a total misconception of what would be the working of a purely metallic circulation;" that he "labours under a misconception fully as great as to what would be the working of a mixed circulation of coin and bank notes administered so as to conform to what would be the working of a metallic circulation;" and that he has formed to himself no adequate conception of "what the working of a mixed circulation of coin and bank notes actually has been, and is, under the existing banking system."

To follow Mr. Tooke through his mazes of unconnected details, would be a tedious operation. The fact, that the errors which in no sparing measure he imputes to others, are in reality his own, will be sufficiently exhibited if I can succeed in showing—

1st. What would be the practical working of a purely metallic circulation under the action of foreign exchanges.

2nd. Under what arrangements a mixed currency of coin and bank notes might be made to coincide with what would be the working of a purely metallic currency.

3rd. The manner and the degree in which, under the actual system of banking of which Mr. Tooke is the advocate, the

* Page 17.

fluctuations in the amount and in the value of the currency exceed the fluctuations to which the currency would be liable were it so regulated as to coincide with a currency purely metallic.

## I. The Working of a purely Metallic Currency.

In order to trace from definite data the working of a purely metallic currency, let us assume the existence of the following circumstances, namely, that the circulation consists exclusively of coin; that no seignorage is charged upon the coinage; that the Mint is always open; that it is divided into two distinct and independent departments—the coinage, or issuing department, and the deposit, or safe custody department; that the function of the coinage department is strictly limited to the issue of coin in exchange for standard bullion; and that the function of the deposit department is confined to receiving for safe custody deposits of bullion, and giving transferable receipts entitling the holder to draw out upon demand the quantity of gold specified upon them.

It is evident that under these circumstances there could exist no difference in value between coin of standard weight and standard bullion. An ounce of gold coined into 3*l.* 17*s.* 10½*d.* would be exactly equivalent to an ounce of uncoined gold of equal fineness. The slightest fall in the market price of gold, as estimated in gold coin, would send bullion to the Mint to be exchanged for coin—the slightest rise in the market price of gold so estimated, would cause the coin to be melted.

Under the circumstances supposed, there would be, as there at present is, a considerable stock of gold in the country beyond that which might be coined into money. Uncoined metals would be in the hands of private persons in the form of plate and ornaments, would exist as the stock in trade and raw material of goldsmiths, jewellers, and manufacturers, and would constitute a portion of the capital of the cambists and merchants who deal in foreign bills, and apportion the precious metals throughout the commercial countries of the world.

A considerable portion of the uncoined metal existing at any time in the country would be lodged for safe custody in the deposit department of the Mint. But wherever the uncoined metals might be lodged, whatever their quantity, or through whatever hands they might pass, their value would necessarily coincide with that of the standard coin—an ounce of gold called a *bar*, would be equal in value to an ounce of gold called *three pounds seventeen and tenpence*. When the Mint is open—when no seignorage is charged upon the coinage—and when the coin is of standard weight, it is impossible that the market price of gold should deviate from the Mint price.

Under a purely metallic currency the proportion between the amount of coined and the amount of uncoined metal, would be ever varying, and could never be very accurately ascertained. A favourable exchange would increase the amount of bullion, without, in the first instance, increasing the circulation; and should bullion be required to supply the consumption of the manufacturer, or to meet the foreign bills of the cambist, the proportion of the inflowing metal ultimately appearing under the form of coin, might be inconsiderable. On the other hand, an unfavourable exchange would diminish the stock of bullion in deposit, without, in the first instance, contracting the circulation; and, had the previous supply of bullion borne a higher proportion than ordinary to the amount of coin, might cause only an inconsiderable portion of the coin to be melted or exported.

The manner in which a favourable exchange would expand, and an unfavourable exchange contract the circulation, would be as follows:—When gold came in, it would, in the first instance, be placed in deposit; and so long as it should be held in deposit for safe custody, it could not enlarge the circulation. But as soon as the quantity held in deposit exceeded the quantity required to supply the demands of the manufacturer and the cambist, the holders would not allow the excess to lie upon their hands as dead stock; they would take it to the coinage department of the Mint, and exchange it for coin to be employed in trade or in loans, or in the purchase of securities. When gold went out, it would be withdrawn, in the first instance, from the bullion in deposit; and so long as there should remain in deposit a sufficient supply of bullion to meet the demands of the merchant and the cambist, no action on the currency would be felt; but as soon as the quantity of bullion remaining in deposit became less than the quantity required to replace the consumption of the arts, and to balance foreign accounts, an action on the circulation would commence, and the coin would be melted or exported.

It would be of little importance, however, whether the action of the exchanges commenced on the portion of the metals circulating as coin, or on the portion deposited as bullion. If the proportion of equilibrium between coined and uncoined gold should be disturbed by an exportation of the coin, it would be restored by the flow of bullion from the deposit to the coinage department of the Mint; if disturbed by the exportation of bullion, it would be restored by the conversion of coin into bullion. In no appreciable period, while the Mint should remain open, and exempt from seignorage, could an ounce of gold called a *bar*, be of more or of less value than an ounce of gold called *three pounds seventeen and tenpence.*

This seems to be the proper place for noticing a singular misconception into which Mr. Tooke has fallen. He says,* "If the views which have been thus far unfolded are correct, it can hardly fail of being seen as a fair deduction from them, that the whole of the ground upon which the theory of the currency [metallic] principle proceeds is unsound. The

* Page 102.

error of supposing that if the currency were purely metallic, every export or import of bullion would be so much taken from or added to the quantity of money in circulation, is so obvious, so palpable, as to make it matter of surprise that such a notion should ever have been entertained."

In this passage Mr. Tooke has shown that he has formed to himself no adequate conception of the theory which he attempts to refute, and which, by a strange misnomer, he designates as the *currency* principle. Those who recommend that the currency should be regulated upon the metallic principle, contend that the central bank should be arranged into two distinct and independent departments,—the department of deposit, and the department of issue ; and that the functions of the department of issue should be strictly limited to holding a fixed amount of securities, and to allowing the circulation to contract or to expand, as bank notes should be presented in exchange for gold, or as gold should be presented in exchange for bank notes. Now it is self-evident, that under the arrangement thus proposed, every export or import of bullion would *not*, as Mr. Tooke imagines, be so much taken from, or added to, the quantity of money in circulation. An influx or an efflux of bullion would increase or diminish the whole aggregate mass of the precious metals existing in the country, and would not act exclusively on that particular portion of the mass, which might have assumed the form of coin. Should the aggregate be 100,000,000*l.*, and the portion of the mass in the form of coin 50,000,000*l.*, an influx or an efflux of 5,000,000*l.* would increase or contract the circulation, not by 5,000,000*l.*, but only by 2,500,000*l.* Were the currency regulated upon the *metallic* principle,—were there a single bank of issue, strictly limited in its functions to giving gold for paper, and paper for gold, millions of bullion might be imported and consumed in the arts and manufactures,—tens of millions might be imported and re-exported for the adjusting of foreign accounts, and the purchase of foreign securities, without producing any effect upon the amount of the circulation,—without causing an additional bank note to be issued or returned.

### *The Effects of Bills of Exchange under a Metallic Currency.*

Were the money or currency of the country purely metallic, bills of exchange would perform the self-same functions which they perform now,—the self-same functions which they performed before bank notes were in existence. They would then serve, as they now serve, to economise the use of money, by adjusting the accounts between one district and another, without any greater transmission of cash than that which might be necessary to pay the accruing balances. They would then serve, as they now serve, as forms and modes of credit, as records of credit transactions, and as written obligations to pay at fixed periods, specified sums in coin. But were the money or currency purely metallic, it could not enter into the imagination of any one, whose opinions were entitled to the slightest weight or authority, that bills of exchange were money. Money or currency is the authorized measure of value—the medium by which, either from positive law or admitted usage, obligations are legally discharged, and transactions finally closed. Money, as the authorized measure of value, is the nominative standard by which all obligations, including those expressed in bills of exchange, are estimated; and, as the universal equivalent which by law or custom constitutes a legal tender, it is that by which all obligations, including those expressed in bills of exchange, are finally fulfilled.

Another of the Tookean fallacies has here to be noticed. While bills of exchange are confounded with money, the following reasons are given for the confusion:—" If, according to the currency [metallic] theory, the circumstance that written promises to pay, being after date or sight, and to order, and therefore requiring an indorsement, are disqualified from being considered as performing the functions of money, on what ground is it that bank post bills, which are after sight and to order, have been always included in the returns of the circulation of the Bank of England?" This question, on which Mr. Tooke appears to lay great stress, is easily disposed of. The difference between bills of exchange and the post bills issued by the Bank of England, and the reasons why the two instruments should not be confounded under a common term, and why the latter should, while the former hould not, be regarded as money, are simply as follows- By universal custom a Bank of England post bill is received as discharging obligations and closing transactions; a bill of exchange, even of the highest credit, is not money, because it is not received as closing transactions and discharging obligations. A Bank of England post bill is money, because it is accepted universally as the final equivalent of a bill of exchange; a bill of exchange is not money, because it is not accepted universally as the final equivalent of a bill of exchange.

Two parties, holding bills of exchange upon each other, balance their account by a payment of the difference in bank notes. This Mr. Tooke considers as a proof that bills of exchange are money. He says,* " If, as a last resort in the argument, it be said that bills of exchange require the intervention of bank notes for the ultimate payment, the answer is that this is a mere fiction; for that, in fact, the adjustment takes place by *settlement*, and that a small amount of bank notes effects the liquidation." This answer, upon which Mr. Tooke relies for proving his position, puts him out of court. Bills of exchange are not money, *because* the adjustment takes place by *settlement*, and because the *liquidation* is effected by the payment of the balance *in some other medium*

* Page 31.

than that of bills of exchange. A holds a bill of exchange upon B for 1000*l*., B holds a bill of exchange upon A for 1200*l*., and an adjustment takes place by A's paying to B 200*l*. in bank notes. If bills of exchange were money equally with bank notes, the final adjustment and liquidation might have been effected by A's giving to B a bill of exchange for 200*l*.

*Effects of Deposits, Cash Credits, and Checks, under a Metallic Currency.*

Bank deposits, checks, and cash credits have so extensive an influence upon the transactions of the market, that it appears necessary, in order to present an accurate view of the working of our monetary system, to examine somewhat in detail the nature and the extent of their operation.

Under a purely metallic currency, the operations of private bankers and of banking companies for economizing the use of money, would be conducted in precisely the same way in which they are now conducted under our mixed currency of coin and bank notes. We should then have, as we now have, deposits, checks drawn against deposits, credits granted to customers, and clearing-houses for settling balances upon transactions effected by bills of exchange and checks. Now, in tracing out the operation of these auxiliary arrangements, it will be distinctly seen that deposits, checks, credits, and adjustments of balances have no exclusive, no peculiar bearing upon our present banking system; that their effects, in economizing the use of money, are common to a metallic and to a paper circulation; and that, in estimating the comparative advantages of a metallic and of a paper circulation, the common quantity should be excluded from the calculation.

Were the currency purely metallic, and were there no bank notes in existence, the overtrading of banks might occasion an undue extension of credit, extravagant speculation, and subsequent reaction, terminating in commercial embarrassment, panic, and insolvency. The liability to these revulsions, and the degree of their intensity when they occurred, would be in proportion to the knowledge and prudence of bankers, and to the extent to which the public might conduct their business through the agency of banks.

The evils resulting from over-banking will be more distinctly seen if we take a simple case, in which the only causes of derangement are an undue extension of accommodation, and a consequent excess in the amount of checks drawn against deposits and credits. We select Birmingham as the locality in which the effects of an excess of auxiliary money are to be exemplified. The circumstances which we assume, as the premises from which our conclusions are to be deduced, are the following:—

Birmingham has but one bank; all the inhabitants, except those who live upon wages, keep their cash at the bank, and make all their payments, amounting to one pound and upwards, by checks drawn against their deposits; the money of the district is purely metallic; the deposits held by the bank amount to 1,000,000 sovereigns; by a regulation, which is effectually enforced, the coin is not allowed to be sent out of the Birmingham district.

Under these circumstances, and so long as the banker did not advance his deposits in loans, or upon securities, the amount of checks which the inhabitants of Birmingham could draw upon the bank, in settling their pecuniary transactions with each other, could not exceed 1,000,000*l.*, being the amount of their deposits; and, consequently, the prices of commodities within the district would be governed by the power of effecting purchases to an amount not exceeding 1,000,000*l.* But this state of things could not continue. The banker, in order to make a profit by his business, would advance a portion, say two-thirds, or 666,666*l.* in discounting bills, and in purchasing available securities. Here a new action upon prices immediately commences. By the supposition, all the inhabitants of the district keep their cash with the banker, and therefore the persons for whom he had discounted bills, or to whom he had made advances in other forms, would leave the amounts placed at their disposal with the banker, under the form of new and additional deposits. The amount of checks which might now be drawn upon the bank, in effecting payments, would be increased by the whole amount of the new and additional deposits. The original depositors, who had placed their 1,000,000 sovereigns with the banker, or to whom, in the course of business, their 1,000,000*l.* might have been transferred, would still be able to draw checks against their deposits to the amount of 1,000,000*l.*; while the secondary depositors, to whom the advances of 666,666*l.* had been made, and placed to their credit in the books of the bank, would have the power of going into the market and of purchasing goods by checks payable to bearer, to the amount of 666,666*l.* Thus the prices of commodities within our Birmingham district, would be governed by the power of effecting payments, not merely to the amount of 1,000,000*l.*, but to the amount of 1,666,666*l.*

Previous to the commencement of the credit system, the banking statistics of the district stood thus :—

| Assets of the Bank. | Liabilities. |
|---|---|
| Gold, £1,000,000 | Deposits, £1,000,000 |

After the bank had made advances and granted credits to the amount of two-thirds of its original deposit, the statistics of the establishment would stand thus :—

| Assets. | | Liabilities. | |
|---|---|---|---|
| Gold, | £1,000,000 | 1st Class deposits, | £1,000,000 |
| Securities, | 666,666 | 2nd Class ditto | 666,666 |
| | £1,666,666 | | £1,666,666 |

Upon the received principles of demand and supply, the auxiliary money or rather the auxiliary medium of exchange thus created by banking accommodation, and consisting of credits to the amount of 666,666*l.*, would raise prices within our Birmingham district, in the same proportion in which they would have been raised had there been an increase of 666,666*l.* in real money, instead of a creation to that amount of auxiliary money. All commodities would rise in price—uncoined gold is a commodity, and therefore uncoined gold would rise in price. But the price of coined gold cannot be less than the price of uncoined gold; and therefore the price of the coin would rise, or in other words, 100 sovereigns lodged in the coffers of the bank would be of greater value than a check for 100 sovereigns drawn upon the bank by a solvent depositor. This state of things could only be momentary. All persons holding the auxiliary money would rush to the bank to exchange it for real money; and the bank, in self-defence, would be compelled to limit its accommodation until the par between 100 sovereigns and a check upon its coffers for 100 sovereigns should be restored.

The contraction of bank accommodation would be regarded as impolitic and injurious by the people of Birmingham. Petitions would be presented to the town council, representing that gold being a commodity in the market, ought, like all other commodities, to be allowed to find its own market price; that it was an arbitrary and most pernicious interference to declare by law, that 3*l.* 17*s.* 10*d.* should be equivalent to an ounce of gold; that money consists of pounds sterling; that a pound sterling is not a specific quantity either of gold or of any other commodity; that it is a pound sterling, and nothing but a pound sterling; that, according to the principle demonstrated by Mr. Tooke, checks upon a bank are money, and do not require to be regulated so as to coincide with a metallic circulation; and that the prosperity of Birmingham could not be restored unless the bank should be relieved from the obligation of paying the checks drawn upon it in gold, at the arbitrary price of 3*l*. 17*s*. 10*d*. per ounce.

The prayer of the Birmingham petition is granted, and the banker is authorised to pay the checks drawn by depositors in gold at the market price estimated by the number of pounds sterling specified in these checks. He has, as before, 1,000,000 of sovereigns lying idle in his coffers, and he is, on the ordinary principles which actuate men of business, desirous of turning this dead stock to profitable account. For this purpose he renews his former operations, and by loans and discounts, accommodates his customers with credits to the amount of twice 666,666*l*. The statistics of his establishment will now stand thus:—

| Assets. | | Liabilities. | |
|---|---|---|---|
| Gold, | £1,000,000 | Primary deposits, representing gold paid in . . . | £1,000,000 |
| Securities, | 1,333,333 | Secondary deposits, representing discounts and loans . . . | 1,333,333 |
| | £2,333,333 | | £2,333,333 |

It will be obvious that, from the well ascertained influence of quantity upon price, that the prices of commodities within our Birmingham district, will rapidly advance as the community acquire the power of making payments, not by drafts limited to 1,000,000*l*. as was the case before the system of credit was supposed to commence, but by drafts increased, through the operation of that system, to the amount of 2,333,333*l*. And it will be equally obvious that, under the circumstances assumed, there can be nothing to cause the extension of credit and the advance of prices to terminate here. The banker might, without danger, continue to lend his still returning advances, until the deposits and book credits amounted to 5,000,000*l*. or to 10,00,0000*l*.; and until the prices of commodities within the district were governed by the power of the community to effect payments by drafts at sight to the amount of 5,000,000*l.* or 10,000,000*l.* Once surrender the cardinal principle of limiting the operations of banking with reference to the efflux of gold, and there will be no assignable limits to the insolvency, even of non-issuing banks, should their checks continue to be payable in specie, or to the depreciation of their auxiliary money, and to the rise of price estimated in it, should they be released from the obligation of paying out their deposits in a metallic standard.

The limits within which a strict adherence to a metallic standard would confine banking accommodation, and the creation of credit mediums of exchange, or auxiliary money, we have now to consider. And here it may be laid down as a general rule that, under a purely metallic currency, the main circumstances which would govern the limits of banking operations, as far as regards deposits and book credits, against which drafts at sight may be drawn, are, the proportion between the bank-dealing and the non-bank-dealing portion of the public, the number of banking establishments, and the efflux of the coin. A brief examination of the specific action of these limiting circumstances may tend to place the subject in a clear light.

Under a perfect adherence to a metallic standard, the power of a single bank to re-issue its deposits, and to grant book credits, would be strictly limited by the proportions in which the money circulating in the country might be held by the bank-dealing and by the non-bank-dealing portion of the public, even though there should be no unfavourable balance of foreign payments, causing an efflux of the metals. To illustrate the operation of this limiting circumstance, let us assume the existence of a district in which the circulation consists of 4,000,000 of sovereigns, held in equal proportions by a single bank, and by the non-bank-dealing public. Under these circumstances, if the bank should either discount bills to the amount of 1,000,000*l.*, or open with its customers book-credits to that amount, one-half of its deposits, or 1,000,000*l.*, would pass from its coffers into the hands of the non-bank-dealing public. For the persons who had obtained accommodations at the bank to the amount of 1,000,000*l.* would pay away one-half of the checks drawn against their deposits or credits, in equal proportions between the bank-dealing and the non-bank-dealing public; the bank-dealing public would pay the checks which they received to their credits with the bank; the non-bank-dealing public would present their checks for payment in gold; and thus the money in the hands of the non-banking public would be increased from 2,000,000*l.* to 2,500,000*l.*, while the cash in the coffers of the bank would be diminished from 2,000,000*l.* to 1,500,000*l.*

This proportion would be maintained so long as the bank should limit its accommodation to the amount of 1,000,000*l.* In this case, when the bank dealers paid away checks to the amount of 1,000,000*l.*, one-half of these checks would be given to bank-dealers, who would place them to their credit with the bank, and it would be the other moiety which would be presented and paid over the counter in sovereigns; while, on the other hand, when the non-bankers paid away 1,000,000*l.*, one-half of the amount would pass into the hands of the bank-dealers, and be by them returned to the bank. The monetary statistics of the district would be as follows:—

| | |
|---|---|
| Gold in the hands of the non-banking public . . . . . . . . . | £ 2,500,000 |
| Gold in the coffers of the bank . . | 1,500,000 |
| Bank credits, against which drafts at sight may be drawn, and over and above the credits represented by the 1,500,000*l.* in the coffers of the bank . . . . . . . . | 1,000,000 |
| Amount of money and auxiliary money acting upon prices . . . . . | £ 5,000,000 |

Should the banker now determine on discounting bills, and opening book credits to the amount of 2,000,000*l*., the gold in the hands of the public would be increased to 3,000,000*l*., while his reserve of treasure would be reduced to 1,000,000*l*. The monetary statistics of the district would now stand thus:—

| | |
|---|---|
| Gold in the hands of the public . . | £ 3,000,000 |
| Gold in the coffers of the bank . . | 1,000,000 |
| Bank credits, over and above those represented by the gold . . . | 2,000,000 |
| Money and auxiliary money acting upon prices . . . . . . . | £ 6,000,000 |

Prices rise, trade is brisk, confidence high, speculators require additional accommodation, and the banker determines to grant discounts and credits to the amount of 4,000,000*l*., that is, to the whole amount of money within the district. In this case the bank-dealers would have the power of paying away checks to the amount of 6,000,000*l*., while the non-bank-dealers, before the bank began to be drained of its gold, would, in the first instance, have the power of paying away cash only to the amount of 2,000,000*l*. But the non-bank-dealers would receive one-half of the checks, or 3,000,000*l*. paid away by the bank-dealers; while the bank-dealers would receive only one moiety, or 1,000,000*l*. of the cash paid away by the non-bank-dealers; and hence 3,000,000*l*. of gold would be drawn out of the bank by the non-bank-dealers, while only 1,000,000*l*. would be paid in by the bank-dealers. The bank held originally 2,000,000*l*.; when 1,000,000*l*. is paid in, and 3,000,000*l*. withdrawn, its coffers are exhausted; the ultimate, the uttermost limits of banking accommodation have been reached, and the discounting of an additional bill, or the opening of an additional credit, might lead to an immediate stoppage of payments and to a sudden and total destruction of the auxiliary money by which prices had been sustained.

Had the proportion between the bank-dealers and the non-bank-dealers been such that, on the commencement of the credit system, the former held three-fourths, or 3,000,000*l.*, while the latter held only one-fourth, or 1,000,000*l.* of the money of the district, the bank might discount bills and grant book credits to the amount of 10,000,000*l.* before the internal drain from the demands of the non-bank-dealers compelled it to stop payment. At this verge of insolvency on the part of the bank the monetary statistics of the district would stand thus:—

| | |
|---|---|
| Gold in the hands of the non-bank-dealing public . . . . . . | £4,000,000 |
| Original credits in the books of the bank in favour of the depositors of cash . . . . . . . . . | 2,000,000 |
| Secondary credits, against which drafts at sight may be drawn . . . | 10,000,000 |
| Total amount of money and credits operating upon prices . . . | £12,000,000 |

At this point the bank would have touched the verge of insolvency. An additional discount, or the granting of an additional credit, would cause the amount of checks presented to exceed the amount of gold paid in, and compel the bank to close.

Let us now consider the manner in which, under a purely metallic currency, the existence of numerous banking establishments counteracts the tendency to the overtrading of bankers, upon the assumption that there is no external drain for gold. Let there be three banks instead of one; let the total amount of money in the district be 4,000,000*l.*; and, previous to the commencement of the credit system, let each of the three banks hold 1,000,000*l.* in deposit for its customers, while the remaining 1,000,000*l.* circulates in the hands of the non-bank-dealing public. Under these circumstances, if all the bankers were to act in perfect concert, and to grant to their respective customers the same proportionate accommodation, the effects of their coinciding operations would be identical with those which would result from the operations of a single bank. There being by the supposition no drain upon their coffers from without, they might go on increasing their discounts and credits until the whole of their gold had passed from their coffers into the hands of the non-bank-dealing public, and thus place themselves on the verge of insolvency. Beyond this verge, this ultimate limit of credit operations, they could not pass without immediate ruin. It will be obvious, however, that the overtrading could not be pushed to this ruinous extent should any one of the banks possess sufficient knowledge and prudence to confine its credit operations within legitimate bounds. Were each of the three banks to open with its customers credits to the amount of 3,000,000*l.*, over and above the credit of 1,000,000*l.* possessed by its original depositors, then the whole of its gold would pass into the hands of the non-bank-dealing public; and each of the three banks would have touched the verge of insolvency. But should bank I. refuse to grant additional discounts and credits beyond the amount of 1,000,000*l.*, banks II. and III. would be compelled to limit their accommodation in the same proportion, by the flow of their gold into the coffers of the more prudent bank. The amount of the drafts paid by the customers of each of the banks II. and III. to the customers of bank I. would exceed the amount of the drafts paid by the customers of I., to each of the customers of II. and III.; and on every adjustment of accounts, II. and III. would be compelled to pay to I. balances in gold.

From the illustrations which have now been given, it will

be apparent that, in the absence of an external drain, the limit to the creation of auxiliary media of exchange, in a district possessing only one bank, is supplied by the efflux of gold from the coffers of the bank into the hands of the non-bank-dealing public; while, in a district possessing many banks, an additional check to overbanking is supplied by the difficulty of establishing that perfect unison amongst the several banking establishments which is necessary in order to prevent disproportionate credits, and a consequent efflux of gold from the coffers of the imprudent to those of the prudent bankers.

And here it may be important to remark that, in a district containing many banks, there will be two antagonist principles or tendencies in operation; the one acting so as to limit, and the other so as to extend, the supplanting of coin by bank credits, and the creation of auxiliary media of exchange. The greater the number of banking establishments, the more instantaneous and the more powerful becomes the compulsion upon each individual banker to limit his transactions within the proportion maintained by the most prudent of the establishments in his neighbourhood; and the more difficult, and the more uncertain it becomes to establish that concert amongst the banks and proportional extension of credit which would be necessary to enable them to extend the auxiliary medium of exchange within a dangerous proximity to that ultimate limit at which the whole of their gold would pass into the hands of the non-bank-dealing public. But, on the other hand, the multiplication of banks has a tendency to increase the proportion which the bank-dealing portion of the public bears to the non-bank-dealing, and thus to enable the banks, should they act in concert, to erect, in the manner which has been already explained, a wider superstructure of credit upon a narrower base of gold. In a district secured from external drain, as has been assumed in our hypothetical case, this might be regarded as comparatively unimportant; but in a country exposed to the vicissitudes of the foreign exchanges, a wide superstructure of credit, resting on a narrow foundation of gold, renders the monetary system a delicate and sensitive machine, requiring to be regulated in strictest conformity with the movements of the metals.

The manner in which, under a purely metallic currency, banking accommodation and the creation of auxiliary money would be limited by the action of the foreign exchanges, remains to be traced. In illustrating this subject let us assume that the currency of the United Kingdom is at par with foreign currencies, when the coin, and the auxiliary money, amount together to 100,000,000*l.*, in the following proportions:—

| | |
|---|---|
| Coin in the hands of the non-bank-dealing public, being one-fifth of the monied classes . . . . | £20,000,000 |
| Coin deposited with the banks, against which drafts at sight may be drawn | 30,000,000 |
| Bank credits and discounts, against which drafts at sight may be drawn | 50,000,000 |
| | £100,000,000 |

It is obvious that, under these circumstances, the banks might effect a large extension of the credit medium of exchange, without incurring the danger of an internal drain upon their coffers. On the principles which have been already fully explained, the banks might grant additional accommodation to their customers, to the amount of 50,000,000*l.*, and yet retain in their coffers 20,000,000*l.* in coin for adjusting their balances with each other; for, on this increase of the auxiliary circulation, the monetary statistics of the country would stand as follows:—

| | |
|---|---|
| Coin in the hands of the non-bank-dealing portion of the public, being one-fifth of the monied classes . . . . . . | £ 30,000,000 |
| Coin in the banks, against which drafts at sight may be drawn . | 20,000,000 |
| Bank credits and discounts, against which drafts at sight may be drawn . . . . . | 100,000,000 |
| Total amount of coin and auxiliary circulation acting upon prices . . . . . . . . | £ 150,000,000 |

Now let us mark the effect which this extension of the auxiliary medium of exchange—an extension, be it observed, involving no danger from an internal drain—would produce upon the foreign exchanges, and through them, upon the stability of the banks. The currency of the United Kingdom was equal in value to foreign currencies, and the exchanges were consequently at par, when the coin and its auxiliaries amounted to 100,000,000*l.* They now amount to 150,000,000*l.* Again, exports balanced imports when domestic prices were acted upon by coin and its auxiliaries, amounting to 100,000,000*l.* Domestic prices are now acted upon by coin and its auxiliaries, to the amount of 150,000,000*l.*; imports exceed exports, and a heavy foreign debt is incurred. To balance this debt a large exportation of the gold is required; and, in order to prevent the creation of new foreign debts as the old one is discharged, the amount of the coin and its auxiliaries, acting upon prices, must be reduced from 150,000,000*l.* to 100,000,000*l.* This inevitable contraction would bring on a commercial crisis, credit would be destroyed, and gold would flow out of the coffers of the banks, not only in consequence of the adverse foreign exchange, but also as the result of domestic panic. It can be shown, with all the evidence of demonstration, that were the currency purely metallic, banks of deposit and discount would be constrained to regulate credit transactions with a reference to the state of the foreign exchanges, by seeing the inevitable danger which would be incurred by a failure to limit their advances and their credits as gold should be withdrawn from their coffers.

Deposits, cash credits, and checks payable to bearer, affect exchanges, and therefore perform one of the functions of money. But they are not measures of value, and they are not the equivalents, the payment of which satisfies engagements and finally closes transactions; they do not perform the most essential functions of money; they are auxiliary media of exchange, but they are not money currency or circulation.

## II.—The Working of a Paper Currency regulated upon the Metallic Principle.

Were the currency purely metallic, very considerable inconvenience would be experienced in effecting large payments in coin. To obviate this inconvenience arrangements would be devised analogous to those which were formerly adopted by the bank of Amsterdam, and which are now in operation in the bank of Hamburgh. The coinage department of the mint, instead of giving coin in exchange for bullion, might, when required so to do, retain the coin in its coffers, and give a receipt entitling the bearer to receive, upon demand, an amount of coin equivalent to the gold paid in. These mint receipts would circulate like the bank money of Hamburgh, and thus the first step towards the establishment of a mixed currency, consisting of coin and paper, would be taken.

It is evident that, if the currency consisted of coin and of mint receipts payable to bearer, on demand, for coin actually deposited in the coffers of the mint, it would be subject to no greater variations, either in amount or in value, than those which would occur were the whole circulation composed of coin. When the quantity of bullion brought in exceeded the quantity required to replace the consumption of the manufacturer, and to balance foreign accounts, the excess would be taken to the coinage department of the mint, and there exchanged either for coin or for coin receipts, and thus the circulation would be expanded. On the other hand, when the quantity of bullion brought in should be less than the quantity required for the manufacturer and the cambist, mint receipts would be returned in exchange for coin, the coin would be melted or exported, and thus the circulation would be contracted.

Under the arrangements which we are now considering, millions of coin might be for ages in the coffers of the mint, as dead unproductive stock, and as little available for any industrial operation as if the gold had remained in the bowels of the earth. This unproductive locking up of treasure would be found to be in a great measure unnecessary. Were the coin lodged in the coffers of the mint, in exchange for mint receipts, to amount to 60,000,000*l.*,* 40,000,000*l.* might be withdrawn and applied to the purchase of Government securities, for the benefit of the public, without endangering the immediate convertibility into coin of such of the 60,000,000*l.* of coin receipts as might be presented to the mint. But it is evident that, if the mint were to issue 40,000,000*l.* of paper upon securities, and 20,000,000*l.* upon coin, and were to increase or to diminish its issues of paper as coin should be paid in or withdrawn, the expansion and contraction of the mixed currency of coin and paper would be identical with those which would occur were the circulation purely metallic.

* Mr. Hubbard, in his valuable publication, "The Currency of the Country," states the paper money of the United Kingdom in 1838 at 55,000,000*l.*; of which about 13,000,000*l.* were supposed to be issued upon bullion or gold coin.

It is equally evident that precisely similar results would be produced were the business of the mint to be confined to the operation of coining, and were the functions of issuing paper upon coin and securities, and of holding deposits of bullion for safe custody, transferred to the Bank of England, provided that establishment should be conducted on the principle of total separation between the departments of issue and of deposit. This is the species of arrangement for the management of the currency which has been recommended by Mr. Loyd and Mr. Norman; and which, under the sanction of such high authorities, I have ventured to advocate. I will endeavour to explain what would be the working of such an arrangement, and to show that the objections which have been urged by Mr. Tooke, against a single bank of issue conducted on the metallic principle, are utterly invalid.

Let us assume that the Bank of England has been invested with the exclusive power of issuing the paper currency; that it is conducted on the principle of total separation between the departments of issue and deposit; that the business of the department of issue is to give upon demand Bank notes in exchange for gold, and gold in exchange for Bank notes; that it has issued 40,000,000*l*. on securities, and 20,000,000*l*. upon gold; and that, while keeping its securities at a fixed amount, it increases its issues of paper as gold is brought in for notes, and allows its issues to contract as notes are returned for gold.

From the considerations which have been already presented it will be apparent that, under the above regulations, a very considerable and even a continuous stream of the precious metals might be directed to this country without having any effect whatever in enlarging the circulation. The bullion in the deposit department of the bank might be increased by a large amount without the presentation to the department of issue of an ounce of gold in exchange for notes. Goldsmiths, jewellers, and manufacturers of plate might place in the deposit department, to be there held in safe custody, that portion of the inflowing treasure which they purchased up as the raw material of their trade. Cambists and dealers in foreign bills, whose business it is to apportion the precious metals throughout the commercial world, would probably place in the deposit department of the Bank those importations of bullion which might be consigned to London as the monetary entrepôt of Europe; and no inconsiderable proportion even of those importations of the metals which come into the country, not merely *in transitu*, but as the profits of trade due to our merchants and manufacturers, might be deposited in the Bank, without having any immediate action on the circulation. The ultimate action of these last-mentioned portions of imported treasure in enlarging the circulation and raising the prices of domestic commodities would be as follows:—

Merchants and manufacturers who receive, as a portion of the profits of their foreign trade, a greater quantity of bullion than they require for the extension of their business, desire to invest their accumulations in some species of securities yielding a return. A part of their securities may seek foreign investment; in which case the imported bullion would not find its way to the issue department of the Bank at all, but would be passed to the cambist in exchange for drafts upon foreign houses, and remitted to pay such drafts. And even that portion of the merchant's or the manufacturer's accumulating bullion which he might desire to invest in British securities might not immediately pass to the department of issue, but might remain in deposit while eligible securities were sought. When it had been presented to the department of issue, and there exchanged for coin or Bank notes, or when, while still remaining in deposit, checks against it should be drawn, then its action upon prices would commence. The notes, or the checks which represented it, would be paid away in the purchase of securities, the value of which would rise under the influence of the increased demand. The Government Funds would probably be the first to rise; and as they rose a motive would be presented to seek a higher rate of interest, by transferring capital from the funds to shares. The share market would thus feel the effects of increased demand; and as the price of shares advanced, and the rate of interest obtainable by investments in them declined, a higher advantage would be sought by speculating in commodities. This would raise wholesale prices; retail prices would speedily participate in the rise; and in this way a general rise of prices would be the ultimate result of the influx of such portions of the precious metals as might be exchanged at the issue department of the mint for coin or Bank notes, or which, while remaining in deposit, might be treated as cash credits, against which drafts payable to bearer might be drawn.

Were the Bank of England the sole issuing body, were its functions kept separate and entirely independent of each other, and were the department of issue to increase the circulation as gold flowed into, and to contract it as gold flowed out of, its coffers, the expansion of the currency resulting from a favourable balance of foreign payments and an influx of the precious metals, would carry within itself the principle of its own limitation. The operation of this limiting principle in preventing any very considerable expansion of the circulation or rise of prices may be easily traced. It only requires to be stated in order to be understood. As prices rose, imports would increase, exports would diminish, and gold, at no distant period, would flow out as copiously as it had flowed in. As the value of British securities exceeded that of foreign securities in more than the ordinary proportion, the export of capital for foreign investment would be a concurrent cause with the diminished export and increased import of commodities in drawing off the excess of the precious metals, and in bringing up the value of the currency to the par-of-exchange level.

The operation of an unfavourable foreign exchange in diminishing the amount and raising the value of the circulation, were it regulated upon the metallic principle by a single bank of issue, I will now endeavour to trace out.

Let us assume that a deficient harvest in England causes an importation of foreign corn, that the importers have an extra demand for foreign bills to the amount of 5,000,000*l*., and that such bills are, consequently, at a premium. The cambists will not be unprepared for this event. During the favourable course of exchange, the low rate of interest in England, and the high price of domestic securities, had induced them to transfer their capital from domestic to foreign securities. These they can now dispose of with advantage to meet the bills sold to the importers of corn. During the favourable course of exchange, too, their deposits of bullion were at the maximum. These deposits they will now withdraw for the purpose of exporting them to meet the drafts drawn upon their foreign correspondents. By these operations a considerable portion of the debt due by England for foreign corn is discharged before any action on the currency commences. As soon, however, as the diminished supply of bullion begins to raise its value in relation to coin, Bank notes will be returned upon the issue department of the Bank in exchange for coin, which will be melted or exported. A contraction of the circulation now takes place. The holders of foreign corn, whether in London or in the outports, will have their deposits with their bankers diminished; while the banks, finding their reserves of cash reduced, are warned to contract their usual accommodation to their customers. A monetary pressure, accompanied by a fall in the value of securities and in the prices of commodities, ensues.

Under a single bank of issue, managing the circulation

upon the metallic principle, a contraction, no less than an expansion, of the currency would carry within itself the principle of its own limitation. In the case which we have been just considering, the merchants, who had employed their capital in importing an extraordinary quantity of corn, would not be in a condition to employ the same amount of capital as before in importing other articles; other merchants, seeing that the high price of corn was diminishing the ability of consumers to purchase other things, would be disposed to limit their foreign purchases; and thus the diminution in the importation of other commodities would partly balance the increased importation of corn, while the fall in the price of domestic productions, together with the premium upon foreign bills, would cause an increase of export. From the combined operation of these several causes, the debt of 5,000,000*l.* incurred for foreign corn might be liquidated, without causing a contraction of the circulation to anything approaching to that amount. A very inconsiderable portion of the coin might be exported. The fall in the value of British securities, and the consequent reinvestment in them of the money, which had been previously placed in foreign securities, would contribute to rectify the exchanges. The cambists and merchants who had possessed early information regarding the state of the crops, and of the probable adverse turn of the exchanges, would have looked forward to a decline in the value of British securities, would have sold out, in anticipation of the fall, and with a view of placing themselves in a position to increase their exportations of British goods, should a decline in domestic prices, and a premium upon foreign bills, render it expedient to do so.

A currency managed by a single bank of issue upon the metallic principle, would have an important action upon the auxiliary media of exchange which it will be expedient to examine. All prudent bankers maintain what they consider to be a safe proportion between the amount of their cash reserves, and the amount of their advances in discounts and credits, against which drafts at sight may be drawn. Were the currency made to expand as a favourable foreign exchange caused gold to be sent to the bank of issue to be exchanged for coin or bank notes, the cash reserves in the coffers of the banks would be increased, and the bankers would feel themselves safe in re-establishing the ordinary proportion between their advances and their reserves, by increasing the amount of their discounts and credits. On the other hand, if the currency were made to contract, as an unfavourable balance of foreign payments caused paper to be returned upon the bank of issue in exchange for gold, the several banks of deposit would have the amounts of their available cash diminished, and would immediately perceive the necessity of limiting the amount of their discounts and credits in a like proportion. Thus, if the currency were regulated upon the metallic principle, the auxiliary media of exchange which are based upon it would partake, with considerable velocity and exactness, in its expansions and contractions. A slight expansion would have an immediate tendency to raise the value of securities and the prices of commodities, while a slight contraction would have an instantaneous tendency to act in the opposite direction. In the one case, the motive to foreign investments, to diminished imports and augmented exports, would be early prescribed, and an excessive influx of the metals early checked. In the other case, the motive to recall foreign investment, to diminish imports, and to augment exports, would be early felt, and an excessive efflux of the metals early arrested. Sudden and deep vibrations upon either side would be prevented.

One of the most important effects of a currency uttered by a single issuer, and regulated upon the metallic principle, would be that of promptly adjusting the circulation of each particular locality, according to the proportion determined by the balance of payments occurring between the several districts of the country. Under a currency thus issued and regulated, when the bills drawn by London on Liverpool exceeded by 100,000*l.* those drawn by Liverpool on London, the account would be immediately balanced, either directly or indirectly, by the remission from London to Liverpool of 100,000*l.* in coin, or in the notes of the single issuing body; and thus the circulation of London would be increased, while that of Liverpool would be diminished by the amount. The reverse process would take place when the bills drawn by Liverpool upon London exceeded those drawn by London upon Liverpool by 100,000*l.* In this case there would be, either by a direct or by an indirect operation, an expansion of the London, and a contraction of the Liverpool circulation by the amount of 100,000*l.* Thus, a mixed currency, consisting of coin and of bank paper, regulated on the same principle upon which a currency consisting exclusively of coin would be regulated, would almost instantaneously obey the impulses of the inter-provincial exchanges; the balance of the circulation would be everywhere preserved; there would be no spasmodic contraction and disturbance; deficient action in one quarter, and congestion in another.*

Should I have been at all successful in tracing out the working of a mixed currency, consisting of coin and of paper, issued upon the same principle upon which coin is issued, the misconceptions and fallacies into which Mr. Tooke has fallen, in his recent publication, will have been made apparent. Were that portion of the currency, which consists of paper, to be issued by a single bank, upon the same principles as the coin is issued by the mint, the circulation would not, as Mr. Tooke most erroneously assumes, expand and contract according to the amount of bullion which might be imported or exported. The principles which Mr Loyd, Mr. Norman, and myself, have contended for, are, as I ventured to explain in a former publication,† that the Bank of England should

* All these advantages will be secured by the Government arrangement for keeping the paper of the provincial banks issued upon securities at a uniform amount.

† Letter to Thomas Tooke, Esq., p. 6, 1840.

be the only issuing body; that its business should be separated into a department of issue and of discount; and that the Directors of that establishment should "keep the securities upon which they issue paper at a fixed and uniform amount, and allow that portion which they advance upon treasure *to increase or diminish as treasure might flow into, or flow out of, their coffers.*" It is evident that, under this arrangement, millions of treasure might be imported without flowing into the coffers of the issuing department of the bank, in exchange for bank notes; and it is equally evident, that millions of treasure might be withdrawn from the coffers of the deposit department, and exported, without causing the efflux of an ounce of gold from the coffers of the issuing department, and a consequent contraction of the paper portion of the circulation. Were the quantity of bullion imported to exceed the quantity required to supply the demands of the manufacturer and cambist, then the surplus, instead of being allowed to remain as a dead stock, would be taken to the mint to be exchanged for coin, or to the issue department of the bank, to be exchanged for notes; and, on the other hand, when the quantity imported fell short of the quantity required to meet the demands of the manufacturer and cambist, then a drain upon the issue department of the bank would commence, and the circulation would be contracted by the return of notes for coin to be melted or exported. Mr. Tooke evidently labours under a total misapprehension when he affirms* that the due regulation of the currency, in the sense in which Mr. Loyd uses the term, must be understood to be a conformity of the amount of bank notes to the amount of bullion. His objections to a system of currency, regulated upon the metallic principle, may be answered in the words which he has applied to the advocates of the system; "he labours under a most egregious misconception of what the working of it would be."

* Page 6.

## III.—The working of a Currency regulated on the principles propounded by Mr. Tooke.

Having thus endeavoured to explain the practical working of a currency managed by a single issuing body, upon the principle of allowing the circulation to expand and contract as the action of the foreign exchanges should cause gold to be paid in exchange for paper, or paper returned in exchange for gold, I proceed to investigate the practical working of a currency uttered by many issuers, and allowed to expand and contract without reference to the action of the foreign exchanges.

Let us assume that the currency of this country has become redundant in relation to foreign currencies, and that a drain upon the coffers of the Bank of England has commenced. We have seen the gradual and easy process by which the adverse exchange would be rectified by a single bank of issue keeping its securities even, and contracting its circulation as gold should be withdrawn from its coffers. Were the bank to disregard this principle of limitation, and manage its circulation in the manner advocated by Mr. Tooke, the process of rectification would be as follows:—

The currency, we assume, is in excess in relation to foreign currencies; the high range of our prices is causing imports to exceed exports; an unfavourable foreign balance is accruing, and gold is flowing out of the coffers of the bank in liquidation of the debt. Under these circumstances, the bank, adopting the theory of currency propounded by Mr. Tooke, disregards the state of the foreign exchanges, and keeps its circulation even by increasing its securities. This arrests the process through which, were the currency allowed to contract as, under the circumstances, a purely metallic currency would do, the foreign debt would be gradually liquidated, and the exchanges restored to par. The amount of cash in the hands of bankers and bill-brokers not being diminished by a due contraction of the circulation, they would not now be warned to limit their credits and discounts; there would be no pressure upon the money market; no advance in the rate of interest, inviting the return of foreign investments; no fall in prices checking imports and increasing exports. All the causes of an adverse exchange would be kept in operation, and gold would flow out in an undiminished stream. The vital question,—how can insolvency be averted? would force itself upon the consideration of the bank directors.

Mr. Tooke contends, that the bank might disregard with impunity the principle of keeping its securities even, and allowing its circulation to contract under the action of the adverse exchange, provided its ordinary reserve of gold when the exchanges were at par should bear a considerably greater proportion to its issues than that which has hitherto been maintained. Now it must be apparent to any person who will attentively consider the causes which produce and keep up an adverse exchange, that no amount of gold held by the bank, though equivalent to half, or to two-thirds, or to three-fourths of its liabilities, could be a security against insolvency, unless a contraction of the circulation should restore the currency to par with foreign currencies. The exportation of 10,000,000*l.* of gold might discharge an existing foreign debt; but, should an excessive issue of paper be maintained, could not prevent the creation of a new foreign debt of equivalent amount.

When, the exchanges having been previously at par, the balance of payments is turned against us by a sudden and unusual importation of some leading article of consumption, the possession of a large amount of treasure by the bank might render it not immediately unsafe, however ultimately injurious, to depart for a time from the sound and scientific principles upon which the issue of paper-money should be regulated, and to allow gold to flow out of the coffers of the bank, without a corresponding contraction of the circulation. Thus, should the bank hold bullion to the amount of 10,000,000*l*., and should an unusual importation of foreign corn create a foreign debt to the amount of 5,000,000*l*. the transfer of 5,000,000*l*. of the treasure held by the bank of issue might liquidate the foreign debt, and thus by restoring the exchanges to par, obviate the necessity of arresting a further drain by a contraction of the circulation. Very different would be the result should an adverse exchange be created by a currency redundant in relation to foreign currencies. In this case, no conceivable amount of treasure held by the bank would be sufficient of itself to adjust the international accounts; because, if the efflux of the metals should not be accompanied by a contraction of the circulation, the currency would continue to be of less value than foreign currencies, imports would exceed exports, and new foreign debts would be contracted as old ones were extinguished.

When the currency is in excess in relation to foreign currencies, the only possible means by which we can avert a suspension of cash payments is to restore the currency to par with foreign currencies; and the only practical questions for consideration are—shall we apply the remedy at an early or at a late period? Shall we at one time keep the circulation in excess, while the treasure in the coffers of the bank is sinking from a safe maximum to a dangerous minimum, and at another time keep the circulation deficient, while the reserve of treasure is reascending from the level of danger to the level of safety? Or shall we at all times adhere to the principle of allowing the circulation to contract or expand as the metals ebb or flow, and thus rectify, upon the instant, the first incipient deviations of the currency from the par of the commercial world? These questions are of such vital importance at the present juncture, that it seems expedient to contrast, in detail, the practical workings of the arrangements for the management of the currency which have been respectively recommended in the publication of Mr. Tooke, and in those of Mr. Loyd, Mr. Norman, Mr. Sampson Ricardo, Mr. Hubbard, Sir William Clay, and others. The arrangement advocated by Mr. Tooke is, that the present system of union of the two departments of the bank should be retained, with greater security against the risks of suspension; and that in order to attain this greater security, the bank directors "discarding the rules which were professed about keeping the securities even, and of investing, in a full state of the currency, two-thirds of their liabilities, should undertake to hold in reserve a much higher average amount of bullion than they have hitherto considered it necessary or consistent with the interest of their proprietors to maintain." The arrangement insisted upon by the other economists to whom I have alluded is, that the rules for keeping securities even should be adhered to, and that the circulation should be allowed to expand and contract, as gold should flow out of or into the coffers of the issuing department of the bank. The following figures will exemplify in palpable contrast the effects which would be produced by these different arrangements. The status of the bank is assumed to be as follows, the exchanges being at par:—

| | Liabilities. | | Assets. |
|---|---|---|---|
| Circulation | £18,000,000 | Securities | £20,000,000 |
| Deposits | 12,000,000 | Bullion | 10,000,000 |
| | £30,000,000 | | £30,000,000 |

This being the previous state of things, let the exchanges turn against us, and let the bank directors, adhering to the rule of keeping their securities even, allow the circulation to contract as their notes are returned in exchange for gold.

The following results, as already explained, would almost instantaneously ensue. The cash at the command of the private bankers and bill-brokers being diminished, they would see the expediency of restoring the ordinary proportion between the amount of their immediately available funds and their immediate liabilities, by limiting their discounts and credits, or by disposing of their securities ; the merchants and dealers who employed bankers, finding their cash balances reduced, and their accustomed amount of discounts diminished, would abstain from purchases, or dispose of securities to complete them ; and from all these several causes the prices of commodities would decline, and the rate of interest advance. The causes which had created the adverse exchange would begin to be counteracted the instant their effects were felt. It is probable that through the diminution of imports, the increase of exports, the recall of foreign investments, and the contraction of the auxiliary media of exchange, the currency might be restored to the foreign par, and the drain of gold arrested before 1,000,000*l*. had been abstracted from the coffers of the bank.

Let us trace the very different effects which would result from the adoption of the system of management advocated by Mr. Tooke. His system is, that the bank directors, disregarding the rule of keeping their securities even, should hold a reserve of bullion of 10,000,000*l*. when the currency is at the par level, and should allow the reserve to increase to 15,000,000*l*. under a favourable, and to decrease to 5,000,000*l*. under an adverse exchange ; reducing the rate of discount when the reserve reaches the maximum of 15,000,000*l*., and increasing it as the reserve falls to the minimum of 5,000,000*l*. The result of this system of management, under the action of the foreign exchanges, would be as follows :—

The previous circumstances being as before, an unfavourable exchange occurs, which not being checked by an adherence to the rule of keeping the securities even, goes on until the reserve of bullion is reduced from 10,000,000*l.* to 5,000,000*l.* The status of the bank is now as follows:—

| Liabilities. | | Assets. | |
|---|---|---|---|
| Circulation . | £18,000,000 | Securities . | £25,000,000 |
| Deposits . . | 12,000,000 | Bullion . | 5,000,000 |
| | 30,000,000 | | 30,000,000 |

Thus, while the bullion in the coffers of the bank is reduced from 10,000,000*l.* to 5,000,000*l.*, the circulation remains, as before, at 18,000,000*l.* Now it is obvious that (the adverse exchange having been caused, not by an extraordinary importation of some article of general consumption, but by a previous process of overtrading, reducing the value of the currency below that of foreign currencies) no reaction tending to restore the circulation to the foreign par has as yet been induced. The diffusion throughout the markets of the world, of the 5,000,000*l.* of gold abstracted from the coffers of the bank, could have no perceptible effect in lowering the value of foreign currency; the maintenance of an undiminished circulation prevents a rise in the value of the home currency; and, consequently, the efflux of treasure from the coffers of the Bank proceeds as before. Mr. Tooke's grand instrument of rectification is now set at work, and the bank directors seek to arrest the drain upon their coffers by raising the rate of their discounts. The effect is inconsiderable. The general rate of interest cannot be materially raised while the amount of the circulation remains undiminished. Its amount is not in the first instance diminished by the rise in the rate of interest. Private bankers and bill-brokers hold the same amount of disposable cash as before; and rather than allow it to remain unproductive in their coffers, employ it in discounts at the same rate of interest as before. No immediate contraction, either of the currency, or of the auxiliary medium of exchange resting upon it, takes place; gold continues to flow out, and the bank directors, in order to protect their establishment from insolvency, are compelled to resort to a sudden and violent contraction of their issues. A panic in the money-market now commences, a general fall in prices, and in the value of securities, arrests the drain, and the convertibility of the bank note is secured through a calamitous commercial revulsion.

Periodical panics and commercial revulsions are not the most formidable results which it would be reasonable to anticipate from the adoption of Mr. Tooke's arrangements for the regulation of the currency. Were the directors of the Bank of England, acting on the principle he has propounded for their guidance, to allow their reserve of bullion to be reduced from 10,000,000*l*. to 5,000,000*l*., an unfavourable foreign balance, created during the period in which the currency was allowed to continue redundant, might cause a further efflux of bullion, beyond the power of their delayed precaution to control. A deficient harvest, requiring an importation of foreign corn to the amount of 4,000,000*l*., at a time when their treasure had been reduced to 2,000,000*l*., might compel them to stop payment.

## IV. Working of a Paper Currency uttered by numerous Issuers, regardless of the principle of keeping their Securities at a uniform Amount.

Having shown what would be the working of a mixed currency of coin and bank paper, managed by a single issuing body, upon the principle of keeping its securities at a fixed amount, and of allowing its circulation to expand or contract as the foreign exchanges caused its reserve of treasure to increase or to diminish; and having contrasted the effects of this system of management with those which would be produced were the Bank of England to disregard the principle of keeping its securities at a fixed amount, and to seek to place itself in a position of safety by increasing its reserve of bullion to an amount which might be deemed sufficient to secure the convertibility of its paper under all the vibrations of the exchanges, I will now endeavour to explain the working of a mixed currency, committed to the management of many issuing bodies, disregarding the principle of keeping their issues upon securities at a uniform amount.

I venture to believe that in the preceding pages I have succeeded in establishing the proposition, that paper money should be so managed as to maintain the currency in the same state, with respect to amount and to value, in which it would exist were it exclusively metallic. Now a careful examination of this important branch of the subject will furnish us with abundant evidence that no management on the part of the directors of the Bank of England can by possibility maintain the currency in this sound and healthy state, so long as the numerous banks of issue throughout the provinces shall continue to act upon their avowed principle, of uttering their paper without reference to the action of the foreign exchanges, and without regard to the principle of keeping the securities at a uniform amount. One or two examples will be sufficient to establish this position.

Under the existing system, when the provincial banks issue their paper to excess, the currency of the provinces becomes redundant, not only in relation to the currency of London, but also in relation to the currencies of other countries; the exchanges between the provinces and London, and also between the provinces and foreign parts, are turned against the provinces; and the merchants of the provinces are compelled to provide themselves with an extra amount, not only of London bills, but also of foreign bills. The process is thus:—The merchants who require the extra amount of bills draw out their deposits with the provincial banks of issue, or return the notes of such banks in exchange for bills upon London; and the banks, by drawing out the balances, or by selling the securities which they hold in

London, provide for the payment of the bills in London currency. Now this portion of the process, while it contracts the currency of the provinces, leaves the currency of London exactly as before. The next step of the process, however, contracts the currency of London, by creating a drain upon the coffers of the Bank of England. The merchants of the provinces, who had obtained the command of London currency in the manner just described, and who had the foreign balances to pay, would go into the market and purchase the extra amount of foreign bills which they required; and the London cambists, in order to provide for the extra amount of foreign bills which they granted, would return the notes of the Bank of England in exchange for gold for exportation.

From this illustration, it will be apparent that so long as there shall be many banks of issue, regardless of the principle of keeping their securities at a uniform amount, and allowing their circulation to be governed by the exchanges, the Bank of England will be under the necessity of providing a supply of treasure sufficient, not only to meet the drains of gold occasioned by a fall in the value of the London currency, as compared with foreign currencies, but also to meet the drains of gold occasioned by the over-trading of all the banks of issue throughout the kingdom. This is a state of things which, while it is highly prejudicial to the Bank of England, inflicts frequent and serious injury, not only on the commercial classes trading within the metropolitan district, but also upon the commercial classes throughout the country. Though the currency of the metropolis may be at par with foreign currencies, yet over-trading by the provincial banks of issue may turn the foreign exchanges against this country, and compel the Bank of England to protect its coffers by contracting its issues, and creating an otherwise unnecessary scarcity of money. This is a cause of monetary derangement and commercial pressure, which is inherent in a system of many banks of issue, not regulated upon the metallic principle; and which the most judicious and scientific management on the part of the directors of the Bank of England cannot by possibility remove.

It is believed in many quarters that provincial banks of issue have a beneficial operation in the agricultural districts. Upon a strict examination of the subject, it will be found that this belief is utterly delusive; and that numerous issuing bodies, regulating the provincial currencies in reference, not to the state of the foreign exchanges, but to the local demands for accommodation in their respective districts, so far from affording any real encouragement or permanent assistance to the farmer, serve but to multiply and to aggravate the periodical returns of agricultural depression. The manner in which the provincial banks of issue produce this injurious effect I will endeavour to explain.

When the supply of an article so indispensably necessary as corn becomes deficient, its price is raised in a considerably greater proportion than that in which its quantity is diminished. On this principle, when a deficient harvest occurs, the balance of payments, as between London and the agricultural districts, is turned in favour of the latter; and cash balances greater than ordinary have to be remitted from London to the provincial banks;—the circulation of the rural districts is increased at the expense of the metropolitan circulation. Now, if the currency were issued by a single body, upon the metallic principle, the amount of cash transmitted from London to the provinces, in consequence of the increased price of agricultural produce, would be limited by the contraction of the circulation caused by the unfavourable exchange consequent upon the deficient harvest. This limitation to the amount of currency which could be remitted to the provinces would operate as a limit to the rise of prices in the agricultural districts. Thus, with a currency regulated upon the metallic principle by a single issuing body, the unfavourable balance of foreign payments, occasioned by the debt incurred for foreign corn, would raise the value of money in this country, and check the rise in the price of British corn. This is supposed to be an evil, and constitutes, with many, an objection to a currency, regulated by a central body, upon the metallic principle.

With numerous banks of issue throughout the agricultural counties, the limit to the rise in the prices of agricultural produce, as above described, could not exist. Under these circumstances, which are, in fact, the existing circumstances, the banker sees it at once safe and profitable to increase his advances to the farmer as the value of the farmer's stock increases. Hence, while the London circulation is contracting, under the action of the adverse exchange, the circulation of the provinces expands, under the action of advancing prices. The increased pecuniary accommodation which the farmer is able to command, as a consequence of the increased value of his produce, becomes the antecedent of a still further rise, by enabling him to hold back his stock, in expectation of an improving market. The results thus produced are supposed to be beneficial, and are urged by many as constituting an irresistible argument in favour of the continuance of many banks of issue.

This argument might be valid, provided the species of encouragement thus afforded to the agricultural class by the provincial banks of issue could be obtained without inducing subsequent reaction and collapse. But this is manifestly impossible. The higher range of prices maintained by the increased accommodation afforded to the farmer necessarily occasions an increased importation of foreign corn; this increased importation increases the amount of the unfavourable balance of foreign payments, prolongs the drain upon the coffers of the Bank of England, and compels that establishment to resort to a still further contraction of the circulation. Ultimately, but inevitably, and at no very great interval, the contraction of the provincial currencies conforms to the contraction of the central currency, in which all balances are adjusted. What is the equivalent which the farmer has now to pay for the temporary accommodation which he received? The increased importations of corn, and the increased exportations of gold, have rendered the prices of agricultural produce lower than they would otherwise have been. The provincial banks of issue, which had aided the farmer in his prosperity, will not, or cannot aid him in his distress. The issues and the credits which were extended on the rise of prices must be contracted on their fall. An increased glut of corn, an increased scarcity of money, and a diminished amount of credit, at the very moment when credit is most required, are the equivalents which the farmer has to pay for the temporary and deceptive advantage afforded by local banks of issue. It amounts to a perfect demonstration, that the artificial, and therefore temporary elevation of prices which the advances of provincial banks of issue enable the farmer to maintain, is the antecedent of agricultural depression more severe and more protracted than that which would occur under the steady and uniform action of a currency regulated upon the metallic principle. The establishment of a currency thus regulated, would be the greatest boon which the agricultural interest could receive from the hands of Government.

### *The grand Tookean Fallacies*

Mr. Tooke concludes with a summary of seventeen conclusions, in which nothing is concluded. The most astonishing of the many astounding fallacies which he has put forth on the present occasion is presented in the conclusion No. 12:—" That the prices of commodities do not depend upon the quantity of money indicated by the amount of Bank notes, nor upon the amount of the whole circulating medium; but that, on the contrary, the amount of the circulating medium is the consequence of prices." The logical accuracy of this conclusion may be tested by affirming the analogous proposition, that the prices of commodities in Europe, after the discovery of the mines of South America, did not depend upon the quantity of money indicated by the amount of coin, nor by the amount of the whole of the supply of gold and silver; but that, on the contrary, the mines of South America, and the increased amount of gold and silver obtained therefrom, were the consequence of the subsequent rise of prices.

Mr. Tooke has written volumes on the effect of quantity on price; and has shown, by the most elaborate details, that on all the remarkable occasions upon which a decline of prices has occurred, the decline was occasioned, not by an appreciation of the currency, but by an increase in the quantity of the leading articles of consumption brought to market. He rests the deserved reputation, which even he himself cannot destroy, upon having traced, by an extensive induction from existing and from historical facts, that the value of everything declines as its quantity is increased in relation to the demand; and he turns his back upon himself by affirming, that the value of money does not decline, as its quantity is increased in relation to the demand.

Mr. Tooke is an advocate for charging a seignorage upon the coin equivalent to the cost of coinage; and at the same time he professes to be a strenuous opponent to a depreciation of the currency. Now, how is it that the currency is kept from depreciation when a seignorage is charged upon the coin? Upon what principle is it that coin upon which a seignorage is charged is not reduced in value in proportion to the reduction in its weight? Why is an ounce of gold less by the reduction of the seignorage, equivalent to an ounce of gold from which nothing has been deducted? Mr. Tooke cannot but admit that the only answer which can be given to these questions is, that coin upon which a seignorage is charged bears a circulating value greater than its bullion value, because the charge for seignorage causes the supply of coin in relation to the demand for coin to be less than the supply of bullion in relation to the demand for bullion. Let there be an adverse exchange, creating a demand for coin for exportation, and it instantly falls to its bullion value—the depreciation of the currency becomes exactly equal to the seignorage charged upon the coin.

Mr. Tooke admits, that the value of an inconvertible paper currency is lowered by an increase in its quantity; but he denies that a convertible currency can be lowered by an increase of its quantity. Here he falls into a manifest contradiction. The effects of an increase of quantity, so far as the increase can be carried in both cases, is in both cases precisely the same. The difference between the two cases is this:—The increase in the quantity of inconvertible paper is unlimited; the increase in the quantity of convertible paper is limited by the power of the holder to exchange it for gold, as soon as, from the increase of quantity, its value in relation to gold begins to decline. If the increase in the quantity of convertible paper had no effect in lowering its value in relation to gold, the holder could have no motive to exchange it for gold. The fact that an undue increase in the quantity of convertible paper causes it to be converted, is a practical demonstration that the increase in its quantity lowers its value. The act of conversion limits the quantity, and therefore limits the fall in value. Mr. Tooke falls into the misconception of imagining that the limitation to a further decline of value which convertibility imposes, prevents the previous existence of the decline which it subsequently arrests. He fails to perceive, that before a decline of value can be arrested, there must have been a decline of value to arrest.

The effect of an increase in the quantity of money in lowering its value, or in other words, in raising prices, may be demonstrated in another way. Let us suppose that in the first instance the currency is exclusively metallic; and that in the second instance, the banks commence the issuing of promissory notes payable upon demand in coin. Now we know, from universal experience, that under these circumstances a proportion of the coin would be displaced. The result is unquestionable; and the manner of its production admits of the simplest explanation. Previous to the issuing of promissory notes by the banks, the amount of coin in circulation would have been, upon the average, just sufficient to keep the currency equal in value with foreign currencies, to maintain the exchanges at par, and to render the average trade with foreign countries a trade of barter. Now this having been the previous state of things, the increase in the amount of the currency occasioned by the issues of the banks, lowers its value in relation to foreign currencies, turns the exchanges against us, and causes gold to be exported. Now why should gold be exported? The answer is, only because its value in relation to exportable commodities has fallen; in other words, only because the prices of commodities have risen. Before the quantity of money was increased by the issue of bank notes, our imports were paid for by the export of commodities; because at the then existing low range of prices, commodities were the cheapest instruments by which foreign payments could be effected. After the quantity of money has been increased by the issue of bank notes, our imports are paid for by the exportation of gold; because at the now existing higher range of prices, gold is the cheapest instrument by which foreign payments can be effected. Had Mr. Tooke understood the laws which govern the foreign exchanges, he could not have ventured to affirm, that an increase in the quantity of money does not cause an increase of prices.

Mr. Tooke's curious reasons for his curious conclusions, that an increase in the quantity of inconvertible paper money does, and that an increase in the quantity of convertible paper does not, cause an increase of prices, require to be noticed. He says,*

"When a government issues paper money inconvertible, and compulsorily current, it is usually in payment for—

"1. The personal expenditure of the sovereign or the governing power.

"2. Public works and buildings.

"3. Salaries of civil servants.

"4. Maintenance of naval and military establishments.

"It is quite clear that paper created and so paid away by the government, not being returnable to the issuer, will constitute a fresh source of demand, and must be forced into, and permeate, all the channels of circulation. Accordingly, every fresh issue beyond the point at which former issues had settled in a certain rise of price and of wages, and a fall of the exchanges, is soon followed by a further rise of commodities and wages, and a fall of the exchanges; the depreciation being in the ratio of the forcibly increased amount of the issues.

"It will hence appear that the difference between paper money so issued and bank notes such as those of this country, consists, not only in the limit prescribed by their convertibility to the amount of them, but in the mode of issue. The latter are issued to those only who, being entitled to demand gold, desire to have notes in preference, and it depends upon the particular purposes for which the notes are employed, whether a greater or less quantity is required."

Fallacies "permeate all the channels" of the passages above quoted. In the first place it is a fallacy that convertible paper is issued to those only who, being entitled to demand gold desire to have notes in preference. In a large number, perhaps in a majority of cases, convertible paper is issued

* Page 69.

to persons who are not, at the time of issue, entitled to demand gold, and whose title to demand it is created by the paper they obtain. The merchant who discounts a bill of exchange at the bank is entitled to demand gold, not because he was the holder of the bill, but because the bank has advanced convertible notes upon it. An advance of convertible notes upon securities is a new creation of paper money, just in the same way in which an advance of inconvertible notes by government is a new creation of paper money.

There is no conceivable difference as regards the nature and character of the action upon prices between the action produced by convertible, and that produced by inconvertible, paper. There is, however, a difference between the degree and extent of the action; the effect being, in the one case, unlimited, and in the other, limited by the speedy diminution in the quantity of the convertible paper money as soon as its value in relation to gold begins to decline. Mr. Tooke's argument, when fairly analyzed, amounts to this—An increase in the quantity of convertible paper cannot reduce its value, because, when the increase of quantity has reduced its value, a diminution in its quantity will raise its value; therefore the quantity of convertible paper has no influence upon its value.—Q. E. D.

Mr. Tooke contends that the increase of an *inconvertible* currency would increase wages and prices, because it would be expended in the personal expenditure of the sovereign or governing power in salaries and in public works and buildings; and because, thus expended, it would permeate all the channels of circulation. Now the increase of a *convertible* currency would produce the same identical effects, through the same identical process, which would be produced by the increase of an inconvertible currency. Were a nobleman to obtain from the Bank of England 100,000*l.* upon the mortgage of his estate, and were he to expend the amount thus obtained in enlarging his domestic establishment, in maintaining an additional retinue of servants, and in erecting a mansion and ornamental buildings, this convertible paper, thus expended, would, like an inconvertible paper expended by Government upon analogous objects, raise wages and prices, because it would " permeate all the channels of circulation." Were this nobleman to expend the loan advanced by the Bank of England in improving his estate, in draining, planting, and reclaiming wastes, exactly similar results, as regards wages and prices, would be produced; while results exactly similar, as far as regards wages and prices, would be produced were a master manufacturer to obtain discounts and other advances from the neighbouring banks of issue, and to expend the amount thus obtained in erecting new factories, in purchasing additional materials, and employing additional hands. In all these cases an increased quantity of convertible currency would "permeate the channels of circulation" in the same way in which an increased quantity of inconvertible currency would permeate them. The nature and character of the effect would be the same, whether the increased quantity of currency should be convertible or inconvertible, though its extent and degree in the two cases would be different. In the case of the inconvertible paper the effect would be unlimited; in the case of the convertible paper the effect would be confined within narrow limits, because a slight action upon prices and on the exchanges would cause the increased quantity of convertible paper to be withdrawn from circulation, by being returned upon the banks in exchange for coin now demanded for exportation. But why should the coin be demanded for exportation? Simply because the increased quantity of convertible paper had reduced the value of the currency, or, in other words, had increased prices. The withdrawal of an increased issue of convertible paper from the channels of circulation is the effect of the reduced value of the currency or increased range of prices, which, in the first instance, that increased issue had occasioned. Mr. Tooke's process of reasoning amounts to this,—that the existence of the effect proves the non-existence of the cause.

Another Tookean fallacy, scarcely less gigantic than that which we have just dismissed, is enunciated in the following passages:—

"The object in tracing thus far the operation hypothetically suggested by Sir Robert Peel is to show that the Bank of England cannot, any more than the country banks, at its pleasure, or for the purpose of employing productively, that is, in securities, a larger than usual portion of its deposits or of its bullion, cause an enlargement of the circulation; and that the usual phraseology, by which the Bank of England and the country banks are said to enlarge their circulation, as a voluntary act, is incorrect, so far as implying a power which they do not possess of directly adding to the amount of bank notes remaining in circulation, passing from hand to hand among the public, and performing the functions of money in daily transactions."*

"The conclusion from the view here presented is, that neither the country banks, nor the Bank of England, have a *direct* power (their advances being on securities, and their paper convertible) of enlarging their circulation; and that the inference from the mere fact of an increase or diminution of the amount of bank notes in circulation as being an indication of a designed enlargement or contraction of issue by the Bank of England, to the extent of the difference, proceeds on a false analogy, by neglecting a consideration of the distinction between issues, used synonymously with advances 'on securities,' and issues of Government bank notes or assignats. It is only the latter description of circulation of bank notes which admits of being increased in amount at the will of the issuers."†

* Page 55. † Page 66.

Mr. Tooke endeavours to establish these positions by quoting an opinion delivered by Mr. Gurney in 1833, "that while the transactions of London are abundantly supplied with notes, the effect of an additional 5,000,000*l.* would be, that it would remain inoperative, or rather idle in the tills of the bankers;" and by extracting from the evidence before the Committee of 1840 on Banks of Issue, the answers given by the late Mr. Page to questions put by Sir Robert Peel. Mr. Tooke is induced to remark upon the opinions of Sir Robert Peel as conveyed in his questions to Mr. Page, "because it should seem that the examination of the Committee upon Banks of Issue, of which he was a member, and in which he took part, had not shaken his belief that it was in the power of the bank, by an attempt at a forced issue, to increase the amount of the circulation, either in gold or notes, and so to depreciate the currency."

What the examinations of the Committee upon Banks of Issue failed to accomplish, Mr. Tooke undertakes to perform. The question put by Sir Robert Peel to Mr. Page was, "Supposing that 20,000,000 of notes issued upon the discount of bills of exchange, or advances to Government, to remain the same, and that the Bank were suddenly to throw 5,000,000 of sovereigns into active circulation, as advances upon landed securities, would there be no effect produced upon the currency of the country?" The answer which was given to this question appearing not to have shaken Sir Robert Peel's belief that it was in the power of the bank to increase the amount of the circulation either in gold or bank notes, and so to depreciate the currency, Mr. Tooke proceeds to correct the misconceptions of Sir Robert Peel, and to demonstrate, by his own peculiar method, "that the amount of the currency would not be increased, were the Bank of England to issue 5,000,000 of sovereigns on mortgage, in addition to its existing circulation. The demonstration is as follows:—

"By the supposition, it (the issue of 5,000,000) is a

forced operation of the bank. In effecting its purpose of making advances to that extent on mortgage, it would have to displace the existing capital (because the hypothesis assumes that things were in a sound and quiescent state, in other words *in equilibrio,* there being no new circumstances to induce fresh borrowers on that description of securities at the existing rate of interest), which had been previously advanced and was absorbed in mortgages. This could not be effected without a great reduction of interest on that description of securities, by way of sufficient inducement to fresh borrowers, or to the existing mortgagees (mortgagors), to pay off their loan, and borrow from the bank at the reduced rate of interest.

"The mortgagees being unexpectedly, and to them inconveniently, paid off, would of course seek other investments ; but those they could not readily find, unless by offers of capital at a still lower rate of interest. This would only remove the difficulty of finding employment for the capital by a single step, or rather shift it; for whatever securities were purchased by the capitalists, whose mortgages had been paid off and transferred to the bank, would set afloat just so much capital as would be produced by the transfer of those securities.

"The result would not be materially varied if the supposed advances made by the bank on mortgage were to parties who were buying land, speculatively or otherwise. There would, of course, while the operation was in progress, be a temporary rise in the number of years' purchase of landed property. In this case the sellers of the land would probably, after paying off incumbrances, seek investment for the remainder of the amount in securities at home or abroad, and would, in the first instance, with the mortgagees, who were paid off, deposit the sovereigns so received at their bankers. In either, or in both cases, the deposits in the Bank of England, or other banks, would be increased. *The deposits so accumulated would, by a greatly reduced rate of interest, gradually find employment as capital, at home or abroad, without necessarily having in the mean time produced the slightest effect in increasing the amount of the circulation, or depreciating the currency.*"

It will be immediately perceived that the conclusion at which Mr. Tooke thus elaborately arrives, involves a manifest inconsistency, not to say a positive contradiction of terms. It is certain that the 5,000,000*l.* advanced by the bank would not be annihilated, and that they would gradually find employment as capital, either at home or abroad. So far Mr. Tooke's reasoning is conclusive. But if the 5,000,000 sovereigns find employment as capital at home, they must "permeate the channels of circulation," increase the amount of the currency, and, as by the supposition the currency had previously been at the par-of-exchange level, must reduce its value, or in other words, enhance prices. And if the 5,000,000*l.* find employment as capital abroad, the same result will have been produced; for the 5,000,000 of sovereigns could not be exported unless their issue by the bank should turn the foreign exchanges against us; and the foreign exchanges could not be rendered adverse unless the currency, as compared with foreign currencies, had been issued in excess, its value reduced, and domestic prices enhanced.

Throughout the whole of his reasoning in support of his position, that banks of issue have not the power of increasing the amount of a convertible currency, Mr. Tooke appears unable to perceive that the effect of convertibility is, not to prevent the occurrence of excess and depreciation, but, on the contrary, to limit and to check excess and depreciation after they have occurred.

After a careful examination of Mr. Tooke's recent publication, I cannot discover any very essential or practical difference between his principles and those of the Birmingham economists. Once deviate from the golden rule of causing the fluctuations of our mixed circulation to conform to what would be the fluctuations of a purely metallic currency and the flood-gates are opened, and the landmarks removed. Between the abandonment of a metallic standard as recommended by the Birmingham economists, and the adoption of arrangements hazarding the maintenance of a metallic standard recommended by Mr. Tooke, the difference in the practicable result might ultimately be nothing.

Though there may be little of practical difference between the Birmingham economists and Mr. Tooke, yet there is a theoretical difference between them. Mr. Tooke is a less consistent reasoner than Mr. Attwood. Mr. Attwood would not bind up, with his own lucubrations, the economical tracts of Mr. Pennington, for the purpose of presenting to the public a second volume of "Gemini." Mr. Tooke, however, delights in heterogeneous masses and incompatible mixtures. In a paper formerly communicated to Mr. Tooke, and also in a letter more recently addressed to Mr. Kirkman Finlay, on the subject of corn and currency, Mr. Pennington urged some objections against the expediency of dividing the business of the Bank of England into a department of issue, and a department of deposit, as advocated by Mr. Loyd, Mr. Norman, and myself. Mr. Tooke appends these papers of Mr. Pennington to his pamphlet on the "Currency Principle," with the following observations:—"As I consider Mr. Pennington's knowledge of the principles and working of the currency to be both profound and accurate, and as my views of the effects of a separation of issue from banking correspond with those which he has stated in the paper here alluded to, I am induced again to insert it, and accordingly refer the reader to it in the Appendix (D), with the addition of some remarks made by him on the letter addressed to me by Colonel Torrens."* In passing this merited encomium upon Mr. Pennington, Mr. Tooke passes a judgment on himself.

* Page 112.

He fails to perceive, that in the papers which he reprints and adopts, Mr. Pennington differs from him in almost every particular, except that of separating the functions of the Bank of England. Mr. Pennington is a distinct and decided supporter of the principle of keeping the issues of the Bank upon securities at a uniform amount, and of allowing the issues upon bullion to expand and contract under the action of the exchanges; and therefore Mr. Pennington must be regarded as being distinctly and decidedly opposed to the views of Mr. Tooke. If Tooke agrees with Pennington, he disagrees with Tooke.

My personal respect for Mr. Tooke renders me desirous of alluding to him in terms more courteous than those which he prof. sely applies to his opponents. He can afford to lose some reputation by his present publication; because, in his "History of Prices," he has a deposit and a book credit with the Bank of Fame, against which he can largely draw.

---

I here reprint, without alteration, the letter and the suggestions regarding the provincial banks of issue which I addressed to Mr. Tooke in 1840.

My dear Sir,

I have read with great interest your valuable publication entitled "A History of Prices, and of the Circulation, in 1838 and 1839." In performing this instructive task, my principal attention was naturally directed to the chapter, "On the proposed "total separation of the business of issuing bank notes from that "of the deposits and other mere banking operations." From the doctrines contained in that chapter I am compelled to dissent. After having reconsidered, with all the attention of which I am capable, the expediency of requiring the Bank of England to effect a total separation between its business as a bank of issue and its business as a bank of deposit and discount, I still adhere to the opinion in favour of that functional separation, which, on a former occasion, I ventured to suggest, and which Mr. Loyd, Mr. Norman, and Mr. Sampson Ricardo, have enforced with such superior ability and knowledge. Under the shelter of these authorities, I shall not be deemed presumptuous if I attempt to reply to the arguments which you have urged against the proposed separation of the business of the Bank of England into two departments, acting independently of each other.

I believe I may assume it as a principle universally admitted, that if banks of issue were to advance one portion of their notes upon securities bearing interest, and were to issue another and a sufficient portion of them by the purchase of treasure; and if they were to keep that portion of their notes which they utter upon securities at a fixed and uniform amount, and to allow that portion which they advance upon treasure to increase or diminish as treasure might flow into or flow out of their coffers, paper currency would be subject to no greater fluctuations in amount and in value than those to which metallic currency is liable. Now the separation of the business of the Bank of England into a department of issue and a department of deposit and discount, would enable the directors of that establishment to keep the securities upon which they issue paper money, at a fixed and uniform amount, and to allow that portion of their issues which is represented by bullion to expand or contract, as the foreign exchanges become favourable or adverse. The separation of the functions of the Bank of England, in the manner which has been proposed, would render the currency of the metropolitan district, except inasmuch as it might be affected by the provincial issues, liable to no fluctuations beyond those to which a purely metallic currency would be liable. Therefore, when you contend that the present system under which the Bank of England conducts its business is preferable to the proposed system of functional separation, you, in effect, maintain that a paper currency " not under a strictly metallic variation " is preferable to a paper currency, contracting and expanding as a metallic currency would contract and expand.

Are you prepared to deny that paper money should be so regulated as to maintain the currency in the same state, with respect to amount and to value, in which it would exist were it exclusively metallic? And if not prepared to controvert the fundamental principle that paper money should invariably conform to its metallic standard, with what consistency can you maintain that an additional amount of paper money may be issued, not in exchange for inflowing treasure, but for the purpose of paying back deposits, or of making advances in the way of discount or loan?

You urge, as an objection to the proposed separation of the functions of the bank, "That it might, under some conceivable "circumstances, be attended with a whimsical effect. Supposing "the deposit department to have no convertible capital beyond "its *rest*, and to have advanced on securities an undue proportion "of its deposits, a sudden demand might, under circumstances of "no improbable occurrence, arise from the depositors, to an extent "beyond that which the reserve of notes or bullion, or of securities "immediately available could satisfy. In such a case the deposit "department might apply to the issuing department for an advance "of bank notes or gold; but the latter department must be sup-"posed inexorable, and so the banking department, under the "same establishment, might stop payment, while the issuing "department would go on as usual."

Now I submit that this supposed case furnishes an illustration, not of the injurious, but of the beneficial consequences which would result from the proposed separation of the functions of the bank. Were the circumstances assumed actually to occur, without the functional separation which has been proposed, not one, but both departments of the bank might stop payment. Let the bank go on advancing its deposits upon securities, until a sudden demand arises from the depositors to an extent beyond that which the reserve of notes, or bullion, or securities, immediately convertible, can satisfy; and let the issuing department create additional supplies of paper money to discharge the liabilities of the deposit department, and the necessary consequences must be, redundant circulation, adverse exchanges, exportation of bullion, and exhausted coffers. I give you your supposed case. I admit, for the sake of the argument, that the bank directors may overtrade to the reckless extent which you have described, and I contend, that the legitimate inference from the admission is, that under the circumstances assumed, the union of functions would occasion a suspension of cash payments.

Your principal objection against the proposed separation is contained in the following passage:—

"If an examination were entered into of the manner in which "the system of separation would have worked, if it had been in "operation in 1835–6, it would be found that, while it would "have presented *no obstacle whatever* to the phenomena of the "low rate of interest, the speculations in shares, and the over-"trading with the United States and the East Indies and China, "and the extravagant credits granted by the American houses, it

" would infallibly, when the turn came (*as it must equally have* " *come*), causing a demand for gold, both for export and for in- " ternal purposes, have been attended with a recoil much more " abrupt and violent than that which was experienced.

" I have before had occasion to observe, that as far as regards " the bank notes in circulation, the amount in 1835–6 was not " above that which would have existed under a separate and me- " tallic variation; while the banking or deposit and discount " department, receiving so very large an accession of deposits as " it then did receive, would equally have invested the same pro- " portion as it did in securities, the same reasons applying. Con- " sequently, the rate of interest would have been as low, and the " facilities of credit, and the motives for making use of it in over- " trading, would equally have existed, without any check from the " issuing department, inasmuch as gold was still flowing in till " an advanced period of the spring of 1836. When, however, " the demand for export of gold arose, such demand, operating " in an immediate contraction of the circulation of bank notes, " would, in all probability, have rendered a considerable proportion " of the immense mass of bills of exchange, both foreign and " inland, inconvertible, except at a very much higher rate of " interest than then prevailed. A sudden decrease of two millions, " from the already low amount of the circulation, would have had " a serious effect on the discount market, and perhaps on com- " mercial credit; an effect much greater than a similar reduction " under the present system."

The conclusions contained in the above passages are, as it appears to me, altogether erroneous. I venture to maintain that, had the system of separation been in operation in 1835–6, it would have presented a very considerable obstacle to the phenomena of the low rate of interest, the speculations in shares, and the over-trading with the United States and the East Indies, and China, and the extravagant credits granted to the American houses. Had the system of separation been in operation in 1835–6, and had the bank directors found it impossible to support the deposit department, by advances from the issuing department, the large accession of deposits which they then received would *not* have been re-advanced upon securities in the same proportion in which they were advanced. The reason seems obvious. While the bank directors are enabled to pay the drafts of their depositors by new issues of paper money, they can, without any immediate danger to the deposit department, advance the whole amount of their deposits upon securities; but were the department of issue separated from that of deposit, the directors, being deprived of the power of meeting the demands of their depositors by new creations of paper money, would be compelled to limit their advances on securities, in order to retain in their coffers a sufficient reserve to meet the demands of their customers. In the one case, the *whole* of the deposits lodged with the bank might be re-advanced to the public in the way of discounts and credits; while, in the other, a *considerable portion* of such deposits would be retained in the coffers of the bank as a reserve, or rest.

The difference between us is this: you contend that the proposed separation of the business of the bank into two distinct departments, would check overtrading in the department of issue, but would not check overtrading in the department of deposit; while I maintain, on the contrary, that the proposed separation would check overtrading in both departments. The manner in which the separation would have this twofold effect will be seen by the following illustrative example:—

Let us assume that the bank holds 18,000,000*l.* of securities, and 9,000,000*l.* of bullion, against 18,000,000*l.* of outstanding notes, and 9,000,000*l.* of deposits; and let an adverse exchange require that the depositors should draw out their deposits in bullion, to the amount of 3,000,000*l.*

In this case, if the business of issue were mixed up with that of deposit, the drawing out of the 3,000,000*l.* of deposits, in bullion, would have no other effect than that of reducing both deposits and bullion by the amount of 3,000,000*l.*, while the amount of the circulation and of the securities, and the power of the bank, as its mercantile securities fell due, to continue the discount business to the same amount as before, would suffer no diminution. But let the department of issue be wholly separated from that of deposit, and the result would be widely different.

As soon as the separation was effected, the deposit department, holding 9,000,000*l.* of deposits with 9,000,000*l.* of securities, would be obliged to sell some portion of its securities, say one-third, in order to be prepared to meet the demands of its depositors. The state of the two departments would then stand thus:—

CIRCULATING DEPARTMENT.

| | |
|---|---|
| Circulation . . . . . . . . | £18,000,000 |
| Securities . . . . . . . . . | 9,000,000 |
| Bullion . . . . . . . . . | 9,000,000 |

DEPOSIT DEPARTMENT.

| | |
|---|---|
| Deposits . . . . . . . . . | £9,000,000 |
| Securities . . . . . . . . | 6,000,000 |
| Reserve, in bank notes . . . . | 3,000,000 |

This being the previous state of things, the demand of the depositors for 3,000,000*l*, of gold would produce the following changes:—The 3,000,000*l*. bank notes held by the deposit department, as reserve, would be drawn out by the depositors, and paid into the circulating department in exchange for gold; while the directors of the deposit department, in order to recover a reserve equal to one third of their deposits, would be obliged to sell 2,000,000*l*. out of the 6,000,000*l*. held in securities. The results would be, that in the circulating department the bullion would be reduced from 9,000,000*l*. to 6,000,000*l*., and the circulation from 18,000,000*l*. to 15,000,000*l*.; and that in the deposit department, the deposits would be reduced from 9,000,000*l*. to 6,000,000*l*.; the securities from 6,000,000*l*. to 4,000,000*l*.; and the reserve from 3,000,000*l*. to 2,000,000*l*.* It is self-evident that the effect of these changes would not be only a contraction of the circulation, but a limitation of the power to over-trade in discount and loans. I must therefore dissent *in toto* from your opinion "That had the system of separation been in operation " in 1835-6, it would have presented no obstacle whatever to the " phenomena of the low rate of interest, the speculation in shares, " and the overtrading with the United States and the East Indies " and China, and the extravagant credits granted to the American " houses."

I have considered, with the respectful attention which your opinions are entitled to command, the plan you propose " for " retaining the present system of union of the two departments of " the bank, with greater security against the risks of suspension." This plan, as it appears to me, does not supply the specific remedy required. The arrangement which you would substitute for functional separation is, that the bank directors, " discarding " the rules which were professed about keeping the securities " even, and of investing, in a full state of the currency, two-thirds " of their liabilities, should undertake to hold in reserve a much

* It is evident that the contraction could never be so great as that assumed in the above illustrative case. Practically, a very moderate contraction would turn the exchanges in our favour.

" higher average amount of bullion than they have hitherto con-
" sidered it necessary or consistent with the interests of their
" proprietors to remain." The grounds of my opinion that this arrangement, considered as a substitute for functional separation, would not be effectual in giving steadiness to the circulation, security to the bank, or encouragement to trade, I will endeavour to explain with as much brevity and distinctness as the nature of the subject will admit.

You propose that the average amount of bullion held by the bank shall not be less than 10,000,000*l.*, and that, while the issue and deposit departments of the bank continue to be blended, as at present, there shall be a latitude for variation in the amount of bullion, between 15,000,000*l.* and 5,000,000*l.* In order to exemplify the operation of this arrangement, let us assume, that while the foreign exchanges are at par, the state of the bank is as follows :

| | | | |
|---|---|---|---|
| Circulation, | £18,000,000 | Securities, | £20,000,000 |
| Deposits, | 12,000,000 | Bullion, | 10,000,000 |
| | £30,000,000 | | £30,000,000 |

This being the previous state of things, let us assume, further, that the foreign exchanges turn in our favour. Bullion will now flow in; and as it flows in, the bank directors, in conformity with your system, must sell securities, and withdraw from circulation the notes paid out in exchange for gold, in order to maintain the favourable exchange, until the amount of bullion in their coffers has reached the maximum of 15,000,000*l.*; the affairs of the bank will then stand thus :—

| | | | |
|---|---|---|---|
| Circulation, | £18,000,000 | Securities, | £15,000,000 |
| Deposits, | 12,000,000 | Bullion, | 15,000,000 |
| | £30,000,000 | | £30,000,000 |

The amount of bullion having now reached the assigned maximum, the directors, ceasing to sell securities, will allow the amount of their circulation to increase by the purchase of the gold flowing in. But, in the absence of other causes, the expansion of the currency, occasioned by the purchase of in-flowing treasure, will not do more than bring the foreign exchange to par. In order to bring the foreign exchange to that state which will allow of the exportation of bullion, and enable them to reduce their treasure to the average amount of 10,000,000*l.*, the directors must now purchase securities for some time after the influx of gold shall have ceased. When the amount of the circulation was 18,000,000*l.*, the value of the currency was so much above the value of the currencies of other countries, that it was profitable to import gold; and it will therefore be necessary to effect an increase in the circulation, say to the amount of 2,000,000*l.*, before the value of the currency can be so far reduced below the value of the currencies of other countries, as to render it profitable to export gold. When this requisite increase of the circulation has been effected, notes will flow in in exchange for bullion, and the treasure in the coffers of the bank will be gradually reduced. But, in conformity with your regulations, the bank directors must continue to purchase securities with the notes they receive in exchange for gold, in order to keep up the drain upon their coffers, until their treasure shall be reduced from 15,000,000*l.* to the average amount of 10,000,000*l.* At this point, however, they may commence precautionary measures, and allow their circulation to contract, by ceasing to re-issue upon securities the amount of paper which they receive in exchange for gold. But the effect of such precautionary measures, in arresting the adverse exchange, could not be instantaneous. When the currency is in excess in relation to the currencies of other countries, the debts due to other countries on account of commodities imported, will exceed the debts due from foreign countries on account of commodities exported; and the liquidation of this balance of debt will keep up the efflux of the metals for a period more or less protracted after the value of the currency has been restored to par. If a currency, redundant in relation to foreign currencies, had caused our imports to exceed our exports by 5,000,000*l.*, then a contraction of the circulation, restoring our currency to the foreign par, could not prevent a further exportation of gold, in order to discharge the balance of foreign debt; because the raising of the value of the currency to an equality with the value of foreign currencies, could have no effect beyond that of preventing a further excess of imports over exports, and consequently a further accumulation of foreign debt. The foreign debt of 5,000,000*l.*, assumed to be already outstanding, would have still to be paid, at least in part, by a further transmission of the metals. Nor could a contraction of the circulation, sufficient to raise the value of our currency above that of foreign currencies, and to cause our exports to exceed our imports, have any immediate effect in arresting the efflux of the metals; because the favourable foreign balance, now gradually accruing, would not fall due in sufficient time to liquidate the unfavourable balance previously incurred. Were the directors of the Bank of England, acting upon the principle you have propounded for their guidance, to allow their reserve of bullion to be reduced from 15,000,000*l.* to the proposed average of 10,000,000*l.*, without effecting a reduction in the circulation, an unfavourable foreign balance, created while the currency remained redundant, might cause a further efflux of the metals, beyond the power of their delayed precaution to control; an unfavourable foreign balance of 6,000,000*l.* might reduce their bullion to 4,000,000*l.*; and an importation of foreign corn, to the amount of 5,000,000*l.*, coincident with such a low amount of bullion, might compel them to stop payment.

To allow the metals to flow in and to flow out, unchecked by a simultaneous expansion and contraction of the circulation, is to resign the power of setting limits to the range of the alternate swell and subsidence of the stream.

When the balance of foreign payments, the exchanges having been previously at par, is turned against us by a sudden and unusual importation of some leading article of consumption, the possession of a large amount of treasure by the bank may render it not actually unsafe to depart for a time from the sound and scientific principles upon which the issue of paper money should be regulated, and to allow gold to flow off without a corresponding contraction of the circulation. Thus, if the bank held bullion to the amount of 10,000,000*l.*, and if the importation of corn created a foreign debt to the amount of 5,000,000*l.*, the transmission of 5,000,000*l.* of treasure might liquidate the foreign debt, and thus, by restoring the exchange to par, obviate the necessity of arresting a further drain, by contracting the circulation.* But very different would be the results were an unfavourable foreign balance created by a convertible currency redundant in relation to foreign currencies. In this case no conceivable amount of treasure, held by the bank, would of itself be sufficient to adjust the international accounts; because, if the efflux of the metals were not accompanied by a corresponding contraction of the circulation, the currency would continue to be of less value than foreign currencies;

* Even in this case the temporary facility afforded to trade by not immediately contracting the circulation, would be more than counterbalanced by the necessity which would subsequently arise of effecting such contraction, in order to enable the bank to restore its bullion to the average amount.

the value of the commodities imported would exceed the value of the commodities exported; and new foreign debts would be contracted as fast as the old ones could be extinguished.

When the currency is in excess, in relation to foreign currencies, the only possible means by which we can avert a suspension of cash payments is, to restore the currency to a par with foreign currencies; and the only practical questions for consideration are, Shall we apply the remedy at an early or at a late period? Shall we, at one time, keep the circulation in excess, while the treasure in the coffers of the bank is sinking from a high maximum to a low minimum; and, at another time, keep the circulation deficient, while the reserve of treasure is rising from a low minimum to a high maximum? or shall we at all times adhere to the principle of allowing the circulation to contract or expand, as the metals ebb or flow, and thus rectify, upon the instant, the first incipient deviations of the currency from the par of the commercial world?

It appeared to me, in perusing the volume under review, that in several instances your conclusions were at variance with each other. But I cannot now wait to examine the specks upon the sun. Having endeavoured to explain the grounds upon which I dissent from your doctrine, as respects the mode of conducting the business of the Bank of England, I cannot deny myself the gratification of alluding to the great majority of economical questions upon which my opinions are supported and confirmed by coincidence with yours.

I am, my dear Sir,

Yours faithfully,

R. TORRENS.

*London, March* 14, 1840.

---

The following suggestions "*for Maintaining the Paper Currency of the Kingdom in the same state in which it would exist were it exclusively Metallic*," were appended to my letter to Mr. Tooke:—

In a former publication on the State of the Money Market and on Bank Reform which I had the honour of addressing to Lord Viscount Melbourne, the following propositions were affirmed, and, as I venture to believe, established:—

*First*,—That paper money should be so regulated as to maintain the currency in the same state, with respect to amount and to value, in which it would exist, were it exclusively metallic.

*Second,*—That, in order to maintain the currency in this sound and healthy state, it is necessary that the amount of paper money in circulation should be made to increase or diminish, under the action of the foreign exchanges, in the same proportions in which the amount of coin in circulation would increase or diminish under the action of the exchanges, if the currency were metallic.

*Third,*—That if banks of issue were to advance one portion of their notes upon securities bearing interest, and another portion by the purchase of treasure; and if they were to keep that portion of their notes which they utter upon securities at a fixed and uniform amount, and to allow that portion of their notes which they advance upon treasure to increase or diminish, as treasure flowed into, or flowed out of, their coffers, paper currency would be subject to no greater fluctuations than those to which metallic currency is liable.

*Fourth,*—That the rule by which the directors of the Bank of England profess to regulate their issues is, not to keep the securities upon which they put out their paper at a uniform amount, and to let their circulation expand and contract under the influence of the exchanges, but, on the contrary, is to keep the whole of their securities, including those upon which they lend their deposits, as well as those upon which they issue their paper, at a uniform amount, and to allow the whole of their liabilities, including their deposits, as well as their circulation, to increase or diminish under the action of the foreign exchanges.

*Fifth,*—That while the directors of the Bank of England continue to act upon a rule which violates the only sound principle upon which paper money can be issued, commercial revulsions, arising out of derangements in the money market, will periodically arrest the prosperity of the country.

I assume the foregoing positions as data, because they have received general assent; and because Mr. Horsley Palmer, in his Defence of the Bank of England, did not venture to controvert them. Those who are acquainted with the business, as well as with the science, of banking, and whose opinions on questions connected with the circulation, are, therefore, entitled to the greatest consideration, concur in condemning the conduct of the directors of the Bank of England, and in urging reform in our monetary system. Mr. Samuel Jones Loyd, in publications evincing that union of practical with speculative ability, by which

Franklin and Ricardo were distinguished, has traced the causes of the recurring derangements in the money market, and has pointed out the means by which those causes may be removed. Public opinion is prepared for bank reform; and the Legislature and the Government have had the path made straight before them.

The great, and, indeed, the only object to be aimed at in reforming our monetary system, is to cause the amount of the paper currency to vary, as the amount of an exclusively metallic currency would vary under similar circumstances. The most simple and efficacious means of attaining this important object would probably be, to confine the issues of paper money to one single establishment, not connected with commerce, and made responsible to Parliament for a strict adherence to the principle of issuing, in the first instance, a prescribed amount of paper, and of then increasing the currency, by purchasing, at the mint price, all the treasure offered, when the exchange should be favourable, and contracting the currency by selling, at the same price, all the treasure demanded when the exchange should be adverse. But the establishment of a single bank of issue, however desirable, had we to legislate upon the subject *de novo*, might be inexpedient and impracticable, now that there have grown up, under legal sanction, numerous banks of issue, the extinction of which might, perhaps, involve an inconvenient and even calamitous change in the established usages and course of business throughout the country. It is probable that the only measure of banking reform which could, under existing circumstances, be brought forward with a reasonable prospect of success, would be, to place the existing banks of issues under such regulations as would secure the constant and uniform application of the cardinal principle, of making the paper currency expand and contract as an exclusively metallic currency would expand or contract, under similar circumstances. The following plan for the regulation of banks of issue, is therefore submitted, not under the presumptuous expectation that the machinery is complete, but in the hope that, should it be found to be constructed upon sound principles, those who possess superior knowledge of business, combined with science, may supply the improvements necessary to render it practically efficacious.*

* The plan here referred to comprised regulations for keeping the paper of the provincial banks, issued upon securities, at a uniform amount; and for allowing their paper, issued upon gold, to vibrate with the exchanges.

# REPLY,

*&c.*

---

The high authority, on all subjects connected with economical inquiry, of the reputed author of the article, 'Currency Question,' in the recent number of the 'Westminster Review,' and the influence which the weight of that authority is calculated to exert upon public opinion, render it expedient, at the present juncture, to examine in careful detail the objections which he has urged against the Government plan for the renewal of the charter of the Bank of England. These objections may be conveniently expressed in the following propositions :—

1st. That it is not in the power of banks of issue, including the Bank of England, to increase the amount of notes in circulation.

2nd. That an increase in the amount of the circulating medium does not increase the purchasing power, which determines the prices of commodities.

3rd. That a total separation of the business of issue from that of banking is calculated to produce greater and more abrupt transitions in the rate of interest, and in the state of commercial credit, than the present system of the union of the departments.

I proceed to examine the validity of these objections in the order in which I have enumerated them.

1st. *On the question—Have Banks of Issue the power of increasing the amount of notes in circulation?*

The following passage presents the grounds upon which the Westminster Reviewer decides that banks of issue have not the power of increasing the circulation:—

"The country bankers unanimously disclaim any arbitrary power over their issues, and declare that in certain states of the markets they *cannot* extend their circulation; if they attempt it, the increase comes back to them, either in deposits or by being presented for payment. They are, it may be said, interested witnesses. But they must mean something by this assertion. It cannot be a mere falsehood. It is confirmed, too, by many persons of the greatest experience, who have no interest in banks of issue,—Mr. Samuel Gurney, for example, and the late Mr. Rothschild. There must be some fact at the bottom of what is asserted. It may be a fact partially stated or misunderstood, and they may be entirely wrong in their explanation of it; but a fact of some sort there must be. We have not seen, on the other side of the question, any attempt to clear up the difficulty, or show the origin of the supposed mistake. We have met with nothing except a flat denial.

"For our own part, we see no incredibility in the assertion of the bankers. We believe it to be in the main correct. It appears to us perfectly consistent with the theory of the subject."

Now it is perfectly true, as stated by the Reviewer in the above passage, that there must be some fact at the bottom of the assertions of the country bankers, and of such disinterested witnesses as Mr. Samuel Gurney and the late Mr. Rothschild. But the fact amounts to nothing more than this,—that there must be two parties to a loan—a party willing to lend, and a party willing to borrow. The country bankers declare, that "in certain states of the market they cannot extend their circulation," which, being interpreted, means, that when no one will borrow no one can lend. This is a proposition which will not be disputed. But it does not touch the real question actually before us. That question is,—Can banks of issue, in those states of the market in which persons of good credit are desirous of obtaining increased accommodation, so increase their issues as to give to the circulation a greater degree of expansion than that which it would receive, under a similar state of trade, were the currency purely metallic? Now this is a question which the country bankers have not answered in the negative. On the contrary, it is a question which they have answered in the affirmative. Mr. Stuckey, the head of the banks of Somersetshire, distinctly states in his evidence, as quoted by Mr. Tooke, that the issues of the country banks "depend upon the state of agriculture;" that when the landed interest is in a comfortable state, he considers the issues to be increased; and that the circulation would not be altered by the foreign exchanges. Now it is quite certain, that were the currency purely metallic, an adverse exchange, withdrawing gold from the coffers of the banks, would contract the circulation; and it follows as a necessary inference, that when the country bankers affirm that they regulate their advances by the state of agriculture, and increase their issues in the teeth of an adverse exchange, they do in point of fact affirm, that they possess the power of so increasing their circulation as to give to the currency a greater degree of expansion than that which it would possess were it purely metallic.

Again, it is not disputed that banks of issue have the power of selling securities. Neither is it disputed that the sale of securities has the effect of causing a *temporary* increase in the amount of the circulation. On this subject the Reviewer quotes, with assent and approval, the following passage from Mr. Tooke's very valuable work, the 'History of Prices:'—

"That an additional issue by the Bank of a million or of five millions on securities would, *cœteris paribus,* reduce the market rate of interest, may be granted; but it is not self-evident, or consistent with experience, that prices of commodities would therefore necessarily rise. The persons who obtained such an increased price for their securities as induced them to sell, would doubtless, upon receiving the money, seek some other investment for it. There might not be, nor would it be likely that there should be, anything in the state of supply and demand in the market of commodities, to induce persons not habitually in them, or so disposed, to speculate in goods; while the probability is, and such has been the course of experience, that as by the supposition, the market rate of interest in this country would by such an operation by the Bank, be depressed below its ordinary rate relatively to other countries, there would be every inducement to individuals who had their capital disengaged to seek investment in securities abroad, whether public or private. As there would not, by the operation of the Bank, be necessarily any additional inducement to export commodities, the capital to be transmitted abroad for such investments would be remitted in bullion. The effect, therefore, of the issue of the million or five millions of bank notes by the Bank, might merely be their return upon the Bank for bullion to be exported. This was, in point of fact, the process in 1834, when the Bank increased its securities by between three and four millions, and reduced its treasure by the same amount; while the markets for commodities, although the rate of interest was low, and the facility of credit complete, were in the most quiescent state possible, and the corn markets falling."—*History of Prices,* vol. iii., pp. 373-4.

I fully agree with the Reviewer that no one would contest the possibility of the case described by Mr. Tooke in the preceding passage. But I contend that the occurrence of such a case would furnish a perfect proof that banks of issue possess the power of giving to the circulation a *temporary* expansion greater than that which could take place were the currency regulated upon the metallic principle. Why should the five millions of notes issued upon securities "be returned upon the Banks for bullion to be exported?" Simply because they had been issued in excess. The fact, that the Bank *may issue in excess,* is adduced in the case put by Mr. Tooke as a proof that the Bank *has not the power to issue in excess.* No advocate of the metallic principle ever contended that the power of issuing convertible paper can give to the currency a *permanent* expansion greater than that which it would possess were it purely metallic. What they contend for is, that when the Bank fails to keep its issues upon securities at a uniform amount, it produces a *temporary* excess in the circulation, requiring that bullion should be withdrawn from its coffers for exportation. This is the doctrine which they hold; and Mr. Tooke, in the passage quoted by the Reviewer, affirms its correctness in terms the most distinct and unequivocal.

I think the able Reviewer will perceive that the argument upon which he founds his objections to the Government plan for the regulation of the currency involves the admission of the fact, that the Bank has the power of causing a *temporary* extension of the circulation beyond that which would occur were it exclusively metallic. Under an exclusively metallic circulation the Bank of England would be a bank of deposit and discount; and when an adverse exchange caused a portion of its deposits to be withdrawn for exportation, it would be compelled to sell so much of its securities as might be necessary to maintain a safe proportion betweeen its reserve and its liabilities. Now, under the Government plan of a separation of functions, the deposit department will be compelled to act on the self-same principle. When an adverse exchange acts upon its deposits, it will no longer be able to recruit its reserve by aid from the department of issue, and will be compelled, in the same way as if the circulation were wholly metallic, to sell a portion of its securities, and thus to contract the circulation in the hands of the public. To this the Reviewer objects. He says, "under the proposed system, the department of deposit must rest upon its own resources. The reserve in the deposit department could derive no aid from the issue department; while it would have to bear the first brunt of the whole action intended to be exercised through it upon the latter. As it would be prohibited from meeting this demand *by creating more notes,* or even by having the notes which it paid out, and which then went to the issue department for gold, returned to it, either the reserve of the deposit department alone will require to be as great as is now requisite for the deposits and issues together, or it will be compelled *to suspend its discounts and sell its securities* much earlier and more abruptly than is necessary under the present mixed system."

It will not be disputed that this objection turns upon the admission of the fact, that under the present mixed system the Bank possesses the power of "meeting a demand by creating more notes," and of thus maintaining, *for a time,* a more extended circulation than that which would exist under a purely metallic currency. This, I repeat, is all that the advocates of the metallic principle have ever contended for. They have never for a moment imagined that banks of issue possess the power of so forcing out their notes as to give to the currency, while convertible into gold upon demand, a *permanent* expansion greater than that at which a purely metallic currency could be maintained.

2nd. *On the question—Can an increase in the circulation cause an increase in the power of purchasing which determines prices?*

Having thus shown, as I venture to believe, that under the existing system, the Bank has the power of causing a temporary extension of the circulation, I proceed to the consideration of the further question—Whether a temporary increase of the circulation can have the effect of causing a temporary increase in the power of purchasing, which determines the prices of commodities? In reference to this question, the Reviewer says, "It will at once be seen that the controversy involves a very important question in the theory of currency; one, indeed, which has not to our knowledge been subjected to thorough examination, or put precisely in issue before. This question is—With what limitations, if any, the proposition is true, that an increase in the quantity of the currency raises prices?" This remark of the scientific Reviewer appears to be perfectly just. In endeavouring to arrive at a correct solution of the important question which he has raised, I will present his views of the subject in his own words, and then proceed to explain the grounds upon which I feel myself compelled to dissent from his opinions.

"The purchasing power of an individual at any moment is not measured by the money actually in his pocket, whether we mean by money the metals, or include bank notes. It consists, first, of the money in his possession; secondly, of the money at his banker's, and all other money due to him and payable on demand; thirdly, of whatever credit he happens to possess. To the full measure of this three-fold amount he has the power of purchase. How much he will employ of this power depends upon his necessities, or, in the present case, upon his expectations of profit. Whatever portion of it he does employ, constitutes his demand for commodities, and determines the extent to which he will act upon price.

"Now, of these three elements of money demand, the first alone is grounded upon a corresponding amount of money actually *in esse*. The second, or the deposit at his banker's, is in part grounded upon actual money, namely, to the extent of about one-third, that being the proportion which prudent bankers profess to keep in their coffers to meet the drafts of their depositors. The third element of money demand, namely credit, has no basis of actually existing money at all. It is an additional money demand, created over and above that which is constituted by all the money in actual circulation. But it is exactly as operative upon prices as the money itself, provided the possessor chooses to make use of the purchasing power which it confers. This explains why periods of general confidence, when large prospects of gain seem to be opening themselves, and when there is a disposition among dealers to employ not only all their money but all or much of their credit in enlarging their operations, are attended with so great a rise of general prices. The effect is sometimes ascribed to the bills of exchange and other transferable paper which these transactions generate, and which are said to perform the functions of currency. Those who use this language mistake the effect for the cause. Bills of exchange are mere evidences of credit. The credit itself is the operating cause. It is manifest that when buyers are willing to employ their credit as well as their money in making purchases, their demand for commodities becomes so much greater, and prices must rise. They would rise if no such thing as a transferable acknowledgment of debt had ever been known in the country.

"If the views now stated be sound, it seems not easy to understand how an increased creation of the written evidences of credit called bank notes, can, of itself, create an additional demand, or occasion a rise of price. Admitting bank notes to be money (which is, in truth, a mere question of language), what does the person do who issues them, but take so much from the third element of purchasing power, namely, credit, and add it to the first element, money in hand—making no addition whatever to the total amount? More properly, he merely converts so much credit from an unwritten into a written, and from a cumbrous into a convenient, form. Bank notes are to credit precisely what coin is to bullion; the same thing, merely rendered portable and minutely divisible. We cannot perceive that they add anything, either to the aggregate of purchasing power, or to the portion of that power in actual exercise."

Such is the reasoning by which the Reviewer supports his position, that an increase in the amount of the circulation has no effect in raising general prices. It appears to me that it involves an obvious fallacy. I fully agree with the Reviewer, while he maintains that the purchasing power of an individual is not measured by the money in his pocket, whether we mean by money the metals, or include bank notes;—that it consists, first, of the money in his possession; secondly, of the money at his banker's, and all other money due to him and payable on demand; and thirdly, of whatever credit he happens to possess; and that to the full measure of this three-fold amount he has the power of purchasing. But while I travel thus far with the Reviewer, I part company with him at the point at which he affirms the propositions,—"that, admitting bank notes to be money, the person who issues them does nothing more than take so much from the third element of purchasing power, namely, credit, and add it to the first element, money in hand; and that bank notes cannot add anything either to the aggregate purchasing power, or to the portion of that power actually in exercise." From these propositions I entirely dissent. I maintain the directly opposite position, that an increased issue of bank notes not only increases the element of purchasing power which consists of money in hand, but also increases, it may be in a much greater proportion, the element which consists of credit.

I proceed to explain the grounds upon which I dissent from the doctrines advanced by the Reviewer; and I enter the more willingly upon the task, because I entertain the conviction that, should my reasoning be erroneous, his superior lights will show me where my error lies; and that, should my conclusions prove correct, the unbiassed love of truth, which is the moving power in the mind of this eminent thinker, will draw him to my side. It seems altogether unlikely that we should continue to discuss the important question at issue without coming to an agreement upon it.

Metallic money performs a double function—it constitutes the element of purchasing power which consists of money in hand; and it forms the basis of a large portion of the element of purchasing power which consists of credit. The manner in which money supports a superstructure of credit, and in which every increase in the quantity of money may cause an extension of credit, I will endeavour to exemplify.

Let us assume the existence of a district possessing 1,000,000*l*. in coin, and having only one bank of deposit and discount, with which the whole of the monied class keep their cash, and through which they make their payments; and let us assume further, that the bank, while holding 1,000,000*l*. in coin, discounts bills and opens cash credits to the amount of 2,000,000*l*. Now it is evident that in this case the 1,000,000 sovereigns deposited with the bank perform a double function. They constitute a money-in-hand power of purchasing, as regards the original depositors, who may draw them out on demand; and they form the basis of the credit-power of purchasing, which the holding of them enables the banker to extend to the customers to whom he grants discounts and cash credits.

Let us now suppose that the money of the district is increased from 1,000,000*l*. to 1,500,000*l*., and that the whole is deposited with the bank as before. The banker now finds himself at liberty to increase the amount of his advances to his customers, while the state of trade renders his customers desirous of obtaining further accommodation; and consequently discounts and book-credits are extended, until the proportion between the banker's reserve and his liabilities again becomes as one to three. The money-in-hand power of purchasing is thus increased from 1,000,000*l.* to 1,500,000*l.*, while the credit-power of purchasing is also increased from 2,000,000*l.* to 3,000,000*l.*

It cannot be contended that in this case the increase in the power of purchasing conferred on those to whom increased discounts and book-credits have been granted, is obtained by a diminution of the credit-power previously existing, so as to leave the aggregate power of purchasing the same as before. It is self-evident, that those who have deposited 1,500,000*l.* of gold with the bank, and who are at liberty to draw it out upon demand, have a ready-money power to the amount of 1,500,000*l.*; and it is also self-evident, that those who have obtained discount and book-credits to the amount of 3,000,000*l.*, and who can draw checks against them to an equivalent amount, can now effect ready-money purchases to the extent of 3,000,000*l.* Equally evident is it, that their increased power of making purchases by checks payable to bearer on demand has in no way diminished any power which the parties may have previously possessed of purchasing goods upon credit. A directly contrary effect would probably be produced. The fact of their being able to obtain increased accommodation from the bank would be calculated, not to diminish but rather to increase the public confidence in their available resources, and thus to enable them to obtain a greater quantity of goods upon credit than before.

Let us now vary our illustration. Let us assume that our banker, finding that he has 1,500,000*l.* in gold lying unproductive in his coffers, determines to convert his establishment into a bank of issue; and that, in pursuance of this design, he disposes of one million of sovereigns in the purchase of government securities, and replaces them by creating one million of notes convertible upon demand.

Now these alterations can have no conceivable effect in reducing the aggregate power of purchasing in our district. The creation of the bank notes, though issued upon the credit of the bank, will not be a deduction from the credit-power of purchasing possessed by the customers of the bank. They have now, as they had before, the power of effecting by checks against their book-credits ready-money payments to the amount of 3,000,000*l.*; and they have now, as they had before, the power of obtaining goods upon credit to the extent of the confidence reposed in their stability. It is self-evident, too, that those who have deposited their cash with the banker to the original amount of 1,500,000*l.*, and who may draw it out upon demand, retain undiminished their original ready-money power of purchasing to that amount. As regards the amount of the purchasing power which determines prices, the effects of an increase in a purely metallic circulation, and the effects of an increase in a convertible paper circulation, are in the strictest sense identical.

Let us now take another illustration. Let us assume that a period of unusual confidence occurs; that there is an expectation of increased demand and of a general rise of prices, and a consequent increased desire to effect purchases throughout our district. Now it will be apparent that although, under these circumstances, there will be an increased desire to effect purchases, yet (the whole of the money of the district being by the supposition kept at the bank) the power of making immediate payment must be limited to the amount of checks payable upon demand which the original depositors, and those who have obtained discounts and cash credits, can draw upon the bank. But it will now be in the power of the banker to enlarge this limit. He may meet the wishes of his customers by extending his discounts and book-credits; and he may maintain the due proportion between his liabilities and his reserve, by an additional creation of notes. Previous to the occurrence of the increased activity of trade, his reserve consisted of

500,000*l.* in gold, and 1,000,000*l.* of bank notes; and his liabilities of 1,500,000*l.* of original deposits, and of 3,000,000*l.* of secondary deposits, represented by discounted bills and book-credits. If he now creates additional notes to the amount of 200,000*l.* and extends his discounts and cash-credits by 600,000*l.*, his reserve will bear the same proportion to his liabilities as before; namely, that of 1 to 3. On this being effected, the aggregate power of purchasing in the district will be increased by 600,000*l.* No one will have less power of purchasing than before; while those who obtain the increased amount of accommodation by discounts and book-credits, will have acquired an increased power of effecting immediate payments to the extent of the increased accommodation afforded by the banks, without suffering any diminution of the power which they previously possessed of obtaining goods upon credit.

It may be here objected, that the increased power of effecting immediate payments acquired by those who have obtained the increased discounts and book-credits from the bank, has its origin, not in the creation of the additional notes, but simply in the additional credit which the bank accords; that this additional credit might have been accorded without any additional creation of notes; and that therefore the whole process resolves itself into this—that the bank transfers to its customers, under the form of a money-in-hand power of purchasing, a portion of the credit-power of purchasing which it previously possessed.

This objection goes directly to the root of the question under consideration; and it might be regarded as a valid objection, *provided it were a fact, that banks of issue could secure the safety of their establishment without maintaining a due proportion between their reserves and their liabilities.* But the fact is otherwise, and therefore the objection is invalid.

In the cases which we have hitherto taken for illustration,

we have assumed, in order to avoid complicated statements of figures, that all persons keep their money with the bank, and that all payments are effected by checks and by transfers in the banker's books; and, therefore, in these cases the necessity of increasing the amount of the banker's reserve with every increase in his liabilities does not very prominently appear. This necessity will become immediately manifest if we will trace the process which takes place in all those actual cases in which a portion of the circulation is held by persons not employing a banker.

We will take for our first illustrative example, a district containing a purely metallic circulation of 2,000,000*l.*, one-half of which is deposited with the bank by the bank-dealing portion of the monied class; while the other half is in the hands of the non-bank-dealing portion of that class. In this case, half the checks drawn by the bank-dealers will be paid away to the non-bank-dealers, and drawn out by them; while half the payments of the non-bank-dealers will be made to the bank-dealers in cash, which cash will be returned by them into the bank; so that one-half of the money of the district will, upon the average, be in the coffers of the bank.

This being the previous state of things, let us assume that a period of commercial excitement occurs, and that the banker accommodates his customers with discounts and book-credits to the amount of 1,000,000*l.* This, in the first instance, would increase by 1,000,000*l.* the money-in-hand power of purchasing possessed by the bank-dealers to whom the accommodation is afforded; while that possessed by the non-bank-dealers remains, as before, at 1,000,000*l.* But as one-half of the incomes and property of the district is in the hands of the non-bank-dealers, the non-bank-dealers will receive one-half of the larger payments made by the bank-dealers who have obtained the accommodation; while the latter will be the recipients of one-half of the smaller payments made by the former. The bank-dealers will continue to pay more than they receive; and more cash will be drawn out of, than returned to, the bank, until the money and the credits representing money become equally distributed between the two equally monied sections of the district. The money statistics would then be as follows:—

*Status as regards Bank-Dealers.*

| | £. |
|---|---|
| Original Deposits, against which Checks may be drawn. . | 1,000,000 |
| Secondary Deposits remaining after one moiety of the advances by the Bank were withdrawn by Non-Bank-Dealers, to whom checks had been given . . . . . . | 500,000 |
| | 1,500,000 |

*Status as regards Non-Bank-Dealers.*

| | |
|---|---|
| Coin in the hands of the Public . . . . . . . | 1,500,000 |

*Status of the Bank.*

| Assets. | £. | Liabilities. | £. |
|---|---|---|---|
| Reserve of Coin after the withdrawal of £500,000 by Non-Bank-Dealers. . . | 500,000 | Original Deposits . . | 1,000,000 |
| Securities . . . . | 1,000,000 | Secondary deposits, after the withdrawal of £500,000 by Non-Bank-Dealers . . . | 500,000 |
| | 1,500,000 | | 1,500,000 |

Here it will be seen that the banker's reserve bears to his liabilities what the Reviewer regards as a safe proportion, namely, of 1 to 3. But should the banker, in compliance with the continued desire of his customers for increased accommodation, extend his discounts and book-credits to 2,000,000*l*., not only would the safe proportion between reserve and liabilities be destroyed, but the whole of the reserve would pass from the coffers of the bank into the hands of the non-bank-dealing public. In this case, as in that just detailed, the amount of cash drawn out of the bank would exceed the amount paid into it, until the power of effecting immediate payments should be equally distributed between the bank-dealing and the non-bank-dealing classes. On this equality being established, the status of the bank would be as follows:—

| Assets. | £. | Liabilities. | £. |
|---|---|---|---|
| Reserve . . . . . | 000,000 | Original Deposits . . | 1,000,000 |
| Securities . . . . | 2,000,000 | Secondary, after half the advances of the Bank were drawn out by Non-Bank-Dealers . | 1,000,000 |
| | 2,000,000 | | 2,000,000 |

The illustrations which have now been given will be sufficient to present a distinct view of the manner in which the advances of banks must be regulated and controlled, by the proportion which they may be able to maintain between their reserves and their liabilities. That a due proportion between reserves and liabilities must be maintained by every banker who would secure the safety of his establishment, is a proposition respecting which no controversy can be raised. The only question at issue (and it is indeed the pivot question on which the main difference between the Reviewer and myself would seem to turn), is, whether the power of creating notes convertible upon demand enables banks of issue to keep up, for some limited period, a larger reserve than that which, were the circulation exclusively metallic, banks of deposit and discount would, under similar states of the market, be enabled to maintain. If this question can be correctly answered in the affirmative, the Reviewer will not continue to contend that banks of issue cannot increase the purchasing power which determines the prices of commodities.

We resume our former illustration. The banker has, as specified in the former case, granted discounts and other credits to his customers, to the amount of 1,000,000*l.*, and holds a reserve of 500,000*l.* against his liabilities of 1,500,000*l.*; while the bank-dealers have the power of drawing checks against their deposits and credits to the amount of 1,500,000*l.*, and while the non-bank-dealers have in their hands coin amounting also to 1,500,000*l.* These being the previous circumstances, and the activity of trade, and the desire to obtain additional accommodation continuing, the banker determines on complying with the wishes of his customers, by granting additional discounts and credits to the amount of another 1,000,000*l*. The state of the foreign exchanges, however, deprives him of the power of increasing his reserve of coin, so as to maintain it at the requisite proportion to his liabilities. He overcomes the difficulty by converting his establishment into a bank of issue, and recruits his reserve by a creation of promissory notes, convertible upon demand. Under these operations the amount of coin and of notes withdrawn from the bank will, in the manner already explained, exceed the amount returned to it, until the money in the hands of the non-bank-dealers becomes proportionate to the checks which the bank-dealers are empowered to draw against their deposits. By the supposition, the proportion between the incomes and property of the two classes is that of equality; and therefore one moiety of the additional advances afforded by the banker to the bank-dealers, will be paid over to the non-bank-dealers, and will be drawn out by them. On this being effected, the following will be the monetary statistics of the district:—

*Status of the Bank.*

| In its Coffers. | £. | Liabilities. | £. |
|---|---|---|---|
| Gold . . . . . . | 100,000 | Original Deposits . . | 1,000,000 |
| Notes . . . . . . | 600,000 | Secondary, after deducting the moiety of credit drawn out by Non-Bank-Dealers | 1,000,000 |
| Securities . . . . . | 2,000,000 | Notes in the hands of the Public . . . | 100,000 |
| | 2,700,000 | | 2,100,000 |

*Status of Bank-Dealers.*

| | £. |
|---|---|
| Original Credit on account of Deposits . . . . . | 1,000,000 |
| Secondary Credits, after deducting from the 2,000,000*l*. of Credits opened by the Bank the 1,000,000*l*. drawn out by Non-Bank-Dealers . . . . . . . . | 1,000,000 |
| | 2,000,000 |

*Status of Non-Bank-Dealers.*

| | |
|---|---|
| Coin . . . . . . . . . . . . | 1,900,000 |
| Bank Notes . . . . . . . . . . . | 100,000 |
| | 2,000,000 |

It will be seen, by a reference to these figures, that the bank, by issuing 600,000*l*. to the public in its promissory notes, has been enabled to maintain the due proportion of 1 to 3 between its reserve and its liabilities, while increasing by 1,000,000*l*. the power of purchasing which determines prices. The non-bank-dealers and the bank-dealers have each acquired an increased power of effecting immediate payments to the extent of 500,000*l*.; while neither class has suffered any diminution of its previously existing power of obtaining goods upon credit.

It will also be apparent that the bank could not have created this increased power of purchasing, had it been restricted from issuing notes. Under a state of the foreign exchanges causing an efflux, or even preventing an influx of the precious metals, it could not, as a bank of deposit and discount, have increased its discounts and book-credits without unduly reducing its reserve.

Had our bank, while acting only as a bank of discount and deposit, extended its discounts and credits from 1,000,000*l*. to 2,000,000*l*., the whole of its treasure would have passed, in the manner which has been already shown, into the hands of the non-bank-dealing public. In this status it might, it is true, have continued to transfer book-credits from one bank-dealer to another; but upon the presentation of the first check which might have passed into the hands of a non-bank-dealer, it must have suspended its payments, and the whole superstructure of credit which had rested on the base of a duly proportioned reserve would have been at once destroyed.

The illustrations which I have now given will be sufficient to explain the essential difference which exists between bank notes and the forms of credit which are represented by checks and bills of exchange. Bank notes are, by law or by custom, the immediate substitutes of coin: though they are not money in the strictly scientific sense, yet, practically considered, they perform the functions of money, inasmuch as they are the instruments by which balances are adjusted, and transactions finally closed. They are, Sir William Clay has happily expressed it in his very instructive publication upon the currency, the feet upon which checks and bills of exchange are enabled to travel. The argument might be further pursued; but on the present occasion I will not further pursue it, because, should the views which I have attempted to present be correct, the very able and the very candid Reviewer will at once perceive and at once admit their correctness.

3rd. *On the question—Is a total separation of the business of issue from that of banking calculated to produce greater and more abrupt fluctuations in the rate of interest and the state of commercial credit than the present system of union of departments?*

The Westminster Reviewer concurs in the conclusion sought to be established by Mr. Tooke,—that the Government measure for the renewal of the Charter of the Bank of England will cause more sudden and violent fluctuations in the rates of interest, and in the state of commercial credit, than those which have resulted from the existing system. The grounds upon which he adopts this conclusion are stated by the Reviewer in the following passage:—

"It is a fact, attested by experience, that a drain of gold upon the bank for exportation takes place, in most cases, mainly by drawing out deposits. As in the proposed system there is nothing to cause any change in this respect, we must suppose that this would still be the case, and that the demand for gold would be first felt in the deposit department.

"Now, under the present arrangements, in case of a run upon the deposits, the bank has to rely, not only on the portion of reserve which it retains, like other bankers, against the deposits themselves, but also on the gold in reserve on account of its issues. Until all the gold in possession of the bank is exhausted, it is in no danger of stopping payment. But under the proposed system, the department of deposit must rest upon its own resources. The reserve in the deposit department could have no aid from the issue department, while it would have to bear the first brunt of the whole action intended to be exercised through it upon the latter. As it would be prohibited from meeting this demand by creating new notes, or even by having the notes which it paid out, and which went to the issue department for gold returned to it, either the reserve of the deposit department alone will require to be as great as is now requisite for the deposits and issues together, or it will be obliged to suspend its discounts, and sell its securities, much earlier and more abruptly than is necessary under the present mixed system. If the demand for gold were to the extent of three or four millions, no merchant, banker, or money-dealer could, for a moment, have a doubt as to the extremity of the pressure which would ensue. While the circulating department was still abundantly supplied with gold, the deposit department might have no alternative but to stop payment."

For these reasons the Reviewer concurs with Mr. Tooke, that "in the main difference (next to solvency and convertibility) between one banking system and another, namely, the greater or less liability to abrupt changes in the rate of interest and the state of commercial credit, the present arrangements, under the condition of a larger bank reserve, have a decided advantage over the new system."

The reasoning by which the Reviewer arrives at this conclusion proves too much. It involves the affirmation of two very startling propositions, namely, that a purely metallic currency is more liable to abrupt fluctuation than a convertible paper currency; and that under the proposed separation of functions, the deposit department of the Bank of England will be less secure than the private banks of the metropolis hitherto have been. The first logician of the age will admit that if these propositions are untenable, some fallacy must lurk in the reasoning from which they are deduced.

Were the currency purely metallic, the Bank of England, no longer possessing a department of issue, would be a joint stock bank of deposit and discount, with the command of an enormous capital; and would be, to all intents and purposes, in the same state and condition in which its deposit department will be placed, upon the adoption of the proposed separation of functions. Assuming that under a purely metallic circulation the Bank of England might hold 15,000,000*l*. of deposits, and that it should act upon the rule which the Reviewer states to be that adopted by prudent bankers, of maintaining the proportion of one-third between its reserve and its liabilities, then its status would be as follows:—

| Liabilities. | | Assets. | | |
|---|---|---|---|---|
| | £. | | £. | £. |
| Deposits . . . . | 15,000,000 | Securities | 10,000,000 | 15,000,000 |
| | | Coin . . | 5,000,000 | |

An adverse exchange now occurs, and the customers of the bank draw out their deposits to the amount of 3,000,000*l*. This reduces both liabilities and assets from 15,000,000*l*. to 12,000,000*l*.; while the reserve, instead of bearing the proportion of one-third, bears that of only one-sixth to the liabilities. The bank directors, in order to restore the safe proportion, sell securities to the amount of 2,000,000*l*., and then the status of the bank consequently becomes—

| Liabilities. | | Assets. | | |
|---|---|---|---|---|
| | £. | | | £. |
| Deposits . . . . | 12,000,000 | Securities | 8,00,0000 | 12,000,000 |
| | | Coin . . | 4,000,000 | |

Now these results will be found to coincide in every

particular with those which would be produced by an adverse exchange, under the Government arrangements for rendering the deposit department independent of the department of issue. Let us assume that upon the separation of departments, the deposit department holds 15,000,000*l*. of deposits, with 10,000,000*l*. of securities, and a reserve of 5,000,000*l*. of notes; and that while this is the previously existing status, an adverse exchange causes the depositors to draw out 3,000,000*l*. of notes, in order to return them to the department of issue, in exchange for bullion for exportation.

In this, as in the former case, the deposit department, in order to preserve the due proportion between its liabilities and its reserve, will sell 2,000,000*l*. of its securities; in this case, as in the former, its deposits will be reduced from 15,000,000*l*. to 12,000,000*l*.; and in this case, as in the former, the circulation in the hands of the public will be reduced by 2,000,000*l*. Therefore if the fluctuation in the rate of interest and in the state of commercial credit would be more abrupt and violent under a separation of departments than under the existing system, it follows as a necessary consequence, that these fluctuations would be more violent and abrupt under a purely metallic currency than under the existing system. I cannot but think that this is a proposition which the able Reviewer would hesitate to affirm.

Again, after the separation of functions, the business of the deposit department of the Bank of England will be conducted on the same principles as the numerous private banks of deposit in the metropolis. Private banks, acting on the principle of keeping their reserves at one-third of their liabilities, are not endangered, because their customers, on the occurrence of an unfavourable exchange, draw out a portion of their deposits in order to procure bullion for exportation. If a private banker having 1,200,000*l*. of deposits, 800,000*l*. of securities, and 400,000*l*. of reserve, should have 300,000*l*. withdrawn from his coffers, he would sell securities or diminish discounts to the amount of 200,000*l*., and would be in no greater danger of stopping payment while holding, as he would now do, 900,000*l*. of deposits, 600,000*l*. of securities, and 300,000*l*. of reserve, than he was in while holding 1,200,000*l*. of deposits, 800,000*l*. of securities, and 400,000*l*. of reserve. On what principle, then, can it be contended, that after the separation of functions the deposit department of the Bank of England will be in danger of stopping payment from the operation of causes which are found in no way to endanger the stability of a well-regulated private bank?

The argument in support of the proposition, that the separation of departments will occasion greater fluctuations in the rate of interest and in the state of commercial credit than those which occur under the existing system of union, must be held to be fallacious, because it involves conclusions obviously at variance with facts.

I proceed to present the more direct evidence against the correctness of the conclusion adopted by the Reviewer, that, under the proposed arrangements for the regulation of the currency, the fluctuations in the rate of interest, and in the state of commercial credit, will be greater than they have been under the existing system of a union of departments.

Fluctuations in the rate of interest, and in the state of commercial credit, so far as they are connected with the alternate expansions and contractions of the currency, are produced by the action of the foreign exchanges in causing an alternate influx and efflux of the precious metals.

An adverse exchange, causing bullion to be withdrawn from the coffers of the bank for exportation, may be produced by two distinct and very different causes: it may be produced by an undue increase in the amount of the currency, reducing the value of money in the home market below what may be called the trade-of-barter level; or it may be produced without any increase in the amount of the currency, and without any general rise of prices in the home market, by any alteration in the state of our commercial relations which should create in the British market an increased demand for foreign productions without creating in foreign markets an equivalent increase in the demand for British goods. An adverse exchange, resulting from the latter of these causes, is that which is most favourable to the side of the question espoused by the Reviewer; I will, therefore, in the first instance, proceed to show that, on the occurrence of an unfavourable balance of payments, originating not from an extension of the currency, but from an extraordinary importation of some leading article of consumption, the fluctuations in the rate of interest and in the state of credit would be far less considerable under the proposed than under the existing system.

I take the following illustrative case:—The currency is at par with foreign currencies; exports balance imports; the departments of deposit and issue continue united; the Bank acts upon the rule of keeping a large reserve of bullion, and of allowing it to fluctuate from 15,000,000*l.* to 5,000,000*l.*, and it has in actual possession the medium amount of 10,000,000*l.*

This being the previous state of things, a deficient harvest turns the exchanges against us, and a foreign debt to the amount of 5,000,000*l.* is incurred. Gold is now demanded for exportation; the demand is mainly supplied by drawing out deposits from the Bank; the directors, disregarding the principle of allowing the currency to contract as treasure is abstracted from their coffers, keep their circulation undiminished; the rate of interest is not raised; the general scale of prices is not reduced; and the foreign debt is liquidated by the transmission of 5,000,000*l.* of gold without any sensible disturbance in the money market or in the state of commercial credit having been occasioned.

This would be a safe and pleasant process were the Bank Directors possessed of the wishing-cap of Fortunatus, and could they waft back, by a volition, the treasure withdrawn from their coffers. But a painful re-action must now be induced: the bullion in the Bank is reduced to the minimum of 5,000,000*l.*; another deficient harvest might bring the establishment to the verge of insolvency; decisive measures are imperatively called for to turn the exchanges in our favour, and bring back the gold. The rate of interest is now raised; money is made scarce; speculation in commodities is checked; prices fall; exports overbalance imports; and, during the commercial inactivity and depression of trade thus induced, gold again flows in. But the screw cannot yet be relaxed. It is essentially necessary, in order to ensure the immediate convertibility of the bank note upon demand, that the Bank should provide an amount of treasure sufficiently large to give scope to the recurring oscillations of the foreign exchanges. The rate of interest is kept high, and prices are kept low, and commercial depression is continued until the bullion in the coffers of the Bank has accumulated to the maximum amount of 15,000,000*l.*

During this protracted period of commercial revulsion the evil would fall with aggravated severity upon the agricultural districts. When the supply of an article so indispensably necessary as corn falls short, its price rises in a considerably greater proportion than that in which its quantity is diminished. Hence, as I have elsewhere explained, when a deficient harvest occurs, the agricultural districts, though supplying the metropolis and other towns with a smaller quantity of produce than before, will have a larger amount of money to receive: the balance of payments as between metropolitan and country dealers is turned in favour of the latter, and cash accounts to a greater amount than ordinary are held by the London for the provincial banks. Under these circumstances the provincial circulation expands in the teeth of the adverse exchange; the agriculturists, in the expectation of a continued advance in prices, are desirous of obtaining increased accommodation in order to be enabled to hold back their produce; while the country bankers, confident in the improving prospects of the farmer, are willing to afford the desired advances, and the expansion of the currency and the progressive advances create a fictitious and delusive prosperity throughout the agricultural districts. But the excitement induced by the artificial stimulus is the precursor—the admonitory symptom—of a dangerous collapse. The higher range of prices (again to repeat myself) maintained by the increased accommodation necessarily occasions an increased importation of foreign corn; this increased importation increases the amount of the unfavourable balance of foreign payments, prolongs the drain upon the coffers of the Bank of England, and compels that establishment to protect itself by more stringent measures for the contraction of the currency. Ultimately, but inevitably, and at no distant interval, the contraction of the provincial currencies conforms to the contraction of the central currency, in which all balances are adjusted. An increased glut of foreign corn, an increased scarcity of money, and a diminished amount of credit, at the very moment when credit is most required, are the equivalents which the farmer now must pay for the delusive advantage which in the first instance he derived from a currency prevented from duly conforming to the par-of-exchange level.

Such, as experience has too frequently proved, are the ruinous effects, as regards the state of commercial credit and the state of agriculture, which, under the existing system, are produced by the occurrence of an unfavourable balance of foreign payments. Let us now contrast these effects with those which, on the occurrence of an unfavourable foreign balance, may be expected to result from the adoption of the Government plan for the reform of our banking system.

We take the following illustrative case:—The functions

of issue and of deposit (issues upon securities being kept at a uniform amount) are rendered independent of each other; the deposit department of the Bank of England holds 15,000,000*l.* of deposits, and 5,000,000*l.* of reserve; an extraordinary importation of corn creates a foreign debt of 5,000,000*l.*; deposits are drawn out in order to be returned to the department of issue in exchange for gold.

Under the circumstances thus assumed, the following process would take place. As deposits were withdrawn the Bank would sell securities, in order to preserve the safe proportion of 1 to 3 between its reserve and its liabilities. The withdrawal of deposits to the amount of 1,000,000*l.*, would be followed by a sale of securities to the amount of 666,666$\frac{2}{3}$*l.*, and these changes would reduce the deposits from 15,000,000*l.* to 14,000,000*l.*, the reserve from 5,000,000*l.* to 4,666,666$\frac{2}{3}$*l.*, the bullion in the issue department by 1,000,000*l.*, and the notes in the hands of the public by 666,666*l.*

Other changes would follow. The sale of securities would have some effect in varying the rate of interest, and in causing a withdrawal of capital from foreign investments, while the contraction of the currency would have, to a certain extent, a two-fold action in reducing prices—first, by directly diminishing the money-in-hand power of purchasing possessed by the public; secondly, by indirectly diminishing that power by reducing the balances of the private bankers, and thus warning them to be more abstemious in their discounts.

In the agricultural districts analogous charges would be produced. The provincial banks would be no longer able to increase their issues in the teeth of an adverse exchange; and this limitation to the amount of the currency would enhance the value of money in the provinces, and prevent the price of corn from rising as high as it would otherwise have risen. This check to the rise in the price of British corn would operate as a check to the importation of foreign corn; and the check to the importation of foreign corn would limit the growing amount of the unfavourable balance of foreign payments.

From the conjoint operation of the several causes which have been thus enumerated,—the sale of securities as deposits were withdrawn;—the immediate limitation of bank notes in the hands of the public and of private bankers,—the rise in the rate of interest, inviting the return of foreign investments,—and the fall of prices acting as a bounty upon exports, and as a tax upon imports,—from the conjoint operation of these several causes, the far greater portion of an unfavourable foreign balance, amounting to 5,000,000*l.*, would in all probability be liquidated under the action of a system of currency regulated upon the metallic principle by the exportation of one million of treasure. It may be assumed, not as merely probable but as certain, that under the proposed arrangement for regulating the currency in conformity with the metallic principle, a foreign debt, amounting to 5,000,000*l.*, would be fully discharged, through the aid of increased exports and diminished imports, before gold to the amount of 3,000,000*l.* should be withdrawn from the issue department of the Bank.

Should the drain of gold fall in the first instance wholly on the department of deposit, the withdrawal of 3,000,000*l.* of gold from the department of issue would be accompanied (to resume our former figures) by a reduction of the deposits of the banking department from 15,000,000*l.* to 12,000,000*l.*, and of its reserve from 5,000,000*l.* to 2,000,000*l.*; and this would lead the directors, in order to restore the due proportion of 1 to 3 between their reserve and liabilities, to sell securities to the amount of 2,000,000*l.*, and consequently to withdraw from the hands of the public and the private bankers notes to a similar amount.

Let us assume, for the sake of argument, the existence of a case, the occurrence of which, under the Government arrangement, would be obviously impossible. Let us suppose that the whole of the foreign debt is discharged by a transmission of gold, and that the drain of gold falls in the first instance exclusively upon the deposit department. Under this supposition the following charges would occur: — As deposits were gradually withdrawn securities would be gradually sold. Now, as the withdrawal of 5,000,000*l.* from the deposit department would reduce the deposits from 15,000,000*l.* to 10,000,000*l.*, and the original reserve from 5,000,000*l.* to nothing, a new reserve to the amount of 3,333,333*l.* would have to be created by the sale of securities to that amount; but the deposit department would now be in a position of security as perfect as that in which it had previously stood. It would be in no greater danger of stopping payments when its liabilities were 10,000,000*l.* and its reserve 3,333,333*l.* than it had been in when its liabilities were 15,000,000*l.* and its reserve 5,000,000*l.*

Let us now contrast the different processes through which, under the proposed and under the existing systems, the gold withdrawn from the Bank in payment of a foreign debt would be subsequently returned into its coffers.

In the case which we have been just considering, the payment of the foreign debt, by the transmission of 5,000,000*l.* in gold, caused a sale of securities to the amount of 3,333,333*l.*, and the consequent withdrawal of notes from the channels of circulation to the like amount. Now, by this supposition, the foreign debt of 5,000,000*l.* was incurred by an extraordinary importation of corn at a period when the exchanges had been previously at par; or, in other words, when the currency was equivalent to foreign currency. But if the value of the currency was equal to that of foreign currency previous to the contraction, its value will be greater than that of foreign currencies after the contraction. It follows as a necessary consequence, that on the liquidation of the foreign debt by the exportation of 5,000,000*l.* in gold, the exchanges will turn in our favour until the value of the currency shall be again reduced to the foreign par. From the natural and necessary law of equilibrium, which determines the movements of the precious metals, and without effort on the part of the Bank, the gold which had been abstracted from its coffers for the liquidation of the foreign debt will now flow in as rapidly as it had flowed out.

We have seen that, under the existing system, the exhausted coffers of the Bank must be replenished through a very different process. The advocates for the continuance of this, with the suggested improvement of a larger reserve of treasure than that which has hitherto been maintained, contemplate fluctuations in the amount of bullion between the maximum of 15,000,000*l*. and the minimum of 5,000,000*l*. And, when the minimum has been touched, how is the maximum to be regained? Simply by a forcible elevation of the rate of interest—a superinduced and long-protracted depression of commercial credit. Under the existing system, the adjustment of the currency in due proportion to foreign currency, by which alone extreme fluctuations can be prevented, is committed to the knowledge and to the discretion of a varying body of directors, instead of being left under the government of those permanent uniform laws by which the precious metals are distributed in their proper proportions throughout the commercial world. In whatever degree the currency is made to deviate in amount and in value from the state in which it would exist were it exclusively metallic, in that same degree the tendency to fluctuations in the rate of interest and in the state of commercial credit will be increased.

We proceed to contrast the effects of the two systems upon the rate of interest and the state of credit, under the action of an adverse exchange, resulting, not from an extraordinary importation of some leading article of consumption, but from a fall in the value of the currency in relation to foreign currencies.

Under a purely metallic currency, an adverse exchange resulting from the latter cause would be a rare occurrence; and, when it did happen to occur, would be almost instantaneously corrected. Except in the countries of the mines, a purely metallic currency of standard weight cannot be made to contract or to expand except through the laws which govern international exchange; and its amount and its value must be determined, not by causes originating in itself, but by causes operating from without. But a convertible paper currency, issued upon securities at a uniform amount, and issued against bullion to an indefinite amount, would be governed, as regards amount and value, by the self-same laws by which the precious metals are maintained, with only slight and temporary deviations, in a state of equilibrium throughout the commercial world. Under the proposed system for the regulation of the currency, an adverse exchange, originating in the currency itself, will be a rare occurrence, and any considerable or permanent deviation from the par-of-exchange equilibrium an impossible event. Practically considered, fluctuations in the rate of interest and in the state of commercial credit, so far as they can result from alterations in the value of the currency, may, under the operation of the proposed system, be taken at *nihil*.

Very different are the results under the existing system. Under this system the circulation may deviate, for protracted periods, from the par-of-exchange equilibrium. When a currency consists of coin, and of bank notes convertible into coin upon demand, and when an increased issue of notes creates an expansion greater than that which, under similar circumstances, a purely metallic currency would receive, the value of the aggregate mass, including coin as well as notes, is lowered in relation to foreign currencies. The value of the bank note, indeed, cannot be reduced below that of the coin into which it is convertible; but the value of the coin is reduced below its bullion value in the foreign market. The coin is consequently exported. But no exportation of coin, to whatever extent it may be carried, can restore the equilibrium of the currency and rectify the exchanges while the bank, instead of allowing the circulation to contract as gold is withdrawn from its coffers, sustains its reserve by an additional creation of notes. Under the operation of this system 20,000,000*l.* of treasure held by the bank would be no more effectual than 5,000,000*l.*, or than 1,000,000*l.*, in liquidating the constantly accruing unfavourable balance of payment, and in averting a sudden and violent revulsion. So long as the Bank of England aided its banking department by advances from the department of issue, and so long as the country issuers increased their circulation in the face of the adverse exchange, so long would imports exceed exports, and so long would new foreign debts be contracted as fast as the old ones should be discharged. No procurable amount of bullion would be sufficient to supply the drain; no contraction of the currency, however sudden and violent; no rise in the rate of interest, and no pressure upon commercial credit, however embarrassing and ruinous,—might prove effective in preventing a suspension of payments.

The larger the amount of bullion held by the bank at the commencement of the drain, and the more protracted the period during which the previous accumulation of treasure might enable the directors to meet the drain, and to sustain the vaunted process of averting the sale of securities by recruiting their reserve from the department of issue, the greater the danger of ultimate insolvency might possibly become. When the currency is redundant, and when in consequence the rate of interest is low, and the scale of prices high in the home market, a more than ordinary inducement is held out to speculation in foreign commodities. The longer the inducement is continued the more extensive the speculation will become. When foreign trade is conducted on a system of credit, the contracts entered into for consignments of foreign goods during a protracted period of high prices and speculative demand may exceed by an enormous amount the demand for British goods in foreign markets. In such a case as this, the most stringent efforts of the bank to avert the drain might come too late to save; a suspension of payment might become inevitable, and a universal disruption of commercial credit might ensue.

These are not hypothetical conjectures; they are legitimate conclusions from actual events. In December 1838, the bullion in the bank was about 9,000,000*l.*, and in September 1839 it was reduced, under the action of the existing system, to 2,000,000*l.* But this transmission of 7,000,000*l.* was insufficient to liquidate the unfavourable foreign balance which had been previously incurred. The Bank of England would have stopped payment had it not obtained a loan of 2,000,000*l.* from the Bank of France.

The following question has been asked:—"If, under the proposed plan, 14,000,000*l.* had been issued on securities, and if 8,000,000*l.* was the amount in which notes had been issued on gold, making the present circulation of the bank 22,000,000*l.* and if a time should again occur when so large a sum as 7,000,000*l.* should be taken from the bank in the short space of nine months, what would be the effect of such a violent collapse?"* The proper answer to this question is, that when the Government plan shall have been carried into effect, the abstraction of 7,000,000*l.* of treasure from the coffers of the bank in a period of nine months will be morally impossible. The violent fluctuation which occurred between December 1838, and September 1839, was the result of the system which the querist would desire to uphold.

The Westminster Reviewer objects to the Government measure on the ground that it will not have the effect of

* Speech of Mr. Hawes on the second reading of the Bill for the renewal of the Bank Charter.

preventing the recurrence of those commercial revulsions to which the country would be liable were the currency exclusively metallic. The proper answer to this objection is, that the object of the proposed measure is to prevent the recurrence of those revulsions only which have had their origin in a currency fluctuating alternately above and below the level to which a purely metallic currency would conform. If it should accomplish this object, it will have performed all the work which it was intended or expected to perform. I believe that it will fully accomplish this object, and that it will effectually prevent the recurrence of those cycles of commercial excitement and depression of which our ill-regulated currency has been the primary and exciting cause; and so believing, I continue to retain, after an attentive and patient consideration of all the objections urged by the able and scientific Reviewer, the opinion which I formerly expressed, that the adoption of Sir Robert Peel's plan for the renewal of the Charter of the Bank of England will be the most important improvement in our monetary system which has been effected since the passing of the Act of 1819, for the resumption of cash payments.

# POSTSCRIPT.

SINCE the preceding pages were written, I have heard some further objections, to which it may not be inappropriate to advert, urged against the Government plan.

An apprehension has been expressed in some quarters that, under the proposed regulations, a large demand for gold by a foreign Government, or by the contractors for a foreign loan, might cause so considerable a portion of the bullion to be withdrawn from the bank, as to limit the circulation to the 14,000,000*l.* allowed to be issued upon securities. The answers to this objection are the following: —

1st. If gold were demanded by a foreign Government, or by the contractors for a foreign loan, it would be drawn, not from the coffers of the Bank of England exclusively, but, on the contrary, in due proportions, from the general markets of the world. 2nd. If the demanders of gold were to draw the required supply exclusively from England, the value of gold would be rendered higher in England than in other countries; and the contractors would pay a high price for that which they could obtain with equal facility for a low price. 3rd. Were the demanders of gold, by acting thus foolishly, to raise the value of gold in England above its level in other countries, the exchanges would be instantly turned in favour of England, and gold would flow back until the equilibrium should be restored. 4th. If the demanders of gold for foreign objects were to act so absurdly as to come to the Bank of England for that which they could obtain cheaper in foreign markets, the cambists and money-brokers who supplied the gold would act more wisely, and would buy the gold cheap in the foreign market for the purpose of selling it dear in the English market. The apprehension lest the Bank of England should be deprived of its treasure through the operation of any cause save that of a depreciation of the currency by excessive issue of paper, is altogether chimerical.

A large and influential portion of the private bankers of the metropolis have addressed a letter to Sir Robert Peel, in which they urge the following objection against that provision of the Government plan which limits the circulation of the Bank of England to 14,000,000*l.* upon securities.

" We are apprehensive that the absolute limitation of the issue to 14,000,000*l.* upon securities, whether that amount be in itself a proper amount or not, will create a general feeling of uneasiness throughout the country, and, by preventing the satisfactory reception of the measure, will deprive the scheme of many of the advantages it possesses, and interfere with its success.

" We respectfully submit that the effect of such an absolute limitation will be to restrict the business of the country by leading to a general withdrawal of legitimate accommodation, unless some power be reserved by the bill for extending the issue, with the sanction of the authorities (the first Lord of the Treasury, the Chanceller of the Exchequer, and the Master of the Mint) above alluded to, in cases of emergency, to be made apparent to such authorities."

The suggestion of the private bankers amounts simply to this,—that in cases of emergency, to be judged of by the financial ministers for the time being, the separation of functions shall be suspended, and that on the occurrence of an adverse exchange, the directors of the Bank of England shall be enabled to recruit the reserve of the banking department, not by a sale of securities, but by advances from the department of issue of additional notes created for that purpose. Now it will be obvious, upon a moment's consideration, that this would be no more nor less than a return to the old system; and a return to it, too, under those very circumstances in which, as experience has fully shown, its operation has been most decidedly and extensively mischievous. Have the private bankers of the metropolis forgotten altogether the occurrences of 1838 and 1839? The system to which they are desirous of providing a means of returning was then in full operation. There was no limitation of issues upon securities, no separation of functions; and the banking department had unrestricted power to replenish its coffers from the department of issue; and what were the results? A drain of 7,000,000*l.* within a period of nine months, an exhaustion of coffers to the very verge of insolvency, and an actual stoppage of payments prevented only by a charitable loan of treasure from the Bank of France. Had the Bank of England in 1838 and 1839 been limited to the issue of 14,000,000*l.* upon securities; had there been functional separation; had the department of banking been denied all aid from the department of issue; and had a gradual contraction of the circulation consequently commenced with the first efflux of bullion, it would have been utterly impossible that the drain should have extended to 7,000,000*l.*; utterly impossible that the pressure upon the money market, consequent on the suspension of confidence and the stagnation of trade, should have been so severe and so protracted as they unfortunately became. The proofs of these positions I have detailed in the preceding pages, and need not here repeat.

A mutual friend has remarked upon the tone in which the controversy between Mr. Tooke and myself has been conducted. I was not the assailant. I occupied a defensive position, wielding the weapons placed by my opponent in my hands. Mr. Tooke commenced the onslaught with charging the parties to whom he was opposed, with a total misconception of the principles which they advocated, and of all that has been, and is, under the existing banking system ; he gave to their doctrines the nickname of 'The Currency Principle,' and to themselves the nickname of 'Currency Doctrinaires;' and it certainly did not occur to me that I was making an over-payment in the coin I had received, when I used the expression 'Tookean Fallacies.' If I have paid more than was due, I shall be most happy to recall the unprofitable advance; and to have it regarded as having been made in a convertible currency, returnable upon the issuer for the more sterling and indestructible medium of respect and consideration which must ever be justly due to the author of 'The History of Prices'—the co-labourer with Horner and Ricardo.

# 3

# The currency question

J. S. Mill, 'The currency question', *Westminster Review*, vol. XLI (June 1844), pp. 579–98.

One of the masters of nineteenth century politics, philosophy and economics, his *Principles of Political Economy* (1848) stands as one of the great contributions to classical economic thought. This piece, which appeared in the *Westminster Review*, at the height of the controversy over the 1844 Act, is essentially a defence of Tooke's statement of the Banking School position against the onslaught contained in Torrens' response. The chapter in Mill's *Principles*, dealing with the question of convertible paper currency has been described by Robbins as 'the pure milk of the Banking School' and this piece, written some four years earlier, betrays a similar attitude. It allows that 'on some minor questions', Torrens has provided a powerful argument, although it is fiercely critical of the general tenor of the Act. It contends mostly with the question of the amount of paper currency to be issued, and contains a strong defence of the law of reflux, by which it is argued that any paper currency issued in excess of the required amount of business will automatically be returned to the banks. The relationship between notes and bullion is protected by convertibility: 'bank notes are to credit precisely what coin is to bullion; the same thing, merely rendered portable and minutely divisible. We cannot perceive that they add anything, either to the aggregate of purchasing power, or to the portion of that power in actual existence...that bank notes, as such, have any peculiar power on prices, we see no reason whatever to believe' (p.355 of the original article)

Mill's position on the question of economic stability and the contribution of the banking system to the amplitude of successive economic crises is clear – he urges that the best way to ensure the maintenance of convertibility and confidence in the currency is the holding of a larger reserve, rather than the separation of the banking and issue departments of the Bank. He predicted – with some prescience, it would appear from the conduct of the crises of 1847 and 1857 – that the main effect of the constraints on the Bank's ability to maintain circulation in a crisis would be to worsen the difficulties.

# The Currency Question

MR. TOOKE is known to all who are conversant with the discussions of the last twenty-five years on commercial topics, as an authority, on all such subjects, of the highest order. Beyond, perhaps, any other man, he brings to the consideration of mercantile phenomena an intimate practical knowledge of the elements upon which they depend, combined with habits of reflecting, or, to give the operation its proper name, of theorizing, which qualify him to discriminate and analyse the influences of those various elements. Owing to this union of qualifications, those who are interested in such inquiries have found in his various publications (and particularly in the "History of Prices,"[*] which is a summary of them all) a scientific explanation of those complex and apparently anomalous phenomena of prices, which the commercial history of the last half century presents in so great abundance, and which, until shown by him to be exemplifications of those very principles and laws with which they seemed to conflict, were perplexing even to those who best understood the subject, and often dangerously misleading to those who did not. The opinions, therefore, of Mr. Tooke upon the questions raised by the new ministerial scheme for the reform of the currency are entitled to an attentive, and, from all who are capable of appreciating what he has previously written, a respectful hearing.*

In the first of the pamphlets[†] named at the commencement of this

[**A History of Prices, and of the State of the Circulation, from 1793 to 1837*. 2 vols. London: Longman, Orme, Brown, Green, and Longmans, 1838; and *A History of Prices, and of the State of the Circulation, in 1838 and 1839*. London: Longman, Orme, Brown, Green, and Longmans, 1840.]

*We should have deemed it superfluous to re-assert Mr. Tooke's claims to attention, if we were addressing only persons in some degree conversant with the subject; but others may have received an erroneous impression from a flippant attack, continued through two numbers of a weekly paper somewhat extensively read. The assailant, who appears to think that strong writing consists in contemptuous language, has not deemed it necessary to prove himself a competent judge, by either answering or showing that he understands any one of Mr. Tooke's arguments or statements. [See Anon., "Mr. Thomas Tooke on the Currency Principle," and "Currency Crochets," *Examiner*, 13 & 27 Apr., 1844, pp. 226–7, 259–60.]

[†*Inquiry into the Currency Question.*]

article, Mr. Tooke has taken the field against the system of doctrines on which the ministerial measure is founded, and which derives its commonest designation from the names of two of its most distinguished supporters—Mr. Jones Loyd and Mr. Norman.[*] To represent the other side of the dispute, we have prefixed the latest pamphlet of the indefatigable Colonel Torrens, who was, we believe, the first promulgator of the theory in question, and who has come forward as its champion against "the fallacies advanced by Mr. Tooke."[†]

For any influence which further discussion can have upon the decision of parliament, it is evidently useless. Parliament has made up its mind. The measure of Sir R. Peel[‡] has been received with approbation by nearly all, in parliament and the press, by whom any opinion has been expressed on it; and with acquiescence, if not satisfaction, by the public. There is not the smallest chance of its undergoing material alteration in its way through either house. That the attention, therefore, of thinkers should be directed to the views contained in Mr. Tooke's pamphlet, is of importance rather as a matter of abstract discussion, essential to the right understanding of commercial phenomena, than with a view to any direct practical result. The question has ceased to be a practical one, and cannot again become so for ten years to come. But it involves highly important questions of theory; the practical bearing of which, as of all theories, far transcends the limits of any single application.

What was affirmed by Cicero of all things with which philosophy is conversant, may be asserted without scruple of the subject of currency—that there is no opinion so absurd as not to have been maintained by some person of reputation. There even appears to be on this subject a peculiar tenacity of error—a perpetual principle of resuscitation in slain absurdity. There are at this day numerous persons who can read and write, and some who think themselves oracles of wisdom, who see no harm in emancipating a paper currency from the restraint of convertibility, and from every definite principle of limitation, provided only that it is grounded on the security of actual property; forgetful that even the *assignats* were issued on no less a security than the principal portion of the soil of France, and that a paper so guaranteed is no more protected from depreciation, if issued in excess, than the land itself would be if offered for sale in unusual quantity. There

[*See, e.g., Loyd, Samuel Jones. *Thoughts on the Separation of the Departments of the Bank of England*. London: Richardson, 1844; Norman, George Warde. *Remarks upon Some Prevalent Errors, with respect to Currency and Banking*. London: Richardson, 1838.]

[†I.e., part of the title of Torrens' *Inquiry into the Practical Workings. . . .*]

[‡See 7 & 8 Victoria, c. 32.]

are writers of pretension, not only out of Bedlam, but even, we can assure Sir Robert Peel, out of Birmingham, who think it the duty of the legislature periodically to degrade the standard (or to authorize an increase of inconvertible paper exactly equivalent) in proportion as the progress of industry creates an increase of productions and a multiplication of pecuniary transactions. But it is not against these extravagant aberrations that it is now necessary to contend. In the discussions which we are here concerned with, both sides admit, that the proper standard of currency is the precious metals, at an unalterable mint valuation; that a pound (precisely as stated by Sir Robert Peel) should mean a fixed quantity of gold of a given fineness; and that no one who has contracted to pay that given quantity, should be allowed on any pretext to discharge his debt by paying a smaller quantity, or making over paper equivalent to a smaller quantity. Gold is not an ideally perfect standard—a commodity absolutely unchangeable in cost of production; but it approaches nearer to that abstract perfection of a measure of value, than any other production of nature or industry; and if it were far more subject to fluctuation than it is, it would be less so than the policy of a government,—especially one which takes for its principle of guidance "the wants of trade," which in this case simply means the convenience of debtors.

Assuming then—as conceded by all persons whom it is at present necessary to reason with—that the value of a paper currency must be maintained at par with the coin which it professes to represent, and that to effect this the issuers must be compelled to give coin for their notes whenever demanded; there is an ulterior question, on which those who are entitled to be considered authorities on the principles of the circulating medium, part company. According to one opinion, steadiness of value in a paper currency is sufficiently secured by ready and immediate convertibility. This was, until lately, the prevailing, if not the exclusive doctrine, among those by whom the theory of money had been successfully cultivated. Within the last few years another doctrine has sprung up, of which Colonel Torrens was, as we have said, the originator, Mr. Loyd, Mr. Norman, and Mr. McCulloch among the chief propounders, and to which Sir Robert Peel and his cabinet have become proselytes.

According to this doctrine, the check of convertibility acts too slowly, and admits of great mischief from excess of issues before it begins to operate. Convertibility, it is contended, is a security only against *permanent* depreciation. When an increased issue of paper has sunk the value of the currency below its regular proportion to the currencies of other countries, the exchanges turn, gold becomes an article of export, and, to obtain it, notes are returned upon the Bank. But the increase of issues has, in the meantime, raised prices; which, when the excess of paper is removed, relapse to their former level. This is already a mischief; it deranges mercantile calculations, creates unexpected gains to some at the expense of others, and adds to the gambling character in a certain degree inherent in all the great operations of commerce. But the evil seldom ends here. All advance of prices tends to encourage speculation; especially when the same cause which creates the advance (being increased issues made by bankers, in the form of increased advances to their customers) occasions, as its very first effect, a reduction of the rate of interest. The conjunction of rising markets and a low rate of interest leads to speculative purchases, by which the rise itself is heightened and prolonged. The rise, however, not being grounded on any permanent cause of increased price (such as a deficiency of supply); in proportion to its continuance, the fall, when the tide turns, is from a greater height, and also to a lower depth. Those who during the rise of prices obtained credit upon the apparently increasing value of the goods which they held, are only enabled to fulfil their engagements by parting with the goods at almost any sacrifice, and prices sink for a time as much below their accustomed rate as they had previously been raised above it.

To avert these evils, in the opinion of Colonel Torrens and Mr. Loyd, and we may now add of Sir Robert Peel, something more than convertibility is necessary. Their remedy is to place the issuers under a legal impossibility of ever increasing their issues (beyond a certain moderate minimum), except in exchange for bullion, which, if refused to them, would probably be sent to the mint and coined. By this contrivance the paper currency is prevented from being arbitrarily increased. It can only, under such a system, be extended, when, if the augmentation were not made, an equivalent increase would probably take place in the portion of the currency which consists of coin.

But it is not enough, according to these authorities, to prevent increase of issues, otherwise than in exchange for bullion; it is also necessary to prevent the currency from being diminished, otherwise than by not re-issuing the notes which are presented for payment. Under the present system, the Bank, when it finds its treasure leaving it, does not remain passive, and allow the exchange of notes for specie to go on until, the needful contraction having been effected, the drain stops of itself. It becomes alarmed, and endeavours by calling in its issues to stop the efflux of bullion in an earlier stage. It diminishes its loans to merchants, depriving them in a period of falling prices of the accustomed accommodation, which is then more than usually necessary. Or it throws some of its securities upon the market, and by absorbing a portion of the capital which is seeking investment, deprives the merchants of an equivalent amount of pecuniary advances. By either process, it raises the rate of interest and increases the difficulty of obtaining loans, at a period which is already one of pressure; thus heightening all the evils of a commercial revulsion.

By the plan proposed, that of compelling the issuers to keep their securities at a fixed amount, and to let the currency contract or expand only by the exchange of gold for notes and of notes for gold, the paper will, according to this theory, be preserved exactly the same in quantity as the metallic money which would otherwise circulate in its place; this identity of quantity being, it is supposed, indispensable to secure identity of value.

It is generally assumed, as essential to this mode of regulating the currency, that the privilege of issue should be confined to a single establishment. But the rule of holding an unvarying amount of securities, and of issuing notes beyond that amount only in exchange for bullion, might be applied to a multiplicity of issuers; and a scheme for that purpose was, in fact, devised by Colonel Torrens. Sir Robert Peel cuts the knot by prohibiting to the country banks any issues whatever beyond the average of the last two years. He does not apply to them, as he does to the Bank of England, the other half of the proposed system, by preventing arbitrary diminution as well as increase; either because he thinks that in preventing over-issue he has guarded sufficiently against revulsion, or because he deems more minute precautions superfluous in an arrangement which is avowedly preparatory to the suppression of all banks of issue other than the Bank of England.

Under the system thus established, we are confidently told that the calamity of almost periodical recurrence, commonly known by the name of a "commercial crisis," will be greatly diminished both in frequency and in severity. Some permit themselves to use language which at least seems to import that these convulsions will be rendered impossible. Colonel Torrens looks upon the measure as one which "will effectually prevent the recurrence of those commercial revulsions, those cycles of excitement and depression, which as Mr. Loyd has so felicitously explained, result from the alternate expansion and contraction of an ill-regulated circulation."[*] He admits, indeed, that undue speculation, and the consequent reaction, might prevail to a great extent even under a metallic currency. But he attributes to the measure now proposed, an efficacy in counteracting those evils, sufficient to constitute that measure "the most important and the most salutary, as regards the reform of our monetary system, which has been brought under the consideration of parliament since the act of 1819 for the resumption of cash payments." [*Ibid.*]

We shall examine presently how far the measure deserves to be considered—again in the words of Colonel Torrens—as "the reform of a banking system hitherto, perhaps, the most defective in Europe." [*Ibid.*] But

[*Torrens, *Inquiry*, p. iv.]

whatever may be its recommendations, that of preventing, or even greatly alleviating commercial revulsions, can scarcely be one of them; since commercial revulsions are as frequent and as disastrous where this so bitterly-condemned banking system does not exist. Not to mention Amsterdam or Hamburg, the currency of France differs as little from a purely metallic currency as that of any civilized country can well do in this industrial era. France has no country banks of issue, no notes below twenty pounds (a large sum measured by the standard of French incomes), and nobody has ever imputed to the single issuing body which exists in France, any depreciating action on the currency. Even the custom of making payments by cheques is not yet generally adopted. Metallic money is the common medium of payment. Yet commercial revulsions are as severe, in proportion to the amount of mercantile business, in France as in England, and fill quite as large a space in public discussion and in the meditations of statesmen and of economists. An evil common to all commercial countries, in the ratio of the extent of their transactions, cannot depend upon a cause peculiar to England and the United States. What a currency actually metallic does not prevent, it is impossible that making the paper conform exactly to the variations of a metallic currency can cure.

As the notions of persons unacquainted with trade on what constitutes a commercial crisis are generally rather vague and obscure, we will, before going further, state as distinctly as possible what are its principal characteristics.

A commercial crisis is the recoil of prices, after they have been raised by speculation higher than is warranted by the state of the demand and of the supply. Speculation is almost always set in motion by something which affords apparent grounds for expecting either an extra demand or a deficient supply. But the anticipation may, in the first place, be erroneous; in the second, however rational it may be, the speculation (especially where the prospect of gain is considerable) is very likely to be overdone, each speculator conducting his operations as if he alone knew the circumstances on which the hope of profit is grounded. The rise consequent upon the speculative purchases attracts new speculators, insomuch that, paradoxical as it may appear, the largest purchases are often made at the highest price. But at last it is discovered that the rise has gone beyond the permanent cause for it, and purchases cease, or the holders think it is time to realise their gains. Then the recoil comes; and the price falls to a lower point than that from which it had risen, because the high price has both checked the demand, and, by stimulating production or importation, called forth a larger supply. Besides, many of those who during the high price have contracted engagements, which they trusted to a further rise for giving them the means of fulfilling, are unable to hold on until the crisis is past, but must sell at any sacrifice.

When this series of effects is confined to some one article of commerce, individuals may be ruined, but the mercantile world generally is not disturbed. When, however, as in 1825 and at several other periods in the present century, the opening of new markets, or some expected deficiency of supply extending to various important articles, has set speculation at work in several great departments at once, the spirit is apt to become general, and other commodities rise in price without any reasonable cause whatever. In such cases, the ultimate revulsion is most extensive and calamitous.

As long as the seasons vary, as markets fluctuate, and men miscalculate, or the passion of gain (as in gamblers) over-rides their calculations, so long will these alterations of ebb and flow, these "cycles," as Colonel Torrens calls them, "of excitement and depression,"[*] continue. They are worse in America than in England, because American commerce is conducted in a more gambling spirit; they are worse at Liverpool than in London, for the same reason. But whatever aggravates the natural fluctuations of the markets, or creates fluctuations when they would not otherwise exist, increases both the frequency and the destructiveness of such convulsions. This the corn laws do; and it is one of their principal evils. This it is also affirmed that the currency, as at present regulated, does; and the merit claimed for the system now to be introduced is, that this artificial cause of fluctuation will be cut off.

It is here that Mr. Tooke and the authors of the new scheme are irreconcilably at variance. He denies *in toto* the evils imputed to the existing system.

The imputations are—First: That the banks, by arbitrary extension of their issues, raise prices; and thus create fluctuation, and speculation, and ultimate revulsions, where such would not otherwise exist.

Secondly: That when speculations have commenced from causes unconnected with the banks, they, by extending their issues, concurrently with the rise of prices, prevent the rise from being checked in an early stage. And when the rise of prices, by its operation on the exports and imports, has caused an efflux of gold, they hasten to stop it by a contraction of the currency equal to or beyond the previous expansion; which contraction being effected by a forced operation upon the loan market, aggravates the difficulties of persons already distressed.

Mr. Tooke disputes both these assertions.

He denies that an extension of issues can be arbitrarily made by the banks; or that, if made, it has any necessary tendency to raise prices.

He denies that, when prices are rising, the extension of issues, which frequently takes place simultaneously, retards the action of the causes which tend to check the rise; or that by preventing such increase of issues,

[*Torrens, *Inquiry*, p. iv.]

improvident speculation would be earlier arrested, and the consequent calamities confined within a narrower range.[*]

It is at once seen that this controversy involves a very important question in the theory of currency; one, indeed, which has not, to our knowledge, been subjected to thorough examination or put precisely in issue before. This question is—With what limitations, if any, the proposition is true that an increase in the quantity of the currency raises prices?

That it is true in some sense and in some circumstances, no one thinks of disputing; but that it is a universal principle, and true without any limitation, may perhaps have been too easily taken for granted.

If—to adopt an illustration sometimes used—every person in England were to awake one morning with a sovereign in his pocket, no one could doubt that the rise of prices would be immediate. All or most would hasten to expend their sovereign, either for pleasure or profit; and as there would be no more commodities to be distributed than before, each would bear a higher price.

On the other hand, suppose that a foreigner lands in England, bringing with him five thousand pounds in gold. This additional purchasing power, being brought into the market, would raise prices, but at first only the prices of those commodities which it was employed in purchasing. It might happen not to be employed in purchasing anything, and then it would not raise prices at all. We scarcely think that any one would contest the possibility, at least, of the case described by Mr. Tooke in the following passage. We quote from his "History of Prices," because the statement of the same principle in his pamphlet is somewhat more imperfect, and gives an advantage to Colonel Torrens to which we do not think that the merits of the case entitle him:—

That an additional issue by the Bank of a million or of five millions on securities, would, *cæteris paribus*, reduce the market rate of interest, may be granted; but it is not self-evident, or consistent with experience, that prices of commodities would therefore necessarily rise. The persons who obtained such an increased price for their securities as induced them to sell, would doubtless, upon receiving the money, seek some other investment for it. There might not be, nor would it be likely that there should be, anything in the state of supply and demand in the markets for commodities to induce persons not habitually in them nor so disposed, to speculate in goods; while the probability is, and such has been the course of experience, that, as by the supposition the market rate of interest in this country would, by such an operation of the Bank, be depressed below its ordinary rate relatively to other countries, there would be every inducement to the individuals who thus had their capitals disengaged to seek investment in securities abroad, whether public or private. As there would not, by the operation of the Bank, be necessarily any additional induce-

[*Tooke, *Inquiry*, pp. 55 ff.]

ment to export commodities, the capital to be transmitted abroad for such investments would be remitted in bullion. The effect, therefore, of the issue of the million or five millions of bank notes by the Bank, might merely be their return upon the Bank for bullion to be exported. This was, in point of fact, the process in 1834, when the Bank increased its securities by between three and four millions, and reduced its treasure by the same amount; while the markets for commodities, although the rate of interest was low, and the facility of credit complete, were in the most quiescent state possible, and the corn markets falling. (*History of Prices*, vol. iii, pp. 273–4.)

Or suppose another case, of frequent occurrence. A country bank issues an extra amount of notes in advances to farmers, to enable them to hold their corn, in hopes of getting a higher price. With the notes received from the bank the farmer pays his rent, and withholds the corn by the sale of which he would otherwise have paid it. But, for every farmer who has not sold his corn, there is a miller or corn dealer somewhere who has not bought it. The notes which this miller or corn dealer was prepared to pay, he now puts into deposit, or repays to the banker from whom they had been borrowed. By as much as the one is enabled to postpone his sale, by so much does the other his purchase. There may have been not a pound more expended in consequence of the transaction, nor any action on prices, except to render more gradual the rise which was taking place from other causes in the price of corn.

If the declaration of innumerable witnesses merits any confidence, the *modus operandi* of country issues must very often be of this sort. The country bankers unanimously disclaim any arbitrary power over their issues, and declare that in certain states of the markets they *cannot* extend their circulation; if they attempt it, the increase comes back to them, either in deposits or by being presented for payment. They are, it may be said, interested witnesses. But they must mean something by this assertion. It cannot be a mere falsehood. It is confirmed, too, by many persons of the greatest experience, who have no interest in banks of issue,—Mr. Samuel Gurney, for example, and the late Mr. Rothschild.[*] There must be some fact at the bottom of what is asserted. It may be a fact partially stated or misunderstood, and they may be entirely wrong in their explanation of it. But a fact of some sort there must be. We have not seen, on the other side of the question, any attempt to clear up the difficulty, or show the origin of the supposed mistake. We have met with nothing except a flat denial.

For our own part, we see no incredibility in the assertion of the bankers. We believe it to be in the main correct. It appears to us perfectly consistent with the theory of the subject.

[*See Gurney, and Rothschild, "Evidence taken before the Committee of Secrecy on the Bank of England Charter," *Parliamentary Papers*, 1831–32, VI, pp. 249–69, 381–93.]

The notion that every increase in the amount of the circulating medium must raise prices, proceeds, as it seems to us, upon the erroneous supposition, that an increase of money must be an increase of purchasing power.

The purchasing power which determines prices is of two kinds,—*ultimate* purchasing power, which determines permanent prices; and the portion of that power which is in actual exercise at a given time; this determines the fluctuations of prices.

The ultimate purchasing power of the community is, in the words of Mr. Tooke, "the quantity of money constituting the revenues of the different orders of the state, under the head of rents, profits, salaries, and wages."[*] We think he should rather have said their "gross incomes," to include that portion of their receipts which is employed in replacing material, and in renewing machinery and buildings as they wear out. The whole of these incomes is destined to be, and is, expended in purchases, either for personal consumption or for reproduction. The aggregate of money incomes, compared with the whole annual produce of the country, determines general prices, as between the dealer and the consumer. If you add to the currency in a way which increases the aggregate of incomes, you raise prices; but this condition can be satisfied by nothing short of a permanent increase* of the quantity of money in the country; either from an influx of the metals, caused by a diminution in the cost at which they can be produced and imported, or from increased issue of an inconvertible paper currency. We say inconvertible, because it is admitted that of that alone could any increase have the character of permanence.†

But though an extension of issues may not increase the aggregate money incomes of the community, nor raise general prices between dealer and consumer, upon which prices all dealers depend for their ultimate returns, and on the anticipation of which they necessarily ground all their transactions with one another; some may suppose that it must increase the money

[*Tooke, *Inquiry*, p. 71.]

*To be scientifically accurate, it must be admitted that if the increased issues were made in advances to employers of labour (for instance, in a loan to a manufacturer, who expends them in the direct payment of wages to his work-people), there would be, to that extent, as long as the expenditure was going on, an increase of the aggregate money income of the community, and hence a corresponding rise of prices. But this supposition is not applicable to our present currency, of which the smallest notes are of too high a denomination to be employed, in any extent worth considering, for the payment of wages.

†We may add, with Mr. Tooke [*Inquiry*, pp. 68 ff.], that the issues of a *Government* paper, even when not permanent, will raise prices; because Governments usually issue their paper in purchases for consumption. If issued to pay off a portion of the national debt, we believe they would have no such effect.

demand for commodities at the particular moment; because the person who obtains the bank notes does so for the purpose of using them, and may be supposed to bring them immediately into the market and make purchases to their full extent.

This opinion seems to us to rest upon a great misconception of what constitutes the money demand for a commodity.

It seems to be thought by many people that the purchase of commodities implies the direct transfer of so much money from hand to hand in return for so much produce; and that the limit to the possible demand for a commodity at any moment, is the quantity of money then and there waiting to be exchanged for it.* With this mode of thinking it is no wonder that any one should suppose that whenever you add to the money at that place physically present, you add as much to the demand, and consequently to the price. But this is a very inadequate notion indeed of what constitutes purchasing power.

The purchasing power of an individual at any moment is not measured by the money actually in his pocket, whether we mean by money the metals, or include bank notes. It consists, first, of the money in his possession; secondly, of the money at his banker's, and all other money due to him and payable on demand; thirdly, of whatever credit he happens to possess. To the full measure of this three-fold amount he has the power of purchase. How much he will employ of this power, depends upon his necessities, or, in the present case, upon his expectations of profit. Whatever portion of it he does employ, constitutes his demand for commodities, and determines the extent to which he will act upon price.

Now, of these three elements of money demand, the first alone is grounded upon a corresponding amount of money actually *in esse*. The second, or the deposit at his banker's, is in part grounded upon actual money, namely, to the extent of about one-third, that being the proportion

*There is (as it seems to us) an almost whimsical exemplification of this common fallacy in Colonel Torrens's pamphlet, which we have not room to extract, but which those who wish to refer to it may find in pages 10–17. Having assumed, for the purposes of his argument, that Birmingham has a metallic currency composed of one million sovereigns, he says [p. 10], "consequently the prices of commodities within the district would be governed by the power of effecting purchases to an amount not exceeding 1,000,000*l*.," forgetting that the million sovereigns may serve, by successive payments, to represent and circulate incomes to the amount of many millions, and that it is this, and not the one million of sovereigns, which constitutes the purchasing power of the community. We admire the ingenuity and polemical acuteness of Colonel Torrens, which have never been more highly manifested than in this pamphlet; but we think in this particular instance he will find, on reconsideration, that he has built an elaborate superstructure upon a foundation of sand.

which prudent bankers profess to keep in their coffers to meet the drafts of their depositors. The third element of money demand, namely credit, has no basis of actually existing money at all. It is an additional money demand, created over and above that which is constituted by all the money in actual circulation. But it is exactly as operative upon prices as the money itself, provided the possessor chooses to make use of the purchasing power which it confers. This explains why periods of general confidence, when large prospects of gain seem to be opening themselves, and when there is a disposition among dealers to employ not only all their money but all or much of their credit in enlarging their operations, are attended with so great a rise of general prices. The effect is sometimes ascribed to the bills of exchange and other transferable paper which these transactions generate, and which are said to perform the functions of currency. Those who use this language mistake the effect for the cause. Bills of exchange are mere evidences of credit. The credit itself is the operating cause. It is manifest that when buyers are willing to employ their credit as well as their money in making purchases, their demand for commodities becomes so much greater, and prices must rise. They would rise if no such thing as a transferable acknowledgment of debt had ever been known in the country.

We may observe, parenthetically, that these considerations remove the puzzle which has been made of whether deposits, and cheques, and bills of exchange, are to be considered as money. With those who think that money alone confers power of purchase, these questions are very pertinent. When they ask whether deposits, or whether anything else, is money, they mean, does it operate on money prices? If it does, they think it a necessary consequence that it should be called money. But when once it is clearly seen that credit, so far as employed in the purchase of commodities, operates upon prices in exactly the same degree as money, the question what forms of credit should be called money, becomes extremely unimportant. It would probably be best that no form whatever should be so called.

If the views now stated be sound, it seems not easy to understand how an increased creation of the written evidences of credit called bank notes, can, of itself, create an additional demand, or occasion a rise of price. Admitting bank notes to be money (which is, in truth, a mere question of language), what does the person do who issues them, but take so much from the third element of purchasing power, namely credit, and add it to the first element, money in hand—making no addition whatever to the total amount? More properly, he merely converts so much credit from an unwritten into a written, and from a cumbrous into a convenient, form. Bank notes are to credit precisely what coin is to bullion; the same thing, merely rendered portable and minutely divisible. We cannot perceive that they add anything, either to the aggregate of purchasing power, or to the portion of that power in actual exercise. The person to whom the notes are advanced is proved by that very fact to have credit, and his requiring the advance proves that to that extent he intends to use his credit in making purchases. Is it supposed that having credit, and intending to buy goods by means of it, he will be disabled from doing so because a banker is prohibited from one particular mode of giving him credit?*

It must be conceded, and Mr. Tooke does fully concede,[*] that if bankers, urged by competition or caught by the contagious confidence of speculative times, make advances to persons who otherwise have *not* credit and cannot give good security, in that case the foregoing arguments do not apply. To that extent they do create a new purchasing power, a new demand, and, as its consequence, a rise of price. The American banks did raise prices by reckless advances; by lending money to persons who could not repay them. No one is more aware of this than Mr. Tooke. It is not, however, by their notes, as such, that banks thus misconduct themselves. Imprudent advances of their deposits, or of their private capital, or imprudent indorsement and guarantee of the engagements of their customers, have precisely the same effect. All extension of credit, legitimate or illegitimate, tends, in proportion as it is made use of, to a rise of price. And all contraction of credit produces an equivalent collapse.

That bank notes, as such, have any peculiar power on prices, we see no reason whatever to believe: and we hold with Mr. Tooke, that when they are increased, their increase is a consequence of a rise of prices, not a cause.[†] It is a known fact that the country issues almost invariably increase when the prices of agricultural produce are rising. The reason is, that the buyers, having larger payments to make, apply for more notes to make them with, it being the custom in the provision and cattle markets not to buy on credit, but to pay immediately in bank notes. A rise of other prices does not necessarily lead to increased issues; because, in almost all other transactions between dealers, bank notes are already superseded by cheques, or book credits; and these would soon be introduced into the markets for agricultural produce, if the obtaining bank notes were rendered difficult. Even the small quantity of bank notes which are employed at the clearing house or elsewhere, to effect the ultimate liquidation of these cheques and credits by the payment of balances, might, as Mr. Tooke remarks,[‡] have their place supplied by exchequer bills (as in Scotland), or by drafts on the Bank of England.

Whether the credit which necessarily exists in a commercial country

*See note, *infra*, page 358.

[*E.g., *Inquiry*, pp. 81–2.]

[†E.g., *ibid.*, pp. 76, 123–4.]

[‡E.g., *ibid.*, pp. 22, 32.]

assumes the form of bank notes or no, is, in short, a mere matter of convenience. In whatever form or vesture the credit is given, its influence on price is the same. He who has credit, and desires to employ it in purchases, will find the means of doing so without bank notes, and will act upon prices accordingly; while if he does not think the time favourable for making purchases, even having the notes in his possession will not induce him to do it; he will either keep them by him until they are wanted, or they will go into deposit.

It appears, then, that any increase of issues which is likely to take place under the present system of convertibility, is in itself quite inoperative to raise prices,* and cannot, therefore, be an exciting cause of commercial revulsions; but that a spirit of speculation, or an undue extension of credit, does raise prices, and raises them equally whether bank notes are generated by it or not; and that by preventing the increase of bank notes during such periods, nothing would be done to check the rise, since it is not bank notes which, as it is sometimes expressed, *sustain* prices, but the state of credit generally. No mode of regulating bank notes would either arrest the rise, or moderate the subsequent revulsion, which is always proportional.

There is, however, one way in which the present administration of the currency does heighten the evils of a commercial revulsion. The rise of prices in periods of exaggerated confidence checks exportation and greatly increases importation. A balance has to be paid in gold, and this is demanded from the Bank. To stop the drain, it hastily contracts its issues, that is, it sells securities and diminishes its loans, thus aggravating, in a period of difficulty, the already existing pressure upon the loan market; and this, it is urged, will be prevented by the ministerial measure, since the bank will not be permitted to contract its issues, except by not re-issuing the notes which have been returned to it for payment. But, as Mr. Tooke remarks,[*] to attain this object it is only necessary that the bank should habitually hold so large a reserve of bullion as will admit of allowing any probable drain to proceed until it has reached its limits. Whatever amount of reserve is needed for this purpose will be equally necessary on the plan of Sir Robert Peel, since the bullion, against which all notes beyond the fixed amount of securities are to be issued, must be sufficient to meet the

*We say *likely* to take place—not any increase which *can* take place; because there have been instances, both with joint-stock banks and private bankers, of imprudent advances, on insufficient security, resembling, on a smaller scale, the gigantic mismanagement of the American banks. These must have tended, as we have already admitted, to raise prices: and though it was not peculiarly in their character of issuers that the banks thus misconducted themselves, their issues, no doubt, enabled them to do so on a larger scale.

[*See *Inquiry*, pp. 108 ff.]

greatest drain which can ever be supposed to occur. We shall see presently that, in reality, the amount of reserve which would suffice on Mr. Tooke's plan will not be sufficient on Sir Robert Peel's.

We think, then—although with unfeigned diffidence, considering the high authorities by which we are opposed—that the reasons urged in recommendation of the contemplated changes, and in proof of the theory on which they rest, are all untenable, and that the system about to be adopted is in no way preferable to the present system, if improved as Mr. Tooke proposes, by making it imperative on the Bank to keep a larger reserve of bullion. But though not preferable, whether it is in any way inferior is another consideration. That question must be determined, not by its effects on price, for these we believe to be null, but by its operation upon the rate of interest, for that is real. Fluctuations of price do not, we believe, depend upon bank issues; but the operations of banks, as of other money-lenders, of course act upon the loan market, or as it is improperly called, the money market; in other words, upon the rate of interest, and what is almost synonymous, the prices of securities.

Mr. Tooke does not share the common opinion, that increased issues, by lowering the rate of interest, operate as a stimulus to speculation. He thinks it a vulgar error

That a facility of borrowing at a low rate of interest, not only confers the power of purchasing, but affords the inducement, applies the *stimulus* to speculation in commodities. If by facility of borrowing be meant a laxity of regard to security for repayment on the part of the lender, there is every probability that money so borrowed will be hazardously, if not recklessly employed; and whether in the purchase of shares, or of foreign securities, or of merchandize, or in any other mode of adventure or enterprise, or in mere personal expenditure, is a matter of chance, depending on the disposition and views of the borrower. Such borrowers are not *stimulated* to purchase commodities speculatively, merely because they can borrow on low terms; they are but too happy if they can borrow at all. But to suppose that persons entitled to credit are likely to be induced—*stimulated* is the favourite term—by the mere circumstance of a low rate of interest, to enter into speculations in commodities (using the term speculation in its obnoxious sense), argues a want of knowledge of the motives which lead to such speculations. These are seldom, if ever, entered into with borrowed capital, except with a view to so great an advance of price, and to be realized within so moderate a space of time, as to render the rate of interest or discount a matter of comparatively trifling consideration. (Pp. 81–2.)

The truth is, that the power of purchase by persons having capital and credit is much beyond anything that those who are unacquainted practically with speculative markets have any idea of. (P. 79.)

A person having the reputation of capital enough for his regular business, and enjoying good credit in his trade, if he takes a sanguine view of the prospect of a rise of price of the article in which he deals, and is favoured by circumstances in the outset and progress of his speculation, may effect purchases to an extent perfectly enormous, compared with his capital.* (P. 136.)

But why should this purchasing power be directed to the purchase of commodities, if there was nothing in the state of supply relatively to the rate of consumption, to afford the prospect of gain on the necessary eventual resale? The error is in supposing the *disposition* or *will* to be co-extensive with the power. The limit to the motive for the exercise of the power is in the prospect of resale with a profit. (P. 79.)

But although the issues of banks may not have the effect imputed to them, of stimulating speculation by lowering the rate of interest, there is no doubt that the mode of issuing and the mode of recalling them may and does produce *fluctuations* in the loan market.

Fluctuation is an evil in the interest of loans, as well as in the prices of commodities; and that is the best banking system (solvency and convertibility being first provided for) under which there is least liability to such fluctuations.

*Mr. Tooke illustrates this statement by some most remarkable instances, which we append, because they are also illustrative of what has formerly been said on the immense purchasing power which may be exercised, and the great rise of prices which may be produced, by credit not represented by bank notes, or even bills of exchange.

Among the earliest speculators for an advance in the price of tea, in consequence of our dispute with China in 1839, were several retail grocers and tea dealers. There was a general disposition among the trade to get into stock, that is, to lay in at once a quantity which would meet the probable demand from their customers for several months to come. Some, however, among them, more sanguine and adventurous than the rest, availed themselves of their credit with the importers and wholesale dealers, for purchasing quantities much beyond the estimated demand in their own business. As the purchases were made in the first instance ostensibly, and perhaps really, for the legitimate purposes and within the limits of their regular business, the parties were enabled to buy without the condition of any deposit; whereas speculators, known to be such, are required to pay 2*l.* per chest to cover any probable difference of price which might arise before the expiration of the prompt, which, for this article, is three months. *Without, therefore, the outlay of a single farthing of actual capital or currency in any shape*, they made purchases to a considerable extent; and, with the profit realised on the re-sale of a part of these purchases, they were enabled to pay the deposit on further quantities when required, as was the case when the extent of the purchases attracted attention.

In this way, the speculation went on at advancing prices (100 per cent. and upwards), till nearly the expiration of the prompt, and if at that time circumstances had been such as to justify the apprehension which at one time prevailed, that all future supplies would be cut off, the prices might have still further advanced, and, at any rate, not have retrograded. In this case, the speculators might have realised, if not all the profit they had anticipated, a very handsome sum, upon which they might have been enabled to extend their business greatly, or to retire from it altogether, with a reputation for great sagacity in thus making their fortune. But instead of this favourable result, it so happened that two or three cargoes of tea which had been transhipped were admitted, contrary to expectation, to entry on their arrival here, and it was found that further indirect shipments were in progress. Thus the supply was increased beyond the calculation of the speculators; and, at the same

In this respect it is Mr. Tooke's opinion that the system about to be introduced is decidedly inferior to the old:—

> That a total separation of the business of issue from that of banking is calculated to produce greater and more abrupt transitions in the rate of interest, and in the state of credit, than the present system of union of the departments. (P. 124.)

The ground of this opinion deserves attention.

It is a fact, attested by experience, that a drain of gold upon the Bank for exportation takes place in most cases mainly by drawing out deposits. As, in the proposed system, there is nothing to cause any change in this respect, we must suppose that this would still be the case, and that the demand for gold would be first felt by the deposit department.

Now, under the present arrangements, in case of a run upon the deposits, the Bank has to rely, not only on the portion of reserve which it retains, like other bankers, against the deposits themselves, but also on the gold in reserve on account of its notes. Until all the gold in the possession of the Bank is exhausted, it is in no danger of stopping payment. But under the proposed system the department of deposit must rest upon its own resources. The reserve in the deposit department could derive no aid from the issue department, while it would have to bear the first brunt of the whole action intended to be exercised through it upon the latter. As it would be prohibited from meeting this demand by creating more notes, or even by having the notes which it paid out, and which then went to the

---

time, the consumption had been diminished by the high price. There was, consequently, a violent reaction on the market: the speculators were unable to sell without such a sacrifice as disabled them from fulfilling their engagements, and several of them consequently failed. Among these, one was mentioned who, having a capital not exceeding 1,200*l*., which was locked up in his business, had contrived to buy 4,000 chests, value above 80,000*l*., the loss upon which was about 16,000*l*.

The other example which I have to give is that of the operation on the corn market between 1838 and 1842. There was an instance of a person who, when he entered on his extensive speculations, was, as it appeared by the subsequent examination of his affairs, possessed of a capital not exceeding 5,000*l*., but being successful in the outset, and favoured by circumstances in the progress of his operations, he contrived to make purchases to such an extent, that when he stopped payment his engagements were found to amount to between 500,000*l*. and 600,000*l*. Other instances might be cited of parties, without any capital at all, who, by dint of mere credit, were enabled, while the aspect of the market favoured their views, to make purchases to a very great extent.

And be it observed, that these speculations, involving enormous purchases, on little or no capital, were carried on in 1839 and 1840, when the money market was in its most contracted state; or when, according to modern phraseology, there was the greatest scarcity of money. (Pp. 137–8.)

Sir Robert Peel talks of preventing credit from being converted into money. What, by being converted into money, could it do, more than was done in these instances?

issue department for gold, returned to it; either the reserve of the deposit department alone will require to be as great as is now requisite for the deposits and issues together, or it will be obliged to suspend its discounts and sell its securities much earlier and more abruptly than is necessary under the present mixed system. If the demand for gold were to the extent of three or four millions, no "merchant, banker, or money dealer," says Mr. Tooke,

> Could for a moment have a doubt as to the extremity of pressure which it would cause. I am most intimately persuaded that it would be within the mark to suppose that a rate of discount (assuming that the doors of the Bank and the ears of the directors were irrevocably closed against all applications) of twenty per cent. and upwards, would in many cases be submitted to, and sacrifices of goods, if any large proportion were held on credit, would be made at a still greater loss. And after all, it might be a question whether even this effort of the Bank on its securities would be effectual in restoring its reserve in sufficient time to meet the exigency.

While the circulating department was still abundantly provided with gold, the deposit department might have no alternative but to stop payment.

> And all this inconvenience may have been purely gratuitous, as a sacrifice to the currency principle; because the utmost demand for gold might have been satisfied by an export of 3,000,000*l.* or 4,000,000*l.*, which, under a system of issuing and banking, would have been attended, as in the instances of 1828–29, and 1831–32, with no inconvenience whatever. (Pp. 109–10, 111.)

Indeed, if the purpose for which the new arrangements are intended is to be carried out, the deposit department must in any case begin selling its securities the moment a drain upon it commences; because if it does not, the notes which will be returned to the issue department in exchange for gold will not have been taken from those in circulation among the public, but from the reserve in the deposit department; and the cherished object of making the currency vary in quantity exactly as would be the case with a metallic currency will not be effected.

We have now stated partly, in the words of Mr. Tooke, partly and more often in our own, the grounds on which, in common with him, we have adopted the following conclusions:—

That the proposed changes in the mode of regulating the currency will be attended with none of the advantages predicted; that, so far as intended to guard against the danger of over-issue, they are precautions against a chimerical evil; that the real evil of commercial vicissitudes, of "cycles of excitement and depression,"[*] is not touched by them, nor by any regulations which can be adopted for bank notes or other mere instruments of credit; and that in what Mr. Tooke justly calls (next to solvency and

[*See Torrens, *Inquiry*, p. iv; cf. Tooke, *Inquiry*, p. 55.]

convertibility) "the main difference between one banking system and another," namely, "the greater or less liability to abrupt changes in the rate of interest and in the state of commercial credit,"[*] the present arrangements, under the condition of a larger bank reserve, have a decided advantage over the new system.

We have left ourselves little room for any observations on Colonel Torrens's reply to Mr. Tooke.

Colonel Torrens is one of the first living economists, and, as he says of Mr. Tooke, "can afford to lose some reputation by his present publication,"[†] though we do not think that such a result is to be apprehended. In clearness and precision of statement, and in that closeness of discussion which is a great part both of argumentative power and of dialectical dexterity, Colonel Torrens has never more distinguished himself. Not a single exposed point in his adversary escapes him; and on some minor questions we think he has successfully answered Mr. Tooke. That we cannot entertain a similar opinion of his main argument, we have sufficiently shown: and the grounds of our difference have been so fully explained as to dispense, we hope, with any detailed controversy.

[*Tooke. *Inquiry*, p. 106.]
[†Torrens, *Inquiry*, p. 55.]

# 4

# On the accounts of the Bank of England under the operation of the Act 7 & 8 Vict., c.32

J. T. Danson, 'On the accounts of the Bank of England under the operation of the Act 7 & 8 Vict., c.32', *Journal of the Statistical Society*, vol. X (1847) pp. 132–53.

This article is valuable is a number of respects. It tries to take a dispassionate approach to an examination of the impact of the Act of 1844 on the relationship between the currency in circulation and the reserves. Unlike many other analyses of this issue, it is both enlightening and convincing. The article opens with a clear and concise statement of the views held by the banking and currency schools, and identifies the crucial issue as the extent to which the seeking for automaticity of the relationship between notes and bullion had been established. He reaches the conclusion that the fixed relationship did not operate, and offers two possible explanations for this finding, "either of which...is of course fatal to the theory upon which the Act of 1844 is founded" (p. 153; original article).

The important element in Danson's analysis is that he identifies the twin difficulties of the Act, and therefore the nature of the fallacy underlying the automatic principle. He is clear that, by not including the total of deposits in calculating the Bank of England's liabilities, the largest part of those liabilities was being ignored. Coupled with the extent of discretion which lay in the Banking Department's management of its reserves, it is clear, he suggests, that the Bank was able to expand credit while reducing its reserve in the same way as it had in the 1830s. Danson then applies the strictures of the Act to the operation of the Bank in 1836 and 1839, and concludes that they would have had little impact on lessening the drains.

*On the Accounts of the Bank of England under the Operation of the Act 7 & 8 Vict., c.* 32. By J. T. DANSON, Esq., F.S.S., *of the Middle Temple.*

[Read before the Statistical Society, 18th January, 1847.]

It is the purpose of the present paper to place upon record, in a collected form, and in as clear and simple a manner as the nature of the subject admits of, the principal facts necessary to a just appreciation of the influence of the Act 7 and 8 Vict., c. 32, upon the business of the Bank of England, during the two years extending from the beginning of September, 1844, (when the Act came into operation,) to the beginning of September, 1846.

The subject obviously derives its interest mainly from two considerations; 1st, the very great influence the operations of the Bank of England have upon the commercial transactions of this country, and incidentally upon those of other countries; and, 2ndly, that the legislative measure referred to rests upon a theory of the currency which, whether it be true or false, is very generally admitted to stand upon debateable ground.

Were there a general concurrence of opinion among the highest authorities upon the subject of the currency, as to the truth of the propositions upon which the Act is founded, and consequently as to the propriety of its enactments, it would still, it is conceived, be desirable to ascertain, by an examination of its actual effect upon the business of the Bank, how far the admitted theory was confirmed in practice. But as the highest authorities were not only divided in opinion when the Act was under discussion, but continue to be so, there is an additional and more urgent reason for marking with care every indication the actual operation of the Act may furnish of the truth or fallacy of the particular theory it embodies, and of the validity of which its operation is avowedly regarded by both parties as a test.

It does not, of course, fall within the scope of the present paper, as embracing the results of an investigation purely statistical, to consider the points in dispute between the supporters and the opponents of the Act of 1844, further than as the views of either party may be illustrated, or their correctness tested, by the facts before us. It may, however, be desirable, before entering upon the facts themselves, to state shortly the leading features of the view of the subject generally understood to be taken by each party. They are gathered on the one hand from the writings of Mr. Jones Loyd and Colonel Torrens, and the speeches of Sir Robert Peel in favour of the measure, and, on the other, from the writings of Mr. Tooke and Mr. Fullarton against it, and are comprised in the following propositions. It is held by the former—

1. That the amount of the circulating medium in the hands of the public may be greater or less than is properly required for the transaction of the current business of the community; and that when greater, it tends, by the excess, to make the use of the circulating medium too cheap.

2. That as the value of all other commodities is measured by that of the circulating medium, prices, or the nominal expressions of their value, are at such periods enhanced.

3. That such enhancement, by reducing exports, and stimulating

imports, turns the foreign exchanges against us, and leads to a drain of bullion.

4. That if, on the other hand, the amount of the circulating medium be reduced *below* that properly required for the time, a contrary effect will ensue, producing favourable exchanges, and an influx of bullion.

5. That one principal cause, and that which has heretofore been the most common in this country, of an undue expansion of the circulating medium, is the putting or keeping in circulation, by their issuers, of too large an amount of bank notes payable on demand.

6. That the issuers of such notes can regulate at will the amount of them in circulation; and

7. That if the bank notes in circulation be kept in strict proportion to the bullion in the hands of their issuers, the amount of the circulating medium will be prevented from becoming greater than it should be, and the mischief held to arise from its becoming so will be averted.

The counter propositions of those who hold that the Act of 1844 is not founded upon correct views of the currency may, for the present purpose, be sufficiently stated as follows:—

1. That no greater amount of the circulating medium, whether in coin or notes, is ever in actual use, or therefore in circulation, than is required by the current transactions of the community; for that so much of it as there is no present use for goes either into hoards or into bankers' deposits. That if hoarded, it ceases to have any effect as circulating medium; and that if deposited with bankers, it can only pass again into use *at interest*, which interest will only be paid by those who have a profitable use for it.

2. That while a large portion of the circulating medium is dependent solely upon the credit of its issuers, its extension can, in fact, only be limited by the state of that credit on the one hand, and by the aggregate demand of those who are willing to pay for its use on the other.

3. That while there is a large fund of deposits in every part of the country payable on demand, an issuing banker cannot affect the aggregate amount of the circulating medium by issuing or withdrawing his notes.

4. That the amount of bank notes in circulation, representing only one portion of the addition made by the operations of bankers to the amount of the circulating medium, through the agency of their credit with the public, a restriction upon the amount of the addition so made must be ineffectual, unless it be accompanied by a like restriction on such of their other operations as have the same or a similar effect; and that, therefore, the omission of any regard to deposits, and their effect in supplying, readily and extensively, the place of a portion of the circulating medium of this country, must render the restriction now placed upon the bank notes in circulation ineffectual to limit the amount of the circulating medium, whenever it shall become practically inconvenient either to bankers or to the public.

5. That the true measure of the voluntary addition made by a banker to the amount of the circulating medium is found, *not* in the amount of his notes in circulation, but in the terms upon which he makes advances, or in other words, upon the price he charges for the

use of so much of the circulating medium as he happens to command, either by the actual possession of money, or by his credit; and

6. That any attempt to control the issuing banker by law in the management of this branch of his business would be, in fact, an attempt to fix the price of the use of money, or of credit held sufficient to represent money, which, like all other prices, is, and must continue to be, governed by influences wholly beyond the control of the Legislature.

The Act 7 and 8 Vict. c. 32 (as well as the other measures subsequently applied by Parliament to the banking system of the United Kingdom) was based upon a series of resolutions introduced into the House of Commons by Sir Robert Peel, and there discussed early in the Session of 1844. Three of these resolutions (the 2nd, 3rd, and 4th,) stated, in few words, the main purposes of the Act. They were as follows:—

"2. That it is expedient to provide by law that the Bank of England should henceforth be divided into two separate departments, one exclusively confined to the issue and circulation of notes, the other to the conduct of banking business.

"3. That it is expedient to limit the amount of securities upon which it shall henceforth be lawful for the Bank of England to issue notes payable to bearer on demand; and that such amount shall only be increased under certain conditions, to be prescribed by law.

"4. That it is expedient to provide by law that a weekly publication should be made by the Bank of England of the state both of the Circulation and of the Banking Departments."

The manner in which these resolutions were subsequently embodied in the Act will be best gathered from a short statement of such of its provisions as are material to the present inquiry.

The first section enacts that, after 31st August, 1844, the issue of promissory notes shall be kept wholly distinct from the general banking business of the Company, and be carried on separately as "The Issue Department of the Bank of England."

By section 2 the Governor and Company are directed, after the same date, to set apart securities to the value of £14,000,000, and appropriate them to the Issue Department. Of this sum the debt of the Government to the Company is to be taken as part. And, in addition to the securities, there is to be placed in the Issue Department so much of the gold and silver coin in the possession of the Bank as shall not be required in the Banking Department. Thereupon an equal amount in notes (including those in circulation) shall be issued from the Issue Department to the Banking Department; and the whole amount shall be deemed to be issued on the credit of such securities, coin, and bullion.

And by section 6 an account, in a prescribed form, is to be rendered by the Bank of England, weekly, to the Commissioners of Stamps and Taxes, to be by them published in the next succeeding *London Gazette*.

The following tables exhibit, in the order of date, every item of the accounts of the Bank as rendered and published weekly under this Act, from the time it came into operation (1st September, 1844) down to 5th of September, 1846.

It may be necessary to observe, that before the Act of 1844 came into operation the accounts of the Bank were also published, but less frequently, and in another and shorter form. And as the accounts in the form directed by the new Act are, partly from their increased detail, and partly from their appearing in two separate parts, somewhat less generally intelligible than in the old form, and as uniformity is also requisite to any comparison of the state of the accounts before and after the Act, and such comparisons may be found necessary to a right apprehension of the fluctuations now to be observed, the accounts just given are repeated in the old form. And for the sake of additional clearness in this more simple view of the accounts, five figures on the left hand of each sum are omitted throughout, leaving the millions to stand as whole numbers, and the next figure on the right as a decimal fraction.

It will be noticed that the sums given in the second series of tables are none of them to be found in the accounts as stated in the new form. It is therefore proper to state how they are obtained.

The "*circulation*" is obtained by deducting from the "notes issued" from the Issue Department the "notes" remaining in the Banking Department, and adding to the remainder the "seven days' bills." Properly speaking, these bills should not be included in a statement of the circulation made use of in testing the operation of the Act of 1844; for though they commonly circulate as bank notes for some time after the expiration of the period for which they are drawn, and, from the first, serve nearly the same purposes as bank notes, they do not come within the definition of what constitutes the "circulation" advanced by the supporters of the Act. They were, however, always included by the Bank in the returns of her note circulation made before the Act, and must therefore be so given in any continuation of the old form of her accounts. And as their amount happens to be tolerably uniform during the period under review, seldom exceeding or falling much short of one million, the addition does not materially affect the apparent variations of the circulation in reference to the remaining items of the account; and the more correct amount may always be obtained, very nearly, by a simple deduction of that sum.

The "*deposits*" are obtained by adding together the amounts now given, separately, as "public deposits" and "private deposits," in the Banking Department.

The "*securities*" are obtained by adding together the "Government debt" and "other securities" in the Issue Department, and the "public" and "other securities" in the Banking Department, and deducting from the sum the amount returned as "capital" in the Banking Department.

The "*bullion*" is obtained by adding the "gold" and "silver" bullion in the Issue Department to the "coin" in the Banking Department.

The "*reserve*" is an item furnished to aid the purpose of the present inquiry. It is obtained by adding together the "notes" and "coin" in the Banking Department. It exhibits the amount of the reserve held at any given time against the sum of the deposits and seven days' bills, and thus marks the proportion of available assets to liabilities payable on demand, fixed by the Bank in the exercise of the discretion left to her in the Banking Department.

ISSUE DEPARTMENT.

| Week ending | Notes. | Government Debt. | Other Securities. | Bullion. | |
|---|---|---|---|---|---|
| | | | | Gold. | Silver. |
| 1844. | £ | £ | £ | £ | £ |
| Sept. 7 .... | 28,351,295 | 11,015,100 | 2,984,900 | 12,657,208 | 1,694,087 |
| „ 14 .... | 28,500,880 | 11,015,100 | 2,984,900 | 12,806,794 | 1,694,086 |
| „ 21 .... | 28,582,705 | 11,015,100 | 2,984,900 | 12,888,619 | 1,694,086 |
| „ 28 .... | 28,362,830 | 11,015,100 | 2,984,900 | 12,668,744 | 1,694,086 |
| Oct. 5 .... | 28,082,905 | 11,015,100 | 2,984,900 | 12,388,819 | 1,694,086 |
| „ 12 .... | 27,838,085 | 11,015,100 | 2,984,900 | 12,149,367 | 1,688,718 |
| „ 19 .... | 27,731,910 | 11,015,100 | 2,984,900 | 12,043,192 | 1,688,718 |
| „ 26 .... | 27,545,730 | 11,015,100 | 2,984,900 | 11,897,842 | 1,647,888 |
| Nov. 2 .... | 27,498,580 | 11,015,100 | 2,984,900 | 11,875,969 | 1,622,611 |
| „ 9 .... | 27,400,995 | 11,015,100 | 2,984,900 | 11,790,467 | 1,610,528 |
| „ 16 .... | 27,507,795 | 11,015,100 | 2,984,900 | 11,914,184 | 1,593,611 |
| „ 23 .... | 27,528,875 | 11,015,100 | 2,984,900 | 11,935,264 | 1,583,611 |
| „ 30 .... | 27,786,190 | 11,015,100 | 2,984,900 | 12,192,579 | 1,593,611 |
| Dec. 7 .... | 27,817,505 | 11,015,100 | 2,984,900 | 12,223,894 | 1,593,611 |
| „ 14 .... | 28,003,705 | 11,015,100 | 2,984,900 | 12,410,094 | 1,593,611 |
| „ 21 .... | 28,151,730 | 11,015,100 | 2,984,900 | 12,558,119 | 1,593,611 |
| „ 28 .... | 28,200,165 | 11,015,100 | 2,984,900 | 12,606,554 | 1,593,611 |
| 1845. | | | | | |
| Jan. 4 .... | 28,087,055 | 11,015,100 | 2,984,900 | 12,493,444 | 1,593,611 |
| „ 11 .... | 28,163,130 | 11,015,100 | 2,984,900 | 12,543,092 | 1,620,038 |
| „ 18 .... | 28,133,080 | 11,015,100 | 2,984,900 | 12,480,235 | 1,652,845 |
| „ 25 .... | 28,128,310 | 11,015,100 | 2,984,900 | 12,463,197 | 1,665,113 |
| Feb. 1 .... | 28,232,485 | 11,015,100 | 2,984,900 | 12,548,405 | 1,684,080 |
| „ 8 .... | 28,447,835 | 11,015,100 | 2,984,900 | 12,552,401 | 1,895,434 |
| „ 15 .... | 28,537,255 | 11,015,100 | 2,984,900 | 12,638,987 | 1,898,268 |
| „ 22 .... | 28,679,520 | 11,015,100 | 2,984,900 | 12,755,367 | 1,924,153 |
| March 1 .... | 28,952,105 | 11,015,100 | 2,984,900 | 12,943,918 | 2,008,187 |
| „ 8 .... | 29,040,075 | 11,015,100 | 2,984,900 | 13,008,880 | 2,031,195 |
| „ 15 .... | 29,148,060 | 11,015,100 | 2,984,900 | 13,102,753 | 2,045,307 |
| „ 22 .... | 29,213,555 | 11,015,100 | 2,984,900 | 13,177,831 | 2,035,724 |
| „ 29 .... | 29,471,410 | 11,015,100 | 2,984,900 | 13,380,953 | 2,090,457 |
| April 5 .... | 29,352,145 | 11,015,100 | 2,984,900 | 13,260,543 | 2,091,602 |
| „ 12 .... | 29,216,950 | 11,015,100 | 2,984,900 | 13,143,380 | 2,073,570 |
| „ 19 .... | 29,184,220 | 11,015,100 | 2,984,900 | 13,110,947 | 2,073,273 |
| „ 26 .... | 29,253,945 | 11,015,100 | 2,984,900 | 13,180,672 | 2,073,273 |
| May 3 .... | 29,167,095 | 11,015,100 | 2,984,900 | 13,088,142 | 2,078,953 |
| „ 10 .... | 29,222,935 | 11,015,100 | 2,984,900 | 13,124,113 | 2,098,822 |
| „ 17 .... | 29,340,425 | 11,015,100 | 2,984,900 | 13,237,395 | 2,103,030 |
| „ 24 .... | 29,412,545 | 11,015,100 | 2,984,900 | 13,309,515 | 2,103,030 |
| „ 31 .... | 29,635,735 | 11,015,100 | 2,984,900 | 13,532,705 | 2,103,030 |
| June 7 .... | 29,732,600 | 11,015,100 | 2,984,900 | 13,605,716 | 2,126,884 |
| „ 14 .... | 29,917,115 | 11,015,100 | 2,984,900 | 13,785,460 | 2,131,655 |
| „ 21 .... | 30,051,610 | 11,015,100 | 2,984,900 | 13,911,607 | 2,140,003 |
| „ 28 .... | 30,047,470 | 11,015,100 | 2,984,900 | 13,907,467 | 2,140,003 |
| July 5 .... | 29,891,935 | 11,015,100 | 2,984,900 | 13,751,932 | 2,140,003 |
| „ 12 .... | 29,682,660 | 11,015,100 | 2,984,900 | 13,542,657 | 2,140,003 |
| „ 19 .... | 29,393,700 | 11,015,100 | 2,984,900 | 13,394,306 | 1,999,394 |
| „ 26 .... | 29,243,520 | 11,015,100 | 2,984,900 | 13,244,126 | 1,999,394 |
| Aug. 2 .... | 29,196,760 | 11,015,100 | 2,984,900 | 13,206,991 | 1,989,769 |
| „ 9 .... | 29,141,605 | 11,015,100 | 2,984,900 | 13,151,836 | 1,989,769 |
| „ 16 .... | 29,075,905 | 11,015,100 | 2,984,900 | 13,086,136 | 1,989,769 |
| „ 23 .... | 29,022,310 | 11,015,100 | 2,984,900 | 13,032,541 | 1,989,769 |
| „ 30 .... | 29,009,005 | 11,015,100 | 2,984,900 | 13,019,004 | 1,990,001 |

BANKING DEPARTMENT.

| Week ending | Capital. | Rest. | Deposits. | | Seven Days' and other Bills. | Securities. | | Notes. | Coin. |
|---|---|---|---|---|---|---|---|---|---|
| | | | Public. | Private. | | Public. | Other. | | |
| 1844. | £ | £ | £ | £ | £ | £ | £ | £ | £ |
| Sept. 7 | 14,553,000 | 3,564,729 | 3,630,809 | 8,644,348 | 1,030,354 | 14,554,834 | 7,835,616 | 8,175,025 | 857,765 |
| " 14 | 14,553,000 | 3,565,796 | 4,417,067 | 8,475,101 | 1,007,670 | 14,554,834 | 8,146,689 | 8,620,220 | 696,891 |
| " 21 | 14,553,000 | 3,567,007 | 5,293,615 | 8,511,771 | 972,959 | 14,554,834 | 8,802,714 | 8,964,545 | 576,259 |
| " 28 | 14,553,000 | 3,568,518 | 6,010,235 | 8,286,772 | 1,052,280 | 14,554,834 | 9,795,840 | 8,460,705 | 659,426 |
| Oct. 5 | 14,553,000 | 3,552,704 | 6,202,322 | 8,225,082 | 1,081,258 | 14,554,834 | 10,510,120 | 7,930,010 | 619,402 |
| " 12 | 14,553,000 | 3,059,645 | 8,147,290 | 8,230,673 | 1,107,985 | 16,352,834 | 10,528,785 | 7,610,025 | 606,919 |
| " 19 | 14,553,000 | 3,102,033 | 3,965,196 | 8,506,798 | 1,074,673 | 15,676,037 | 8,418,826 | 6,648,665 | 458,172 |
| " 26 | 14,553,000 | 3,105,387 | 3,556,646 | 8,291,481 | 1,065,712 | 15,408,775 | 8,387,508 | 6,224,845 | 551,098 |
| Nov. 2 | 14,553,000 | 3,131,881 | 3,471,119 | 8,757,379 | 1,051,941 | 15,070,775 | 8,675,659 | 6,678,715 | 540,171 |
| " 9 | 14,553,000 | 3,133,564 | 3,653,893 | 8,340,444 | 1,019,350 | 14,409,775 | 8,731,567 | 6,844,275 | 714,631 |
| " 16 | 14,553,000 | 3,137,195 | 3,879,458 | 8,029,934 | 989,320 | 13,539,775 | 9,398,630 | 6,927,045 | 723,457 |
| " 23 | 14,553,000 | 3,139,027 | 4,812,191 | 7,864,144 | 965,990 | 13,539,775 | 9,547,462 | 7,410,400 | 836,715 |
| " 30 | 14,553,000 | 3,140,040 | 5,226,633 | 8,345,610 | 949,133 | 13,539,775 | 9,958,645 | 7,943,850 | 772,146 |
| Dec. 7 | 14,553,000 | 3,110,069 | 5,795,572 | 8,442,809 | 966,455 | 13,540,619 | 10,193,713 | 8,286,105 | 827,468 |
| " 14 | 14,553,000 | 3,105,886 | 6,385,654 | 3,381,188 | 994,174 | 13,540,619 | 10,293,154 | 8,745,540 | 840,589 |
| " 21 | 14,553,000 | 3,110,513 | 7,075,258 | 8,348,738 | 967,934 | 13,540,619 | 10,763,777 | 8,959,630 | 791,417 |
| " 28 | 14,553,000 | 3,113,267 | 7,411,605 | 8,265,079 | 984,540 | 13,540,619 | 11,031,821 | 9,076,800 | 678,251 |
| 1845. | | | | | | | | | |
| Jan. 4 | 14,553,000 | 3,127,278 | 7,366,643 | 8,037,320 | 1,015,166 | 13,539,720 | 11,426,996 | 8,418,125 | 714,566 |
| " 11 | 14,553,000 | 3,194,623 | 4,123,966 | 8,877,905 | 1,019,528 | 14,386,839 | 9,001,544 | 7,772,930 | 612,709 |
| " 18 | 14,553,000 | 3,208,159 | 3,069,572 | 8,803,570 | 1,079,821 | 13,843,692 | 8,627,598 | 7,588,085 | 654,747 |
| " 25 | 14,553,000 | 3,209,696 | 2,787,253 | 8,714,052 | 1,058,727 | 13,651,692 | 8,561,399 | 7,418,075 | 691,562 |
| Feb. 1 | 14,553,000 | 3,298,944 | 2,852,124 | 8,713,690 | 1,085,065 | 13,541,692 | 8,652,751 | 7,642,235 | 666,145 |
| " 8 | 14,553,000 | 3,302,806 | 3,715,171 | 9,732,193 | 1,068,046 | 13,476,160 | 10,065,958 | 8,128,350 | 700,748 |
| " 15 | 14,553,000 | 3,302,136 | 4,630,247 | 9,944,408 | 1,031,922 | 13,474,379 | 10,821,457 | 8,395,065 | 770,812 |
| " 22 | 14,553,000 | 3,252,281 | 5,237,999 | 9,941,556 | 985,035 | 13,522,379 | 10,784,494 | 8,889,215 | 773,783 |
| March 1 | 14,553,000 | 3,575,172 | 5,476,984 | 10,323,799 | 983,328 | 13,474,379 | 11,707,400 | 8,952,545 | 777,959 |
| " 8 | 14,553,000 | 3,577,267 | 5,879,753 | 10,379,610 | 982,386 | 13,474,379 | 11,720,459 | 9,340,815 | 836,363 |
| " 15 | 14,553,000 | 3,579,429 | 6,451,283 | 9,994,572 | 980,378 | 13,474,379 | 11,836,377 | 9,451,385 | 796,521 |
| " 22 | 14,553,000 | 3,581,884 | 6,890,121 | 10,452,425 | 992,192 | 13,474,379 | 12,535,169 | 9,673,205 | 786,869 |
| " 29 | 14,553,000 | 3,584,054 | 7,321,855 | 10,713,052 | 1,023,977 | 13,589,379 | 13,126,469 | 9,747,280 | 732,810 |
| April 5 | 14,553,000 | 3,586,219 | 6,924,106 | 10,445,950 | 1,063,189 | 13,474,379 | 13,123,678 | 9,252,350 | 722,057 |
| " 12 | 14,553,000 | 3,147,578 | 4,355,166 | 11,753,022 | 1,085,969 | 15,147,495 | 11,069,829 | 8,001,434 | 675,977 |
| " 19 | 14,553,000 | 3,151,333 | 3,218,350 | 11,531,267 | 1,122,066 | 14,471,966 | 10,654,085 | 7,791,345 | 658,620 |
| " 26 | 14,553,000 | 3,176,289 | 2,643,448 | 10,781,637 | 1,181,547 | 13,921,966 | 9,680,272 | 8,101,770 | 631,913 |
| May 3 | 14,553,000 | 3,183,817 | 2,712,041 | 10,355,640 | 1,139,238 | 13,616,966 | 9,857,686 | 7,827,925 | 641,159 |
| " 10 | 14,553,000 | 3,183,822 | 3,391,477 | 10,065,486 | 1,106,626 | 13,416,966 | 10,104,644 | 8,140,050 | 638,751 |
| " 17 | 14,553,000 | 3,188,579 | 4,357,386 | 10,276,032 | 1,060,598 | 13,385,797 | 10,656,808 | 8,734,045 | 658,945 |
| " 24 | 14,553,000 | 3,191,461 | 5,051,007 | 10,087,531 | 1,021,487 | 13,384,898 | 10,644,537 | 9,014,845 | 860,206 |
| " 31 | 14,553,000 | 3,181,245 | 5,352,114 | 10,865,704 | 1,030,555 | 13,464,898 | 11,558,992 | 9,182,485 | 776,243 |
| June 7 | 14,553,000 | 3,136,091 | 5,745,482 | 10,564,624 | 1,018,497 | 13,384,898 | 11,470,805 | 9,382,505 | 779,486 |
| " 14 | 14,553,000 | 3,136,239 | 6,261,465 | 10,315,111 | 976,405 | 13,384,898 | 11,305,902 | 9,854,015 | 696,805 |
| " 21 | 14,553,000 | 3,140,557 | 6,951,773 | 10,147,586 | 1,001,282 | 13,384,898 | 11,984,420 | 9,837,175 | 587,705 |
| " 28 | 14,553,000 | 3,143,841 | 7,398,420 | 10,154,148 | 1,026,853 | 13,384,898 | 12,619,663 | 9,717,270 | 554,431 |
| July 5 | 14,553,000 | 3,164,433 | 7,330,309 | 10,041,440 | 1,045,502 | 13,384,206 | 12,944,496 | 9,279,785 | 526,197 |
| " 12 | 14,553,000 | 3,218,008 | 3,456,089 | 11,356,519 | 1,081,545 | 13,800,344 | 11,282,221 | 8,068,970 | 513,626 |
| " 19 | 14,553,000 | 3,234,268 | 2,834,528 | 10,934,390 | 1,091,953 | 13,456,776 | 10,815,121 | 7,890,610 | 485,632 |
| " 26 | 14,553,000 | 3,321,972 | 2,933,908 | 10,745,613 | 1,085,211 | 13,539,344 | 10,607,877 | 7,942,485 | 549,998 |
| Aug. 2 | 14,553,000 | 3,338,246 | 3,215,363 | 10,960,214 | 1,072,260 | 13,321,844 | 11,403,003 | 7,849,785 | 503,851 |
| " 9 | 14,553,000 | 3,340,750 | 4,034,767 | 10,187,780 | 1,050,220 | 13,321,844 | 11,634,159 | 7,682,465 | 528,049 |
| " 16 | 14,553,000 | 3,348,596 | 4,969,963 | 8,973,401 | 1,374,346 | 13,441,844 | 11,679,359 | 7,494,205 | 603,808 |
| " 23 | 14,553,000 | 3,349,282 | 5,393,936 | 8,408,887 | 1,383,566 | 13,321,844 | 11,353,577 | 7,832,955 | 580,295 |
| " 30 | 14,553,000 | 3,588,888 | 5,830,311 | 8,571,253 | 1,059,606 | 13,347,570 | 11,712,811 | 7,959,390 | 583,287 |

ISSUE DEPARTMENT.

| Week ending | Notes. | Government Debt. | Other Securities. | Bullion. | |
|---|---|---|---|---|---|
| | | | | Gold. | Silver. |
| 1845. | £ | £ | £ | £ | £ |
| Sept. 6 .... | 28,953,300 | 11,015,100 | 2,984,900 | 12,982,591 | 1,970,709 |
| „ 13 .... | 28,790,195 | 11,015,100 | 2,984,900 | 12,819,486 | 1,970,709 |
| „ 20 .... | 28,798,230 | 11,015,100 | 2,984,900 | 12,863,507 | 1,934,723 |
| „ 27 .... | 28,557,990 | 11,015,100 | 2,984,900 | 12,717,050 | 1,840,940 |
| Oct. 4 .... | 28,355,670 | 11,015,100 | 2,984,900 | 12,514,730 | 1,840,940 |
| „ 11 .... | 28,068,820 | 11,015,100 | 2,984,900 | 12,253,289 | 1,815,531 |
| „ 18 .... | 27,778,955 | 11,015,100 | 2,984,900 | 12,018,447 | 1,760,508 |
| „ 25 .... | 27,415,690 | 11,015,100 | 2,984,900 | 11,758,159 | 1,657,531 |
| Nov. 1 .... | 27,267,115 | 11,015,100 | 2,984,900 | 11,661,681 | 1,605,434 |
| „ 8 .... | 27,202,365 | 11,015,100 | 2,984,900 | 11,670,074 | 1,532,291 |
| „ 15 .... | 26,974,685 | 11,015,100 | 2,984,900 | 11,478,722 | 1,495,963 |
| „ 22 .... | 27,036,550 | 11,015,100 | 2,984,900 | 11,441,931 | 1,594,619 |
| „ 29 .... | 26,733,810 | 11,015,100 | 2,984,900 | 11,159,981 | 1,573,829 |
| Dec. 6 .... | 26,540,480 | 11,015,100 | 2,984,900 | 10,992,631 | 1,547,849 |
| „ 13 .... | 26,626,350 | 11,015,100 | 2,984,900 | 11,054,501 | 1,571,849 |
| „ 20 .... | 26,819,390 | 11,015,100 | 2,984,900 | 11,240,465 | 1,578,925 |
| „ 27 .... | 26,771,510 | 11,015,100 | 2,984,900 | 11,189,484 | 1,582,026 |
| 1846. | | | | | |
| Jan. 3 .... | 26,675,925 | 11,015,100 | 2,984,900 | 11,093,869 | 1,582,056 |
| „ 10 .... | 26,541,200 | 11,015,100 | 2,984,900 | 11,006,127 | 1,535,073 |
| „ 17 .... | 26,573,910 | 11,015,100 | 2,984,900 | 11,025,956 | 1,547,954 |
| „ 24 .... | 26,525,025 | 11,015,100 | 2,984,900 | 10,974,471 | 1,550,554 |
| „ 31 .... | 26,587,355 | 11,015,100 | 2,984,900 | 11,028,945 | 1,558,410 |
| Feb. 7 .... | 26,698,620 | 11,015,100 | 2,984,900 | 11,140,210 | 1,558,410 |
| „ 14 .... | 26,800,325 | 11,015,100 | 2,984,900 | 11,177,282 | 1,623,043 |
| „ 21 .... | 26,973,255 | 11,015,100 | 2,984,900 | 11,346,130 | 1,627,125 |
| „ 28 .... | 27,015,295 | 11,015,100 | 2,984,900 | 11,353,065 | 1,662,230 |
| March 7 .... | 27,079,270 | 11,015,100 | 2,984,900 | 11,417,040 | 1,662,230 |
| „ 14 .... | 27,117,805 | 11,015,100 | 2,984,900 | 11,407,524 | 1,710,281 |
| „ 21 .... | 27,264,475 | 11,015,100 | 2,984,900 | 11,554,194 | 1,710,281 |
| „ 28 .... | 27,269,245 | 11,015,100 | 2,984,900 | 11,558,964 | 1,710,281 |
| April 4 .... | 27,181,980 | 11,015,100 | 2,984,900 | 11,460,445 | 1,721,535 |
| „ 11 .... | 27,030,255 | 11,015,100 | 2,984,900 | 11,308,300 | 1,721,955 |
| „ 18 .... | 27,031,510 | 11,015,100 | 2,984,900 | 11,250,593 | 1,780,917 |
| „ 25 .... | 27,049,510 | 11,015,100 | 2,984,900 | 11,256,880 | 1,792,630 |
| May 2 .... | 27,072,295 | 11,015,100 | 2,984,900 | 11,279,130 | 1,793,165 |
| „ 9 .... | 27,244,995 | 11,015,100 | 2,984,900 | 11,451,830 | 1,793,165 |
| „ 16 .... | 27,520,215 | 11,015,100 | 2,984,900 | 11,633,619 | 1,886,596 |
| „ 23 .... | 27,706,865 | 11,015,100 | 2,984,900 | 11,782,453 | 1,924,412 |
| „ 30 .... | 27,993,880 | 11,015,100 | 2,984,900 | 12,062,597 | 1,931,283 |
| June 6 .... | 28,325,000 | 11,015,100 | 2,984,900 | 12,192,710 | 2,132,290 |
| „ 13 .... | 28,603,395 | 11,015,100 | 2,984,900 | 12,371,105 | 2,232,290 |
| „ 20 .... | 29,005,160 | 11,015,100 | 2,984,000 | 12,592,403 | 2,412,757 |
| „ 27 .... | 29,273,105 | 11,015,100 | 2,984,900 | 12,849,579 | 2,423,526 |
| July 4 .... | 29,322,200 | 11,015,100 | 2,984,900 | 12,905,074 | 2,417,126 |
| „ 11 .... | 29,266,360 | 11,015,100 | 2,984,900 | 12,844,442 | 2,421,918 |
| „ 18 .... | 29,139,905 | 11,015,100 | 2,984,900 | 12,703,642 | 2,436,263 |
| „ 25 .... | 29,312,945 | 11,015,100 | 2,984,900 | 12,875,243 | 2,437,702 |
| Aug. 1 .... | 29,292,320 | 11,015,100 | 2,984,900 | 12,854,618 | 2,437,702 |
| „ 8 .... | 29,386,305 | 11,015,100 | 2,984,900 | 12,935,426 | 2,450,879 |
| „ 15 .... | 29,456,535 | 11,015,100 | 2,984,900 | 12,958,912 | 2,497,623 |
| „ 22 .... | 29,653,990 | 11,015,100 | 2,984,900 | 13,145,719 | 2,508,271 |
| „ 29 .... | 29,875,890 | 11,015,100 | 2,984,900 | 13,199,102 | 2,676,788 |
| Sept. 5 .... | 29,760,870 | 11,015,100 | 2,984,900 | 13,057,997 | 2,702,873 |

BANKING DEPARTMENT.

| Week ending. | Capital. | Rest. | Deposits. | | Seven Days' and other Bills. | Securities. | | Notes. | Coin. |
|---|---|---|---|---|---|---|---|---|---|
| | | | Public. | Private. | | Public. | Other. | | |
| 1845. | £ | £ | £ | £ | £ | £ | £ | £ | £ |
| Sept. 6 | 14,553,000 | 3,608,180 | 6,474,705 | 8,507,213 | 1,021,689 | 13,468,643 | 11,967,081 | 8,255,505 | 473,558 |
| „ 13 | 14,553,000 | 3,611,164 | 7,319,619 | 8,316,750 | 963,995 | 13,348,643 | 12,391,188 | 8,430,700 | 593,997 |
| „ 20 | 14,553,000 | 3,616,685 | 8,222,109 | 8,110,787 | 1,020,324 | 13,348,643 | 13,297,048 | 8,327,895 | 549,319 |
| „ 27 | 14,553,000 | 3,621,711 | 8,802,110 | 8,070,212 | 1,000,311 | 13,348,643 | 14,149,003 | 7,946,995 | 602,703 |
| Oct. 4 | 14,553,000 | 3,629,978 | 8,703,497 | 8,167,961 | 1,088,160 | 13,348,643 | 15,188,965 | 7,095,615 | 509,373 |
| „ 11 | 14,553,000 | 3,140,006 | 8,782,975 | 8,474,856 | 1,081,206 | 13,348,643 | 15,133,966 | 7,037,600 | 511,834 |
| „ 18 | 14,553,000 | 3,188,641 | 4,488,419 | 9,835,604 | 1,123,843 | 13,203,138 | 14,049,529 | 5,525,510 | 411,330 |
| „ 25 | 14,553,000 | 3,212,133 | 4,323,662 | 8,930,134 | 1,000,472 | 13,203,138 | 12,931,115 | 5,389,575 | 585,573 |
| Nov. 1 | 14,553,000 | 3,224,453 | 4,487,058 | 9,099,737 | 1,106,405 | 13,203,138 | 13,429,813 | 5,219,775 | 617,927 |
| „ 8 | 14,553,000 | 3,234,595 | 5,340,731 | 9,134,243 | 1,133,320 | 13,203,138 | 14,234,438 | 5,437,730 | 520,583 |
| „ 15 | 14,553,000 | 3,244,733 | 6,524,834 | 8,899,130 | 1,101,349 | 13,203,138 | 15,041,397 | 5,483,110 | 595,401 |
| „ 22 | 14,553,000 | 3,252,209 | 7,363,168 | 9,024,223 | 1,063,589 | 13,201,863 | 15,454,390 | 6,076,985 | 522,951 |
| „ 29 | 14,553,000 | 3,246,426 | 7,670,581 | 8,992,719 | 1,045,574 | 13,201,863 | 15,871,054 | 5,932,345 | 503,038 |
| Dec. 6 | 14,553,000 | 3,209,394 | 8,110,401 | 9,022,019 | 1,004,471 | 13,201,863 | 16,224,712 | 5,945,840 | 526,870 |
| „ 13 | 14,553,000 | 3,215,596 | 8,684,374 | 9,089,705 | 943,591 | 13,201,863 | 16,135,637 | 6,506,345 | 642,421 |
| „ 20 | 14,553,000 | 3,221,636 | 9,408,044 | 8,715,667 | 960,094 | 13,201,863 | 16,329,285 | 6,768,340 | 558,953 |
| „ 27 | 14,553,000 | 3,227,443 | 9,698,409 | 8,482,239 | 961,859 | 13,201,863 | 16,252,051 | 6,914,660 | 554,376 |
| 1846. | | | | | | | | | |
| Jan. 3 | 14,553,000 | 3,254,660 | 9,369,630 | 8,350,465 | 959,967 | 13,201,072 | 16,262,593 | 6,418,510 | 605,547 |
| „ 10 | 14,553,000 | 3,314,454 | 5,191,017 | 10,656,207 | 1,020,503 | 13,137,047 | 15,273,096 | 5,672,855 | 652,183 |
| „ 17 | 14,553,000 | 3,341,777 | 4,710,957 | 11,254,618 | 1,009,030 | 13,137,047 | 15,773,124 | 5,393,745 | 565,466 |
| „ 24 | 14,553,000 | 3,356,690 | 4,464,806 | 14,208,608 | 1,028,388 | 13,137,047 | 18,381,010 | 5,416,380 | 677,055 |
| „ 31 | 14,553,000 | 3,451,151 | 4,389,810 | 17,036,830 | 987,102 | 13,137,047 | 21,466,997 | 5,112,860 | 700,989 |
| Feb. 7 | 14,553,000 | 3,462,787 | 5,054,436 | 18,912,445 | 963,888 | 13,137,047 | 22,908,661 | 6,263,625 | 637,025 |
| „ 14 | 14,553,000 | 3,474,577 | 5,738,873 | 18,018,523 | 945,332 | 13,137,047 | 22,251,906 | 6,674,075 | 667,277 |
| „ 21 | 14,553,000 | 3,477,016 | 6,202,903 | 18,091,320 | 918,282 | 13,137,047 | 22,539,192 | 6,887,810 | 678,472 |
| „ 28 | 14,553,000 | 3,689,430 | 6,296,535 | 18,647,068 | 947,432 | 13,136,440 | 23,242,035 | 6,984,485 | 760,505 |
| March 7 | 14,553,000 | 3,757,708 | 6,502,355 | 17,828,778 | 898,176 | 13,136,440 | 22,118,987 | 7,576,625 | 707,965 |
| „ 14 | 14,553,000 | 3,767,623 | 6,804,524 | 17,476,998 | 887,487 | 13,136,440 | 21,923,787 | 7,712,120 | 717,285 |
| „ 21 | 14,553,000 | 3,780,009 | 7,065,422 | 17,356,203 | 921,887 | 13,136,440 | 21,806,194 | 8,033,665 | 700,222 |
| „ 28 | 14,553,000 | 3,789,971 | 7,319,625 | 17,103,928 | 953,579 | 13,136,731 | 22,181,392 | 7,683,690 | 718,290 |
| April 4 | 14,553,000 | 3,799,508 | 7,074,026 | 16,763,047 | 965,446 | 13,136,440 | 22,058,631 | 7,316,415 | 643,541 |
| „ 11 | 14,553,000 | 3,352,391 | 4,210,976 | 18,069,993 | 959,379 | 14,437,065 | 19,438,782 | 6,728,120 | 541,772 |
| „ 18 | 14,553,000 | 3,359,084 | 3,197,029 | 17,710,987 | 986,017 | 13,957,865 | 18,736,602 | 6,515,990 | 595,660 |
| „ 25 | 14,553,000 | 3,364,576 | 2,698,953 | 16,978,110 | 962,415 | 13,528,065 | 17,884,532 | 6,488,140 | 656,317 |
| May 2 | 14,553,000 | 3,396,540 | 2,578,451 | 16,780,380 | 965,730 | 13,303,065 | 17,901,148 | 6,408,470 | 661,418 |
| „ 9 | 14,553,000 | 3,406,284 | 3,031,375 | 16,256,526 | 981,417 | 13,023,065 | 17,734,025 | 6,836,405 | 635,107 |
| „ 16 | 15,553,000 | 3,418,272 | 4,084,117 | 16,354,017 | 963,128 | 12,988,065 | 18,222,548 | 7,497,460 | 664,461 |
| „ 23 | 14,553.000 | 3,426,036 | 4,809,183 | 15,947,268 | 970,401 | 12,988,065 | 18,236,480 | 7,774,925 | 706,478 |
| „ 30 | 14,553,000 | 3,378,878 | 5,228,640 | 16,165,620 | 890,192 | 13,008,065 | 18,460,493 | 8,043,560 | 704,212 |
| June 6 | 14,553,000 | 3,379.044 | 5,753,512 | 15,927,013 | 852,008 | 12,988,065 | 18,321,641 | 8,468,180 | 686,691 |
| „ 13 | 14,553,000 | 3,386,810 | 6,537,132 | 15,518,397 | 862,665 | 12,988,065 | 18,122,098 | 9,011,510 | 736,331 |
| „ 20 | 14,553,000 | 3,396,774 | 7,313,539 | 15,293,909 | 832,981 | 13,090,946 | 17,984,603 | 9,631,235 | 683,419 |
| „ 27 | 14,553,000 | 3,405,354 | 7,807,802 | 15,034,361 | 851,222 | 12,987,946 | 18,257,149 | 9,664,090 | 742,554 |
| July 4 | 14,553,000 | 3,424,178 | 7,794,200 | 14,402,460 | 887,364 | 12,987,142 | 18,145,319 | 9,303,090 | 625,651 |
| „ 11 | 14,553,000 | 3,482,541 | 3,489,416 | 15,661,286 | 941,566 | 12,962,147 | 16,143,726 | 8,425,630 | 596,306 |
| „ 18 | 14,553,000 | 3,504,138 | 3,162,696 | 14,904,973 | 989,462 | 12,962,560 | 15,382,397 | 8,139,020 | 630,292 |
| „ 25 | 14,553,000 | 3,508,378 | 3,438,401 | 14,305,311 | 940,024 | 12,962,560 | 14,583,407 | 8,562,695 | 636,482 |
| Aug. 1 | 14,553,000 | 3,597,679 | 3,793,610 | 13,449,388 | 943,423 | 12,961,735 | 14,068,257 | 8,796,875 | 510,233 |
| „ 8 | 14,553,000 | 3,603,683 | 5,014,200 | 12,456,737 | 952,056 | 12,961,735 | 13,984,578 | 9,075,160 | 558,203 |
| „ 15 | 14,553,000 | 3,611,298 | 6,135,636 | 10,794,523 | 905,994 | 12,961,735 | 13,848,421 | 8,601,335 | 588,960 |
| „ 22 | 14,553,000 | 3,613,216 | 6,843,002 | 10,074,026 | 920,016 | 12,961,735 | 13,012,824 | 9,506,025 | 522,676 |
| „ 29 | 14.553,000 | 3,354,370 | 7,142,212 | 9,161,868 | 885,680 | 12,961,735 | 12,395,457 | 9,449,760 | 490,178 |
| Sept. 5 | 14,553,000 | 3,864,479 | 7,318,919 | 8,557,109 | 935,830 | 12,961,735 | 12,523,550 | 9,231,095 | 512,957 |

| Week ending | Bullion. | Circulation (including Bank Post Bills.) | Deposits. | Securities. | Reserve. |
|---|---|---|---|---|---|
| 1844. | | | | | |
| Sept. 7 | 15·1 | 21·2 | 12·2 | 21·8 | 9·0 |
| ,, 14 | 15·1 | 20·9 | 12·8 | 22·1 | 9·3 |
| ,, 21 | 15·1 | 20·6 | 13·8 | 22·8 | 9·5 |
| ,, 28 | 15·0 | 20·9 | 14·2 | 23·7 | 9·1 |
| Oct. 5 | 14·6 | 21·1 | 14·4 | 24·5 | 8·5 |
| ,, 12 | 14·3 | 21·3 | 16·3 | 26·3 | 8·2 |
| ,, 19 | 14·1 | 22·1 | 12·4 | 23·5 | 7·0 |
| ,, 26 | 14·0 | 22·3 | 11·8 | 23·2 | 6·7 |
| Nov. 2 | 14·0 | 22·2 | 12·2 | 23·1 | 7·1 |
| ,, 9 | 14·1 | 21·6 | 11·9 | 22·5 | 7·5 |
| ,, 16 | 14·2 | 21·5 | 11·8 | 22·3 | 7·6 |
| ,, 23 | 14·3 | 21·0 | 12·6 | 22·5 | 8·2 |
| ,, 30 | 14·5 | 20·7 | 13·5 | 22·9 | 8·7 |
| Dec. 7 | 14·6 | 20·5 | 14·2 | 23·1 | 9·1 |
| ,, 14 | 14·8 | 20·2 | 14·7 | 23·2 | 9·5 |
| ,, 21 | 14·9 | 20·1 | 15·4 | 23·7 | 9·6 |
| ,, 28 | 14·8 | 20·1 | 15·6 | 24·0 | 9·7 |
| 1845. | | | | | |
| Jan. 4 | 14·8 | 20·6 | 15·3 | 24·4 | 9·1 |
| ,, 11 | 14·7 | 21·4 | 12·9 | 22·8 | 8·3 |
| ,, 18 | 14·7 | 21·6 | 11·8 | 21·9 | 8·2 |
| ,, 25 | 14·8 | 21·7 | 11·4 | 21·5 | 8·1 |
| Feb. 1 | 14·8 | 21·6 | 11·5 | 21·6 | 8·3 |
| ,, 8 | 15·1 | 21·3 | 13·4 | 22·9 | 8·8 |
| ,, 15 | 15·3 | 21·1 | 14·5 | 23·7 | 9·1 |
| ,, 22 | 15·4 | 20·7 | 15·1 | 23·7 | 9·6 |
| March 1 | 15·7 | 20·9 | 15·7 | 24·6 | 9·7 |
| ,, 8 | 15·8 | 20·6 | 16·2 | 24·6 | 10·1 |
| ,, 15 | 15·9 | 20·6 | 16·4 | 24·7 | 10·2 |
| ,, 22 | 16·0 | 20·5 | 17·3 | 25·4 | 10·4 |
| ,, 29 | 16·2 | 20·7 | 18·0 | 26·1 | 10·4 |
| April 5 | 16·0 | 21·1 | 17·3 | 26·0 | 9·9 |
| ,, 12 | 15·8 | 22·3 | 16·1 | 25·6 | 8·6 |
| ,, 19 | 15·8 | 22·5 | 14·7 | 24·5 | 8·4 |
| ,, 26 | 15·8 | 22·3 | 11·4 | 23·0 | 8·7 |
| May 3 | 15·8 | 22·4 | 13·0 | 22·9 | 8·4 |
| ,, 10 | 15·8 | 22·1 | 13·4 | 22·9 | 8·7 |
| ,, 17 | 15·9 | 21·6 | 14·6 | 23·4 | 9·3 |
| ,, 24 | 16·2 | 21·4 | 15·1 | 23·4 | 9·8 |
| ,, 31 | 16·4 | 21·4 | 16·2 | 24·4 | 9·9 |
| June 7 | 16·5 | 21·3 | 16·3 | 24·3 | 10·1 |
| ,, 14 | 16·6 | 21·0 | 16·5 | 24·1 | 10·5 |
| ,, 21 | 16·6 | 21·2 | 17·0 | 24·8 | 10·4 |
| ,, 28 | 16·6 | 21·3 | 17·5 | 25·4 | 10·2 |
| July 5 | 16·4 | 21·6 | 17·3 | 25·7 | 9·7 |
| ,, 12 | 16·1 | 22·6 | 14·8 | 25·5 | 8·5 |
| ,, 19 | 15·8 | 22·5 | 13·7 | 23·7 | 8·3 |
| ,, 26 | 15·7 | 22·3 | 13·6 | 23·5 | 8·4 |
| Aug. 2 | 15·7 | 22·4 | 14·1 | 24·2 | 8·3 |
| ,, 9 | 15·6 | 22·5 | 14·2 | 24·4 | 8·2 |
| ,, 16 | 15·6 | 22·9 | 13·9 | 24·5 | 8·0 |
| ,, 23 | 15·6 | 22·5 | 13·7 | 24·1 | 8·4 |
| ,, 30 | 15·5 | 22·1 | 14·4 | 24·5 | 8·5 |

| Week ending | Bullion. | Circulation (including Bank Post Bills.) | Deposits. | Securities. | Reserve. |
|---|---|---|---|---|---|
| 1845. | | | | | |
| Sept. 6 | 15·4 | 21·7 | 14·9 | 24·8 | 8·7 |
| ,, 13 | 15·3 | 21·3 | 15·6 | 25·1 | 9·0 |
| ,, 20 | 15·3 | 21·4 | 16·3 | 26·0 | 8·8 |
| ,, 27 | 15·1 | 21·6 | 16·8 | 26·9 | 8·5 |
| Oct. 4 | 14·8 | 22·3 | 16·8 | 27·9 | 7·5 |
| ,, 11 | 14·5 | 22·1 | 17·2 | 27·9 | 7·5 |
| ,, 18 | 14·1 | 23·3 | 14·3 | 26·6 | 5·9 |
| ,, 25 | 14·0 | 23·1 | 13·2 | 25·5 | 5·9 |
| Nov. 1 | 13·8 | 23·1 | 13·5 | 26·0 | 5·8 |
| ,, 8 | 13·7 | 22·8 | 14·4 | 26·8 | 5·9 |
| ,, 15 | 13·5 | 22·5 | 15·4 | 27·6 | 6·0 |
| ,, 22 | 13·5 | 22·0 | 16·3 | 28·1 | 6·5 |
| ,, 29 | 13·2 | 21·8 | 16·6 | 28·5 | 6·4 |
| Dec. 6 | 13·0 | 21·5 | 17·1 | 28·8 | 6·4 |
| ,, 13 | 13·2 | 21·0 | 17·7 | 28·7 | 7·1 |
| ,, 20 | 13·3 | 21·0 | 18·1 | 28·9 | 7·3 |
| ,, 27 | 13·3 | 20·8 | 18·1 | 28·9 | 7·4 |
| 1846. | | | | | |
| Jan. 3 | 13·2 | 21·2 | 17·7 | 28·9 | 7·0 |
| ,, 10 | 13·1 | 21·8 | 15·8 | 27·8 | 6·3 |
| ,, 17 | 13·1 | 22·1 | 15·9 | 28·3 | 5·9 |
| ,, 24 | 13·1 | 22·1 | 18·6 | 30·9 | 6·0 |
| ,, 31 | 13·2 | 22·4 | 21·4 | 34·0 | 5·8 |
| Feb. 7 | 13·3 | 21·3 | 23·9 | 35·4 | 6·8 |
| ,, 14 | 13·4 | 21·0 | 23·7 | 34·8 | 7·3 |
| ,, 21 | 13·6 | 21·0 | 24·2 | 35·1 | 7·5 |
| ,, 28 | 13·7 | 20·9 | 24·9 | 35·8 | 7·7 |
| March 7 | 13·7 | 20·3 | 24·3 | 34·6 | 8·2 |
| ,, 14 | 13·8 | 20·2 | 23·2 | 34·5 | 8·4 |
| ,, 21 | 13·9 | 20·1 | 24·3 | 34·3 | 8·7 |
| ,, 28 | 13·9 | 20·5 | 24·4 | 34·7 | 8·3 |
| April 4 | 13·8 | 20·8 | 23·8 | 34·6 | 7·9 |
| ,, 11 | 13·5 | 21·2 | 22·2 | 33·3 | 7·2 |
| ,, 18 | 13·6 | 21·5 | 20·9 | 32·1 | 7·1 |
| ,, 25 | 13·6 | 21·5 | 19·6 | 30·8 | 7·1 |
| May 2 | 13·7 | 21·6 | 19·3 | 30·6 | 7·0 |
| ,, 9 | 13·8 | 21.3 | 19·2 | 30·0 | 7·2 |
| ,, 16 | 14·1 | 21·1 | 20·3 | 30·6 | 8·1 |
| ,, 23 | 14·4 | 21·1 | 20·7 | 30·6 | 8·4 |
| ,, 30 | 14·7 | 20·8 | 21·3 | 30·9 | 8·7 |
| June 6 | 14·9 | 20·7 | 21·6 | 30·7 | 9·1 |
| ,, 13 | 15·3 | 20·4 | 22·0 | 30·5 | 9·7 |
| ,, 20 | 15·6 | 20·2 | 22·6 | 30·4 | 10·3 |
| ,, 27 | 16·0 | 20·4 | 22·8 | 30·6 | 10·4 |
| July 4 | 15·9 | 20·9 | 22·1 | 30·6 | 9·9 |
| ,, 11 | 15·8 | 21·7 | 19·3 | 28·5 | 9·0 |
| ,, 18 | 15·7 | 22·0 | 18·0 | 27·7 | 8·7 |
| ,, 25 | 15·9 | 21·7 | 17·0 | 26·9 | 9·1 |
| Aug. 1 | 15·7 | 21·4 | 17·2 | 26·4 | 9·2 |
| ,, 8 | 15·9 | 21·2 | 17·4 | 26·3 | 9·6 |
| ,, 15 | 15·9 | 21·7 | 16·9 | 26·2 | 9·1 |
| ,, 22 | 16·1 | 21·0 | 16·9 | 25·4 | 10·0 |
| ,, 29 | 16·3 | 21·2 | 16·3 | 24·8 | 9·9 |
| Sept. 5 | 16·2 | 21·4 | 15·8 | 24·9 | 9·7 |

Before noticing the fluctuations shown in these accounts, it may be well to observe the effect of the payment of the dividends on the public funds quarterly. The periodical changes produced by these payments in the state of the Bank accounts, though of a perfectly legitimate nature, serve occasionally to give an apparent exaggeration to fluctuations of a different description, and, unless carefully regarded, are apt to falsify inferences drawn from a comparison of the accounts of one period with those of another. But in reference to the object of the present inquiry, it is more particularly to be observed, that previous to October, 1844, a period nearly coincident with that at which the Act of 1844 came into operation, the manner in which the payment of dividends was distributed over the quarters of the year had, to a much greater extent than at present, the effect of aiding occasional disturbances of the currency, and diminishing in some degree the power of the Bank in the use of the discretion she was then generally supposed to have, and was held bound to exercise over it. The sum annually payable in England upon the funded debt before that date may be stated in round numbers at about £27,000,000. If paid in four equal parts, it would therefore cause, four times a-year, a payment or transfer from public deposits of about £6,700,000. But the dividends being payable half-yearly, and about two-thirds in amount being payable in January and July, the payments made at the Bank of England at those quarters, previous to October, 1844, were not far from nine millions in amount, those of April and October being considerably less than five millions. And as the revenue, whence the public deposits were replenished, came in much more equably, there was usually a deficiency to be made up by extra advances from the Bank in January and July, which were repaid as the revenue came in subsequently. When (in 1844) the 3½ per cent. stock was reduced the annual charge of the funded debt was diminished by about £625,000; and at the same time the days for payment of the dividends upon a part of the reduced stock, amounting to upwards of four millions yearly, were moved from January and July to April and October. The effect was to make the amount of the dividends payable by the Bank, on account of the Government, nearly the same at each of the four quarters, and therefore to render more equal the quarterly fluctuations of the circulation exhibited in the Bank accounts.

The bearing of this alteration upon the management of the affairs of the Bank will be obvious when it is considered that the immediate effect of each payment of dividends is to diminish, to some extent, the proper basis of the operations of the Bank, as a body making profit by the advance of capital held in deposit. The payment of some eight or nine millions twice a-year in the first days of January and of July acted upon the public deposits precisely as cheques to that amount upon private deposits. And though a part of it passed at once into the private deposits, and the advances of the Bank were always so timed as to anticipate the operation as to the rest, the periodical and unavoidable necessity of so heavy a draft upon deposits (necessarily preceded, when the revenue was deficient, by a large advance upon Government securities) had an evil influence upon the position of the Bank in times of difficulty. The equalization of the quarterly payments of dividends is therefore to be allowed for in

# DIAGRAM

## TO ILLUSTRATE THE ACCOUNTS OF THE BANK OF ENGLAND UNDER THE OPERATION

*Of the Act 7 & 8 Vic: C. 32.*

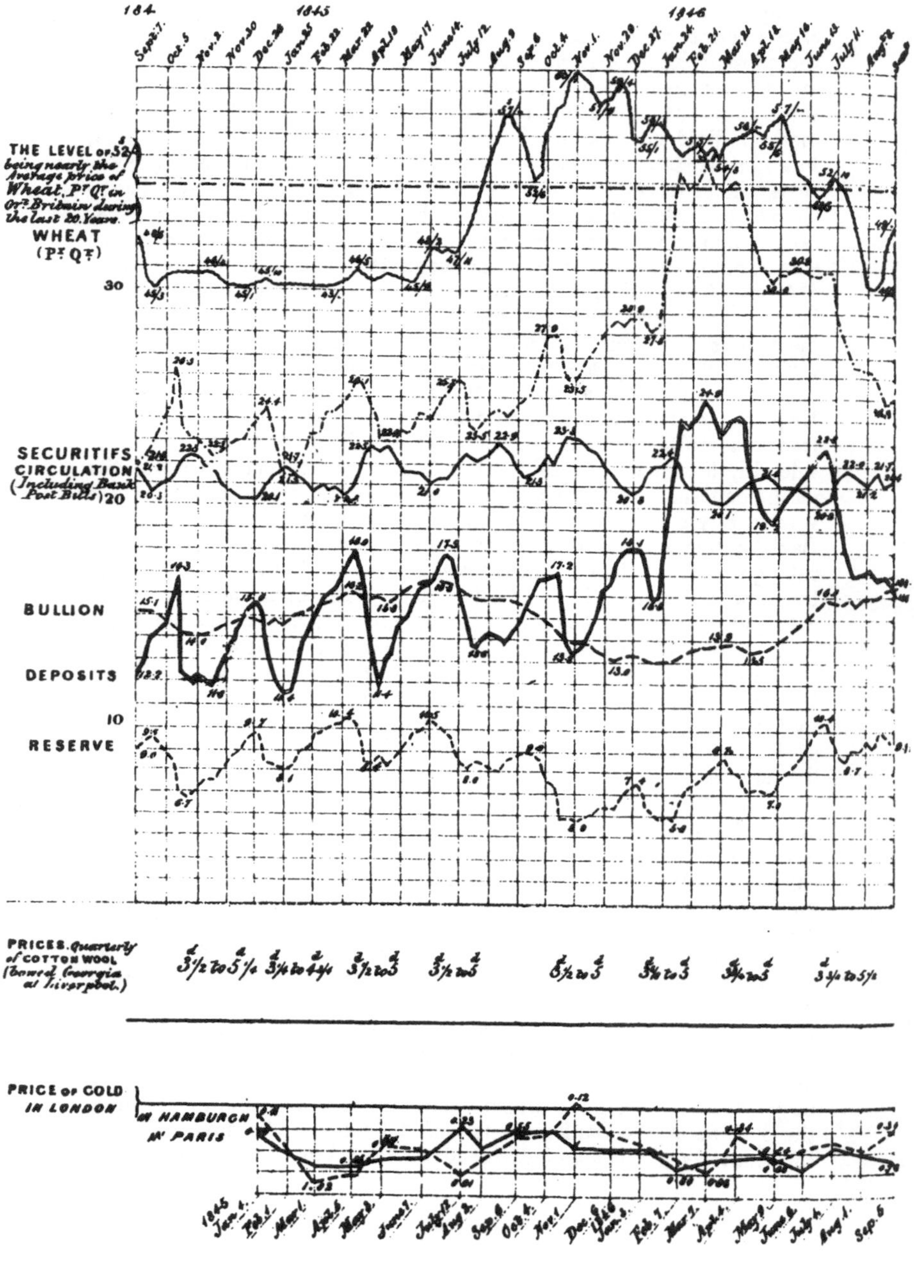

comparing the accounts of the Bank now exhibited with those of any period anterior to October, 1844, as leaving the amount of bank notes in the hands of the public less liable to sudden expansions twice a-year.

Prior to entering upon a review of the facts apparent upon the face of these tables, it is also desirable that notice should be taken of some other facts more or less connected with and bearing upon these—as the rate of interest, the state of the foreign exchanges, the cost of food, and the state of trade, during the two years under review.

From September, 1844, to January, 1845, the advances of the Bank were made upon bills having ninety-five days to run at 2½ per cent. From January to March the same rate of interest was continued, but upon bills limited to eighty-five days. In March the term of ninety-five days was resumed, and the rate of interest still continued at 2½ per cent., but only *as a minimum*, the actual rates charged varying thenceforward with the character of the security. On the 16th of October, 1845, the minimum rate was raised to 3 per cent., and on the 6th of November to 3½ per cent. It continued at that rate till a few days before the close of the two years under review, viz., 27th August, 1846, when it was reduced to 3 per cent.

The *current* rate of interest on first-class bills was, in September, 1844, 2 per cent; in October, 2½ to 3 per cent. In the beginning of 1845 it was lower—2¼ to 2½ per cent.—and continued so till near the end of August, when the railway speculations of that year attained about their greatest extent. In September it began to rise, and slowly but steadily continued to do so, till the end of February, 1846, when the deposits at the Bank of England on account of railways were completed. It then reached 5 per cent. Thenceforward it fell gradually through the remainder of the period embraced by these tables, and at the close of it was at 2¾ to 3½ per cent.

The foreign exchanges, as indicated by the relative values of gold in London, Paris, and Hamburgh, were in favour of this country during the whole of the two years, with a single exception in November, 1845, when, for a week or two, the exchange with Hamburgh was slightly adverse*.

The harvest of 1844 is believed to have been the largest ever produced in this country. There was also a general abundance in Europe and America, with one exception (caused by heavy rains just before the harvest) in the Low Countries; where, however, the deficiency was amply made up by the surplus of Northern Europe. There was also a large quantity of old wheat on hand. Accordingly, from September, 1844, to the end of June, 1845, the price of wheat in England averaged about 46*s*. per quarter. But about the end of June, 1845, the failure of the potato crop became generally known, and it began to be anticipated that the grain crops would prove deficient. During the six weeks ending the 9th of August, 1845, the imperial average price of wheat rose from 47*s*. 11*d*. to 57*s*†. It receded by the middle of September to 52*s*. 6*d*. It was then fully ascertained that the crop of 1845 was deficient both in quantity and in quality, and the price rose again, till it reached 60*s*. 1*d*. on the 1st of November. Thenceforward, to the middle of May, 1846, the general average was

* See Diagram No. 1. † Ibid.

about 57*s*. After May it fell pretty regularly, till it reached 45*s*. 1*d*. on the 15th of August; and when the two years under review closed, the average price of wheat was at 49*s*., and rising under anticipations of scarcity.

Of the state of trade it may suffice to observe, that the year 1845 was an unusually busy and profitable one, alike to the capitalist and the labourer, in every branch of production. The quantity of raw cotton imported and retained for consumption in that year was the largest on record. The same may be said of wool. The quantities of sugar, coffee, and tea imported and consumed in this country were also larger than in any previous year. The declared value of the principal articles of British produce exported also exceeded that of any previous year. And lastly, the aggregate tonnage of the shipping which entered and cleared out from the ports of the United Kingdom showed a similar increase. During the first eight months of the year 1846, included in these tables, the returns of the progress of our trade are not equally satisfactory. There was a diminution, as compared with the same period of 1845, in the value of British produce exported. This, however, is attributed with much apparent correctness, to the large amount of profitable employment offered to labour and capital in the construction of railways. The consumption of imported commodities generally, and of coffee and tea in particular, still showed an increase. That of sugar was diminished. At the same time the imports of provisions of all kinds were increased, and the quantity of timber imported (chiefly in connexion with the construction of railways) was fully 30 per cent. greater than in the same period of 1845.

Altogether, it may be said that during the greater part of the two years included in these tables the productive powers of the country were very fully and profitably employed; that during the whole of it, with the exception of the few months from the revulsion in the Share Market in October, 1845, to the completion of the arrangements for receiving and readvancing the railway deposits by the Bank in March, 1846, money for ordinary commercial purposes was abundant at a comparatively low rate of interest, and that the general condition of the people was, throughout, one of decided prosperity.

The extraordinary railway speculations of 1845, and their relation to the present subject, will be referred to in a subsequent part of the paper.

---

In looking at these accounts, the question likely to occur first to one desirous of ascertaining how far the Act of 1844 has operated upon the affairs of the Bank, and produced the effect intended, is this:—Has the amount of Bank of England notes in circulation fluctuated with the amount of bullion in the coffers of the Bank? If we accept that definition of the bank note circulation which is commonly in use, it needs little more than a glance to show that it has not.

For example, in the third weekly return made under the Act (21st September, 1844,) the bullion is stated at 15·1, the circulation at 20·6. Five weeks afterwards we find the bullion has fallen to 14·0, while the circulation has risen to 22·3. Thus, while bullion to the amount of £1,100,000 runs out, the note circulation is not reduced, but increased by £1,700,000.

Thenceforward, to the close of the year, the bullion rises slowly to 14·8, while the circulation falls, more rapidly, to 20·1.

At the opening of 1845 the bullion is 14·8, and the circulation 20·6. At the end of the first three months (29th March) the bullion has risen to 16·2, and the circulation is very nearly where it was, being 20·7.

Again, we find that on the 14th of June, 1845, the bullion is at 16·6, being the highest amount it reached during the two years, and the circulation 21·6, that the bullion thenceforward falls gradually till the 29th of October, when its amount is reduced to 14·0; and that during the same period the circulation rises from 21·6 to 23·3. This happens to be the highest amount the circulation reached during the two years; and it is remarkable that it was attained at a time when the bullion had been falling continuously for more than four months. While the bullion sank 2·5 the circulation rose 2·1.

A similar want of uniformity in the fluctuation of these two items is observable all through the accounts. The obvious conclusion is, that either those provisions of the Act, the purpose of which is to cause the circulation to fluctuate with the bullion, have not been in operation during these two years, or being in operation, have failed to produce the effect intended.

This view of the accounts favours the opinion of the opponents of the Act that it would be found ineffectual for its purpose of causing the circulation to fluctuate with the bullion. It is, however, to be observed, that the conclusion stated depends upon a particular definition of the word "circulation"—that namely which limits the term, as applied to Bank of England notes, to the notes in the hands of the public, excluding those retained in the Banking Department. The use of the term under this definition, for the present purpose, is justified by its having been similarly used, hitherto, both by the supporters and by the opponents of the Act. On the other hand, it is to be observed, that the separation of the Issue Department from the Banking Department appears to have been intended to place the latter in the same position, in reference to the Issue Department, as any other banking establishment in London, and therefore seems fairly to include the idea that the notes in the drawers of that department are as much in circulation as though they were in those of any other bank. If the word "circulation" be used in this sense, the question whether the circulation has fluctuated with the bullion must of course be answered in the affirmative.

But whether the affirmative thus obtained be conclusive as showing that the purpose of the Act has been fulfilled, depends upon one or two further considerations.

That, by the machinery described, the Bank must be prevented from issuing a single note in excess of £14,000,000 against which she shall not hold bullion, is self-evident. This, therefore, can neither be the proposition disputed by the opponents of the Act, nor the one which has been advanced by its supporters.

Again, if this definition of the bank note circulation be admitted, it follows that the Act can only check the operations of the Bank when those operations call for the actual use of an amount of notes exceeding the amount of bullion in the Bank plus £14,000,000.

If notes are retained in the Banking Department, it is clear they are retained quite irrespectively of the provisions of the Act, and only in the exercise of a discretion on the part of the Bank which the Act leaves perfectly unfettered.

It was also an avowed purpose of the authors of the Act to prevent the Bank being again placed in certain positions, undoubtedly dangerous, in which she has stood in times past, and into which she has been brought, as is asserted, through a want of due care in the exercise of the discretionary power entrusted to her *before* the passing of this Act.

The Act purports to cure the evil by taking from her the power she has misused.

But if the "circulation" which it is the purpose of the Act to make fluctuate with the bullion, includes every note out of the Issue Department, it requires but little examination of these tables to show that the scope still left to the voluntary operations of the Bank is wide enough to enable its managers to place the establishment in a position quite as improper, in reference to the maintenance of its credit, as any it has occupied during the period from which the instances of mismanagement most commonly adduced have been drawn.

In proof of this it may be sufficient to state, by way of comparison with the tables before given, some of the particulars of the Bank accounts under the two drains of 1836-7 and 1839; being those usually referred to as best illustrating the danger of leaving to the Bank the entire control of its business of issue.

| Date of Weekly Account. | Deposits. | Securities. | Circulation. | Maximum limit of the Circulation, had the Act 7 & 8 Vict., c. 32, been then in operation. | Bullion. |
|---|---|---|---|---|---|
| 1835. | | | | | |
| Sept. 22 | 13·4 | 27·1 | 17·3 | 20·2 | 6·2 |
| Oct. 13 | 20·0 | 33·8 | 17·2 | 20·1 | 6·1 |
| Nov. 10 | 17·9 | 31·2 | 17·3 | 20·6 | 6·6 |
| Dec. 8 | 18·4 | 30·7 | 16·9 | 21·3 | 7·3 |
| 1836. | | | | | |
| Jan. 5 | 20·4 | 32·0 | 16·7 | 21·6 | 7·6 |
| Feb. 2 | 15·2 | 28·8 | 18·3 | 21·6 | 7·6 |
| March 1 | 13·9 | 27·2 | 18·1 | 21·9 | 7·9 |
| „ 29 | 12·8 | 25·5 | 17·6 | 22·0 | 8·0 |
| April 26 | 13·9 | 27·6 | 18·5 | 21·5 | 7·5 |
| May 24 | 12·2 | 25·2 | 17·5 | 21·3 | 7·3 |
| June 21 | 15·2 | 28·0 | 17·1 | 21·0 | 7·0 |
| July 19 | 15·8 | 31·8 | 19·1 | 19·9 | 5·9 |
| Aug. 16 | 13·1 | 29·0 | 18·5 | 19·4 | 5·4 |
| Sept. 13 | 12·0 | 27·2 | 17·4 | 19·1 | 5·1 |
| Oct. 11 | 15·8 | 30·7 | 17·1 | 18·9 | 4·9 |
| Nov. 8 | 12·2 | 27·7 | 17·4 | 18·6 | 4·6 |
| Dec. 6 | 14·8 | 31·0 | 17·0 | 17·9 | 3·9 |
| 1837. | | | | | |
| Jan. 3 | 16·6 | 32·4 | 17·0 | 18·2 | 4·2 |
| Jan. 31 | 11·2 | 29·8 | 19·1 | 17·8 | 3·8 |
| Feb. 28 | 10·0 | 27·2 | 18·0 | 18·0 | 4·0 |

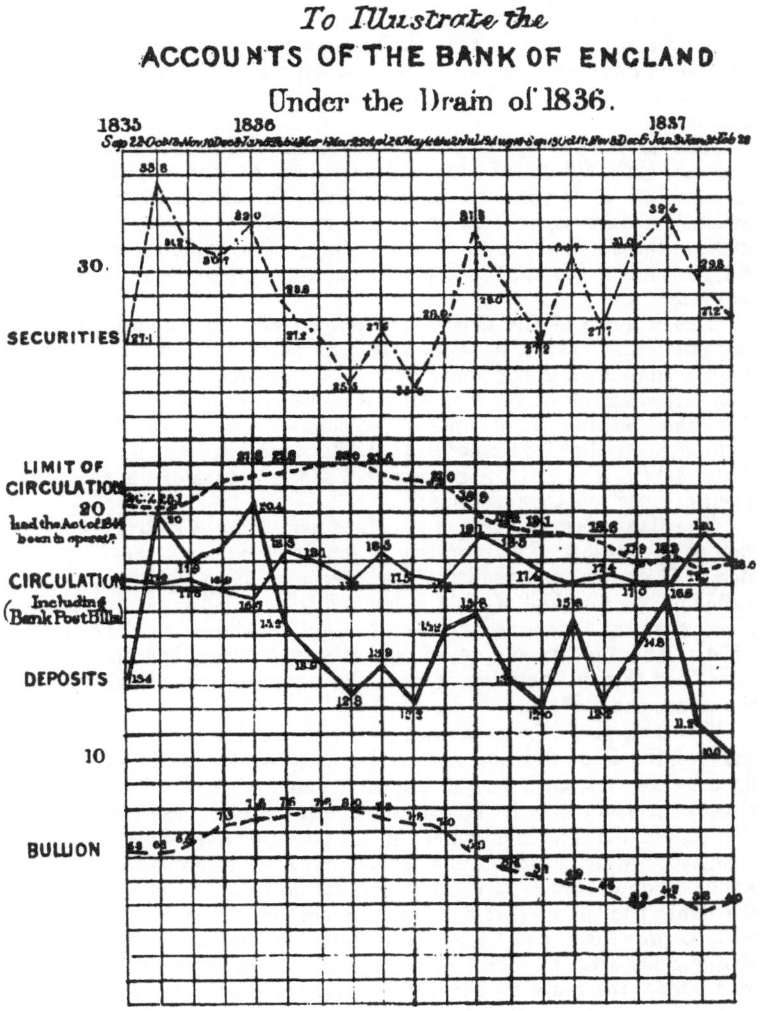
To Illustrate the
ACCOUNTS OF THE BANK OF ENGLAND
Under the Drain of 1836.
1835
1836
1837
30.
SECURITIES
LIMIT OF CIRCULATION
20
had the Act of 1844 been in operat.
CIRCULATION
(Including Bank Post Bills)
DEPOSITS
10
BULLION

The preceding table shows the state of the Bank accounts at intervals of four weeks, from September, 1835, to February, 1837, including, as will be observed, a period of eight months, from the end of March to the beginning of December, 1836, during which the bullion sank from £8,000,000 to £3,900,000. In addition to the four items furnished by the Bank accounts, as then published, a fifth is given, showing the maximum limit which would have been imposed upon the amount of notes out of the Issue Department, had the present Act been then in operation.

The most striking feature in this series of returns is the great increase, in the autumn of 1835, and during the greater part of 1836, of the amount of *deposits* and of *securities*. The circulation was little affected, if we except the usual increase for a short time after the payment of the dividends in January and July. The bullion rose steadily till the end of March, 1836, and fell rapidly during the remainder of the year*.

The increase of the deposits, as is generally known, arose partly from the Bank having, in 1835, agreed to allow interest for the large sums accumulated in her hands by the East India Company when the commercial affairs of the Company were being wound up, and partly from the reception of deposits on account of a loan of £15,000,000 contracted by the Government about the same time (under the Act 5 and 6 Wm. IV. c. 45, 31st August, 1835,) preparatory to the payment of the Slave Compensation.

The Bank deemed it proper to extend her advances with this extension of her means. The propriety of her doing so is not here in question. The extent and facility of her advances during the latter half of 1835 and the first half of 1836 is asserted to have led to, or materially aided, the very serious reduction of her bullion shown at the close of 1836. And the present question is simply whether, had the Act of 1844 been then in operation, it would have prevented the Bank taking the course she did*.

The table given above shows that the whole circulation out of the walls of the Bank did not exceed the limit which would have been fixed by the Act, until late in January, 1837, when the bullion had already reached nearly its lowest point. And if it be observed that in the "circulation," as here stated, is included the *seven days' bills*, the amount of which, though not stated, may be safely estimated at £600,000 or £700,000, it will be seen that down to the close of 1836 the Bank, had the present Act been in operation, would have complied with its provisions, and have held at least a million of reserve in the Banking Department. But in truth it would not be just towards the managers of the Bank at that period to take this extreme view of the case. Assuming that they had unduly extended their advances during the autumn of 1835 and the spring of 1836, it is to be observed that in July 1836 they changed their course. They then raised the rate of interest to 4½ per cent., and in August to 5 per cent. And the question at once arises—Would the Act have caused an earlier or more effective restriction of the advances? The facts seem to answer this question with a decided negative. When the rate of interest was

* See Diagram No. 2.

raised in July, the bullion amounted to nearly six millions, and the drain had only run about half its course, while the "circulation," even including the seven days' bills, and notwithstanding its expansion by the payment of the July dividends, was considerably within the limit imposed by the Act of 1844, and by the end of the year was brought still more within that limit.

It seems evident, therefore, admitting to the fullest extent that the indiscretion of the Bank Directors caused the drain of 1836, that it would not have been prevented by the strictest enforcement of the provisions of the Act 7 and 8 of Vict. c. 32.

But the instance of want of uniformity between the circulation and the bullion most commonly brought forward to justify the restrictions of the Act of 1844 is exhibited in the Bank accounts for 1839, which are stated in the following table in the same manner as in the one preceding.

| Date of Weekly Account. | Deposits. | Securities. | Circulation. | Maximum limit of the Circulation, had the Act 7 & 8 Vict., c. 32, been then in operation. | Bullion. |
|---|---|---|---|---|---|
| 1838. | | | | | |
| Nov. 27 | 8·8 | 19·5 | 17·8 | 23·5 | 9·5 |
| Dec. 24 | 11·0 | 21·5 | 17·5 | 23·5 | 9·5 |
| 1839. | | | | | |
| Jan. 22 | 9·8 | 23·9 | 19·3 | 21·8 | 7·8 |
| Feb. 19 | 7·9 | 22·2 | 18·4 | 20·8 | 6·8 |
| Mar. 19 | 7·7 | 21·6 | 17·5 | 20·3 | 6·3 |
| April 16 | 8·5 | 25·2 | 18·8 | 18·7 | 4·7 |
| May 14 | 7·3 | 24·0 | 18·3 | 18·1 | 4·1 |
| June 11 | 6·7 | 22·8 | 17·3 | 17·9 | 3·9 |
| July 9 | 12·5 | 30·6 | 18·6 | 17·4 | 3·4 |
| Aug. 6 | 7·7 | 27·0 | 18·4 | 16·4 | 2·4 |
| Sept. 3 | 6·1 | 24·6 | 17·8 | 16·4 | 2·4 |
| Oct. 1 | 5·5 | 23·0 | 16·8 | 16·5 | 2·5 |
| Oct. 29 | 6·3 | 24·1 | 17·3 | 16·5 | 2·5 |
| Nov. 26 | 5·6 | 20·9 | 15·9 | 17·4 | 3·4 |
| Dec. 24 | 8·0 | 22·0 | 15·8 | 18·5 | 4·5 |

A review of the manner in which the Bank exercised her discretion in making advances during the period covered by this table certainly leads to the inference that the drain was accelerated by it. In February, 1838, the current rate of interest for the best bills was about 3½ per cent. At that time the Bank rate, having previously been 5 per cent., was reduced to 4. For some weeks afterwards the demand for money declined; and in May, 1838, the Bank rate being 4 per cent., that current out of doors did not exceed 3. After May the demand for money steadily increased. In November the market rate of interest had risen to a level with that of the Bank—4 per cent. And then came that course of conduct on the part of the Bank which has been so much blamed. On the 23rd of November a notice was issued offering advances till the 23rd of January at 3½ per cent.; and that, not only

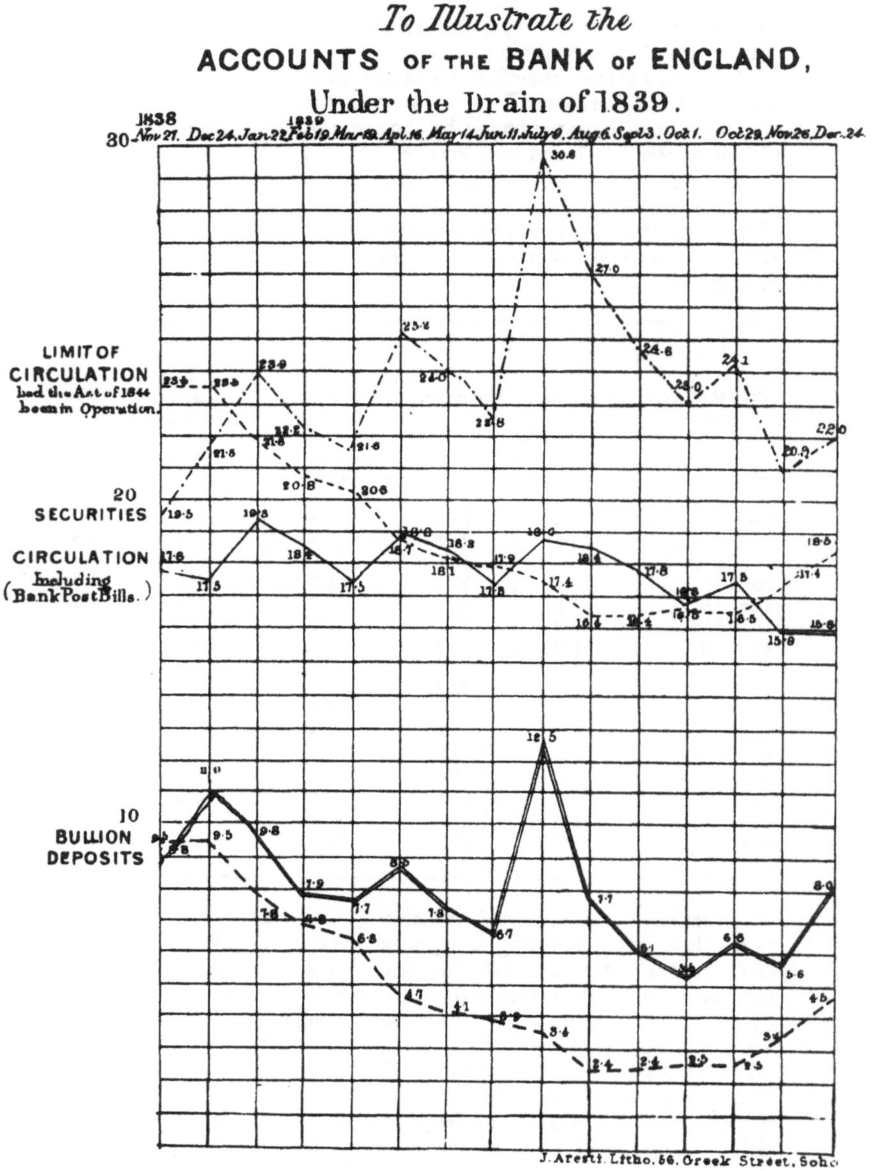
To Illustrate the
ACCOUNTS OF THE BANK OF ENGLAND,
Under the Drain of 1839.
1838
1839
Nov. 27. Dec. 24. Jan. 22. Feb. 19. Mar. 19. Apl. 16. May 14. Jun. 11. July 9. Aug. 6. Sept. 3. Oct. 1. Oct. 29. Nov. 26. Dec. 24.
30
20
10
LIMIT OF CIRCULATION had the Act of 1844 been in Operation.
SECURITIES
CIRCULATION Including (Bank Post Bills.)
BULLION
DEPOSITS
J. Arestt. Litho. 56. Greek Street, Soho

upon Bills of Exchange, but upon Exchequer Bills, East India Bonds, and other approved securities. As this made the Bank rate of interest lower than that current out of doors, it was immediately followed by a large increase of the securities. Thenceforward, through the first months of 1839, while the current rate of interest went on rising, the foreign exchanges declining, and the bullion running out, the Bank continued her advances under the notice of November. On the 28th of February another notice appeared, not raising the rate, but continuing the terms of the notice of November till the 23rd of April. Now mark the result upon the column of securities. When the rate of interest was reduced in November the securities were 19·5. In the weekly return of the 9th of April they reached 26·6, showing an increase of more than £7,000,000. During the same period the bullion had fallen continuously from 9·5 to 5·2, showing a loss of £4,300,000*.

On the 16th of May the Bank took the first step towards checking the drain by raising her rate of interest from 3½ to 5 per cent. But it was still lower than the current rate. On the 20th of June the Bank rate was raised to 5½ per cent., and again limited to Bills of Exchange. On the 13th of July the dead-weight annuity was offered for sale; and on the 1st of August the rate of interest was further raised to *six* per cent.

The question now presented is, whether, had the Act of 1844 been then in operation, it would have prevented the Bank from lowering her rate of interest and increasing her securities in the manner shown, or would have compelled a restriction of her advances at a period so much earlier, and in a manner so much more gradual and decisive, as to have averted the necessity for the extraordinary pressure upon commercial credit exerted by the Bank in the latter months of 1839.

The table last given shows that, had the Act been then in force, the conduct of the Bank would not, down to a period so late as the 19th of March, 1839, have been in any manner contrary to its provisions†.

At that period, if we allow £700,000 for the amount (not published) of the seven days' bills, included in the return of the circulation, the reserve of notes and coin retained in the Banking Department would have been about £3,500,000, an amount amply sufficient, according to the usage of the Bank, as the deposits were then only £7,700,000. Yet at this time the bullion had already fallen from £9,500,000 to £6,300,000; all the principal causes of the drain were fully and palpably in operation; and the imputed indiscretion of the Bank Directors had been carried nearly to its full extent. It is therefore apparent that the drain of 1839, so far as it was due to any want of caution on the part of the Bank down to the middle of March, 1839, would not have been affected by the provisions of the Act of 1844, had it then been in operation.

And indeed a reference to the proximate causes of the drain in question, as they have been explained by the supporters of the Act themselves, tends strongly to show that it was not so much an arbitrary limit upon the mere present conduct of the Bank that was called for as a regard to the shadows of coming events; which, as it could

* See Diagram No. 3. † Ibid.

only result from a process of reasoning, could not have been supplied by previous legislative enactment.

The Directors were blamed for a dangerous state of the ship—not in reference to the then present weather, but in reference to that which they might have foreseen. Passing events boded a coming storm. But it is apparent that the most significant of these events would not have effected in any appreciable degree the index of danger furnished by the Act of 1844. Apart from the knowledge that the Bank rate of interest was, from November, 1838, to March, 1839, *below* that of the market; and that the securities were increasing to an unusual extent (of neither of which circumstances the Act would have taken cognizance) there were the important facts, then well known, that the harvest of 1838 had been greatly deficient, and that large and sudden importations of foreign grain were being made during the autumn of that year and the spring of the next, which, under the circumstances, could not fail to have a depressing effect on the foreign exchanges. These facts, known to the Bank Directors, loudly counselled caution; but not materially affecting any item of the Bank accounts, as limited by the machinery of the Act of 1844, they could have had no effect in calling the restrictions of that measure into play. That from the beginning there was danger impending, of a heavy and palpable description, is evident. But it seems equally clear that to meet the danger required the forethought of intelligent men—not the restrictive mechanism of an Act of Parliament.

---

A careful consideration, then, of the Bank accounts given in the above tables, in conjunction with those of the twelve years immediately preceding, which embrace all the more remarkable instances of danger charged by the supporters of the Act of 1844 to the indiscretion of the Bank, appears to lead to the conclusion that the provisions of that Act are not sufficient to prevent the recurrence of similar events.

It is apparent that whenever danger has arisen which could be justly attributed to the conduct of the Bank, it has been traceable to an undue expansion of her securities; or, in other words, to a reduction of the reserve held against *her liabilities to pay in gold on demand*, to an amount dangerously small. These liabilities include the notes and bills in circulation and the deposits. But the Act embraces only a part of them—the *bank notes*. The deposits and bills are left untouched. These, and the reserve held against them, the Bank is therefore still at liberty to deal with as she thinks proper. And as the use of deposit accounts extends year by year with the growth of our commercial transactions and the more scientific management of their details, the power of the Bank to increase her advances and liabilities in this direction may be expected also to increase.

It is well known that bills may be discounted, and liabilities to pay in gold on demand be incurred, by the granting of deposit credits as readily and effectually as by the issue of bank notes, and that such credits may often be used more conveniently, and quite as efficiently, by way of transfer from one account to another, as by drawing out notes or coin. And thus the Act of 1844, though it effectually provides for the payment in gold of every note issued to the public in excess of £14,000,000, only provides for the meeting of a portion of the liabilities of the Bank to pay in gold on demand; and a portion, too, which may sometimes at the will of the Bank become the smallest.

It follows that by indiscretion in the Banking Department—an improper increase of the securities, and diminution of the reserve against the total liabilities to pay on demand—the establishment may at any time be placed in a position as dangerous as any it has been placed in in times past.

The nature and extent of the discretion thus left to the Bank is very clearly illustrated in the tables before us by the state of her accounts during the extraordinary expansion of her banking business in the early part of 1846, by the reception and management of the railway deposits. The amount paid into the Bank of England upon this account in the previous year (1845) was about £3,444,000; but as the bank rate of interest was held rather above the current rate, and money was abundant, only a portion of this amount was advanced upon securities, the remainder going to increase the reserve. The amount paid in on account of railways in 1846 was £11,396,000; and as the Bank rate of interest was kept at 3½, and the current rate was from 4 to 5 per cent., what was added to the deposits went to increase the securities. Whether the course taken by the Bank in the disposal of these deposits was wise or unwise is, of course, not here in question. But the fact that it *was* taken proves that the Bank retains, under the Act of 1844, that discretionary power in the use of any large addition to her deposits, her exercise of which was found fault with in 1836-7, when she held the deposits on account of the East India Company and the Slave Compensation Loan.

---

The following statement places in a striking point of view the result of the discretionary extension of the advances of the Bank during the two years under review, as affecting *the proportion of the reserve to the deposits* only.

By the return of 3rd May, 1845, the deposits, public and private, amounted to £13,067,000—the public deposits being £2,712,000, and the private £10,355,000. The reserve, in notes and coin, was £8,468,000.

On the 21st of June, 1845, the deposits were £17,098,000—the public deposits being £6,951,000, and the private £10,147,000. The reserve was £10,424,000.

On the 6th of December, 1845, the deposits were £17,132,000—public, £8,110,000; private, £9,022,000. The reserve was £6,471,000.

And on the 28th of February, 1846, the deposits were £24,943,000—public, £6,296,000; private, £18,647,000. The reserve was only £7,744,000*.

It will be observed that these four periods have been selected so as to exhibit every material variation of the proportion of public to private deposits. In the first instance the public deposits are unusually *low;* in the second, of a *medium* amount; in the third, *high;* and the private deposits do not much vary from a common average. In the fourth instance the public deposits are of a medium amount, and the private unusually high. The following figures show the proportion of reserve to deposits at each period:—

* See Diagram No. 4.

| | Deposits. | Reserve. | Proportion of Deposits held in Reserve. |
|---|---|---|---|
| 1845. | | | |
| May 3 ........... | 13·0 | 8·4 | 64 per cent. |
| June 21 ........... | 17·0 | 10·4 | 61 ,, |
| Dec. 6 ........... | 17·1 | 6·4 | 37 ,, |
| 1846. | | | |
| Feb. 28 ........... | 24·9 | 7·7 | 30 ,, |

The latitude of discretion here shown in the reduction of the reserve is nearly, if not quite, equal to that exhibited by the Bank at any period within the twelve years immediately preceding the passing of the Act of 1844; and there is nothing upon the face of that measure, or in its practical operation, which opposes any obstacle to a still further reduction of the reserve, should the Bank think proper to make it.

---

The bearing of the Act upon the "circulation," in the sense in which that term was commonly used before the measure was introduced, and also in the sense in which it includes every note out of the Issue Department, having been thus tested, it only remains to mark its bearing upon the course of those commercial transactions which are known to require the use of a circulating medium, as viewed entirely apart from any particular definition of the Bank "circulation."

And here, in the first instance, our attention is irresistibly attracted by the railway speculations during the period under review.

Between March and September, 1845, joint stock speculations for the immediate investment of capital were set on foot, involving a larger aggregate amount than had ever before been so involved in this country. The amount to raise which, for railways alone, the sanction of Parliament was actually applied for in the following Session, exceeded 340 millions. And if we include all the other schemes in which scrip or letters of allotment were actually selling in the market at a premium in July, August, and September, 1845, the amount cannot be estimated at less than 500 millions.

Many of the schemes of 1845 reached a high premium within a few weeks; and all those first in the market, and having any substantial merit, were raised considerably above their true value. For instance, the Leeds and Thirsk Railway—£50 shares, with only the deposit of £2 10*s*. paid—were selling in March at £3 10*s*.; in September, at £23 15*s*.; and in November at £4 15*s*. per share. Again, the Bolton, Wigan, and Liverpool—£40 shares, with £4 paid—were selling in January, 1845, at £4 10*s*.; in September, at £42 15*s*.; and in December (when £9 had been paid), at £20 per share. If we assume an average premium of £10 per cent. upon the schemes then in the market, the property temporarily created by these speculations (and the repeated purchase and sale of which, on commission, furnished profitable employment to some thousands of brokers) must have been at least 50 millions.

And to this there is to be added an increased value during the same period of the shares in the established lines of railway. For instance—

The Midland Stock—amount £4,180,000—was selling in January, 1845, at 114 per cent.; and in July at 188 per cent., showing a rise of 74 per cent., and an increase in the aggregate value of the stock of £3,098,000.

The Great Western—share capital issued £8,160,000—£100 shares selling in January, 1845, at £156; and in July at £228; and (allowing for a call of £5 per share in the interim) showing a rise of 67 per cent., and an increase in the aggregate value of the shares of £5,467,000.

The Manchester and Leeds—share capital £4,660,000—£100 shares selling in January, 1845, at £126; and in August at £215, showing a rise of 89 per cent, and an increased value in the aggregate of £4,147,000.

The average increase in the value of £100 shares in these three lines was £76; and the total increase of value in August and September was upwards of 12 millions.

To determine to what extent the circulating medium of the country was actually expanded under these speculations might, with the existing means of information, be found extremely difficult; but that it was very great cannot be doubted; and its probable amount may be strikingly illustrated, though it cannot be proved. For instance, if we accept the estimate of the whole annual income of the inhabitants of Great Britain, given in a recent pamphlet by Mr. Smee, of the Bank of England, we may assume that it is about £370,000,000. The whole annual expenditure of the country on consumable commodities must, of course, fall within this sum, in its ultimate form. And we may safely assume that the whole amount of property the subject of purchase and sale, say within one week, at any period of the year, in reference to the annual production and consumption of the country, is considerably less in value than £370,000,000; and as it is well known that the transactions of this class form, by far, the larger part of all those in which the use of the circulating medium is necessary, it seems clear that the additional transactions connected with the purchase and sale of Railway property in 1845 must have caused, for the time, an addition to the aggregate amount of the circulating medium called into use, very large in proportion to its ordinary amount.

But it will be seen, on reference to the tables, that during those months in which the purchases and sales of railway property were most numerous and extensive, while everybody was buying and selling shares, and the current rate of interest was only 2½ per cent., that portion of the circulating medium which consisted of Bank of England notes was but very slightly, if at all, increased, and that it reached its greatest amount when the prices of shares were lowest—when everybody had ceased to speculate—when the number and amount of current transactions were reduced to the lowest point by discredit, and the current rate of interest for first-class bills had risen from 2½ to 4½ per cent.

It seems to follow, therefore, either that an increase in the amount of the circulating medium is not necessary to support the most extensive speculations, or that the amount of Bank of England notes in circulation affords no index to the amount of the circulating medium; either of which conclusions is of course fatal to the theory upon which the Act of 1844 is founded.

# 5

## Currency of the United States

C. H. Carroll, ' Currency of the United States', *Hunt's Merchant's Magazine*, vol. XLIII (1860), pp. 574–83.

One of the most outspoken critics of the American banking system in the period before the Civil War, Carroll conducted a ferocious campaign against fractional reserve banking. In a series of articles in *Hunt's Merchant's Magazine* and the *Bankers' Magazine*, he provided trenchant criticism of the banking system and its ability to issue 'debt currency', which he described as 'a fiction of money manufactured virtually out of nothing, and is...in excess of all the money and property in the world' (p.577; original article). His conviction was clear; money was a fiction, and the banks who traded in money were rapacious exploiters of ignorance; 'the paper money system... rests upon and is wholly sustained by, the idea – the delusion, in fact – that the wants of trade require more money than can be supplied in gold and silver' (Money and Banking, *Hunt's Merchants Magazine* (XXXVII) 1857 p.308).

This article, which seeks to show that 'the nation is just as rich with little money and low prices, as with much money and high prices' contains two arguments characteristic of his general attack on banking. The first was his view that the creation of bank deposits in excess of reserves raised prices in the United States, encouraged imports and thus had an immediate impact on the balance of trade and resulted in an outflow of specie. Banks, by creating money, were directly responsible for many of the difficulties in the domestic economy. Carroll's solution to this problem was clear; one hundred percent reserve backed bullion banking, wherein: 'the banks would be under no immediate liabilities without coin in reserve, dollar for dollar, to meet them...it puts an end to the present unjust and ruinous principle of lending the same dollar several times over' (p.582; original article) This last suggestion is important, because it was to reappear at various times throughout the discussions of banking reform in the United States.

## Art. IV.—CURRENCY OF THE UNITED STATES.

*To the Editor of the Merchants' Magazine:—*

THE currency of the United States consists of all the metallic money not in absolute hoards, and the sum of the immediate liabilities of the banks, except the coin in their coffers. The sum total of currency in money and bank debt is *permanently* the same as would be present in the nation and be offered, or in readiness to be offered, in gold and silver, in exchange for commodities and property, and in the payment of debts. When it exceeds this the course of exchange is against us, and money runs away. Buried treasure, or money so absolutely withdrawn from business and from circulation, as to have no influence upon the owner's mind in directing his expenditure, is not currency; it is an absolute hoard, having no more effect upon prices or upon business than if it did not exist. But we must not confound this miserly store with the stocking deposit of the Dutch farmer, for example; which, although a reserve fund, influences his expenditure, and, as there is more or less of it, induces him to hold his commodity at a higher, or sell it for a lower price. The proportion of money thus at rest, in relation to the volume of currency, is not greater than the proportion of commodities at rest, in relation to the whole circulating property which necessarily remains on hand waiting the right customer or a satisfactory price; and the line between the currency and the hoard is not more imperfectly defined than that between the property in and out of circulation. There is always a considerable quantity of property not in circulation, that is to say, not offered for sale, that some large price would tempt the owner to part with, and there is about the same proportion of money in idleness that may be tempted into action by offering for it a sufficient quantity of property. These two opposite exchangeable values neutralize each other.

We have, then, a controlling measure of price in the volume of currency, the public instrument of exchange. As that volume increases in relation to the circulating property, the value of money falls in a general or average rise of prices; and as it decreases in relation to the circulating property, the value of money rises in a general or average fall of prices. So far as price is concerned, of course the effect is the same if the circulating property increases or diminishes in relation to the volume of currency; for as it increases in quantity its price falls, and as it diminishes in quantity its price rises; but it is not by any means the same in regard to value or wealth; for the variation in the volume of currency merely alters the value of money, it does not affect the absolute value of other property, and the nation is just as rich with little money and low prices, as with much money and high prices; but when the property of the country diminishes in quantity the public wealth declines, although prices rise; and when the property increases in quantity the public wealth increases, although prices fall. This is more apparent in an isolated community or nation, such for example as Japan has been for two centuries past. Every nation is quite as well off with little money as with much; but a commercial nation or community, such as Japan has now become, is vastly better off with the less money or more limited currency. Japan, with a limited currency, having a plenty of circulating property, has now the most valuable money in the world; it is valuable because of the quantity of property it will exchange for, and nothing but war or non-intercourse can prevent her from becoming an immense exporting nation. I think Europe and America will be astounded at the extent of production, activity of business, and increase of wealth, in Japan in a very few years, if the empire escapes internal dissention and external war.

It is the quantity and quality of cultivated land, dwellings, warehouses, ships, steamers, factories, schools, utilities of all kinds, and everything that contributes to human enjoyment, which constitute wealth; this wealth is the same in value at any price; it is not, therefore, of the least importance what volume of currency we possess, so that the coins are not too diminutive or too large for convenient use, excepting the less currency the better for the convenience of handling, and because where there is the least currency relatively, money will buy the most, and where money will buy the most, business will go. As with individuals so with nations; where the best bargains are to be had customers are plentiest and make the largest purchases. What we want, then, is to increase our stock in trade and not our currency; for money itself will come fast enough by the increase of commodities; no earthly power and no contrivance can keep it out of the country, excepting this that we employ, of cheapening it with an admixture of fiction. The little child, soon as he learns the meaning of a cent, knows enough to go to the shop where he can get the most taffy for his money; and when he grows to manhood he pursues the same simple principle in buying goods; but the sophistication of the currency system blinds him to the fact that the increase of currency and cheapening of money locally by his community, more than elsewhere, adds cost to his goods, enhances their price without increasing their value, and drives his customers into other shops, in other cities, or in other countries. The cheapening of money is a local loss of business and wealth, infallibly.

The effect of change in the volume of the currency follows an immutable law, however delayed by longer or shorter maturing credits, or however obscured to the mind of the unpracticed observer. It is therefore a matter of the greatest importance to know what the currency is and where to look for it.

We must look for it precisely where it would rest if the whole were exclusively metallic, to which volume it must ultimately return from every aberration; the true money or specie measure being determined and marked by the par of exchange on London of 9¼ per cent, or $4 86 65 to the pound sterling. It will be observed, that with a pure metallic currency, the banks could not be under demand liabilities, either to the public or to each other, without coin in hand dollar for dollar against them; each debtor bank must therefore hold the coin; so that the balances due *to* banks, as well as *to* individuals, are *currency* occupying the place of coin, and the balances due *from* banks, as well as *from* individuals, are loans. Thus, taking the returns at Washington, with an approximate estimate of the amount of specie in circulation outside of the banks, I find the national currency, with a proper nomenclature, as follows, nearest to January 1, 1860:—

| | | |
|---|---|---|
| Bank notes in circulation | 207,102,477 | |
| Bank credits inscribed for discounts without money.. | 170,207,562 | |
| Bankers' credits in California inscribed for discounts without money, estimate | 2,000,000 | |
| Balances due to banks | 55,932,918 | |
| Total of *debt currency*, that is, currency exceeding the money in the nation | | 435,242,957 |
| Bank deposits absolute in specie | 83,594,567 | |
| Government treasury, including balances at credit of disbursing officers, specie | 10,160,000 | |
| In circulation among the people including bankers in California, estimate... | 84,002,476 | |
| Total of money in the currency | | 177,757,043 |
| Total currency of the nation | | $613,000,000 |

IMMEDIATE LIABILITIES OF THE BANKS.

| | | |
|---|---|---|
| Debt currency, as above | | $435,242,957 |
| Absolute deposits, as above | $83,594,567 | |
| Absolute deposits with California bankers, say | 2,000,000 | |
| Money in banks | | 85,594,567 |
| Total of immediate liabilities | | $520,837,524 |

It follows that the ratio of their money to their immediate liabilities is as 16.43 to 100. The ratio of money, outside of the hoards, to the total currency of the nation, is as 29 to 100; and this indicates the method of doing business; the exchanges at wholesale and retail being effected approximately with money 29 per cent, and debt 71 per cent; besides some that are made by the direct barter of commodity for commodity, without the intervention of debt or money. Obviously debt must be created and discounted to bring the debt currency into existence, and it is kept alive by continued renewal or *kiting* of the notes and bills of customers, against the notes and inscribed credits of the banks. The bank debt is, therefore, merely a portion of the circulating debt of the community, which compels the exchanges to pass through a circuit of debt and credit, by removing so much money from the country, which circuit would otherwise be made with money. This circuit is made by the transfers of raw material, and articles partially and wholly finished, through the hands of manufacturers and tradesmen to the consumers, and the return of the consumer's commodity or produce to close the transaction, when the two producers and consumers are mutually paid. Approximately these transfers are five each way; so that we cannot be far wrong in estimating *ten* exchanges to the circuit. Consequently we maintain a commercial debt upon the above figures of $4,352,000,000, or ten-fold the sum of the *debt-currency*, that need not and could not exist with a currency exclusively of money. Every merchants' stock of goods greatly exceeds the sum of currency he retains on hand; and this law of the exchanges in the circuit of money seems to determine the ratio of goods offered for sale, with other circulating property, to be approximately as 10 to 1 of the currency throughout the country.

So completely has the idea of money in the debt currency taken possession of the public mind, that it is difficult for people to comprehend how the above incubus of debt is created, or why there is any more of it than would exist with a money currency. But money is a value purchased with another value in goods, and comes in return for merchandise sold to California and to other countries; debt has no part in its creation. The debt currency is not a value: it is a fiction of money manufactured virtually out of nothing, and is, when created, like every other debt, in excess of all the money and property in the world. An illustration will show how this worse than useless load of debt and embarrassment is entailed upon us. You have 100 yards of cloth for sale at $5 per yard that I want; and I have 2,500 pounds of wool for sale at 20 cents per pound that you want; either commodity amounting to $500. Simple barter would effect the exchange in the most economical manner, and satisfy us both, without debt or embarrassment; but we do not know each other's wants, and do not meet in the market; a middle man or merchant is therefore necessary to us both. If he has $500 of money, as he would have under a money currency, to pay for your cloth that you can pay for my wool, the exchange may be effected without debt or delay of settlement. It is triangular barter; gold, a third commodity of value, being employed as a medium of exchange; but, by the present system, we expel the gold, and thence comes the necessity of debt to create the debt currency and maintain the banks. A merchant gives his note for your cloth, and the same or another gives his note for my wool; then, according to the present custom of making the utmost possible use of banking, you give your note for the wool, and I give my note for the cloth; and now the bank is ready to *accommodate* all parties in accommodating itself. You and I get the merchant's notes discounted; he gets our notes discounted, and the bank gives in exchange—what? Certainly not money, for that yields no profit; it must lend what has no existence, and make a currency of its debt, over and above its money and capital, on which to charge interest as money, to make dividends; of course, it lends its debt in the form of notes or inscribed credit. You and I now owe $500 each; the merchant owes $1,000, and the bank owes $2,000; and here, on $1,000 of value, by reason of the absence of $500 of money in the currency, is $4,000 of debt created, more useless and unnecessary than a fifth wheel to a coach; $2,000 of it is *debt currency* which infallibly drives from the country $2,000 of gold, and compels the next traders to go through the same operation of running in debt to effect their exchanges. And what capital is employed in these transactions? Clearly not a dime but yours and mine; your cloth and my wool: our capital maintains the merchant and the bank, and all their clerks and rent and charges; we are entangled in a useless debt, with the fluctuating values of a currency continually expanding and contracting to accommodate the cupidity or necessities of the bank, and we run the risk of bankruptcy, out of the proceeds of our own labor, which, under a money currency, would have been exchanged without any risk whatever. Every time the cloth or the wool is exchanged in its progress to the consumer, more debt and more currency of the same sort are created, and an oppressive mass of debt is thus built up and maintained to expel money, postpone payments, and embarrass everybody.

There is no objection to the merchant in this business; he is a necessary and economical agent in finding and opening markets and effecting exchanges, securing to the producer uninterrupted employment at home; and, in transferring a commodity from where it is of less, to where it is of greater, value, he performs a service equivalent to the production of so much value; employing labor and tools of wood, iron, wind, steam, &c., differing in form but not in principle from those employed by the producer himself. Indeed, it is to the merchant we owe the variety and increase of employments that maintain labor and produce wealth; but to the bank of the debt system we owe nothing but obstruction to labor, loss of national capital, bankruptcy, and distress. It is the system, and not the banks, that I condemn, and it is the people, not especially the bankers, who are responsible for it; but it is most especially the duty of the economist and the legislator to speak plainly, and put public opinion right upon this momentous subject.

I have taken occasion to say in these pages repeatedly that commerce consists of an exchange of material and immaterial products upon the simple principle of barter; commodity pays for commodity, and service for service, and the nearer we come to a direct exchange the less is the tax upon both producer and consumer, and the better it is for the community. Merchants and money are necessary to an economical accomplishment of exchanges, but not mere speculators nor a currency of debt. If the natural law of value be not interfered with, business will provide the true and necessary volume of currency for itself in real money; less we cannot have permanently, and more we cannot permanently retain; the debt currency does nothing but sink the value of money, and drive so much money away; it is a false intruder of the most damaging character.

The population of the United States has been estimated of late at 32,000,000; on this estimate the currency as above would be $19 16 *per capita;* but the progress of the census of 1860 thus far seems to indicate that this is an overestimate of the population; probably the currency at the beginning of the year was $20 for each inhabitant, approximately.

The estimate of $84,000,000 of specie outside of the banks is, I am aware, very much below that of other writers, but I feel very confident there is not over $200,000,000 of money in the whole nation, including the California currency and the hoards. Estimates in round numbers very generally exceed the truth, and are often wild. In the inveterate paper-currency States, like those of New England, where one dollar notes are in circulation, it is rather difficult to find change for a dollar in the hands of any family; the omnipotent bank note of one to five dollars is everywhere, and is counted upon to buy the smallest commodity; there is a constant running about for change from house to house, and the till of the retailer is poorly supplied. There seems to be a penchant for *shin plasters* in New England, and money flees from them as from a pestilence. I doubt if there is an average of three dollars of real *money* to a family in the State of Massachusetts outside of the banks, including the money-drawers of the shops, sums in the hands of money dealers, and all reserves outside of the hoards; of hoards, there are a few among the foreign population. In the South, and of course in those States where the circulation of bank bills below the denomination of five dollars is prohibited, there is some money to be found; but I defer considerably to official estimates in placing the average so high as *fifteen* dollars to each family in the nation, deducting the slaves, and make no doubt it is an overestimate sufficient to counterbalance any amount the slaves may have in possession.

Supposing we have a free population of 28,000,000—an extravagant estimate, I think—and allowing five members to each family, there are 5,600,000 families, to whom I assign $15 each, making $84,000,000. There must be large reserves—not hoards—somewhere, and large sums in the hands of money dealers, travelers, and immigrants, to make up so large an amount as this, outside of the banks; for there is a bank wherever a bank can be planted throughout the country, to gather all the money in its neighborhood. The New York *Journal of Commerce* cyphers up $283,000,000 in the whole country. I cannot conceive where they find it; but I believe Mr. Snowden of the Mint thinks with me, that $200,000,000 is a large estimate. At any rate, I do not think the *money* in the *currency* can exceed the sum I have named. With such a leak as there is in the course of exchange, that we keep almost constantly adverse to ourselves, which is neither more nor less than keeping money cheaper here than elsewhere, specie must run out in ways that cannot be discovered, or brought within the range of statistical investigation.

Some writers have placed promissory notes and bills of exchange in the category of currency, but it is altogether a mistake; their affinity is with circulating property, not with money. They may be exchanged for property, and so might the property upon which they are drawn; and if offered for sale for money they are still more like property; they are exchanged against money, and are more likely to have the effect of increasing the exchange value of money than of reducing it, as they would if they were of the nature of currency. They are, however, neither money, nor currency, nor property, but mere records of an unfinished bargain; the purchase money is not paid, and these are memoranda or written evidences of what the debtor is to do to complete the contract. One species of property exchanges for another; this is barter, the fundamental principle of trade; and when promissory notes and bills of exchange are exchanged for money, they take the position of property as essentially different from money as the goods that were delivered for them, or for the fund upon which they are drawn.

We must clearly understand, and I therefore repeat, that the currency is that, and only that, which ought to be money, and would be if not interfered with by an abnormal legislation that authorizes debt to take its place. The public mind should be disabused as to the existence of capital or value in promissory notes and bills of exchange; then people would comprehend that there is neither money, capital, nor value in the debt currency erected upon them, or into which they are converted, nor in the so-called "bank capital," which stands upon no other foundation. He who buys 1,000 barrels of flour for $5,000, holds the capital in the flour; and if he pays for it in gold, it is an exchange of capital; he has so much more of one commodity, and so much less of another—more flour and less gold—while the flour seller has so much less flour and more gold. If, instead of paying money, the buyer gives his note for the flour, it is preposterous to say or suppose that he creates a value of $5,000, and that the community are in possession of $10,000 of capital because he has run in debt $5,000, and made his note for the same. And now, if the note be exchangd for gold, or hemp, or cloth, or any other property, there is only a legitimate use of credit in the transaction; it may be exchanged fifty times for value received in each transfer without affecting the value of money, or doing any harm; the payee or original holder of the note simply receives gold, or hemp, or cloth, or some other property in exchange for his flour; the note is all the while nothing but a written evidence of the debtor's verbal promise; adding nothing to the volume of gold, or of currency equivalent in use to gold, or to property of any kind. In effect, the whole is legitimate barter; flour being exchanged for gold, and gold for hemp, and hemp for cloth, &c., through the entire circuit of exchanges. I wish to direct attention particularly to this point, and ask for it the most careful consideration, that there is not in this note an increase of anything but debt; there is nothing in it of the nature of an increase of money, currency, or property, and the transfers effected, as I have described, are merely transfers of pre-existing money or property.

But now let us suppose that the note is discounted in bank, and the bank, instead of delivering the material equivalent, money, that is, gold or silver, for the proceeds of the discount, issues its notes, or inscribes a credit to be checked upon as money in excess of the money in its coffers; it is then a very different thing; the act is the creation of *debt currency*, for which there is no material equivalent; there is no such money or value in existence as the bank promises to pay; and, therefore, although it receives an obligation to return something for nothing, at the ultimate settling day the thing cannot be done; if the bank gets the material equivalent, it belongs to some other obligation that it is required to meet, and somebody must break for it when the bank can no longer maintain the fiction in circulation. The continued existence of this fiction in the currency is absolutely necessary to maintain the price it created in the circulating property, and support the obligations of debt in the circuit of exchanges made by and resting upon it. Its withdrawal by a set-off between the two debtors, the bank and its customer, in the contraction of loans, is inevitable bankruptcy to all these obligations that must fall somewhere upon wholesale or retail dealers within the circuit of its operation, for it is the annihilation of so much currency.

But when it is created, being accepted without bargain or question as money, it degrades the value of all the capital of the community invested in money, precisely as much as it adds to the volume of the currency; this is the sure effect of an increase of bank loans. Obviously, if the bank loan is not increased by the discount; if it be merely relending a fund previously in the currency and just paid in, there is neither an increase of currency nor degradation of the value of money in the discount transaction; but I am treating of the principle of the thing, the construction of the debt currency, and I aver that we might as well make a free gift of so much gold to some other portion of the world, as to organize this note into a currency equivalent in use to money, without a special reserve of coin in the bank, dollar for dollar, against the sum placed at the disposal of the party obtaining the discount; it is converting fiction into a currency of *price* that is not *value*, and is a dead loss of capital to the nation, excepting so far as it adds to the price of our products in foreign countries, which is inappreciable, as the expelled coin flows into the great ocean of the currency of the world. Its effect is entirely adverse to ourselves, because, by raising general local prices, it checks our production and exports, and brings returns in foreign goods with precisely the whole amount of the fiction of money added to their price, which we must pay in the solid value of gold and silver. Your constant readers will excuse the repetition of this truth, which I have presented in previous numbers of this Magazine; it must be repeated, "line upon line and precept upon precept," until our people are fully awakened to its vast importance. It is the absence of money and value in the currency, and of capital thus expelled from the country, that is the cause of the cruel bankruptcy that cankers the life of our business men.

With 613 millions of currency at the beginning of the year, sterling exchange was at par, or somewhat in our favor; we were shipping products but no money. Now, late in August, sterling exchange rules against us, and we are shipping money, twice as much as we receive. Are we short of exportable produce? Certainly not; there is an abundance of it that we want to sell; but we have expanded the currency and cheapened money; 613 millions is no longer the volume of the currency. The city banks of New York and Boston alone have since increased their loans $11,000,000, and the Northwestern States are breeding red dogs and wild cats as fast as possible; new banks are going into operation in all directions, and there is a general expansion of the debt currency, with the single exception of New Orleans, while the increase of gold would expand the currency more than fast enough. There is now currency enough to maintain the prices of many exportable products above the exporters' limits, and to turn the export demand to that extent upon gold and silver—just enough of currency to sink the value of money for the amount of the export of specie. The volume of currency is now above the specie measure, and no human statute, unless by destroying a portion of the debt currency in the contraction of loans, can prevent the excess from being exported in solid money. Who does not see, if we exported merchandise to the amount of $50,000,000 instead of gold, that we should have room for the reproduction of 50 millions more of merchandise; and that we *should* reproduce it, leaving the money in the currency and so much more capital in the nation, than we shall have by the present destructive policy at the close of the year? We want the business of exporting this 50 millions and of producing 50 millions more of merchandise, and the relief from debt that would come with the accession of so much capital.

But the so-called *balance of trade* is now against us. The "balance of trade" is a chimera; money is cheapened by an increased supply like beef, and is exported like beef when it is cheaper here than in the foreign market. It is perfectly in the power of a few gentlemen who control the New York city banks, to turn the so-called balance of trade in favor of the United States in six weeks, and, if judiciously managed, without any considerable disturbance of prices; excepting perhaps among the fancy stocks in Wall-street. The clear reduction of six or seven millions of bank loans would reduce the volume of currency one per cent, and general or average prices one per cent, but for the continued supply of California gold; and even with that, a reduction of seven millions in six weeks, would so enhance the exchange value of money as to reduce sterling exchange below the par rate of 9½ per cent. This is not a mere conjecture, but a matter in which the country has had practical and ample experience, and which intelligent bank directors understand perfectly well; then the "balance of trade" would be in our favor, and we *must* export merchandise instead of money.

The vast power of regulating the value of money, and thence the commerce of the United States, is very properly delegated by the States to Congress in the constitution; it is the chief function of sovereignty, without which, the stipulation for regulating commerce, as well as that for maintaining the inviolability of contracts, is an utter nullity.* But, by reason of the neglect of Congress, this great function is given over to the cupidity of the banks; and to suit first their profits and then their necessities, the value of money is first degraded, then enhanced; the import of foreign goods is, by the same process, first stimulated, then checked; the production, as well as the export, of our domestic merchandise, is first diminished, then increased, inversely as the increase and diminution of the currency; the government revenue is first over supplied to a surfeit, then depleted to starvation; the people are first thrown into debt for a huge sum in *price*, and then compelled, by the inevitable fall in the money value of their assets, to settle the whole sum of *price* in their obligations, above *value*, in bankruptcy. Indeed, the chief object of the business of the nation, or of its conduct, seems to be first to make dividends for the banks, and then save them from the consequences of their cupidity in the suspension of specie payment; while the prosperity and happiness of the people are of secondary consideration, or of none at all. This mighty power over the public welfare is now practically exercised by a few gentlemen who control the discounts of the leading banks of the city of New York, the creditor city and center of the exchanges of the nation.

It would be no hardship to the banks of issue to be converted into "savings banks," and compelled to borrow all they lend in excess of their capital, paying interest on deposits, and making their support and profit out of the difference between the interest they pay and the exchange and interest they receive; because there would then be no limit to the loans in excess of their capital; then they would get *money* without creating a fictitious currency. I presented a statement of this principle of banking in your issue of May last, showing its practicability and profit. The public would be protected in this principle by the bank capital, of which there is none in the present savings banks; and the capital would be *real*, which, to a very great extent, it is not in the present banks of issue. It is in effect *bullion banking*, although the circulation may be in checks and certificates, the deposits being borrowed on stipulated time, and the loans being carefully averaged to be returned before the deposits fall due. There could be no contraction of the currency in this principle of banking; on the contrary, there would be a continual and normal increase of the currency by and with the increase of circulating property; the only way in which it can be steadily or profitably increased. The banks would be under no immediate liabilities without coin in reserve, dollar for dollar, to meet them; for the undrawn loans would be retained on special deposit, with the fund belonging to the circulating certificates, in coin not to be loaned again, while its ownership exists in the loans and certificates. It puts an end to the present unjust and ruinous principle of lending the same dollar several times over, upon which

* Strictly speaking, no human government can regulate the value of money, excepting by restraint upon any interference with it. Money may be diverted from its true course, or obstructed in its natural flow, like the current of a river; and it is vitally important in the matter of money that government shall prevent such diversion and obstruction. It can have no other power to regulate the value of money. Coinage is simply inspection.

the banks now make their support and profit, and which is absolutely necessary to their existence under the present system.

*Finally, it would soon add* $450,000,000 *of real money to our working capital; make the United States, in excess of imports, the greatest exporting nation on the globe: put an end to our "panics" and commercial revulsions, and New York would infallibly become the center of the exchanges and the leading city of the commercial world.*

Such is the vast importance of this currency question. If Congress should think that existing charters, which completely override the constitutional power of regulating commerce and the value of money, are still too sacred to be annulled, they can at least put a stop to their further extension, and to the creation of any more debt currency, by prescribing a limit to the bank loans of each State, and prohibiting the establishment of any more banks to create a fiction of money and lend what has no existence.

I trust the government will never again attempt to be concerned in the business of banking; but, in the exercise of their constitutional control over commerce and the currency, Congress can further the business of bullion banking, which is the only means of regulating, and the only security for both, by establishing a safe depository for coin in the hands of commissioners, independent of the treasury, and beyond the control of the treasury officers, with authority to issue certificates therefor of convenient denominations to furnish a portable, secure, and convenient national currency, to save the loss by abrasion and other cost of handling and of transporting gold. The government must be responsible for the safe keeping of the coin, dollar for dollar, against all outstanding certificates, with a positive restriction of its power to remove the deposits from the custody of the commissioners. The certificates should be payable only where the deposit for the same is made, leaving to bankers and merchants the business of removing the coin on presentation of the certificates, when the same shall be required. But the bullion or coin must be *kept*, at any cost of vaults and bolts and responsible custodians, while its ownership circulates; otherwise it is utterly lost to the nation.

This important subject needs a leading mind in Congress. Is there not some member who will make it his specialty and attend to it? In no other way can he do his country such essential service. C. H. C.

# 6

# Statistical critique of the Bank Charter Act of 1844, and suggestions for an improved system of issue

E. Seyd, 'Statistical critique of the Bank Charter Act of 1844, and suggestions for an improved system of issue', *Journal of the Statistical Society*, vol. XXXV (1872), pp. 458–540.

In the aftermath of the Bank Act, a number of criticisms focused on the large size of the Bank of England, and the dominance which this gave it in the discount market. This paper follows that line of criticism but it takes a novel approach to the role of the Bank of England's reserves. His argument is that the fiduciary issue provides an incentive to the Bank to reduce its reserve below a safe minimum; he argued for an abolition of this fiduciary limit and the introduction of a measure of elasticity. Under his proposals, the quantity of notes would be determined by a sliding scale relating the discount rate to the amount of bullion A discount rate of 2.5 per cent was to be established, and for every half percentage rise above this level, additional notes to the extent of 10 per cent of the amount of bullion held could be issued.

Seyd was a prolific author on monetary and banking issues, and he submitted a lengthy memorandum on reform of the note issue to the Select Committee in 1875. A later version of this Statistical Society paper appeared in book form in 1873, with the title, *Reform of the Bank of England Note Issue*, in which he presented a series of tables containing the weekly returns of the Bank of England between 1844 and 1871. This tabular presentation of the Banking Department data is generally considered to be Seyd's greatest contribution to discussion of these issues.

## STATISTICAL CRITIQUE *on the* OPERATION *of the* BANK CHARTER ACT *of* 1844, *and* SUGGESTIONS *for an* IMPROVED SYSTEM *of* ISSUE.

*By* ERNEST SEYD.

[Read before the Statistical Society, 17th December, 1872.]

THE subject of the Bank Act of 1844 has always been a favourite theme in this Society, and although it has rarely been treated statistically, yet the Society cannot complain of the lack of variety of opinions under which it has been brought before them.

Of the two parties which stand at the extreme ends of diverging views, the one not only utterly condemns the Bank of England Act and its limit of issue, but recommends the introduction of so-called "free banking." The other upholds and praises the Bank Act, but condemns the public for not knowing how to make proper use of it. All the controversy which has hitherto taken place upon the question lies between these two extremes.

One author modifies the extreme suggestion of "free banking" by proposing that the right of issuing bank notes should be conferred only on joint stock banks. Why should such a privilege be granted to joint stock banks, institutions which, but for the fact of their being composed of more than seven partners, and of their falling under a special law designed for their better control by the public, differ in no way from other corporations, partnerships, or individuals constituting firms? The State cannot grant such general privileges to a class, and in making the proposal its authors altogether ignore the very first principles of legislative duties. But supposing it were carried out, the questions would arise: shall these notes have legal tender rights, involving the responsibility of the State, and forcing it to control the securities of the issuers; or shall they not have legal tender rights; shall their acceptance in payment remain optional? The State cannot act as an inspector or spy of the concerns of a number of joint stock banks, and for the safety of the contract basis and the due legal vindication of the contract, it cannot permit the issue of a general currency which has no legal tender rights. "But," says the proposer of such scheme, "we want "this kind of currency principally when there is a crisis and money "is scarce, and our country bankers now issue notes without legal "tender rights." Now whenever a crisis threatens, the issue of the country bankers, it is curious to notice, contracts rather than expands; the more severe the pressure the more does the country banker endeavour to cancel his liabilities by calling in his notes, a perfectly natural result, when it is borne in mind that his issue is nothing more than an ordinary promissory note without legal tender force. And any issue of the kind proposed, instead of being sought during a crisis, would be refused, and a *perfect* currency demanded. In ordinary times our present country bankers' issues are no doubt successful as far as the profits of the issuers are concerned; whether they are really useful to public interests as regards their influence on prices in their international relationship, and in other directions, is a matter of doubt with some parties; my own opinion is that all the pleas as to their local importance are fallacious, and that they are mischievous; but this much is certain, that in the event of a crisis they become, like all non-legal tender moneys, absolutely useless. A further or temporary admixture of this kind of currency without legal tender, with the true circulating medium (gold and Bank of England notes) now vested with legal tender rights, could not be borne. Fortunately, the country issues are confined within their own limited spheres; our great national and international financial centre would, by the mere force of a natural law, sweep them aside, together with all other similar issues proposed as remedies by the class of authors referred to.

Another class of reformers propose to take the issue of bank notes from the Bank, and to transfer it to the Government. The State, through the Treasury, is to make the issue, say, partly on bullion, partly on credit. The Government can take in bullion and print notes, receiving and paying away money in exchange for notes; but what can it do with the fiduciary or credit portion of the issue? To whom are these notes to be given, and for what consideration? Can the State purchase consols or discount bills? This question I ask quite independently of the liability of the State to pay the fiduciary notes. The fact is that all issues of bank notes must be brought into direct contact with commercial interests, and no Government can issue a presumably convertible bank note without becoming a banker, liable to all the chances of that business. A few Governments, in distress for money, have issued *inconvertible* notes from their treasury, but they have speedily dropped them, transferring the right of issue to banks. The most notable case of this kind is that of the United States of America, and the issues, under Government inspection, of their national banks. The Government inspects, investigates, and spies into the assets of these banks as rigorously as possible, and so makes itself responsible for their safety. Would such a system suit England? And bear in mind that this system can only be carried on because the American notes are *inconvertible*, and legal tender at the same time; if they were convertible it could not be maintained.

Wilder schemes than these are now and then proposed, the heroic remedy of the issue of 70 millions of bank notes (the amount of our annual imperial taxation), for the purpose of paying taxes, is frequently suggested by social reformers of a certain type. I do not care to notice them; but one idea I may now set forth, for the consideration of those whose mind is not yet made up as to the relative value of a fiduciary bank note issue, compared to an issue based on the precious metals alone.

If it were an absolute truth that a fiduciary issue is as good as a bullion note issue, there would be no doubt in the matter nor need of any controversy; the absolute truth would assert itself with the unerring force of a natural law, in spite of all endeavours to prevent it, and if that were so, if both issues were equal in value, the fiduciary issue would reign supreme, and set aside the use of metallic money. As this has not taken place, as, on the contrary, all attempts to establish a fiduciary issue have either failed, or, where seemingly successful, have been attended with overwhelming evils, we must conclude that such issue is, to say the least, inferior to the one based on metal. The question of degree of inferiority is of less importance, and whatever that may be, it is quite evident that its evil results do not manifest themselves alone in issues wholly fiduciary, but that in some measure they are present also in all issues in which the fiduciary element forms a part.

I make these remarks in order to define the point of view on which I stand, from which all ingenious combinations proposed as to general issues by banks, or a special issue by the State, or kindred issues by way of seignorage on legal tender coin, are dispelled and placed into the category of financial alchemy. The duty of the State in regard to the provision of legal tender coin is simply that of certifying to its value by the dies of the Mint, and to forbid the issue of similar pieces by other parties. The same attitude, neutral in its main principle, must also be maintained in regard to bank note issues, and if the Government gives way to the pleas upon which a paper issue is demanded, it must retain the power of making a contract with one responsible factor whom it can control on behalf of the public, so as to be justified in giving legal force to the issue, without at the same time involving the direct liability of the State. I indicate thereby that I am in favour of our present bank note issue being retained, and altogether undertaken by a single establishment, the Bank of England; and now face the questions: is the present Bank of England issue so constructed that it satisfies the pleas upon which it has been established? does it meet requirements? is it faulty? and can it be improved?

It is needless for me to point out here the conflict of opinions which, in reference to this matter, has raged for years, and the evidence of the remarkable disturbances in our commercial history since the passing of the Bank Act; it is sufficient to say that in the whole of the controversy I have never met with an *exposé* of the "first "principles" upon which this matter is to be decided, and yet such first principles must exist.

The only attempt to bring out first principles is made by those who defend the Act of 1844 by saying: "The Bank Act is perfect in "every way—but (and here come their so-called first principles) "the public is not good enough for it; our merchants will speculate, "they will draw accommodation bills, and get themselves and our-"selves into trouble; if the public would only act properly the "Bank Act would be a splendid success, and nobody would have "reason to complain." The Pharisee who in his pride set himself so far above the publican is much less to blame than those who pit their system against the whole community and its degree of civilization—who are unable to deal with human nature, unable, therefore, to govern it or to invent a system which will suit human nature. Fancy the prime minister of this country, finding himself in conflict with the British nation, coming forward and saying: "I am not to "blame, it is you, the people, who are bad, and not fit to be governed." And so the defenders of the Bank Act have moralised for years in this strain without improving the public. They have boasted of the convertibility of the note, although we all know by what a contradictory process it has in times of danger been maintained; parliamentary inquiries have taken place, and heavy blue books have been printed thereon. No wonder that all these seemingly authoritative and copious matters should bother the ordinary Englishman; that he should finally shake his head, acknowledging humbly that he is not good enough for the Bank Act. He may wish himself on some other planet with a superior race of beings, and if by chance there should be a similar Bank Act in such higher realms, his report to us on its working would be very desirable.

I think you will agree with me that this line of defence, taken by the admirers of the Bank Act, is in reality its severest condemnation.

Yet bank notes must exist, and must be used. Why and how, that is the point. I shall endeavour, subject to your considerate criticism, here to establish the first principles upon which an issue of bank notes can be conducted; but before I do so, I shall lay before you a closer account of the intention and construction of the Bank Act, together with statistical facts showing how far these intentions have been carried out or not, and the evils which have arisen in connection therewith, so as to prepare the way for "first "principles." And in thus criticising one of your favourite institutions, I trust that you will concede to me the privilege which the native Englishman enjoys, when, though full of respect for his national greatness and prosperity, he yet feels anxious about some matter of public interest.

The first, and to many persons the most important purpose of the Act of 1844 was to secure the convertibility of the bank note. That this has been accomplished I will allow, but not by strict adherence to the Act; on the contrary, whenever the danger of inconvertibility drew nigh, the suspension of the Act had to be resorted to. There is no special merit in the Act, even including the absurdity of its suspension, for having accomplished this, other equally efficient methods of preserving the bullion basis might have been adopted. Other nations and other national banks have maintained the convertibility and par value of their bank notes as well as ourselves. If during the existence of the Act we had been involved in war on our own soil, like America and France, I question whether we should have maintained the convertibility of the note, especially as we have in thoroughly peaceful times been, at all events, very near to its failure. But I will allow that we have so far succeeded in maintaining the convertibility, and I will go so far as to say that, in the next crisis, especially if we again suspend the Act, we may again succeed in doing so. I say this in order to forestall and render unnecessary any discussion on this point. You will, however, I am sure, generally agree with me in this, that if we issue notes against bullion only, and not against bullion *and* Government securities, the convertibility of the note would be absolutely secure, and that, consequently, the extra issue of 15 millions of notes against Government securities does not improve the convertibility.

The Act further carries out the purpose of placing the purchase and sale of gold bullion upon a firm basis, and the firmness of the valuation which has thereby been established as regards gold is one of the principal means of our success as international bankers. That is the best feature in the system. In its practical working it has lately undergone a slight improvement in the way of greater accuracy. The arrangements made by the Bank for the control of our gold coinage are also admirable.

But in addition to the bullion which the Bank purchases as material for the convertibility of the note, and the arrangements connected with the dealings in the precious metals, the Bank also issues 15 millions (originally 14 millions) of bank notes on securities, not bullion. The whole controversy as regards the Bank Act turns upon this extra issue of 15 millions. The advocates of the bullion basis condemn it as too large and unnecessary, the partisans of the fiduciary system say that it is too small and not elastic enough. Now, I am perfectly well aware that, in talking of Bank of England notes generally, the public in its faith makes little distinction between the bases on which they rest, and seems to expect that everybody should do the like. The investigator, however, must inquire into their origin, and to him the two elements present in the Bank of England issue, viz., the bullion and the Government securities, appear as two distinct matters.

The Bank then, as you are aware, besides the notes issued against bullion, also issues 15 millions against 11,015,100*l.* Government securities, and 3,984,900*l.* other securities. Why is this extra issue made? What are its objects, either for the benefit of the State, or the public, or the Bank? I propose to answer these questions in succession.

The Government, some long time ago, it may be said, owed a debt of 11 millions to the Bank, and not finding it convenient to repay this sum, granted to the Bank the privilege of issuing notes to that amount (and 4 millions more) to be used as money, the debt of 11 millions (and 4 millions other securities) serving as guarantee to the public who hold the notes. Whatever may have been the original necessity of the State, it cannot be said that in its present prosperity it requires to borrow 11 millions of the Bank, and this sum might as well be added to the great national debt. The Government, therefore, at the passing of the Act was not, and is not now, under any necessity to use the issue as a means for borrowing money; it might have long since repaid the sum. The main object in keeping the debt standing was the conception that it would serve as security for the issue of the notes. And here let me at once declare that all the controversy in regard to this matter of the debt of the State to the Bank, the proposed repayment, the paradox of such a security, is, as far as this question of the issue of 15 millions is concerned, quite immaterial. It does not matter in the least whether this debt is booked or held by the Bank in consols, or whether it is repaid to the Bank, who with the money thus obtained might replace this security by substituting some other kind for it, for it does not matter what securities the Bank holds against fiduciary issue, so long as they fall within the same category of safety as the 4 millions "other" securities in the issue department.

The primary object of the extra issue itself, undoubtedly, was that of providing money or supposed money for the public wants. At the time when the Bank Act passed, it had been ascertained that the public had been accustomed to a circulation in their hands of some amount of bank notes, for which an issue of fiduciary notes to the amount of 14 millions seemed suitable, and the legislature conceded this amount, and fixed it as a limit. Without referring here to the nature of such an issue as combined with bullion, or to the prudence or imprudence of the limit so rigorously fixed, let me dwell upon the point that the *evident* and *beneficient intention of the law was that of providing the public, through the medium of the Bank, with 15 millions (at first 14) of money beyond that which the nation possessed in coin and coinable bullion, so that the 15 millions should circulate freely, encouraging commerce and industry.* Could the object have been anything else?

If such was the object, I invite you now to look at the returns placed before you of the reserve of bank notes held by the Bank of England, *in its banking department*, during the time the Act has been in existence (see the full returns for the twenty-seven years). You will there find that the greater portion of 15 millions of notes, instead of being in the hands of the public in "circulation," is in "reserve," in the banking department of the Bank of England, idle, inviting employment. There is only one instance out of 1,409 when the whole amount was used by the public; a few when it was fully employed within 2 and 3 millions; more when three-quarters or one-half was made available; but in the vast majority of the 1,409 weeks, or twenty-seven years, a comparatively small proportion came into the hands of the public. On many occasions, almost the whole of the sum lay idle in reserve, on several occasions there was even a surplus beyond it. The following table shows what was in the hands of the public:—

TABLE A.—*Table showing the Amount of Notes held by the Public in Excess of the Bullion in the Issue Department, Weeks and Amounts from 1st January*, 1845, *to 31st December*, 1871.

The amounts issued above bullion being:—

| | £ |
|---|---|
| From 1st September, 1844, to 8th December, 1855 ........ | 14,000,000 |
| „ 8th December, 1855, to 10th July, 1861 ............ | 14,475,000 |
| „ 10th July, 1861, to 21st February, 1866 ............ | 14,650,000 |
| „ 21st February, 1866 ............ | 15,000,000 |

The amounts used by the public have been:—

| | | | | | | | | | | | | |
|---|---|---|---|---|---|---|---|---|---|---|---|---|
| 1 week | between | 15 | and | 16 | millions.* | 175 weeks | between | 4 | and | 5 | millions. |
| 5 weeks | „ | 14 | „ | 15 | „ | 147 | „ | 3 | „ | 4 | „ |
| 1 week | „ | 13 | „ | 14 | „ | 113 | „ | 2 | „ | 3 | „ |
| 11 weeks | between | 12 | „ | 13 | „ | 68 | „ | 1 | „ | 2 | „ |
| 18 | „ | 11 | „ | 12 | „ | 26 weeks | below | | | 1 | million. |
| 37 | „ | 10 | „ | 11 | „ | 5 „ | surplus | under | | 1 | „ |
| 81 | „ | 9 | „ | 10 | „ | 4 „ | „ | over | | 1 | „ |
| 151 | „ | 8 | „ | 9 | „ | 1 week | „ | „ | | 2 | millions. |
| 148 | „ | 7 | „ | 8 | „ | | | | | | |
| 200 | „ | 6 | „ | 7 | „ | 1,409 weeks. | | | | | |
| 217 | „ | 5 | „ | 6 | „ | | | | | | |

* Special issue of 2,000,000*l.*

Roughly dividing the issue into four portions, it can be said that the public had the advantage of it in circulation during the twenty-seven years as follows:—

For 1¾ years of three-quarters of the issue above bullion.
„ 12 „ one-half „
„ 12½ „ one quarter „
„ ¾ „ none at all.

The following table shows the highest and lowest point during each year, and the average calculated on each week.

TABLE B.—*Table showing the Highest and Lowest Circulation of Bank Notes above Bullion in each Year, and Averages of Circulation and Idle Reserve in the Banking Department.*

| | Issued above Bullion. | Highest Circulation above Bullion. | Lowest Circulation above Bullion. | Average Week by Week. | Idle Reserve, Week by Week. |
|---|---|---|---|---|---|
| | £ | £ | £ | £ | £ |
| 1845 .... | 14,000,000 | 8,780,000 | 4,145,000 | 6,105,000 | 7,895,000 |
| '46 .... | „ | 8,887,000 | 4,153,000 | 6,123,000 | 7,877,000 |
| '47 .... | „ | 12,846,000 | 5,723,000 | 9,389,000 | 4,611,000 |
| '48 .... | „ | 6,848,000 | 2,691,000 | 4,892,000 | 9,108,000 |
| '49 .... | „ | 5,889,000 | 1,518,000 | 4,045,000 | 9,955,000 |
| 1850 .... | „ | 4,695,000 | 1,989,000 | 3,455,000 | 10,545,000 |
| '51 .... | „ | 7,350,000 | 1,858,000 | 5,529,000 | 8,471,000 |
| '52 .... | „ | 3,887,000 | *244,650** | 1,778,000 | 12,222,000 |
| '53 .... | „ | 8,988,000 | 2,868,000 | 5,633,000 | 8,367,000 |
| '54 .... | „ | 10,099,000 | 5,647,000 | 7,464,000 | 6,536,000 |
| 1855 .... | „ | 9,737,000 | 2,113,000 | 6,269,000 | 7,731,000 |
| '56 .... | 14,475,000 | 11,924,000 | 7,086,000 | 9,417,000 | 4,958,000 |
| '57 | „ 2,000,000 extra | 13,327,000 | 8,281,000 | 9,816,000 | 4,659,000 |
| '58 .... | 14,475,000 | 7,486,000 | 1,233,000 | 3,093,000 | 11,372,000 |
| '59 .... | „ | 6,120,000 | 1,125,000 | 4,046,000 | 10,429,000 |
| 1860 .... | „ | 9,552,000 | 5,151,000 | 6,768,000 | 7,707,000 |
| '61 | „ 14,650,000 | 9,736,000 | 4,628,000 | 7,844,000 | 6,806,000 |
| '62 .... | „ | 6,538,000 | 4,168,000 | 5,320,000 | 9,330,000 |
| '63 .... | „ | 8,846,000 | 5,172,000 | 6,897,000 | 7,753,000 |
| '64 .... | „ | 9,757,000 | 5,692,000 | 7,819,000 | 6,831,000 |
| 1865 .... | „ | 10,356,000 | 5,119,000 | 7,387,000 | 7,263,000 |
| '66 .... | 15,000,000 | 14,584,000 | 3,625,000 | 9,189,000 | 5,811,000 |
| '67 .... | „ | 5,183,000 | 170,000 | 3,236,000 | 11,764,000 |
| '68 .... | „ | 6,502,000 | 2,009,000 | 4,255,000 | 10,745,000 |
| '69 .... | „ | 8,495,000 | 3,268,000 | 5,679,000 | 9,321,000 |
| 1870 .... | „ | 6,473,000 | 814,000 | 3,449,000 | 11,551,000 |
| '71 .... | „ | 7,713,000 | *2,106,400** | 1,530,000 | 13,470,000 |

* The two items in 1852 and 1871 in *italics* being surplus above the whole issue.

The *average of the whole being* 5,794,000*l.*, *i.e.*, that being the amount of which, *out of the* 14 *and* 15 *millions assigned*, the public has had the use during the existence of the Bank Act. This, of course, includes the years of very high interest and those of crises, during which abnormal times the fiduciary circulation was exceptionally large, as you see by Table A.

The following statement shows the average of notes above bullion in circulation at respective rates of interest:—

| 2 to 2½ per Cent. | 3 per Cent. | 3½ to 4½ per Cent. | 5 per Cent. | 5½ to 8 per Cent. | 9 to 10 per Cent. |
|---|---|---|---|---|---|
| 315 weeks | 318 weeks | 315 weeks | 140 weeks | 230 weeks | 31 weeks |
| £3,500,000 | £4,568,000 | £6,043,000 | £7,694,000 | £8,716,000 | £11,277,000 |

| | | £ |
|---|---|---|
| The average for the ........................................ | 27 years is | 5,794,000 |
| If the exceptional times of crises and high interest from 5½ to 10 per cent. be deducted, viz., 261 weeks or 5 years, the average would be for the remainder ........................................ | 22 „ | 5,000,000 |
| If the interest up to 4½ per cent. be deemed the normal state, the 140 weeks at 5 per cent. deducted, there would remain an average for.... | 18 „ | 4,630,000 |
| Whilst from 2 to 3 per cent., representing 693 weeks, or nearly one-half of the whole time, the average would be for........................................ | 13½ „ | 3,987,000 |

These statements show to what extent the public has profited by the fiduciary issue of 14 to 15 millions by way of circulation. I am aware that some of my hearers are preparing now to urge that the balances thus lying idle at the Bank constitute the reserve, that they are available, that they arise from this and that and the other cause. I beg of them not to forestall me here, for I will deal with all these matters; the simple question which I have so far discussed is, that if the legislature intended that the 14 to 15 millions of extra issue should *circulate* for the benefit of the public, how has this intention been carried out? The figures given speak for themselves.

I think you will agree with me that the balances held as reserve by the Bank, and not in circulation, stand on the same ground as hoarded money—utterly inactive. The facts before us prove what their "availability" amounts to, and even hoarded money is "available" when it meets with proper demand. I shall presently again allude to this so-called "available" character of the reserves; but as far as the practical use in the hands of the community for the current transactions of commerce is concerned, the Bank might as well hold securities or merchandise, or no reserve at all.

In presenting the matter to you in this light, the admirers of the Bank Act may feel disposed to charge me with having forgotten their distinction between the issue department and the banking department; the 15 millions of notes emanating from the former, the reserve accumulating in the latter. They maintain, as you are aware, that the issue department is so entirely separated from the banking as to constitute separate interests. Yet, as we all know, the stockholders of the Bank alone are responsible for the issue, and receive the profit arising therefrom. The State, it is true, owes a debt of 11 millions to the Bank, it also taxes the issue by a certain sum per annum, and it gives the privilege of legal tender to the notes, but it is in no way responsible for the issue department. Indeed, the debt of 11 millions might be converted into consols to be held by the Bank, or the Bank might hold other securities, without any reference whatsoever to the State. The only monetary connection between State and Bank then remaining would be the annual contribution paid by the latter to the Exchequer, and the nature of this connection is none other than that of ordinary licences or duties in taxation. The right of legal tender which the Government has granted to the Bank of England note has nothing to do with the responsibility of the State, or the accountancy at the Bank. The whole weight of the issue department rests upon the shoulders of the Bank itself; and as far as *this question of the amount of notes in the hands of the public is concerned, it matters not a whit to them whether the idle reserve be held in the issue department, or is held in the banking department*, in the left or in the right hand of the Bank—in either case it is not in circulation.

I here introduce and concede the alleged distinction between the issue and banking departments, for it is not only convenient for an investigation of the accounts which are given in that form, but later on I may show also that this same distinction between the departments, or rather the automatic character of the one, can be maintained, as a matter of separate account in connection with an improved bank-note issue.

Glancing now again at the amounts of the fiduciary issue in the hands of the public, and, by way of contrast, at the large reserves in the Bank, the question arises, how do these accumulate? The suggestion nearest at hand is that they are money which the public, or rather the customers of the Bank, have paid in; and if the reserve is small, it follows that the reduction should have been caused by money withdrawn. That means, in other words: an increase in the deposits at the Bank must bring about a corresponding increase in the reserve, and *vice versâ*. Now if you look at the column of "Total "deposits and bills" in the general returns (under which I have united the three items of liabilities—public deposits, private deposits, and seven days and other bills, as money liabilities of the banking department), and at the column of reserve of notes, you will find that this is but very partially the case. The variations in the deposits are caused chiefly by the public accounts (the most unsteady up to 1871), the periodical payments of taxes, dividends on the debt, deductions from the "rest" of the Bank, &c., and if there are numerous cases where an increase or decrease in the deposits means a corresponding effect in the reserve, there are more where this is the case but very slightly, and many where the contrary takes place. The absorption of any sudden increase is met by the temporary investment in or advance on Government and other securities of casual surplus. These movements, with the demand at harvest time, &c., represent but the current transactions within certain reasonable limits, and in accordance with the progressive increase, year by year, of the business. But what we must look to, in order to verify the proposition that the increase or decrease in reserve is tantamount to increase or decrease of deposits by the public, are the larger movements under which at different times the reserve is either insignificant or redundant;—and in doing so, it must be strictly borne in mind that, according to the theory of the separation between issue and banking department, the presence of bullion in the former is an element which can be entirely separated from the latter. For the Bank assumes that its banking department stands on precisely the same ground as every joint stock bank or private banker, the action of the issue department being merely automatic for the sake of the public, of which the banking department is but a member. In the general returns for the twenty-seven years, you will find numerous disproportions between deposits and reserve, in flagrant contradiction with the theory that the latter declines and falls with the former.

Between the 19th December, 1845 and 10th January, 1846, there is a difference of 100,000*l.* in the reserve, but one of 8 millions in deposits. On the 24th July, 1847, the reserve is 1 million, the deposits over 14; on the 5th of August, 1848, the reserve is 8 millions, with 14 millions deposits. Look at 1853-54, and all subsequent years, and you will find still greater variations, not only in the same years, but more so in periods of two, three, or more years. In December, 1857, the reserve is near 1 million, the deposits being 19 millions; four months later, with the same deposits, the reserve exceeds 10 millions. Still more flagrant in the years 1866-67, when with deposits at 27 millions, the reserve is at one time under half-a-million, at another above 14 millions. This independence in the relationship between the reserve (or rather the issue) and the deposits becomes all the more extraordinary at times when the so-called pressure for money brings money to the institution, instead of the contrary, as might be expected. In the table which I now lay before you, I have selected in each half-year the highest and lowest state of the reserve, and placed them in juxtaposition with the deposits of the same week. I have avoided to include the last and first weeks of each half-year, for these exhibit the most abnormal results; for reasons well known, I exclude them so as to escape the charge of forcing my case. There are also numerous instances where the deposits are much larger proportionately than those resulting from the comparison with high and low reserves.

TABLE C.—*Table showing the Highest and Lowest State of the Reserve of each Half-Year from* 1845 *to* 1871 *inclusive (avoiding the extreme Weeks at the End and Beginning of each Half-Year), with Bullion, Deposits, and Percentage of Idle Deposits or Idle Fiduciary Issue.*

[000's omitted.]

| Date. | Bullion. | Reserve of Notes. | Deposits and Bills. | Difference. | Percentage of Idle Deposits. | Percentage of Idle Fiduciary Notes. |
|---|---|---|---|---|---|---|
| 1845. | £ | £ | £ | £ | | |
| 25th Jan. .... | 14,128, | 7,418, | 12,650, | 5,232, | 58 | 53 |
| 14th June .... | 15,917, | 9,857, | 17,552, | 7,695, | 56 | 70 |
| 13th Sept. .... | 14,790, | 8,430, | 16,600, | 8,170, | 51 | 60 |
| 1st Nov. .... | 13,276, | 5,219, | 14,693, | 9,474, | 36 | 38 |
| 1846. | | | | | | |
| 31st Jan. .... | 12,587, | 5,112, | 22,413, | 17,301, | 23 | 37 |
| 13th June .... | 14,603, | 9,011, | 22,918, | 13,807, | 40 | 64 |
| 12th Sept. .... | 15,864, | 9,846, | 17,197, | 7,351, | 57 | 70 |
| 31st Oct. .... | 14,309, | 6,934, | 14,399, | 7,465, | 48 | 50 |
| 1847. | | | | | | |
| 16th Jan. .... | 13,225, | 6,545, | 16,372, | 9,827, | 40 | 47 |
| 17th April .... | 8,801, | 2,558, | 13,925, | 11,367, | 19 | 18 |
| 23rd Oct. .... | 7,865, | 1,154, | 14,293, | 13,139, | 8 | 8 |
| 18th Dec. .... | 11,309, | 7,551, | 18,227, | 10,676, | 41 | 54 |
| 1848. | | | | | | |
| 15th Jan. .... | 12,247, | 7,152, | 15,913, | 8,761, | 45 | 51 |
| 18th March.... | 14,414, | 10,967, | 17,600, | 6,633, | 62 | 78 |
| 5th Aug. .... | 12,690, | 7,998, | 13,966, | 5,986, | 57 | 57 |
| 16th Dec. .... | 13,982, | 11,246, | 18,123, | 6,877, | 62 | 80 |
| 1849. | | | | | | |
| 24th March.... | 14,582, | 10,953, | 18,065, | 7,113, | 61 | 78 |
| 5th May .... | 13,495, | 8,281, | 15,705, | 7,424, | 53 | 59 |
| 21st July .... | 13,834, | 8,111, | 15,218, | 7,107, | 53 | 58 |
| 22nd Dec. .... | 16,284, | 12,481, | 20,801, | 8,320, | 60 | 89 |
| 1850. | | | | | | |
| 23rd March.... | 16,472, | 11,854, | 20,221, | 8,367, | 59 | 85 |
| 20th April .... | 15,873, | 9,537, | 16,732, | 7,195, | 57 | 67 |

TABLE C.—*Highest and Lowest State of Reserve of each Half-Year—Contd.*
[000's omitted.]

| Date. | Bullion. | Reserve of Notes. | Deposits and Bills. | Difference. | Percentage of Idle Deposits. | Percentage of Idle Fiduciary Notes. |
|---|---|---|---|---|---|---|
| 1850. | £ | £ | £ | £ | | |
| 21st Sept. .... | 16,176, | 11,313, | 20,431, | 9,118, | 55 | 80 |
| 19th Oct. .... | 15,406, | 9,304, | 17,219, | 7,915, | 54 | 65 |
| 1851. | | | | | | |
| 22nd March.... | 13,715, | 9,221, | 18,685, | 9,464, | 49 | 64 |
| 22nd April .... | 12,733, | 6,793, | 15,203, | 8,410, | 45 | 49 |
| 19th July .... | 13,283, | 6,649, | 14,723, | 8,073, | 45 | 48 |
| 13th Dec. .... | 16,279, | 11,390, | 19,045, | 7,655, | 60 | 81 |
| 1852. | | | | | | |
| 17th Jan. .... | 17,151, | 10,112, | 17,489, | 7,377, | 58 | 72 |
| 20th March.... | 19,175, | 13,195, | 20,882, | 7,687, | 63 | 94 |
| 25th Sept. .... | 21,132, | 13,619, | 22,044, | 8,425, | 58 | 97 |
| 30th Oct. .... | 20,767, | 10,954, | 18,937, | 7,983, | 58 | — |
| 1853. | | | | | | |
| 19th March.... | 18,596, | 11,132, | 22,430, | 11,298, | 50 | 78 |
| 7th May .... | 17,744, | 8,274, | 17,885, | 9,611, | 46 | 59 |
| 15th Oct. .... | 14,679, | 5,012, | 17,870, | 12,858, | 28 | 36 |
| 17th Dec. .... | 14,729, | 8,124, | 22,376, | 14,252, | 36 | 58 |
| 1854. | | | | | | |
| 18th Feb. .... | 15,513, | 7,858, | 15,704, | 7,846, | 50 | 56 |
| 6th May .... | 11,874, | 3,900, | 14,191, | 10,291, | 28 | 28 |
| 14th Oct. .... | 12,333, | 5,755, | 14,851, | 9,096, | 38 | 41 |
| 16th Dec. .... | 13,369, | 8,330, | 16,739, | 8,409, | 50 | 59 |
| 1855. | | | | | | |
| 20th Jan. .... | 11,509, | 5,463, | 14,138, | 8,675, | 39 | 39 |
| 16th June .... | 17,350, | 11,814, | 19,929, | 8,115, | 59 | 84 |
| 18th Aug. .... | 15,506, | 9,229, | 19,670, | 10,441, | 47 | 66 |
| 27th Oct. .... | 10,689, | 4,262, | 16,007, | 11,745, | 27 | 30 |
| 1856. | | | | | | |
| 3rd May .... | 9,181, | 3,430, | 15,496, | 12,066, | 22 | 27 |
| 14th June .... | 11,437, | 6,678, | 15,105, | 8,427, | 44 | 46 |
| 23rd Aug. .... | 11,751, | 6,287, | 15,626, | 9,339, | 40 | 43 |
| 18th Oct. .... | 9,231, | 2,550, | 15,506, | 12,957, | 16 | 18 |
| 1857. | | | | | | |
| 11th April .... | 8,321, | 3,044, | 16,314, | 13,270, | 18 | 21 |
| 13th June .... | 10,221, | 5,924, | 17,730, | 11,806, | 33 | 41 |
| 12th Sept. .... | 10,592, | 6,194, | 17,622, | 11,428, | 35 | 43 |
| 11th Nov. .... | 6,666, | 957, | 19,133, | 18,176, | 5 | 7 |

TABLE C.—*Highest and Lowest State of Reserve of each Half-Year—Contd.*
[000's omitted.]

| Date. | Bullion. | Reserve of Notes. | Deposits and Bills. | Difference. | Percentage of Idle Deposits. | Percentage of Idle Fiduciary Notes. |
|---|---|---|---|---|---|---|
| 1858. | £ | £ | £ | £ | | |
| 20th Jan......... | 13,764, | 8,199, | 22,289, | 14,090, | 37 | 57 |
| 24th March.... | 17,845, | 13,013, | 22,263, | 9,250, | 58 | 90 |
| 4th Aug. .... | 16,659, | 10,317, | 19,207, | 8,890, | 54 | 72 |
| 15th Dec. .... | 18,377, | 13,106, | 22,896, | 8,790, | 62 | 90 |
| 1859. | | | | | | |
| 16th March.... | 19,295, | 13,349, | 23,260, | 9,911, | 57 | 92 |
| 4th May .... | 16,571, | 8,790, | 22,216, | 13,426, | 39 | 61 |
| 28th Sept. .... | 16,916, | 10,185, | 23,188, | 12,003, | 44 | 70 |
| 19th Oct. .... | 16,368, | 8,355, | 20,445, | 12,090, | 40 | 58 |
| 1860. | | | | | | |
| 11th April .... | 13,914, | 4,922, | 21,155, | 16,233, | 23 | 34 |
| 13th June .... | 15,434, | 8,942, | 21,499, | 12,557, | 42 | 62 |
| 19th Sept. .... | 15,598, | 9,215, | 20,897, | 11,682, | 44 | 64 |
| 14th Nov. .... | 12,532, | 6,338, | 19,186, | 12,848, | 33 | 44 |
| 1861. | | | | | | |
| 16th Jan......... | 11,004, | 5,081, | 17,871, | 12,790, | 28 | 35 |
| 20th March.... | 11,829, | 7,453, | 20,253, | 12,800, | 37 | 52 |
| 17th July .... | 10,711, | 4,913, | 16,913, | 12,000, | 29 | 34 |
| 11th Dec. .... | 14,230, | 9,378, | 19,759, | 10,381, | 47 | 64 |
| 1862. | | | | | | |
| 19th March.... | 15,671, | 10,451, | 21,965, | 11,514, | 47 | 71 |
| 11th June .... | 14,238, | 8,195, | 22,618, | 14,423, | 36 | 55 |
| 24th Sept. .... | 16,333, | 10,482, | 23,892, | 13,410, | 44 | 71 |
| 5th Nov. .... | 14,561, | 8,111, | 22,030, | 13,919, | 37 | 55 |
| 1863. | | | | | | |
| 28th Jan......... | 12,737, | 7,206, | 20,501, | 12,295, | 40 | 49 |
| 25th Feb. .... | 13,720, | 9,253, | 20,967, | 11,714, | 44 | 63 |
| 16th Sept. .... | 14,684, | 8,560, | 27,570, | 13,010, | 40 | 58 |
| 4th Nov. .... | 13,194, | 5,803, | 19,670, | 13,867, | 29 | 40 |
| 1864. | | | | | | |
| 23rd March.... | 13,702, | 8,495, | 22,831, | 14,336, | 37 | 59 |
| 4th May .... | 11,778, | 4,944, | 19,821, | 14,877, | 24 | 34 |
| 3rd Aug. .... | 12,171, | 4,892, | 19,236, | 14,344, | 25 | 34 |
| 14th Dec. .... | 13,354, | 8,825, | 19,920, | 11,095, | 44 | 60 |
| 1865. | | | | | | |
| 18th Jan......... | 13,411, | 7,350, | 19,357, | 12,007, | 38 | 50 |
| 23rd March.... | 14,454, | 9,530, | 24,206, | 14,676, | 40 | 65 |

TABLE C.—*Highest and Lowest State of Reserve of each Half-Year—Contd.*

[000's omitted.]

| Date. | Bullion. | Reserve of Notes. | Deposits and Bills. | Difference. | Percentage of Idle Deposits. | Percentage of Idle Fiduciary Notes. |
|---|---|---|---|---|---|---|
| 1865. | £ | £ | £ | £ | | |
| 11th Oct. | 11,956, | 4,294, | 21,284, | 16,990, | 20 | 30 |
| 29th Nov. | 13,348, | 7,776, | 19,509, | 11,733, | 40 | 53 |
| 1866. | | | | | | |
| 21st March | 13,554, | 7,918, | 19,700, | 11,782, | 40 | 53 |
| 30th May | 11,434, | 415, | 27,199, | 26,784, | 1½ | 2¾ |
| 1st Aug. | 12,932, | 2,412, | 21,644, | 19,232, | 11 | 16 |
| 12th Dec. | 17,497, | 10,403, | 26,255, | 15,852, | 40 | 69 |
| 1867. | | | | | | |
| 8th May | 17,963, | 9,816, | 25,399, | 15,583, | 39 | 65 |
| 12th June | 20,181, | 12,413, | 27,428, | 15,105, | 45 | 83 |
| 25th Sept. | 23,237, | 14,829, | 27,823, | 12,994, | 53 | 99 |
| 6th Nov. | 21,217, | 11,610, | 24,791, | 13,181, | 47 | 78 |
| 1868. | | | | | | |
| 29th Jan. | 21,203, | 12,728, | 26,676, | 13,948, | 48 | 85 |
| 6th May | 19,234, | 9,779, | 25,809, | 16,030, | 38 | 65 |
| 29th July | 20,784, | 11,422, | 25,454, | 14,032, | 45 | 77 |
| 2nd Dec. | 17,007, | 8,497, | 24,223, | 15,726, | 35 | 57 |
| 1869. | | | | | | |
| 5th May | 15,510, | 6,504, | 21,496, | 14,992, | 30 | 45 |
| 16th June | 18,043, | 10,465, | 25,040, | 14,575, | 42 | 70 |
| 25th Aug. | 19,999, | 11,731, | 22,955, | 11,224, | 51 | 78 |
| 3rd Nov. | 17,600, | 8,604, | 21,617, | 13,013, | 40 | 58 |
| 1870. | | | | | | |
| 4th May | 18,701, | 10,026, | 25,060, | 15,034, | 40 | 67 |
| 15th June | 19,917, | 12,313, | 28,876, | 16,563, | 42 | 81 |
| 3rd Aug. | 17,957, | 8,527, | 27,308, | 18,781, | 31 | 57 |
| 14th Dec. | 22,021, | 14,185, | 26,388, | 12,203, | 54 | 95 |
| 1871. | | | | | | |
| 12th April | 21,541, | 12,340, | 29,921, | 17,580, | 41 | 82 |
| 14th June | 25,135, | 16,418, | 29,042, | 12,624, | 56 | 109 |
| 26th July | 26,655, | 16,620, | 32,269, | 15,649, | 51 | 111 |
| 11th Oct. | 18,394, | 7,286, | 27,155, | 19,869, | 27 | 49 |

A further proof that the surplus reserves have little connection with the public may be drawn from the bankers' balances. The bankers are the great factors in whose hands any surplus money would collect and flow into the Bank; but, if you glance at the column of bankers' balances in the general Bank statements appended (which unfortunately only go as far as 1857), you will find that the variations between them cannot have any important bearing on the matter, and that they often have a quite contrary effect, *i.e.*, they increase, when the reserve is dangerously small.

The abnormal conditions in which the bank note reserve is so often placed may further be ascribed to the variations in the bullion at the Bank. I contend that by the theory which maintains the present bank note issue, viz. that of the admixture of a fixed fiduciary issue with bullion, there should be no reference to bullion, as far as the banking department and its reserve is concerned. The separation between the one and the other department implies that the banking department uses "the money" as constituting an indivisible whole. It does not acknowledge the inferiority of the fiduciary portion: on the contrary, it gives it precedence as the original issue, as the basis. Now, if that were correct, and if the 15 millions form an integral part of the 25 to 35 millions of notes issued, and consequently also of the 100 to 120 millions of metallic money in circulation, the demand for money should be regulated by the ordinary means of raising and lowering the rate of interest in some proportion to the actual amount asked for at the Bank as a percentage on the total of 120 to 150 millions in the country, and the store of bullion of the Bank would be of less importance.

But the view is not correct; and, whatever may be the value of the boast as to the independence of the banking from the issue department, the Bank directors cannot, as bankers, apply the ordinary rule as to interest. They must also watch the issue department, wherein a drain of bullion, which represents but a small percentage on the whole metallic wealth of the country, is a large percentage on that stored at the Bank. So, in addition to the necessity of raising or lowering the rate for what we may call ordinary monetary movements in banking, they must make extra efforts, for the sake of the issue, in a double or fourfold measure. Hence the nervous susceptibility of our money market, the extreme spasmodic movements, the consequent exhaustion and flatness, and the large useless reserve of notes.

A reference to Table C shows, under the head of "Bullion," the sums in the issue department at the periods of low and high reserve indicated. If you except the years 1847, 1857, 1866, when the Bank Act was turned upside down, you will find that the variations in the reserve of notes correspond much better with the bullion reserve—that when the latter decreases there is more issue of notes, and *vice versâ*. Nevertheless, the rule shows large divergences, the cause of which is the varying supply of securities in which the Bank finds itself able or unable to invest—a subject to which I shall presently allude.

The fact that our bullion reserve stands in much better relationship to the momentary condition of commerce and its progressive increase with the prosperity of the country, would seem complimentary to the system. In reality the compliment is due to the directors, whose instinctive wisdom has applied heroic remedies, irrespective of their bad influence on other legitimate interests, and who have succeeded somehow to maintain this bullion reserve, such as it has been at times. The disease requiring these rough heroic measures lies in the old misconception that a fiduciary issue is as good as the pure metallic ore. *There are people who actually assert that the surplus of notes in the Bank is due to the increase in bullion, and not to the extra issue. In their eyes the bullion is the scum of our monetary system.* Common sense must repudiate this notion; the highest logical reasoning would dispose of this aberration of thought at once. But, if we admitted the foolish claim that the fiduciary issue thus has precedence over the increase in bullion, we can answer, "The matter is as broad as it is long, "the 15 millions themselves either become superfluous, or, through "their presence, they place so much bullion in that position."

The allegation may be made that if the fixed fiduciary issue did not exist, that is, if the issue were a pure bullion one, there would be the same kind of plethora from time to time, and the same abnormal idle reserves. Unfortunately this country has never tried the pure bullion basis, so that statistics might refute this allegation; but as a matter of fact the state of the note reserve at all times shows that bullion is never in surplus. In 1870 only, from the 7th June to 26th July, there is a surplus of bullion, owing to the exceptional import of gold from France after the war. The case of absolute idleness of metallic money has otherwise been unknown. A lowering of the rate of interest will always give it employment, and although a sudden plethora may require days and weeks for absorption, it will not, like in the case of fiduciary notes, take months and years before use is found for it. The law of exchanges, the great clearing system involved in "arbitrations" of exchanges, rules the equalisation of the value and the stores of solid money with almost mathematical certainty, and makes a permanent surplus of solid international means an impossibility. Unfortunately we do not well understand and appreciate these laws in our banking practice, and our bankers, confining themselves to local national claims, neglect the opportunity of holding and profiting from claims on foreign countries; so that England, the great international trader and banker, holds but a one-sided position in the great system of claims and counter-claims. Independently, however, of the principles of adjustment which a better policy in international trade would turn to account, if any more or less permanent surplus of metallic money were to arise *it would be absorbed by the rise in the prices of commodities, and thus disappear.* Anybody acquainted with the first elements of the theory of prices must admit this. A permanent, or even a more or less permanent, accumulation of solid money, capable of giving an average, becomes an impossibility; the law of prices would absorb it with unfailing certainty, even supposing that the inland intercourse of the country stood entirely apart from the international intercourse.

The fiduciary element has no relationship to international trade, and, whatever value it may be supposed to have in reference to local intercourse, it brings international and national commerce into continual conflict. As far as the British public (which has received so little benefit from it) is concerned, the fiduciary issue of 15 millions might as well be abolished. There have been periods when the variations in bullion exceeded the average of issue, and longer periods of almost total idleness of the sum, tantamount to a practical abolition, and no inconvenience was felt. If it were finally abolished, you will concede to me that, to commence with, all danger of "inconvertibility" of the note, for which we now make such sacrifices, would cease for ever.

I think that I have pointed out to you the slender connection between the fiduciary note issue and the public, it remains for me only to dispose of one other suggestion connected therewith. It may be said: True, the bank note reserve is generally unused and large, but it is *available*, and in times of great pressure it is so used. A reference to the years 1857 and 1866, notably, will show that at such times it is not the note issue which comes to the rescue, but the depositors; and, paradoxical as it may seem, the depositors, at their risk, save both the bank and the note issue.

If, then, the object of the Act, that of benefiting the public by the issue of 15 millions fiduciary notes, has substantially failed, what other object remains? The only other object could be a supposed benefit or monopoly in favour of the Bank itself. Now I utterly repudiate the suggestion that, at the charge of commerce or anything else, the legislature ever intended to confer a privilege of this nature; but let us suppose, that though not intentionally, such were the consequences of the arrangement (a very natural suggestion, for "when one loses, the other wins," it is said). An examination of the results will show the truth of the rule that in matters of general commercial intercourse an identity of interest alone will bring profit to both, by the contrary both will suffer.

Let us therefore start the proposition, "the issue is useful and "profitable to the Bank, both as reserve and as investment."

There are two purposes for which a banker covets a reserve. The first is that of being able to accommodate his customers. Now, if the 15 millions of issue are serviceable for this purpose, the figures given before, as regards the extent to which that issue has been used by the customers of the Bank, will enlighten you. The banking department finds it impossible to move the reserves but within the narrow limits shown, or by the uncontrollable force of panic and confusion. Here the lover of the separation of the issue department from the banking department will smile again in his wisdom and say, "But the banking department has received the "15 millions of notes and invested them, the surplus of notes is quite "another thing." *That is to say, he wants to make out that the 15 millions of notes are gone, that they are involved in the general business, and that the "reserve"* is but the consequence of the notes returned to the Bank by deposits. I have shown the want of connection between the issue and deposits, *nevertheless it suits me*, for the present to throw the onus of the idle surplus on the deposits. Taking, then, his view, we find that the banking department has at its disposal 15 millions of notes *plus* the deposits of its customers to do business with. The first being invested and gone, the deposits have their turn.

Look now at the general returns, viz., the deposits and the reserves supposed to arise from their plethora, and notice how very large a portion of the former would be idle. In Table C you will find column headed "Difference." The use of this will now appear. If precedence is given to the 15 millions as invested and disposed of, the difference between the reserve of notes and the amount of deposits shows the sums which the Bank has been able to employ out of the deposits, and, comparing them with the deposits, the balances being idle, you find that these range from 63 per cent. downwards, the average of the whole twenty-seven years giving 42½ per cent. of idle deposits. If the abnormal times of crises, when nearly all the deposits are used at extra high rates of interest, are deducted therefrom, and calculated over the whole of each week, the result is an average of 51½ per cent. of unused deposits.

Is this right and proper? Separate the question for a moment from that of the safety reserve of the Bank, which I shall presently consider. The banking department, it is pretended again, is independent of the issue, as a banker—so say the advocates of the Act—it stands upon the precise footing as all other banks, and may use its deposits as it pleases. But can any banking concern be conducted when, as is thus frequently the case with the Bank of England, more than half of the deposits are idle? That the Bank does not leave them uninvested as a matter of choice we all know, for it tempts commerce to use them by lowering the rate of interest, at times to an extremely low figure, yet all in vain. And the fact that the Bank pays no interest on deposits does not concern the trade of the country, which requires banking capital. The great principle in every banking system is that the funds which, either as accumulated wealth or as average of balances, are placed in a bank, should, within reasonably safe limits, be used for the development of business; yet here we find that this cannot be done, excepting in the most spasmodic manner. The wealth and strength of the country represented by these deposits, the fruits of our economy and industry, seems half wasted when thus brought into competition with the fiduciary issue. I must leave you to judge which of the two is the more worthy of consideration.

The last column in Table C, headed "Percentage of Idle Notes," proceeds upon my assumption, that the *deposits have precedence*, and that the burden of idleness is thrown on the fiduciary issue, *like an incurable disease*, cheating us into the belief that these idle notes constitute a reserve.

A striking proof of the disadvantages under which the Bank suffers by this hallucination is furnished by the discount business of the Bank. You are no doubt under the impression that the Bank of England, as the great centre of the monetary power of the country, the leader in the rate of discount, does an enormous discount business, and holds in hand the "cream of the cream" of all that is fine in our gigantic system of commercial intercourse at home and with all parts of the world. In the general returns for the years 1845 to 1857 (unfortunately the returns only go so far), under the head "Bills "discounted," you will find that there were times when the Bank held no more than two millions of such bills.

The columns of Table D, which I submit, contain—1st, the total banking funds or liabilities of the banking department, viz., capital, rest, deposit, and bills; 2ndly, deposits and bills separately; 3rdly, the note reserve; 4thly, the investments in Government securities; 5thly, the other securities; and in the sixth and seventh columns the bills discounted and temporary advances. The table starts with the highest and lowest amounts of bills discounted in each year, and gives the corresponding items under the other columns. The amounts, which, under the head of bills discounted, appear large, are exceptional, they would seem to make the average larger; but a reference to the general tables of the Bank returns will show you, notably during the years 1848 to 1854, that the smaller sums are in the greater majority.

TABLE D.—*Table showing the Amount of Total Banking Funds and Bills Discounted and Temporary Advances, &c., from* 1845 *to* 1857 (*the Half-Yearly Weeks avoided*).

[000's omitted.]

| Date. | Capital, Rest, and Total Funds. | Deposits and Bills. | Note Reserve. | Government Securities. | Other Securities. | Bills Discounted. | Temporary Advances. | Percentage to Resources of Bills Discounted and Temporary Advances. |
|---|---|---|---|---|---|---|---|---|
| | £ | £ | £ | £ | £ | £ | £ | |
| 1845. | | | | | | | | |
| 1st Feb..... | 30,502, | 12,650, | 7,642, | 13,541, | 8,652, | 2,030, | 1,175, | 10½ |
| 20th Dec..... | 36,858, | 19,083, | 6,768, | 13,201, | 16,329, | 9,561, | 1,064, | 27 |
| 1846. | | | | | | | | |
| 28th Feb..... | 44,133, | 25,891, | 6,994, | 13,136, | 23,242, | 13,137, | 4,142, | 39 |
| 12th Sept.... | 35,618, | 17,197, | 9,846, | 12,961, | 12,321, | 5,568, | 560, | 17 |
| 1847. | | | | | | | | |
| 9th Jan..... | 34,693, | 16,620, | 6,715, | 12,757, | 14,464, | 7,490, | 970, | 24½ |
| 13th Oct..... | 32,629, | 14,538, | 1,176, | 10,613, | 20,409, | 12,738, | 1,728, | 44½ |
| 1848. | | | | | | | | |
| 15th Jan..... | 34,187, | 15,903, | 7,152, | 11,203, | 15,254, | 7,734, | 1,793, | 28 |
| 9th Dec..... | 35,559, | 17,631, | 10,771, | 13,329, | 10,668, | 3,182, | 1,109, | 15 |
| 1849. | | | | | | | | |
| 20th Jan..... | 34,564, | 16,529, | 9,641, | 13,621, | 10,522, | 3,236, | 919, | 12 |
| 29th Nov.... | 36,380, | 18,663, | 11,571, | 14,338, | 9,660, | 2,308, | 591, | 8 |
| 1850. | | | | | | | | |
| 25th May.... | 35,672, | 18,052, | 10,884, | 14,316, | 9,697, | 2,207, | 656, | 8 |
| 7th Dec..... | 38,186, | 20,540, | 10,642, | 14,228, | 12,722, | 3,695, | 1,740, | 14 |
| 1851. | | | | | | | | |
| 3rd May.... | 33,134, | 15,457, | 6,957, | 14,125, | 11,441, | 3,855, | 680, | 14 |
| 4th Oct..... | 37,622, | 19,460, | 8,958, | 13,464, | 14,624, | 5,883, | 1,668, | 20 |
| 1852. | | | | | | | | |
| 17th Jan..... | 35,344, | 17,489, | 10,112, | 13,269, | 11,388, | 3,569, | 622, | 12 |
| 11th Sept.... | 39,113, | 21,009, | 13,263, | 14,189, | 11,116, | 2,674, | 284, | 7½ |
| 1853. | | | | | | | | |
| 30th July.... | 34,190, | 16,388, | 7,970, | 13,337, | 12,466, | 4,525, | 228, | 14 |
| 15th Oct..... | 35,484, | 17,870, | 5,012, | 12,455, | 17,425, | 9,116, | 319, | 26½ |
| 1854. | | | | | | | | |
| 11th Mar.... | 33,184, | 14,913, | 7,626, | 11,747, | 13,054, | 4,515, | 178, | 14 |
| 10th June | 32,238, | 14,397, | 5,667, | 10,024, | 15,799, | 7,488, | 496, | 25 |
| 1855. | | | | | | | | |
| 16th June | 37,605, | 19,929, | 11,814, | 12,681, | 12,399, | 3,614, | 235, | 29 |
| 20th Oct..... | 34,283, | 16,569, | 4,310, | 10,635, | 18,789, | 9,054, | 811, | 29 |
| 1856. | | | | | | | | |
| 26th July.... | 33,233, | 15,318, | 5,803, | 13,713, | 13,094, | 3,761, | 938, | 14 |
| 15th Nov.... | 33,741, | 15,933, | 3,606, | 10,457, | 19,054, | 9,789, | 632, | 31 |
| 1857. | | | | | | | | |
| 10th Jan..... | 33,083, | 15,275, | 4,603, | 11,513, | 16,342, | 5,833, | 1,978, | 23½ |
| 2nd Dec.... | 39,362, | 21,349, | 2,268, | 5,441, | 31,191, | 17,788, | 3,215, | 53½ |

*Note.*—The reserve of coin is left out.

The table shows that, with banking resources ranging from 30 to 40 millions sterling, the bills discounted frequently fall as low as 2 to 3 millions. In the column "Percentage to resources of bills "discounted and temporary advances," you find the proportions of bills and advances thereon which have been so employed. They range from $7\frac{1}{2}$ per cent. to $53\frac{1}{2}$ per cent., the latter being the extraordinary moment in December, 1857. The average is $21\frac{1}{2}$ per cent., but this includes the two short crises of 1847 and 1857, which, when deducted, leave an average of 17 per cent. During more than one-half of the entire time the average is but $12\frac{1}{2}$ per cent. That is to say, if by "Bills discounted and temporary advances" are meant dealings in those instruments of exchange which form the life and soul of our commerce, with advances thereon, there are periods stretching over several years in which but one-eighth of the banking resources of the great centre are so engaged. But I am justified in going much farther than I have done in this table. The Bank's discount business can be divided into two categories, the one being that for customers with regular current accounts, the other that connected with the general market, through less regular accounts; the former, in which the regular business at branches is included, may be represented by averages of from 2 to 4 millions, and if these be deducted from the percentages given in Table D, it will appear that there are times when the Bank is, for many months together, altogether severed from the general market, so that the whole average is but 10 per cent., and nothing for about one-half the time. Bearing in mind the original intention of the issue of 15 millions, its great resources, and its natural position, the Bank has no right to refuse such fine discount business on capricious excuses, nor does it do so when the market suits it. It is said that since 1866 there have been more bills, more discount on the average, but an increase of 3 or 4 millions even would not much affect the principle of irregularity. Yet lately the proposition was started that the Bank should give up discounting, an indication of the state of doubt and demoralisation into which we have fallen in the controversy. (After 1857 the Bank ceased to make temporary advances, for reasons which were then given: in 1871 they were resumed. It is much to be regretted that the returns do not continue, so as to show us what the Bank has done since, especially in 1865, 1866, and shortly after; as also in 1870-71.)

In general the overwhelming proportion of the Bank's funds is invested in Government securities and in "other securities," not commercial bills and temporary advances. The business of investing in Government securities (and these securities in the banking department are independent of those in the issue), railway, colonial and other securities of that kind, is a very simple one, and hardly requires a large organisation by way of a bank. It is rather the business of the capitalist, not that of the banker. I am far from saying that a banker should never make use of Government stocks of any kind as an investment; indeed he must invest any surplus money in them, and thus maintain a certain percentage of reserve; but they should not be the principal investment, if only for the reason that they vary in price and cannot always be sold without loss. Bills, however, are not subject to variations in price, they are securities continually absorbing and reproducing money by a self-acting process.

The Bank of France, before the war, held 39 millions sterling of bills, and, although the war and sieges intervened, they were all paid, the loss being about one-quarter per cent. The trade of France is not one-half of ours, the Bank of France has no monopoly, for the banks and bankers of Paris and the large towns are comparatively as powerful as our own other joint stock banks and bankers. Nor is the Bank of France compelled, as is erroneously supposed, to discount all bills with three signatures, it simply rejects those without that number, and has full liberty to do as it pleases. Examine the accounts of the Bank of France, or that of Prussia, and you will find that their chief investments are in commercial bills, the true banking security. The Bank of Prussia, on "Lombard" business, *i.e.*, advances on Government securities, railways, &c., charges 1 per cent. above the bank rate. Look at our own banks, bankers and discount companies, several of them hold more than double as much in bills as the Bank of England, the whole aggregate does not probably fall short of 200 millions sterling.

It would almost appear as if our great Bank of England had lost the power of acting upon the principle that good bills are the most valuable, the most legitimate, the most reproductive and equalising security for banking purposes. At one time, or rather for a length of time, it holds between 2 or 3 millions sterling, at another time (1857) it holds 20 millions, as if our trade had suddenly increased eight-fold, and *vice versâ*. Why this irregularity? why cannot the Bank, claiming the total independence of the banking department, at all events keep some kind of regular percentage share in the business of the country, especially as it determines the rate of discount? I am far from proposing that the Bank should only deal in bills (upon a three-signature system or some other absurd plan), and agree with Mr. Hankey, who in his book on the institution, says that the Bank should also promote railway and public enterprises; but to such advances, which endanger a bank, no preference must be given; at all events some reasonable proportion must be maintained in that kind of business for which banking institutions are established. That our Bank makes every effort to obtain these securities we all know; as soon as its reserve reaches a certain figure, it lowers the rate, say, from $4\frac{1}{2}$ to 4, instantly the market rate becomes $3\frac{3}{4}$; the Bank says $3\frac{1}{2}$, the market $3\frac{1}{4}$, and so on, until the Bank says 2 and the market $1\frac{3}{4}$. This process resembles nothing so much as omnibus nursing. Yet the Bank Directors cannot act otherwise, the rule in regard to money or supposed money is absolute, and interest must be lowered. But they obtain no more bills; on the contrary, the reserve increases and remains stationary for years, until the demoralisation, gradually sown, brings on the violent reaction. The fact is, that when the note reserve is large, when consequently the country itself is on the bullion basis, the successful competition of the adulterated currency at the Bank with the bullion basis becomes impossible.

The fits, starts, and extraordinary divergences in the rate of interest often puzzle the public, and create great mischief, not only in destroying legitimate profits, but in causing ruin and failure. To what are they due? When any change in the rate takes place, we endeavour to account for it, by referring either to declines or rises in the bullion, the reserve, the deposits, or the securities; and although we often doubt the necessity for strong measures, we on the whole rely upon the wisdom of the directors. A closer and comparative examination of the actual state of matters will, in reference to this, reveal to you singular facts, and furnish the true explanation of the anomaly. In order to show this I have, in Table G, herewith submitted, put together the moveable items, viz., bullion in issue department, total deposits, Government securities, "other" securities, and reserve in banking department (the others, viz., securities in the issue and capital, being fixed, rest and coin, more or less fixed items), and placed them in juxtaposition to the rate of discount. The test as to the demand for money on the one hand, and the absorption of the Bank's strength on the other hand, is given by the "other" securities in the banking department; and selecting (without any special choice, and avoiding the extreme weeks of each year) three different stages in each year, with the corresponding other items, you can with greater ease glance over the results. In order now to test the demand for money or its value, it must be borne in mind that an *increase* in bullion, in the deposits and in the reserve, a *decrease* in Government and other securities, have the effect of lowering the rate; whilst a decrease in bullion, deposits, and reserve, as well as an increase in the two securities, have the tendency to raise the rate.

TABLE G.—*Table showing "Other" Securities in the Banking Department at Three Different Stages in each Year, and Bullion Deposits, Government Securities, Rate of Discount, Note Reserve, and Bills Discounted and Temporary Advances.*

[000's omitted.]

| Date. | *Issue* Department, *Bullion.* | Banking Department, *Deposits.* | Banking Department, Government Securities. | Banking Department, Other Securities. | Rate of Discount. | Reserve of Notes. | Bills Discounted and Temporary Advances. |
|---|---|---|---|---|---|---|---|
| | £ | £ | £ | £ | | £ | £ |
| 1845. | | | | | | | |
| 25th Jan. | 14,122, | 12,560, | 13,651, | 8,561, | 2½ | 7,418, | 3,178, |
| 5th July | 15,891, | 18,471, | 13,384, | 12,944, | " | 9,279, | 7,162, |
| 6th Dec. | 12,540, | 18,136, | 13,201, | 16,224, | 3½ | 5,945, | 10,512, |
| 1846. | | | | | | | |
| 28th Feb. | 13,105, | 25,891, | 13,136, | 23,242, | 3½ | 6,994, | 17,279, |
| 27th June | 15,273, | 23,693, | 12,987, | 12,257, | " | 9,664, | 12,763, |
| 7th Nov. | 14,235, | 14,729, | 12,808, | 12,153, | 3 | 7,264, | 6,247, |
| 1847. | | | | | | | |
| 3rd April | 9,554, | 16,464, | 11,990, | 18,627, | 4 | 3,699, | 12,606, |
| 3rd July | 9,562, | 18,514, | 11,806, | 18,758, | 5 | 5,158, | 12,977, |
| 20th Nov. | 9,525, | 15,967, | 10,633, | 18,791, | 8 | 4,228, | 12,782, |
| 1848. | | | | | | | |
| 15th Jan. | 12,247, | 15,903, | 11,203, | 15,254, | 5 | 7,152, | 9,527, |
| 10th June | 13,132, | 15,764, | 12,197, | 11,398, | 4 | 9,505, | 5,212, |
| 11th Nov. | 12,961, | 15,727, | 13,329, | 10,758, | 3 | 8,894, | 4,993, |
| 1849. | | | | | | | |
| 31st March | 14,407, | 18,184, | 14,072, | 11,278, | 3 | 10,461, | 4,330, |
| 11th Aug. | 13,648, | 15,783, | 14,282, | 9,551, | " | 8,902, | 2,978, |
| 15th Dec. | 16,137, | 20,528, | 14,350, | 10,803, | 2½ | 12,184, | 4,061, |
| 1850. | | | | | | | |
| 16th Feb. | 16,340, | 18,089, | 14,399, | 9,657, | 2½ | 11,153, | 2,929, |
| 22nd June | 16,192, | 19,927, | 14,375, | 11,115, | " | 11,339, | 4,246, |
| 5th Oct. | 15,831, | 20,861, | 14,443, | 13,389, | " | 10,527, | 6,078, |
| 1851. | | | | | | | |
| 1st March | 13,772, | 18,369, | 14,145, | 13,174. | 3 | 8,536, | 5,674, |
| 5th July | 13,581, | 18,782, | 13,545, | 14,251, | " | 8,036, | 7,387, |
| 15th Dec. | 15,902, | 18,773, | 13,241, | 11,547, | " | 11,048, | 4,570, |
| 1852. | | | | | | | |
| 20th March | 19,175, | 20,882, | 13,567, | 11,722, | 2½ | 13,195, | 3,493, |
| 26th June | 21,587, | 21,699, | 13,874, | 10,755, | 2 | 14,244, | 3,143, |
| 11th Dec. | 20,970, | 21,907, | 13,962, | 12,620, | " | 12,415, | 4,414, |
| 1853. | | | | | | | |
| 5th March | 18,361, | 21,313, | 13,464, | 15,401, | 3 | 10,086, | 7,156, |
| 23rd July | 17,460, | 16,496, | 13,537, | 12,553, | 3½ | 7,852, | 4,836, |
| 10th Dec. | 14,620, | 22,129, | 15,043, | 16,525, | 5 | 7,575, | 8,624, |
| 1854. | | | | | | | |
| 4th Feb. | 15,513, | 15,704, | 11,757, | 13,346, | 5 | 7,858, | 5,396, |
| 30th Sept. | 12,464, | 16,741, | 11,006, | 16,912, | " | 6,499, | 8,545, |
| 2nd Dec. | 13,244, | 15,806, | 11,517, | 13,710, | " | 7,627, | 5,561, |

TABLE G.—*Showing "Other" Securities in the Banking Department, &c.* —*Contd.*

[000's omitted.]

| Date. | *Issue* Department, *Bullion.* | Banking Department, *Deposits.* | Banking Department, Government Securities. | Banking Department, Other Securities. | Rate of Discount. | Reserve of Notes. | Bills Discounted and Temporary Advances. |
|---|---|---|---|---|---|---|---|
| 1855. | £ | £ | £ | £ | | £ | £ |
| 31st March | 14,510, | 17,183, | 11,581, | 14,991, | 5 | 9,129, | 5,431, |
| 1st Sept.... | 14,368, | 19,345, | 13,031, | 15,661, | 3½ | 8,263, | 6,463, |
| 6th Oct..... | 11,765, | 18,956, | 11,413, | 19,791, | 5½ | 5,473, | 10,706, |
| 1856. | | | | | | | |
| 29th March | 9,831, | 19,461, | 11,871, | 20,063, | 5½ | 5,289, | 12,458, |
| 19th July.... | 11,708, | 15,994, | 14,798, | 13,153, | 4½ | 5,321, | 4,760, |
| 15th Nov.... | 9,061, | 15,933, | 10,457, | 19,054, | 7 | 3,606, | 10,412, |
| 1857. | | | | | | | |
| 4th April | 8,570, | 19,181, | 11,645, | 21,699, | 6½ | 3,507, | 12,867, |
| 3rd Oct..... | 10,078, | 19,122, | 10,593, | 21,835, | 5½ | 4,686, | 11,475, |
| 25th Nov.... | 6,784, | 21,555, | 5,807, | 31,350, | 10 | 1,918, | 21,185, |
| 1858. | | | | | | | |
| 20th Jan..... | 13,746, | 22,289, | 9,191, | 22,250, | 5 | 8,199, | — |
| 17th Feb..... | 16,542, | 21,222, | 9,857, | 17,634, | 3 | 11,313, | — |
| 27th Oct..... | 18,510, | 20,321, | 10,809, | 14,783, | " | 11,760, | — |
| 1859. | | | | | | | |
| 27th April | 16,960, | 21,351, | 11,371, | 17,505, | 2½ | 9,496, | — |
| 1st June.... | 17,095, | 23,921, | 11,281, | 19,206, | 4½ | 10,478, | — |
| 5th Oct..... | 17,025, | 22,708, | 11,219, | 19,792, | 2½ | 9,388, | — |
| 1860. | | | | | | | |
| 18th Jan..... | 15,168, | 20,876, | 10,813, | 19,593, | 2½ | 7,589, | — |
| 27th June | 15,770, | 22,339, | 9,814, | 20,263, | 4 | 9,285, | — |
| 21st Nov..... | 12,535, | 19,464, | 9,490, | 20,298, | 6 | 6,613, | — |
| 1861. | | | | | | | |
| 20th March | 11,829, | 20,253, | 10,599, | 19,707, | 8 | 7,453, | — |
| 17th April | 12,368, | 18,268, | 10,272, | 18,415, | 5 | 6,548, | — |
| 13th Nov.... | 13,566, | 17,769, | 10,812, | 16,392, | 3 | 7,477, | — |
| 1862. | | | | | | | |
| 28th May.... | 15,317, | 22,285, | 10,335, | 19,392, | 3 | 9,364, | — |
| 30th July.... | 17,565, | 23,539, | 11,002, | 19,442, | 2 | 10,022, | — |
| 29th Oct..... | 14,695, | 23,266, | 11,763, | 18,978, | " | 8,330, | — |
| 1863. | | | | | | | |
| 13th May.... | 13,731, | 21,077, | 11,151, | 18,952, | 3 | 7,744, | — |
| 28th Oct..... | 13,769, | 20,205, | 10,995, | 19,693, | 4 | 6,547, | — |
| 23rd Dec..... | 13,503, | 23,595, | 10,762, | 21,418, | 8 | 8,496, | — |
| 1864. | | | | | | | |
| 2nd March | 13,264, | 21,992, | 11,124, | 20,708, | 6 | 7,670, | — |
| 25th May.... | 13,041, | 21,304, | 10,785, | 20,414, | 8 | 7,274, | — |
| 9th Nov.... | 12,925, | 19,528, | 9,972, | 19,506, | 9 | 7,184, | — |

*Note.*—The returns of "Bills Discounted and Temporary Advances" cease after 1857.

TABLE G.—*Showing "Other" Securities in the Banking Department, &c.*
*—Contd.*
[000's omitted.]

| Date. | *Issue* Department, *Bullion.* | Banking Department, *Deposits.* | Banking Department, Government Securities. | Banking Department, Other Securities. | Rate of Discount. | Reserve of Notes. | Bills Discounted and Temporary Advances. |
|---|---|---|---|---|---|---|---|
| 1865. | £ | £ | £ | £ | | £ | £ |
| 1st Feb..... | 13,734, | 20,455, | 11,023, | 18,920, | 5 | 7,852, | — |
| 26th July.... | 18,603, | 20,229, | 10,398, | 21,782, | 3 | 6,181, | — |
| 22nd Nov.... | 13,673, | 19,513, | 9,741, | 19,004, | 7 | 7,739, | — |
| 1866. | | | | | | | |
| 16th May.... | 11,851, | 25,086, | 10,837, | 30,943, | 10 | 730, | — |
| 27th June | 14,170, | 29,364, | 11,348, | 30,883, | ,, | 4,346, | — |
| 14th Nov.... | 16,084, | 22,425, | 12,304, | 19,061, | 4 | 7,807, | — |
| 1867. | | | | | | | |
| 29th May.... | 19,287, | 26,584, | 12,886, | 18,883, | 3 | 11,358, | — |
| 31st July.... | 21,725, | 25,982, | 12,830, | 17,322, | 2 | 12,542, | — |
| 13th Nov.... | 21,150, | 24,471, | 12,319, | 16,682, | ,, | 12,000, | — |
| 1868. | | | | | | | |
| 1st April | 19,935, | 27,725, | 13,271, | 20,698, | 2 | 10,767, | — |
| 10th June | 20,943, | 28,185, | 13,294, | 18,850, | ,, | 12,408, | — |
| 18th Nov.... | 17,202, | 24,398, | 15,301, | 16,873, | ,, | 8,713, | — |
| 1869. | | | | | | | |
| 31st March | 16,473, | 25,848, | 14,999, | 20,130, | 3 | 7,862, | — |
| 9th June | 17,468, | 24,583, | 14,148, | 17,331, | 4½ | 9,626, | — |
| 6th Oct..... | 18,626, | 24,082, | 15,211, | 16,377, | 2½ | 9,361, | — |
| 1870. | | | | | | | |
| 11th May.... | 18,735, | 25,615, | 12,931, | 19,018, | 3 | 10,290, | — |
| 10th Aug.... | 18,230, | 26,984, | 12,483, | 22,207, | 6 | 9,449, | — |
| 5th Oct..... | 21,545, | 25,746, | 12,983, | 17,254, | 2½ | 12,270, | — |
| 1871. | | | | | | | |
| 8th March | 21,021, | 32,296, | 12,923, | 23,983, | 3 | 12,874, | — |
| 20th Sept.... | 22,844, | 27,326, | 14,043, | 17,781, | 2 | 13,058, | — |
| 15th Nov.... | 23,237, | 29,041, | 15,001, | 17,583, | 5 | 13,471, | — |

Apply this rule throughout to the table, and you will find that, whether you compare periods within a year, according to bullion or securities, or whether you select different years according to rates of interest, you will find a majority of vast and seemingly inexplicable divergences. And let me state here distinctly, that the increase in business (the doubling and trebling of our trade) has little or nothing to do with this matter; for, in spite of this increase, of which *all* our banks have profited so immensely, the Bank of England has remained nearly stationary. The column of other securities (showing what the Bank has done) is as large in 1845 as in 1868, in 1856 as in 1869, &c. &c. The deposits in 1845, 1852, 1856, are higher than those of 1860, 1861, 1865. The bullion shows similar relations.

From 1865 to 1871 there is a general increase in the bullion, deposits, and other securities; but even this increase is but a small percentage on the colossal development of our commerce. Notable examples of the seemingly inexplicable movements of interest are furnished, among others, by the year 1847. Comparing 3rd April with 20th November, you will find that there is no change in bullion and securities, but a decline of 500,000*l*. in deposits, telling for a rise; a decline in Government securities of 1,300,000*l*., and increase in note reserve of 500,000*l*., in favour of lowering the rate; in all, 1,300,000*l*. in *favour of a decline in interest* from 4 per cent. Instead of that the rate is doubled, viz., 8 per cent. (It is true that three weeks before the 3rd April, reserve was $2\frac{1}{2}$ millions below, but this would have made but $1\frac{1}{4}$ million in favour of a rise.) Take the year 1863, when between 13th May (when the rate was 3 per cent.) and 23rd December bullion agreed, there being a rise in deposits of 2,500,000*l*., a decline in Government securities of 400,000*l*., and a rise in reserve of 700,000*l*., together 3,600,000*l*., for lowering; against a rise of 2,500,000*l*. in other securities for an increase (balance against lowering being 1,100,000*l*.), yet the rate rises from 3 to 8 per cent. Similar examples appear in other years.

It will be evident to you that, upon the ordinary merits of the case, these examples are inexplicable; *but the fact is this:* the Bank is anxious at such times to improve the bullion basis, and raises the rate of interest for that purpose, at any cost to the inland trade. Say that upon bullion of 9 millions it is desirable that 2 millions should be added. The rule of raising the rate to attract "money" is put into operation, and a rise from 4 per cent. to 6 per cent. brings in 2 millions of "money." But, remember that the Bank's money consists of bullion and of notes; so that, say, one-half of the 2 millions coming in is notes, the other half is bullion—only 1 million; and, as 2 millions are wanted, it follows that, instead of jumping from 4 to 6 per cent., the Bank must jump from 4 to 8 per cent. The mathematician will at once understand this case, and he will also perceive that this necessary doubling of the increase of interest beyond legitimate wants must produce the contrary effect when interest is to be lowered, viz., that the decline must be at a double ratio, so as to affect in equal measure two objects, that of the decline in the bullion as well as in the fiduciary reserve. Hence the frequent rapid decline in the rate, so inexplicable to many people, and the long periods of excessively and unreasonably low rates. In the second part of my paper, when speaking of an improved plan, I shall revert to this matter, and show its closer relationship to international exchanges. So far you may have gained the idea that the 15 millions of fiduciary issue act as the "dog in the manger" in both directions.

In the above example I have assumed that a rise in the rate produces an effect of which half falls on bullion, half on fiduciary notes. That can take place only when our foreign relationship stands fairly neutral. As soon as the balance of trade is definitely against us, the effect on bullion becomes less, that on notes more; so that the rate must be more than doubly increased in order to procure bullion. This leads to all sorts of mischief and incomprehensible complications, particularly visible in the years of pressure. Compare, for instance, 25th November, 1857, with 27th June, 1866, when interest stood at 10 per cent. The difference in bullion was 7,400,000*l.*, in deposits 7,200,000*l.*, in reserve 2,400,000*l.*, in other securities 500,000*l.* in favour of 1866, with 5½ millions difference in Government securities against, the balance being 12 millions against lowering the rate in 1866 as compared to 1857, upon a total of other securities of 30 millions; and whilst in 1857 the bullion was 6¾ millions, and rose rapidly, until seven weeks later it had increased 100 per cent., it took, in 1866, twenty weeks until the rate could be lowered to a reasonable figure through an increase of only 30 per cent. on the bullion. I quite admit that, in the latter case, next to our strong international indebtedness, the want of confidence of the foreigner delayed the import of bullion; but this is only an additional element of confusion, caused originally by the speculation fostered through the false issue. Finally, as the results in a crisis show, when all the ordinary means of conforming to the Act prove ineffective—when failures take place on all sides—the whole system becomes like the bull in the china shop, dashing and breaking the crockery about, and threatening to push through the walls, until more room is made by suspending the Act.

The causes of the extreme rates may now be more clear to you, and you may agree with me that the rates must be in conflict with the market at home as well as the markets abroad. Hence the Bank cannot share properly in the life of commerce, and only at certain rare times can it, by way of its exceptional position, profit from such business in a way which is more or less usurious. The year 1872 will be such an example. Obliged to raise (in October and November) to 7 per cent. so as to protect bullion, the market being bare of money, although there were between 8 and 10 millions of reserves at the Bank, it accumulated at the same time "other securities" at a charge for interest of 7 to 7½ per cent. In view of the *seemingly* threatening state of German wants, the Bank may appear to have done right in holding up the rate, but that at the same time it should hold so large a note reserve might seem inexplicable. Through all these misfits and misconceptions, our money market has become so chafed and uncertain as to wear almost the ludicrous aspect of a strong, powerful man, afflicted with hysteria or hypochondria. A movement of a couple of hundred thousands in bullion either for abroad, or for Scotland or Ireland, frightens us—a decline in the reserve of a small percentage causes us to make long faces; and, as far as the Bank itself is concerned, we must suppose that the discount of a quarter of a million of bills, or thereabouts, is made the occasion for raising the rate. Is this right and proper?

The second purpose for which a Bank covets a reserve is that of its own safety. Sudden withdrawals of its deposits may take place, and a cash reserve must be maintained in order to meet such contingencies. In the case of the Bank of England there can be no question as to safety of position, the question of reserve here concerns momentary requirements only. The investments of the Bank of England, partly in other securities, are of such a nature that almost at any time they can be realised at once, in order to meet any decline in the deposits. So, at all events, it appears from the returns furnished. Besides this, the Bank has a large amount (equal nearly to its capital) in Government securities, and the power of moving these appears notably from the year 1857, when from 10 millions on the 4th November, they fell to 5 millions on the 25th November, at which occasion 2 millions of them passed temporarily into the issue department. Nevertheless, when there is a surplus of notes, I quite admit that the Bank can take supply from them without disturbing securities, but let it be distinctly understood that I am speaking here only of ordinary requirements in good times. When extraordinary requirements arise, as in times of crises, I have already stated that the extraordinary feature presents itself, not of a withdrawal of deposits, but of a large increase in them.

For such ordinary requirements, then, in times of peace, we may, notwithstanding the capital and securities at the Bank and their abundance, set aside an amount, which as you all will agree with me, ought to exhibit a certain degree of regularity, and within whatever that may be supposed to be, the fiduciary issue can be said to be available. Bear in mind here that the banking department also holds an amount of gold and silver coin ranging, say, from one-half to $1\frac{1}{4}$ million sterling. This feature I have left altogether out of my calculations. It would make a very large item in favour of all that I have laid before you, and strictly speaking I have the right to regard it as reserve, both from the point of idleness and safety, especially as, by the Act, the Bank can incorporate silver coin with the note issue within the limit of one-fifth of the whole of the bullion. But as it may be pleaded that this reserve of gold and silver coin in the Bank, in spite of its permanent character, is the result of the business across the counter, I have left it out. It is, however, an element when sudden withdrawal of deposits are problematically considered, and can assist in overcoming a sudden dangerous demand. Granted, then, that two or three, or four or more millions of extra notes should be kept idle to meet such a contingency (though presently I may show you how with a better system of issue there would be no need whatever, even for this), what must we think of a reserve which varies from 15 millions downwards to less than one million? Can it be said to be in any way connected with this question of safety for a withdrawal of deposits? It is, as you see, either extravagantly large, or, when both for momentary requirements and for dangerous withdrawals of bullion it is called upon, it proves totally inadequate, the depositors alone save the situation, at their own risk.

The charge that our other banks and bankers in London invest too closely, to within one-eighth or one-tenth of their deposits, whereas the Bank keeps larger reserves, may be true as regards general policy, but the Bank of England itself has no right to make such a charge, for were it not for the privilege of the fixed issue of 15 millions, that institution would have no reserve at all. Supposing any other bank in London had 5 millions of capital, with 15 millions of deposits, holding securities to the amount of 17½ millions, and consequently a cash reserve of 2½ millions, only. If to such a bank the privilege of issuing notes were granted, say, by the transfer of 5 millions in consols, book-debt of the State or "other" securities to an "issue department," that bank would virtually possess a reserve of 7½ millions, viz., 2½ millions cash, and 5 millions fiduciary notes to 15 millions of deposits. The Bank of England has 14½ millions of capital with 3½ millions rest, and (13th November, 1872), 27½ millions deposits, and 460,000*l.* in bills, together 46 millions to invest. Of this sum 13¼ millions are invested in Government securities in the banking department, 23¼ millions in "other" securities, and 15 millions in the securities of the issue department, in all 51¾ millions, against cash capital and deposits of 46 millions. But the privilege of converting the 15 millions invested in and deposited in the issue, gives the Bank the right to issue 15 millions of fiduciary notes to cover this apparent deficiency. Comparing this with the position of a bank with 5 millions, and a similar right of issue, the Bank of England ought to hold 4½ millions in cash, *plus* the 15 millions of notes. Therefore, when the Bank holds in reserve the whole of the 15 millions of notes, it has practically invested its cash resources to a shilling, without margin. What is the nature of such a reserve compared with an actual cash reserve?

Do not permit yourself here to be misled by the usual cry about separation between issue and banking department. The separate or "automatic" character of the issue department has reference only to bullion, and therein it is neutral, but as regards the 15 millions extra issue, its origin and present character, the case is in every respect identical with the supposed case of the Bank with 5 millions capital and the supposed issue thereon.

You are no doubt all familiar with the method of stating the accounts of the Bank as prescribed by Parliament, so as to separate the issue from the banking department. But, let us take, for example, the statement of 13th November, 1872, in the following manner:—

| *Liabilities.* | | *Assets.* | |
|---|---|---|---|
| *Issue Department—* | £ | *Issue Department—* | £ |
| Notes issued against bullion | 18,978,380 | Bullion | 18,978,380 |
| " securities | 15,000,000 | Government and other securities | 15,000,000 |
| *Banking Department—* | | *Banking Department—* | |
| Proprietors' capital | 14,553,000 | Government securities | 13,259,873 |
| Rest | 3,188,605 | Other " | 23,152,710 |
| Public deposits | 7,612,438 | Notes in reserve | 8,481,410 |
| Other " | 19,841,727 | Coin | 762,421 |
| Seven days' bills, &c. | 460,644 | | |
| | 79,634,794 | | 79,634,794 |

That the Bank, and nobody else, is responsible for the whole of these 79½ millions of liabilities, you will admit. That the Bank can discharge all these liabilities we all know, we all agree that it is the best and safest institution, because it has the largest capital and rest of all known banks. The 17½ millions of capital and rest must first be lost before the noteholders and depositors are in jeopardy, and such a contingency need not be thought of. *Nor is this the question before us*, the capital and rest of the Bank is a matter entirely apart from the principle upon which the note issue is conducted. The former, and the risks which it runs, concern the proprietors; the latter is dependant upon a form of contract between the State and the Bank through which the public is to be furnished with a species of currency. The former comes into play when the question of winding up the Bank arises, and for this purpose it can be called a security or reserve *invested*, the latter is a matter concerning a constant or suitable supply of currency, of free uninvested reserve, needful for the regulation of the current necessities and claims upon the Bank. We must be clear upon these points in order to understand the real nature of the controversy. Unfortunately, whenever the principles of the issue are under discussion, the defenders of the system come forward with the capital and rest of the Bank, and although they know well that the issue has its own system and securities, they endeavour to veil its anomalies by an appeal to the capital and rest. No wonder that with the confusion of ideas thus brought about, the public is disposed to lump it altogether, and to listen to the song of "lullaby" in sheer fatigue of the subject. Should the national economist fall into the same snare, and allow this proceeding? Does the large capital of the Bank justify a gigantic error in the issue from which all suffer?

The boast of the Bank's capital and rest frequently takes the form of separating the two items from the liabilities, and representing them as independent reserve. That this is contrary to the rules of accountancy will be conceded, but it is no doubt true that the capital and rest would bear the first brunt of losses, that the shareholders of the Bank would first suffer. But I maintain that the national economist has just as much right to make his voice heard on behalf of the stockholders of the Bank, as he has the right to draw attention to other public matters; and the Bank, as a public institution, is subject to the same control. Bank stock is an important feature in the social and economical arrangements of the country, and requires just the same conscientious guarding as the deposits and notes. Hence any attempt to exclude the capital and rest of the Bank from the liabilities proper must be repudiated and looked upon as tainted with the suspicion of demoralisation, unworthy of the institution.

I think, therefore, that I am justified in maintaining, that, for all the current business of the Bank (and that does not mean the winding up), and all the controversy as regards the issue arrangement, the capital and rest of the Bank stand in the same category as the other liabilities, and being invested, the mere question of free reserve becomes one of *pro rata* on the whole aggregate of liabilities.

Now if you look at the form in which I have given the account, which states the issue department first, and more truthfully, inasmuch as it states the amounts of notes virtually issued against bullion and against securities, you can please your fancy in either adding the whole of the liabilities or assets together, or in keeping the departments separate, in either case you cannot alter the result. The total liabilities being 79½ millions, there are as assets 19 millions of bullion, 9¼ millions of note reserve and coin, together *seemingly a reserve* of 28¼ millions, and 52¼ millions of securities, leaving thus an *apparent* cash reserve of about 35 per cent. Is this view, generally given by the defenders of the Act, a correct one? It is utterly false, for the 19 millions of bullion must be struck out as an item which has entirely lost its character of a free reserve, it is distinctly and clearly pledged for the notes, and the Bank directors have no control whatever over it, the very plea of the "automatic" character of the issue department proceeds upon this ground. The only free "reserve," then, is the $9\frac{1}{4}$ millions of reserve of notes and coin.

If the issue is now separated from the account, the liabilities in the banking department would amount to $45\frac{1}{2}$ millions against a free reserve of $9\frac{1}{4}$—so that about one-fifth (in juxtaposition to other bankers' one-eighth or one-tenth) would seem to be available. The separation of the issue department, however, cannot do away with the fact that 15 millions of claims or assets of the Bank have been transferred to it, that the institution is responsible for their validity, and so I maintain that the actual amount of securities, or assets, or investments effected is $61\frac{1}{2}$ millions against $9\frac{1}{4}$ millions free assets; or between one-seventh and one-eighth, whereas in the case of a supposed bank with 5 millions of capital and 15 millions of deposits —investing $17\frac{1}{2}$ millions in securities and having $2\frac{1}{2}$ millions uninvested, the free reserve would be one-eighth. Can the Bank, under these circumstances, say that it is so immensely more prudent than other "banking houses" as regards free reserve?

Recollect here that I take the $9\frac{1}{4}$ millions of reserve (of which $8\frac{1}{2}$ are notes) as wholly consisting of real cash, passing over the anomaly that in the issue the whole 15 millions of notes against securities are liability—whilst in the banking they act as assets, and that is the reason why I am justified in including the 15 millions of securities as investment. But if the issue department be left out of the account, if the 15 millions be deducted again, leaving the liabilities in the banking department at $45\frac{1}{2}$ millions, the free reserve amounting to $9\frac{1}{4}$ or about one-sixth, then the question must arise again, what is the real nature of this free reserve? The other banker holds his one-eighth free reserve in actual cash, free of any contingency whatsoever, but the one-sixth reserve of the Bank of England arises from a transaction in the issue department, which is a mixture of bullion and securities, in which the notes out in circulation can diminish the bullion, and render the Bank's reserve of less value, until the contingency draws near under which the larger proportion of "Government securities" in the mixture must first be converted into bullion. The best that can be said under the circumstances is that the 15 millions of notes issued on securities, and the 19 millions against bullion, together 34 millions, must share in the 19 millions of bullion—each receiving a percentage—in this case 56 per cent. The actual cash value of the Bank's free reserve of $9\frac{1}{4}$ millions ($8\frac{1}{2}$ notes) then becomes reduced to about $5\frac{1}{2}$ millions —or about one-tenth of real reserve.

I am aware that an outcry will be raised against this method of stating the case, the controversy will turn again upon the point whether fiduciary issue is equal to bullion issue; and I must leave you to decide whether the arithmetical difference of $\frac{1}{24}$th between the absolutely free cash reserve of other bankers of one-eighth, and the fiduciary reserve of the Bank of England of one-sixth, gives to the latter institution a superior claim as to the holding of available reserves. If in addition to this you bear in mind the fact that the other bankers keep their cash reserves at the Bank of England, and that this one-eighth is included in the one-sixth of the latter, which they have the right to withdraw at any time, you can put the climax upon the matter without me.

Now, if this is the state of things when 8 or 9 millions are in "reserve," what is the true position when that reserve is reduced to 2 or 1 million, or when the cry of misery is raised for the suspension of the Act. What rescued the Bank from its dilemma? who else but the depositors and bankers, long before the effects of the rate of interest upon bullion and reserve could manifest themselves. Let me ask you again to separate this question from that of the capital and rest of the Bank; the question here is not that of the last extremity of winding up the institution, but that of the requirements of the moment—and *that of avoiding* this *winding up*, brought near by the deception in the employment of the fixed fiduciary issue, at all hazards, and at a tremendous sacrifice to the welfare of the country.

In my opinion, the Bank when holding even as much as 10 or 12 millions of notes in reserve, when, according to the opinion of some authorities, it is "strong," is in reality in a far more precarious position than the other bankers with their habitually small, but free cash reserves. The situation is extremely artificial and delicate on all points, and were it not for the Bank's strong capital and the general faith of the public in its stability, the system would have broken down long before this.

In Table C, pp. 469—472, I have exhibited the proportions of idle deposits as large. This might lead to the supposition that in spite of what I have said here the Bank keeps large free reserves. Recollect, however, that on p. 476 I distinctly state that this table is made on the supposition that the 15 millions of fiduciary issue have precedence over deposits, that they are gone and invested, leaving the deposits to come after. I accepted the fallacy only in order to show to what unnatural results it must inevitably lead; but to Table D I added another column headed "Percentage of Idle "Fiduciary Issue," throwing the onus of the idleness upon that issue.

Let me here endeavour to bring the common sense of Englishmen back to the truth by another method of illustration. The defenders of the present form of issue allege that the 15 millions are as good as gold, and that as far as the banking department is concerned, no liability whatever is attached to the value of the reserve. If such were the case, *i.e.*, if the Bank could freely use the 15 millions, why does it not cease the more or less precarious discount business and invest the 15 millions again in Government securities? The origin of the transaction is the investment of 15 millions in Government and other securities, placed in the issue against the right of issuing 15 millions of notes. These being "money," the Bank might purchase another 15 millions of securities and profit also from the interest gained thereon, thus killing two birds with one stone. The first investment gives 3 per cent., from that, it is true, expenses of issue and share of profit to the State must now be deducted, but these items have nothing to do with the "security" offered by the investment; the expenses of the issue, if need be, might be much reduced, and the State might resign its share of profit (like the French Government). We should then witness the pleasant spectacle of seeing how 15 millions of money can be manipulated so as to be invested in 30 millions of securities, obtaining the interest on each 15 millions, and yet leaving one of the 15 millions *unpledged* and free in the hands of the investor. Now if this second 15 millions consists of Government and other securities, of the same character as the first, equally valuable, what objection would there be to allowing the investor again to place them in an issue department, and to issue a second batch of 15 millions? Why should not a third, fourth, and more batches, *ad infinitum*, be so created? You will admit the utter absurdity of such a proposal, yet it can be made, if it be maintained that the first 15 millions have an absolutely independent value of their own, founded on such securities; and you must rise to the level of this theory in order to be able to conceive the utter weakness of the allegation that fiduciary notes are as good as gold. If, however, under these reflections you should say, we cannot go so far as to maintain that such notes are quite as good and safe as gold; if you admit only the principle of inferiority, I have gained my case, for the degree of inferiority can be determined between us.

Determine it in this way: the Bank looks upon the 15 millions as an absolutely free and valuable asset, and tries to act with it accordingly; in reality it is an asset subject to the liability of bullion, and moreover to the bankers' balances. The Bank acts like a merchant who with, say 100,000*l.* of assets and 60,000*l.* to 120,000*l.* liabilities (varying according to the state of the bullion in store, the reserve in hand, and the bankers' balances and deposits generally), nevertheless considers himself worth 100,000*l.* These are "singular" views, no doubt, but it is just possible that they fairly represent the case.

No wonder, then, that such singular assets as these 15 millions of fiduciary issue should refuse to do their office, that our generally sound trade should decline to associate itself regularly with it, and leave large unemployed reserves of such "unnatural" money. No wonder that in so false a system the evidence of mutuality and compensatory action is so frequently absent and replaced by irregular profits and conflicting disturbances. No wonder that such a system should give rise to false charges, to doctrines of finance and policy which seem as if they had been dragged by the hair through the thick and thin of all anomalies until, after this process, they are, forsooth, set up as idols destructive of all common sense in the matter. Lead any of the defenders of the Act on to the subject of the large and false reserve of notes, and you will find that he will endeavour to explain it by allegations which I have here refuted, and he is unable to perceive that that which seems natural in his sphere, can possibly be submitted to more general tests. In the same manner he sees nothing but "right" in the course that has been pursued when the reserve becomes small, and is disinclined to entertain the thought that a system which has generated the doctrines to which he is wedded, might possibly be improved so as to give a more natural aspect to all the matters which are connected with the present seemingly complicated state of the question. He cannot realise the fact that the fiduciary issue of 15 millions is liable to heavy claims which have precedence over its usefulness as a banking reserve, that indeed (and this is the mildest form of expression which can be used as descriptive of its character), it is a *mere nominal* and *unavailable*, but *not a practical* and *really available* reserve—a helpless, crippled thing—for the sake of which so many great interests, imbued with vigorous life and having an absolutely free and independent value of their own, are sacrificed.

What is the cause of this failure of the rules of supply and demand, this danger to, and weakness of the Bank of England in the matter, this waste and neglect of the wealth of the country represented by the deposits (and therein lies the wrong to the depositors who practically bear the brunt of both the extremes of the situation), in short of the whole conflict? Here is the largest and most powerful institution in the world, in midst of the richest trading nation, it is managed by the most experienced members of our mercantile community, men who are disinterested and have at heart the public good alone, and that of the Bank. These men should not have a vacillating policy, for if they changed their course, the charge of having done wrong before or doing so now might be made against them. And the outside public, honouring wealth and experience, proud of its own great *quasi* National Bank, is loth to believe, in spite even of the conflict and discomfort which manifest themselves (or whatever term you may choose to apply to the existing feeling of doubt), that there can be anything wrong. Yet the whole grievous disorganisation of their splendid and powerful machinery is due to the uncouth, unscientific notion, that 15 millions of fixed fiduciary issue are as good as 15 millions of gold, and that they must be looked upon and treated as such. I trust I have succeeded in showing that the idea of "stability" which some persons of weak arithmetical education seem to perceive in the "fixed issue" is fallacious, and that this issue acts in no other way than the enticer of the Bank of England itself into danger. This is the sum and substance of the "stability."

I now come to the question of the supposed direct pecuniary profit to the Bank arising from the issue, and what I have to lay before you will go far to confirm that which I have said.

The arrangement which exists is as follows:—The Bank, in its issue department, holds invested 15 millions of securities, on which it receives an annual interest of say 3 per cent., or 450,000*l*. After deducting the expenses of the issue and the share of so-called profit which the State receives, there remains a certain balance to the profit of the issue department. Besides this, then, the Bank receives back its investment (to use this expression) in the shape of 15 millions of fiduciary notes, which it can use as money; and you probably imagine that by this process of investing money twice over—of killing two birds with one stone—the Bank must make a considerable profit. Yet I am prepared to show that the Bank loses a sum by it, which on the average is equal to 100,000*l*. per annum.

In order to make this clear to you, you must bear in mind the fact that the sum of notes issued on bullion brings no profit whatever to the Bank of England. As far as interest or profit on this portion of the issue is concerned, it is immaterial whether the amount in bullion be 5 or 25 millions, or any other sum; indeed it may be said that the Bank, for the convenience of the public, entirely bears the general charges which fall on the issue against bullion for the benefit of the public.

The whole merit of the case of profit and loss rests on the 15 millions of fiduciary notes the use of which as money is supposed to cover the expenses on the total issue, and to leave a profit besides. It is absolutely necessary that you should agree to this as a matter of account, and thus bear in mind the purpose of the 15 millions, not because I seem to you to be opposed to these 15 millions, but because this method of stating the case is the only true one

In a Parliamentary Paper (Bank of England, 7th February,

1861, No. 12, p. 13), the committee makes the following report in reference to the issue:—

" *Issue Department.*

" The expenses of the issue department of the Bank of England, " have been returned to us as follows:—

| | £ |
|---|---|
| Wages | 89,731 |
| Pensions | 8,063 |
| Rent | 25,600 |
| Repairs | 8,568 |
| Directors' allowance | 2,926 |
| Rates and taxes | 2,300 |
| Stationery | 1,811 |
| General charges | 6,790 |
| Bank note paper | 11,623 |
| Interest on cost of machinery | 1,500 |
| Composition paid to bankers | 20,493 |
| Totals | 179,405 |

" This statement shows a great increase of charge over the " amount of the account presented to the Bank Committee in 1832; " and the aggregate is largely in excess of the estimate submitted " to the Chancellor of the Exchequer in 1844. The augmentation is " chiefly explained by the composition paid to country bankers for " issue under the Act 7 and 8 Vict., cap. 32, and the increased " charges for rents, and for the renewal of bank notes.

" The profits of the issue department for the year have been " returned to us as follows:—

| | | £ |
|---|---|---|
| Interest on fixed securities | | 445,117 |
| Gain on foreign coin and bullion | | 10,811 |
| | | 455,928 |
| Deduct expenses as above | | 179,405 |
| Profit | | 276,523 |
| Of this sum the public receives from the Bank— | | |
| 1st. Composition in lieu of stamps | £60,000 | |
| 2nd. For share of profits of the circulation department | 128,078 | |
| | | 188,078 |
| Net profit | | 88,445 |

It is unnecessary here to discuss the correctness of the items of expenditure given; nobody need doubt that they are all perfectly justified and legitimate, appertaining to the issue. The only exception, on principle, might be the last item, " compensation paid to " bankers" who have given up their issue; but as this item forms part of the actual contract, it must be retained.

I must further state that this return refers to a year when the issue stood at 14,475,000*l.* No returns of expenses were published when the issue stood at 14,000,000*l.*, or when, in 1861, it was raised to 14,650,000*l.*, and finally, in 1866, to 15 millions. I am obliged, therefore, to determine the expenses of these other years according to the amount of issue; and, when it is borne in mind that during recent years bankers' compensation has increased, and rent or other charges have risen, the proceeding would seem fair, and serve as a set off against any miscalculation of previous years. I accordingly return the expenses:—

| | £ |
|---|---|
| From 1845 to 1855 | 173,511 |
| „ '55 „ '61 | 179,405 |
| „ '61 „ '66 | 181,574 |
| „ '66 | 185,912 |

Besides the actual expenditure on the issue, the Bank pays to the State a sum in composition of stamp duty, and so-called profits on the issue, which in the first period,

| | £ |
|---|---|
| From 1845 amounted to | 180,000 |
| „ '55 „ | 188,078 |
| „ '61 „ | 192,480 |
| „ '66 „ | 195,078 |

So that the total expenditure may be given,

| | £ |
|---|---|
| Since 1845 | 353,511 |
| „ '55 | 367,483 |
| „ '61 | 374,054 |
| „ '66 | 381,000 |

On the other hand the investment of the "fixed securities," which at the above return were 14,475,000*l.*, yielded 445,117*l.*; calculated at the same *pro rata* manner—

| £ | | £ |
|---|---|---|
| 14,000,000 | would have brought | 430,510 |
| 14,475,000 | „ | 445,117 |
| 14,650,000 | „ | 450,495 |
| 15,000,000 | „ | 461,261 |

In the return submitted there also appears the item, "gain on "foreign coin and bullion, 10,811*l.*," as profit on the issue. I leave this item (which is sometimes larger) out here, for it has no immediate reference to the issue of the 15 millions of notes. It arises solely in connection with the portion issued on bullion, and the Bank can deal in that article without the fiduciary issue. In this view I am confirmed by one of the directors of the Bank of England who at the Bank Inquiry of 1857 (see Report 220, Sess. 2, p. 36, No. 360), said: "The profit upon bullion and coin is entirely irre-

" spective of the issue of notes, and, though it comes to the profit of " the same department, it is in reality not a profit contingent upon " the issue of notes."

I then arrive at the result that the investment of the 14 millions —until the present 15 millions, at the interest here set forth, less expenses—gives an annual balance in favour of the issue department of—

| | £ |
|---|---|
| From 1845 | 76,999 |
| " '55 | 77,634 |
| " '61 | 76,441 |
| " '66 | 80,261 |

That is to say, the Bank, having parted with 15 millions of money by way of investment in certain advances to the State and on other securities, receives, when the expenses are deducted, an annual profit of 80,261*l.*, equal to a rate of interest of $\frac{8}{15}$, or a little more than one-half per cent. per annum on the money laid out.

But you will say, the Bank receives this money (I am careful not to say this "capital," for the meaning can be twisted) back again by the authority to issue the 15 millions of notes. I agree with this, but, naturally, it depends upon the employment of the 15 millions whether the Bank shall make a profit or not. If the whole 15 millions were thus employed at, say, 4¼ per cent. (the average rate of interest), the Bank would make, including the 80,261*l.*, a total profit of 717,761*l.* per annum. A reference to the state of the reserves will show you that this is impossible; but, before I lay the results before you, let me again remind you that the question of what is uppermost—bullion issue or fiduciary issue—will again arise here. The Bank-Act-people will tell you that the surplus is not notes, but bullion; they may say even, "We never gave our " capital, or any capital, in bullion for the securities of the issue, we " paid in notes and hold our capital intact." I must leave it to your common sense whether you agree with them, but even if you should do so, I can maintain that if the surplus is bullion, and bullion instead of notes is consequently idle, it is the fault of the fixed issue of 15 millions fiduciary notes that it is so, and so the matter remains as broad as it is long. I have calculated the total interest which the Bank thus receives from the employment of that portion of the fiduciary issue which it has been able to use, or, if you like it better, of that portion of the total issue, which, after deducting bullion, is put into circulation. In doing so I have taken the Bank rates of discount as they stood from week to week, and although the Bank makes certain advances below that rate, in which the employed proportion has a share, I have—seeing that on rare occasions it makes a higher chargo for long bills—adhered to the current rate.

TABLE F.—*Total of Interest Earned by the Bank on the Notes in Circulation above the Amounts of Bullion held.*

| | £ | | £ |
|---|---|---|---|
| 1845 | 167,207 | 1860 | 285,300 |
| '46 | 204,769 | '61 | 426,930 |
| '47 | 485,567 | '62 | 138,584 |
| '48 | 188,003 | '63 | 310,108 |
| '49 | 121,351 | '64 | 576,180 |
| 1850 | 86,791 | 1865 | 347,814 |
| '51 | 166,005 | '66 | 690,177 |
| '52 | 38,460 | '67 | 88,984 |
| '53 | 222,956 | '68 | 92,986 |
| '54 | 379,351 | '69 | 186,611 |
| 1855 | 300,721 | 1870 | 111,566 |
| '56 | 549,672 | '71 | 59,053 |
| '57 | 675,227 | | |
| '58 | 103,864 | | 7,118,148 |
| '59 | 113,902 | | |

The total for the twenty-seven years gives an average of 263,635*l.*, and if you add thereto the so-called profit of the issue department at the respective rates (according to issue), an average of 77,641*l.*, you obtain 343,276*l.*, which, on the average amount of the issues, gives a return of interest of 2·346 per cent. per annum, or a little over 2⅓ per cent.

That is to say, *the investment of the* 14 *to* 15 *millions at* 3 *per cent.* (or a trifle more), after *allowing for expenses*, together *with the profit* which the Bank makes on the 14 *to* 15 *millions of notes*—the two birds killed with one stone—the *whole business* yields but 2⅓ per cent., equal to an annual loss of 100,000*l.* on the supposed first investment of the money at 3 per cent.

But the question has no great special reference to the investment of the 15 millions in the first instance. That investment is an accomplished fact, yielding, at 3 per cent., 450,000*l.* per annum, and standing as a mere security, the issue might go on, say under some other form of guarantee, without taking into account the rate of interest derived from the investment. Indeed, if that were made a question, I have the good right to say: the Bank might use this money in commerce, at a free rate of interest varying on the average at 4¼ per cent., without being encumbered by the rate of interest imposed by the issue and the expenses attached thereto. In that case the loss per annum might be stated at 287,500*l.*, a matter for the consideration of the proprietors.

The question may be narrowed simply to the expenses of the issue on the one hand, and the profits of its productive element on the other hand, and then according to the average expenditure of 263,635*l.* per annum, against the annual expenditure of 365,688*l.*, the loss is 102,000*l.*, showing about the same result. Putting together the annual expenditure as against the annual produce of interest, the following profit and loss account can be made out.

TABLE H.—*Showing the Annual Charge on the Issue, the Annual Interest, and consequent Profit and Loss per Annum.*

| Years. | Annual Total Charge. | Annual Interest Earned. | Profit. | Loss. |
|---|---|---|---|---|
| | £ | £ | £ | £ |
| 1845 | 353,511 | 167,207 | — | 186,304 |
| '46 | | 204,769 | — | 148,742 |
| '47 | | 485,567 | 132,056 | — |
| '48 | | 188,003 | — | 165,508 |
| '49 | | 121,351 | — | 232,160 |
| '50 | | 86,791 | — | 266,720 |
| '51 | | 166,005 | — | 187,506 |
| '52 | | 38,460 | — | 315,051 |
| '53 | | 222,965 | — | 130,546 |
| '54 | | 379,351 | 25,840 | — |
| 1855 | 367,483 | 300,721 | — | 66,762 |
| '56 | | 549,672 | 182,189 | — |
| '57 | | 675,227 | 307,744 | — |
| '58 | | 103,864 | — | 263,619 |
| '59 | | 113,902 | — | 253,581 |
| '60 | | 285,300 | — | 182,183 |
| 1861 | 374,054 | 426,930 | 52,876 | — |
| '62 | | 138,584 | — | 235,470 |
| '63 | | 310,108 | — | 63,946 |
| '64 | | 576,180 | 202,126 | — |
| '65 | | 347,814 | — | 26,240 |
| 1866 | 381,000 | 690,177 | 309,177 | — |
| '67 | | 88,984 | — | 292,016 |
| '68 | | 92,986 | — | 288,014 |
| '69 | | 186,611 | — | 194,389 |
| '70 | | 111,556 | — | 269,434 |
| '71 | | 59,053 | — | 321,947 |

*Note.*—The only profits are made in years of pressure and crisis.

If interest be calculated on the reserve of gold and silver coin held in the banking department, there would be a loss of 789,211*l.* for the twenty-seven years, or an additional loss of 29,000*l.* per annum, but for reasons already given, I have left this reserve quite out of my calculations.

As regards the expenses in the issue department, I have followed out the method employed in the parliamentary paper, which I should imagine ought also to be that in use at the Bank, for both the expenses of the issue and the Government share of profit belong to the "issue department," and the Act reads in accordance therewith. I mention this because efforts may be made to construe the account differently; the Bank-Act-people, although they fully adhere to the pleasing fiction of the total separation between the two departments, are quite ready to mix them up when it seems suitable for an argument. However they may twist the matter, I challenge them to produce a different result in the account.

A favourite way of puzzling the inquirer is this:—" Here is our

" weekly return, our issue department, in which our 15 millions are " invested (the greater part of our capital as you are pleased to say), " against securities; you think, therefore, it is gone in that, but " look at the banking department, there is our capital again, fully " stated and active in the account." Admitting this as a method of stating an account, what is the actual fact? The Bank has invested 15 millions (capital if you like) in the issue, from which it receives, after deducting charges, a return of one-half per cent. interest per annum only. This capital appears back again by the authority of issuing 15 millions of fiduciary notes, but, as the reserves show, these notes cannot somehow be properly used. In truth, in consideration of an income of 70,000*l.* to 80,000*l.*, or one-half per cent. per annum, in the issue department, the Bank has parted with resources of cash or capital against securities which should be realisable into gold, but are not allowed to be thus converted, taking in return the authority to issue 15 millions of fiduciary notes, upon the supposition that they are as good as gold. Here Hercules stands again at the cross roads, and must decide for himself which is best, gold or fiduciary notes. In my opinion this action on the part of the Bank bears a close resemblance to Esau and his mess of pottage.

The defenders of the Bank Act have another method of stating their case; they say, " The issue department is totally distinct from " the banking, and we have nothing to do with the 15 millions " of issue. Let the State take over the whole issue, bullion and " all, paying us for the securities, or leaving us to sell them, we " should then cease to have anything to do with it." This is true, and the Bank would not only obtain its reserve in cash, it would also be rid of the annual expenditure of 381,000*l.* and I am inclined to think that this would be a very good job for the Bank, for if you look at the present results of the issue at only 263,000*l.*, whilst all the time the reserve of notes shows so large an average of idle notes, you will see that the saving of the 100,000*l.* would enable the Bank to keep an extra reserve of about 2½ millions cash, without reckoning on the one-half to 1½ million of coin now habitually held in the banking department.

Take, for instance, the year 1852, when the interest of the fiduciary issue amounted to but 38,460*l.*—a loss against expenses of 327,000*l.*—interest during that year was at 2 per cent., so that the Bank might have kept an absolutely idle cash reserve in actual coin of over 16 millions sterling, besides the habitual 1 to 1½ million of gold and silver coin. The years 1850, 1867, 1868, and 1871 show similar results.

In pursuit of anomalies, permit me further to point out, that the average result of the interest on the notes in circulation above bullion is given as 263,000*l.* per annum. This average, however, would be much less were it not for the exceptionally high profits on the issue which the Bank makes during the times of panic, crises, and mercantile ruin; for at such times the institution makes its best harvests. The Bank may say: but we are also suffering heavy losses during these times. Would that the Bank were compelled to state the amount so lost—but the plea of these losses does not concern the legitimate traders, who are compelled to furnish the harvest. The years 1847, 1856, 1857, 1864, and notably 1866, are examples of this kind; but bear in mind that they are principally portions of these years, not the whole years which bring these high profits. A reference to the highest or lowest states of the reserves, and the rates of interest during those times of distress, will show what I mean. These extra profits arising from the mercantile community (so far on a fair basis of momentary supply and demand, I admit), ought to be deducted from the average.

Reflect further how this state of things clashes with the fair rules of mutuality which should guide all matters of money and all banking laws. What are the facts in this case? The issue costs the Bank 381,000*l.* per annum. Now, when the fiduciary issue circulates to the amount of, say, 13 millions (leaving but 2 millions in reserve), this charge is equal to about $2\frac{9}{10}$ per cent. per annum. At such times the actual interest rules high, say at 8 per cent., and the bank is brought face to face with the desire to make larger profits. Notably, however, the longest periods are those of quiet; and when the reserve amounts to, say, 14 millions, leaving 1 million over bullion in circulation, the costs on this 1 million are equal to $38\frac{1}{10}$ per cent. per annum, and the Bank cannot get more than 2 or $2\frac{1}{2}$ per cent. in return. No wonder that with these contradictory positions the directors of the Bank must proceed with a degree of prudence and circumspection which brings them into frequent conflict with the real interests of the community.

The defenders of the Act, ready to turn anything into use, may even say this is the very thing we want, but I question whether they could bring forward a string of logical arguments without introducing some hocus pocus as a supposed final blow, with which they would ruthlessly destroy even their own scanty admissions of the force of true reasoning.

I think I have shown to you that in the question of account or profit and loss the Bank is a loser by the Act. But, it may be said, the Bank, by means of its connection with the Government and the right of issue, enjoys other indirect advantages which compensate it for any such drawback. Let us analyse what they are. The Bank of England has the management of the National Debt. For this service it receives a specified sum amounting to about 200,000*l.* per annum (see "Hankey on the Bank of England," p. 57), just like any paid agent, and the State gets rid of a duty which it could not itself perform at the same price. Necessarily, inasmuch as the Bank is the great banker of the State, of other banks and bankers and important persons, more or less connected with governmental money business, there is a great mechanical advantage in this arrangement for all parties concerned. But the whole is a business which stands entirely on its own merits, and for the profit which it brings to the Bank, *ie.*, the *pro rata* salary paid, it has been hinted even that the remuneration is not sufficient. Then it may be said, the Bank keeps the Government account, and this is a set-off. Now, of all the accounts which the Bank keeps, the public accounts are the most irregular. A glance at the general returns will show this. No banker can look upon such an account as being worth more than the interest on the minimum balance. The surplus over the minimum, being simply collected by the State, and already assigned to specific purposes, cannot be actively employed, and for that matter it might as well be held at the Treasury as at the Bank. No wonder that the governor of the Bank stated during last session, when the question of the Bank's paying interest on this account was mooted, that the Bank did not care for the account at all. This account, however, by its violent fluctuations, in spite of its uselessness for commerce, affects the reserve considerably. The Government, besides the mechanical facilities of the account, of course enjoys the advantage of keeping its money with the largest and safest institution, and could not dare to change its bankers.

It has been alleged that the *lost notes* form a considerable item in favour of the Bank. Nothing has been published showing what kind of profit this is, and the Bank is no doubt bound to pay any note which may turn up. The Bank can tell from the half-notes handed in how many of them are lost, and it is well known that it facilitates the recovery of the other halves, and pays the first under certain guarantees. For the notes absolutely lost it must, nevertheless, retain provision until the State settles the question of whether, after a while, the Bank is freed from paying them. In any case, the supposed profit from lost notes would not be a legitimate source of profit to the institution.

It has also been suggested that the Bank of England derives great advantages from old and forgotten deposits, that just as claims for dividends on consols are forgotten, so there might be deposits for which no claimant appears. Certain continental papers occasionally allude to large sums supposed to have been lodged with the Bank of England many years back, and although such allegations are of the "cock-and-bull" class of stories, yet they have given colour to surmises. It is certainly not the business of the managers of the Bank to publish such claims, on the contrary, they must remain quite passive in the matter. Nor (supposing such deposits did exist) have those dealing with the Bank any concern in it, with the exception of the State on behalf of the public at large; for the question arises, whether such forgotten deposits should remain with the Bank or whether they should accrue, after proper steps having been taken, to the Treasury. The view can be maintained that such deposits have been made at the Bank of England because of its character as a *quasi* State bank, and a parliamentary inquiry into the subject seems advisable, if it were only for the purpose of setting at rest all the cock-and-bull stories here and elsewhere. The bank note issue itself has no connection whatever with this matter.

The great position of the Bank, its high credit, its large deposits without interest, and its general influence and monetary power, are due simply to its enormous capital and rest, and to the prudent and superior management of the institution under all circumstances. The fiduciary issue confers no advantage which can be kept secret, which would not at once be made apparent, and stand the test of all criticism in its details and the full light of the sun. The disadvantages, however, which the issue brings, I have endeavoured to point out to you in each single instance or object, and the final question remains, does it answer on the whole "somehow," *i.e.*, if it does not suit one object at one time, does it not suit on the average. This "somehow" reminds me much of the gentleman, who being with his daughter on board an American steamer where all the machinery stood on deck, was asked to explain its principles. Pointing to the steersman he said "You see that man working the "wheel round; well then, there is this crinkum crankum pushing "that iron thing in and out, pumping away at it, and there are the "firemen with long iron pokers pushing in and out, and so you see "they all perspire and push, and so, between them, they shove the "boat along somehow!" If any principle of compensation or counteraction existed between the various objects which the Bank Act is supposed to carry out, it would clearly assert itself in the averages, but the present extremes show clearly that these objects, singly and jointly, are more or less defeated by the system.

But what the fixed fiduciary issue does is this: it disturbs our valuation, it cheats us into the belief that we have plenty of money, for I have met with bankers who looked upon a strong note reserve as indicating strength of the Bank and the situation. I myself look upon this supposed strength as the sign of weakness and consequent danger. The large reserve, although it is chiefly due to the blood-letting and want of animation that has taken place during a crisis, may appear satisfactory for a short time following the upset, but when after a few months it still remains, and continues for years, it becomes the great agent which fosters speculation.

Interest falls very low, and the necessity to use the money arises. Speculation begins from below; for a time bankers and others resist, but when the better class of speculators make money, and securities are shown of more or less legitimate value, one banker or capitalist follows the other in advancing upon them. The prudent bankers (let me admit, however, that many of our bankers know well to keep clear of all speculative things) and the Bank of England resist to the last, but I have it upon hearsay that this institution itself had some interest in the very things which assisted in laying the foundation of the crisis of 1866. The crisis, the strangling process, the loss to legitimate commerce all over the country, the increased pauperism, then follow the deception. If the Bank directors were able to control the reserve, they would, instead of lowering the rate of interest, keep it at a reasonably higher figure long before the crisis is due. But they cannot do this, for however far the directors may be able to see, they cannot overcome the fact that the reserve exists, that the ordinary rules must be applied; the fallacy of the issue acts as a fog, hence the haste and terror when the pursuer suddenly looms through it.

There are many people who would altogether refuse to the Bank of England the title to rule the discount market; and, indeed, as far as the small share which the Bank takes in discount or the actual working business of the country is concerned, this opinion seems justified. And if it is borne in mind that the notes, gold, and silver currency in the country out of the Bank amounts to from 110 to 130 millions, it would seem singular that the demand for a few millions, say even 10 millions, should go so far as to affect, through the rise in discount, the money value of the raw material in Lancashire, Yorkshire and elsewhere, where legitimate non-speculative industry flourishes, the mainspring of the country's wealth. I quite admit that the lead which the Bank takes in altering the rate of discount suits other bankers, for it appears that they can compete successfully in lowering, and can profit only by the raising, of the rate; and, on the other hand, there must be some central institution which has the power of initiating such movements. The question whether they have been initiated fairly does not depend on principle, but on the good judgment of the directors of the Bank, and although we may admit that, at tremendous sacrifices to the commerce of the country, they have succeeded in triumphing over a bad and confused system, yet the good judgment in this respect stands on no other footing than that which might deal with an unrestricted issue—and can be supplemented by a more self-acting process.

As regards the expenditure on the issue, it might here be suggested that the Bank of England conducts it in rather an extravagant manner by the continual destruction of notes, and that otherwise the items might be diminished. The destruction and reprinting of the notes is not a very important item in the expense, as you observe by the statement. The chief expenditure is in salaries, rent, and compensation to bankers whose issue the Bank has taken. Now, where the system of registering the numbers of the notes prevails, a larger staff of employés is required; and the system, with the renewal of the note, is so useful to the public, and serves as so efficient a protection to the Bank, that I am by no means inclined to recommend its abolition. I may mention that the Bank of France now follows the same plan, registering even the 20-franc notes, keeping back the dirty ones, and only reissuing clean notes. And although the Bank of Prussia has hitherto not registered the small and dirty paper money, yet, as soon as the small notes are abolished and larger amounts issued, it will probably follow a plan similar to that of our Bank.

The only item which, properly speaking, does not belong to the general system of issues, is compensation to bankers. But, supposing this were to disappear, and that altogether a considerable reduction in the expenditure of the issue were made, you will agree with me that, although the Bank would not lose as much as it does now, such economy would have no influence whatever on the numerous anomalies consequent on the fixed limit. There is, however, one item in the expenditure of the issue which, in the form that it is levied, merits severe condemnation. The State (by a compromise well known) receives from the issue 195,000*l.* per annum (originally 180,000*l.*), viz., 60,000*l.* in lieu of stamps, and 135,000*l.* so-called profits. This sum is paid regularly, whether the actual or real profit of the Bank is 300,000*l.*, or whether the loss is 300,000*l.* Is this right and fair? I quite recognise the principle that the State should receive a share in the profits of the issue, and shall speak of this later on; but when such a share bears the character of a partnership in profits, it appears to me that it ought to rise and fall in accordance with the actual results. For if in the first a fixed sum be taken as a compromise, the inference lies near that it is liable to error, to the prejudice of either State or Bank. But, it will be said, what does this matter, and of what consequence are 195,000*l.* in a system where so many hundred millions of transactions take place? The country or the Bank can easily pay it! Arguments like this were used in the free-trade controversy; but the freetrader knows that even the smallest regular tax can have the effect of preventing trade—that the smallest grain of sand can disorganise a whole machinery. A trifling tax can stop the importation of one of our commodities into a foreign country; yet, when it is there, the retail trader can put a profit on it twenty times larger than the duty. It is the question of a tax on the first movement, on the embryo of business, which is expected to develop itself, and which, when developed and grown strong, can bear bleeding; whereas the same amount of blood-letting on the embryo itself would prove the ruin of its future. So I look upon the origin of our bank note issue, whose few millions are expected to develop a thousand millions of transactions, as an embryo in principle, and any rough and unscientific treatment or detraction from its growing power has a thousand-fold effect hereafter; and where, as in the case of the Bank of England, a yearly settlement or dividend is contemplated and striven for, this rough tax forms an element which must, though perhaps unconsciously, affect the action of the sytem. The system being that upon which our commerce depends, it is clear that any damage to it injures commerce a hundredfold, and weakens the tax-bearing power of the nation. A more refined plan, then, say, that of the State taking its share in accordance with actual profits made by means of the whole issue system, might improve the banking power of commerce, and might probably give a larger average of profit to the State.

In my discourse so far I have taken the great liberty to criticise the banking department of the Bank of England, that which certain people consider "private," for, beyond the weekly accounts and the returns which Parliament now and then enforces, the Bank of England publishes nothing regular or irregular concerning its business, and shuns criticism, as it has the right to do. Other State banks, like the Bank of Prussia, or *quasi* State banks, like the Bank of France (whose connection with the State is even less than that of the Bank of England, because it has less legal privileges), fully and freely publish their affairs, giving a complete view of all their transactions in each department of action. Our Bank should be compelled to do so likewise; we cannot presume that it is under the necessity of hiding something; the country ought to be rather proud of what is done by it, independently of the instruction and knowledge which this proceeding would distribute. The plea that the Bank of England banking department is as much a *quasi* private matter as that of other banks, cannot be maintained when it is borne in mind that the issue contract between it and the Government, as representatives of the public, gives the latter the full right to look into all its affairs. Mr. Hankey's answer to the wish for publishing banker's balances that, "if it were so " ordered by Parliament, I believe it would lead to no good," &c., belongs to the dark ages, when Parliaments and courts of law were held secretly for similar reasons. Let us hope that some powerful reformer will come forward on behalf of all these matters.

I have shown you that the theory of the fixed fiduciary issue is wrong, but I have shown also that when it is taken as it stands, and that when propositions are made in accordance with, and in supposed explanation of its working according to the wishes of its defenders, that almost every one of such propositions in actual practice meets with flat denial or contradiction, and that the whole exhibits a picture of misconceptions and conflicts in which there are but few accords, and these few accords bear more the character of forcible driving, than that of correspondence or unity of interests.

The errors to which such a system leads in theory and practice manifest themselves on all sides. Just now (December, 1872), when the pressure of October and November has passed away, when bullion has again accumulated, we hear it said, "See how "the Act has triumphed over the difficulty!" Is there anything in the Act itself that provides for the raising of the rate of interest? Certainly not. The action of the rate of interest is a matter standing alone, apart from the Bank Act. Indeed, if you believe in the correctness of the views which I expressed on p. 485, as regards the competition of the 15 millions of fiduciary notes with bullion, you may with me come to the conclusion that it is not the Act which has triumphed, but "that the rule under which "interest attracts bullion has triumphed over the Act." Can business be properly conducted when perversions like the above are accepted as truths?

Without unison and logical connection, no system can work smoothly, and one essential error in construction can throw the whole organisation out of gear. If the existing anomalies could be removed, the power of the Bank, its usefulness to the great commerce of this country would be largely increased, to the benefit of the State, the bankers and merchants, and the community at large, and the shareholders of the Bank itself. The Bank directors have to act according to law, they may be advisers, they cannot be movers in this matter, indeed, they have the right to remain conservative or impassive. But those members of the Government, to whom the initiative in these matters belongs, might be requested to show whether, in their conceptions and actions in reference thereto, they are mere menders of kettles and sharpeners of scissors, or great financial engineers.

It remains for me now to remark that I have purposely abstained from discussing the clauses of the Act of 1844, which relate to the country banker's issue. You may have inferred that I am totally opposed to them, but the question of their abolition can be considered apart from the Bank of England, whose issue might be continued or reformed without reference to such country issues. The only plea for their maintenance is the issue of 1*l.* notes; but, under certain conditions, the Bank of England might issue a limited number of such notes for the accommodation of the public. In any case, the present issues of country bankers are an injustice to the Bank of England.

*Suggestions for an Improved System of Issue.*

My criticism on the Bank of England issue would hardly appear justified, unless I were prepared to lay before you some plan for a better system. Bank notes must be used for certain purposes, the question is what are the clear principles upon which they can be so used? Let these principles be established, and surely there will be little difficulty in constructing a system in accordance with them.

What are the pleas upon which the issues of bank notes or paper money are usually made?

The first and foremost is that of the convenient instrument of exchange. Gold is heavy, paper is light; and if I can carry 10*l.*, or 100*l.*, or 1,000*l.* in a piece of paper instead of in weighty money, I prefer the former. You will observe that this plea is based simply on a natural mechanical law, which will bear no disputing.

The second plea is that bank notes, in their capacity as money, can make an addition to the mediums of exchange for the purpose of assisting commerce. Here the fiduciary element, entirely apart from the above mechanical law, comes into consideration.

The third plea is the necessity of the State. In times of war and distress, the State, compelled to lay out heavy sums, is obliged to create an enormous issue of bank notes, and to give them the force of legal tender. This plea again is distinct from either of the two named above.

In exact accordance with these pleas bank notes may be classified as follows: *Firstly*. The bullion note; the foundation of which is nothing but bullion, so that, say, on a store of 20 millions of bullion 20 millions of bank notes, and no more, are issued, for no other purpose than that of furnishing to the public a convenient medium of exchange, and the presumed object of saving wear and tear in metallic currency. None of the great nations make such an issue, although the relative position of bullion reserves to the notes in actual circulation had frequently, or nearly, brought it about, both in England and France.

*Secondly*. The good bank note; based upon a certain proportion of bullion, the rest of the issue being made on securities, one of the chief objects of such issues being that of poising the admixture of the two elements, so as to maintain, at all events, the convertibility of the note. Our Bank of England issue, the Prussian issue, the French issue before 1870, are examples of this kind; although the manner in which they are severally conducted differs materially as to methods of limitation.

*Thirdly*. The depreciated bank note issues; in which the excessive fiduciary issue has altogether overwhelmed the metallic basis, so that metal has been set aside and risen to a premium. The convertibility of such notes has of course been lost. The value of the metal varies in accordance with political prospects. Modern examples of this kind are the United States, Russia, Italy, Austria, &c., and France seems on the point, by excessive fiduciary issue, to enter the class.

To these three classes may be added the *fourth class*—the valueless bank note—of which Hayti, where 500 to 700 paper dollars are counted as one dollar silver; and the notes of the defunct Confederate States of America, are examples.

I give this last class merely in order to show the rapid descent into nothing. We can dismiss it, as far as England is concerned; and so we might dismiss the third class, the depreciated bank note, for England is at peace, rich and prosperous; and we may trust that it will never again, as it did at the end of last and beginning of present century, issue depreciated bank notes, which the conquest of independence, wealth, and political supremacy, enabled it to set aside. A reflection as to the actual effects upon the prosperity of a country labouring under a depreciated issue may, however, be useful. Why is it that such countries continually lose bullion, and become poorer? Why should the mere addition of paper currency to metallic currency, which in the first instance actually seems to improve prosperity, make such a country the debtor of other nations, and force it to part with gold, thereby increasing the evil of depreciation progressively? The reason for this will appear plain to you when you reflect what is done in such cases. Take a country which carries on its business, say with 100 million pounds of metallic currency. A war breaks out; the Government requires enormous supplies in material, &c., and pays for them, say in 100 millions of its own notes. The currency of the country becomes 200 millions, and it follows that the prices of all commodities must rise in order to correspond with this increase. The increase is not due to industry or some solid equivalent as a neutralising element; it is more or less sudden, without original countervalue. The classes of contractors, and the individuals and traders connected with them, suddenly become rich, and the apparent plethora of money creates throughout the country considerable extravagance. Not only do native commodities rise in price, yielding large profits, but *all foreign produce* benefits by the change; higher prices and higher profits are made. But the great distinction between native and foreign commodities and trade becomes this: the native producer receives his profit in paper currency, whereas the foreign producer, not able to use this currency at home, must take out his profit in gold, and gold leaves the country accordingly in an increasing ratio. At the same time the high prices of native produce prevent its exportation, and the importation of foreign goods is encouraged to the injury of home industry. Hence the extraordinary state of the exchanges, and the great struggles which a nation must make afterwards in order to restore the equilibrium. Where immigration, bringing hundreds of thousands of immigrants—where immense resources in land, mines, and the future generally, are in store, as in the United States—the process of recovery is easier. In other countries less favourably situated, the demoralisation, the struggle, the division of the people into richer and poorer, the labouring and suffering, cannot be overcome for long periods.

Now, if this is correct as regards overwhelming issue, it follows that any issue above the neutral bullion basis must have a similar effect, although in a lesser degree. The mere question of the depreciation or par value and convertibility of the note is dependent on the mere amounts of fiduciary issue; the effects on prices remain, and with the consequent separation between national and international trade, become a question of degree. And so, if we pretend that 15 millions of fixed fiduciary issue are a permanently useful addition to our currency, we are in error, for in reality they operate *permanently against* our bullion basis.

Our choice between the classes of bank notes now lies between the bullion note and the good bank note, or in a compromise between the two. Strictly following the pleas put forth, let us first deal with that of the usefulness of the note as a convenient instrument of exchange. It is often said that bank notes save the currency from wear and tear. This is true; but the expenses of bank note issues are larger than the cost of mintage and wear and tear of coin, as the foot-note annexed will show.*

Nevertheless, the plea that bank notes are such easy instruments of exchange is the most legitimate of all, and they must be maintained, if for this purpose alone, independently of the expense.

* Professor Jevons has calculated that on the average a sovereign in circulation becomes light in eighteen years, *i.e.*, that it loses the legal three-quarters grain and the right of tender. This calculation I have verified by researches as to the sums coined by the Mint since 1816, the light coin taken in at the Bank, the exports and imports, and the proportion of light coins remaining in circulation, and substantially agree with him, although I would extend the period to twenty years. But I will go further than he does. Instead of assuming that on the 123·274 grains 0·750 grain is lost, I will take a whole grain, and allow one-quarter grain for costs of recoinage, so that, within twenty years 1·232 grain, or, say, 1 per cent. are absorbed. This would show that the annual wear and tear on coin costs one-twentieth per cent.

The issue of our bank notes costs 180,000*l.* (exclusive of the 195,000*l.* paid to the State) on a circulation taken as high as 30 millions pounds. Let us reduce this by economies to 150,000*l.*, the annual cost of the issue would be equal to one-half per cent., or ten times as high as on coin.

It will be seen how large a margin is left for further reduction before a bank note issue can be said to be cheaper than the issue of coin on the mere ground of wear and tear of coin versus printing, paper, and administration of paper issue.

Bullion notes, *i.e.*, pure bullion notes, are, however, not issued, for they are not only not profitable to the issuer, but involve the large expenditure of printing and administration. No bank would undertake such a bullion issue unless it secured a profit which, at all events, would cover the cost. A small charge on each bank note used by the public is impracticable in a medium of exchange which must be legal tender. The State cannot be asked to bear the costs, for that would be unfair to certain classes of the community. What remains to be done ? Take, then, the case of an issue of, say, 20 millions of notes against 20 millions of bullion, at a cost of 100,000*l*. per annum. The 100,000*l*., at the rate of interest of, say, 4 per cent. would represent the produce of a capital of 2½ millions, so that if on 20 millions of bullion an issue of 22½ millions of notes were made, all being employed at 4 per cent., the cost of the issue would be recovered. On some such plan, which is not necessarily confined to 20 millions, to 100,000*l*. expense, and 4 per cent. interest, but which must be fitted to the case, can the fiduciary or productive element of bank note issue be used, and a contract for its carrying on be offered and accepted by a bank. Later on I shall modify the suggestion again, but so far you may be willing to admit, that some such arrangement can serve to satisfy the plea of convenience of the note to cover its costs, and that an issue so arranged is the best practical bullion note issue.

The plea of convenience being so disposed of, the question remains: Is a further fiduciary issue for the purpose of encouraging commerce at all advisable ? In the foregoing, I have sufficiently shown that a permanent addition of a fixed fiduciary issue is the great mistake which underlies the whole of our present system. But if that is so, it is all the more clear also that no issue at all, *i.e.*, the flat and absolute bullion basis would, in a certain sense, also be an error. For there are times when harvests fail, when mercantile disturbances take place; at other times great discoveries are made, new industrial channels are opened, requiring money, the contingencies of commerce are numerous, they cannot, as they are irregular, be always brought into accord with the currency whose increase is less spasmodic. For these times a temporary increase in the currency is quite justified, even necessary. But as there are also times when greater regularity in trade prevails, during which profits and currency accumulate, the latter over-reaching the commodities, so must such a temporary allowance of fiduciary issue be withdrawn again. That this is the true state of things, all the movements in commerce and the value of money prove abundantly. Now, if thus at one time 2 millions of fiduciary money can be used, at another 20 millions, would it be right to say: Oh! the average is 11 millions, and this must suffice. Nothing can be more false than such an average, for the very word belies and contradicts its own original basis.

The legislators of 1844 seem to have thought that there were only two ways open to them, viz., either to leave the issue at the discretion of the Bank directors under the old Act—in principle thus granting an unlimited right—or that of establishing a fixed limit. Although the old Act was condemned, yet the discretion which the Bank exercised appears to ~~me to~~ have been quite as efficient as that which they now exercise in forcing the rate of discount. I am far from recommending that we should fall back on the old Act, with its system of liabilities and means, for I fully recognise that discretion, however wisely exercised, is liable to errors, and prefer a machinery with a modicum of discretion only, with less than is now required under the Act of 1844.

Such machinery can be constructed on the two elements:—the *amount of bullion* and *the value of money* or the rate of interest, so as to afford any suitable scale of limitation. If you will kindly listen to me, I will try to lay before you maxims and practical illustrations which may guide you to a conception of the theory involved.

If, as we all know, commerce has its varying phases, which at one time bring about a strong demand for money, indicating a disproportion between the currency and the business to be done, it follows that there are also *neutral times* when both are in due proportion. This level of neutrality we have frequently arrived at in this country; as I have before explained, the large reserves of notes in the Bank show them—and I am entitled I think to leave country bankers' issue out of the question—as far at least as London is concerned. There must have been, consequently, also times when there was a *neutral rate of interest* in connection with the neutral bullion basis. Many people think that this neutral or normal rate of interest may be deduced from that on our national debt, because investments in that are made when money falls to a certain stage of inactivity, viz., 3 per cent. I decline to bind myself to this figure; indeed, in binding oneself in this manner, however plausible the assumption may seem, the first error is committed, and I may presently succeed in showing you that the neutral rate of interest will result from a self-acting process.

In order to start with the two elements, let us suppose there were 20 millions of bullion at the Bank and interest at $2\frac{1}{2}$ per cent. Suddenly (I use this term for convenience of illustration only) there was so strong a demand for money as to make the rate 5 per cent., could we legitimately say: the value of money has doubled, and the 20 millions available must do double duty? If we could say that, we need only issue 20 millions of fiduciary money more to make 40; but then interest should fall back again to $2\frac{1}{2}$ per cent., and so the original cause of the rise would disappear again. In fact, if we doubled the issue with the doubling of the interest, or increased it with the increase of the latter, we should adopt a species of geometrical progression which could not be maintained on its own ground.

But if there were 20 millions of bullion at 2½ per cent., and if interest rose to 5 per cent., would we be justified in issuing 10 millions (only half of the proportionate increase of interest), say, altogether 30 millions, and keep interest at 5 per cent.? I trust you do not look upon this method of opening my case as involving a mere fanciful little arithmetical problem with which I please myself; it rests upon certain principles in mathematics in connection with limits; and I may succeed in showing you that it works in accord with all the contingencies and practical matters that I am required to deal with.

Accept, then, for the present, my proposal "that the Bank shall " have the right to add to the issue made on bullion, an amount of " fiduciary issue equal in proportion to the bullion, to one-half of " the increase on the normal* rate of interest. On the reduction " of the rate of interest, the Bank shall reduce the fiduciary issue in " the same proportion, but the Bank shall not be bound to reduce " the rate of interest."

Test, now, this proposition by ordinary examples. Supposing there were, as before, 20 millions of bullion and the rate of interest rose from 2½ to 5 per cent.: when 10 millions more might be issued. If the rate rose to 10 per cent. the additional issue might be 30 millions more. But the rise in the rate of issue must not be taken upon the 20 millions of bullion, for the rise in the rate of interest is, in the first place, due to a withdrawal of bullion; say, then, that bullion has diminished from 20 to 15 millions, when interest stands at 5 per cent., the additional issue might then be made 7½ millions more, so as to give 22½ millions. And if bullion further diminished, say, to 10 millions, interest being at 10 per cent., the total issue might become 25 millions. If the bullion should fall as low as 7½ millions, a rise in the rate of interest to 12½ per cent. would be required to justify the addition thereto of 15 millions of fiduciary issue. Submit now this system to any further tests with any given amount of bullion, and you will observe that it is capable of affording limits which will regulate and satisfy the *demand and enforce the importation of bullion* at the same time. You will see, therefore, that as far as the cautious idea of limiting excess is concerned, that this system is far more effective; and that, in order to produce a state of disproportion between bullion and notes, such as existed in 1857, when bullion was but one-fourth of the issue, a far higher

* The term "normal" will be explained hereafter.

rate of discount would have prevailed, without absolutely excluding further supplies of money.

The present Act practically and presumably exercises the same effect upon bullion in an irregular and spasmodic fashion, as I have shown, whereas, by the method proposed, the process would become regular and self-acting, causing more gradual and less frequent movements both in the rate of interest and the export of bullion.

A rise in the rate of interest has a twofold effect. It induces money to stay at home, and attracts money from abroad, for the Englishman finds a better remuneration for it here than abroad; and the foreigner, when interest with him is cheaper, realises and sends money over here for investment. Now, it must not be for one moment supposed that these movements involve a direct sending over of cash or bullion; they take effect through the changes in the rates of exchange. The English merchant or banker disposes of his claims and bills on abroad, and asks his correspondent for short remittances in return; and the banker abroad, instead of sending bills to England for discount, prefers to hold them in portfolio, because they give him a higher rate of interest. Thus money is supplied to our market on the one hand; on the other hand the discount market is relieved, because bills are withheld from it; the exchanges turn in our favour because our bills are sought abroad, whilst we ourselves sell our foreign claims. A divergence from the par of exchange in our favour, or in favour of the foreigner, may thus exist for a length of time without reaching the bullion points, *i.e.*, the points at which the rate of exchange covers the expense of shipping or receiving bullion; and other exchanges, favourable or unfavourable to us, may, by arbitration, assist in maintaining the transitory state until either the par is recovered or until bullion must be forwarded. In February, 1870, I had the honour to lay before you (see *Journal of the Statistical Society*, pp. 63 to 69), the exact calculations how such bullion shipments between England and France are made, and what their margins are. Nothing can disturb the absolute right of bullion in these movements; and when, as is now the case in France, a premium is paid on gold, it has the effect merely of influencing the nominal rate of exchange, which is but the bullion rate of exchange with the premium added.

Our requirements or obligations as regards bullion can be followed up from the first departure from the pars until the shipment point. At first measures are required to maintain our existing stock of bullion; subsequently they must be strengthened so as to retain in the country the bullion, or more of the bullion, passing *in transitu* through our market, so as to add to our stock. In the third stage the rates of interest must be forced, so as to attract bullion from abroad, to cover a deficit in what we hold. And, when circumstances are reversed, and we have bullion enough, or can afford to let that *in transitu* pass, or when, finally, we have a surplus, the natural law of arbitration of exchanges will progressively effect a clearance.

All these operations, however, in their adjustment, involve the same principle of compromise that prevails in buying-and-selling prices, *i.e.*, the middle-price is the ultimate result; each sacrifices one-half of the whole margin; and upon that ground I base my proposal that, in increasing the rate of interest in a double ratio, we obtain the half of its effect, namely, the whole of what we require; whereas, in raising the rate merely in accordance with apparent demand, we should only obtain one-half of the supply.

"But," you will say here, "that is what the Bank does now, "according to your own showing on p. 485, as that which is the "cause of the violent movements in the rates of discount." The essential difference between the present fiduciary issue and my proposal will now appear. On p. 485, I state that the Bank is obliged to raise the rate of interest in double ratio, because, when thereby it attracts "money" in the general sense, it obtains half in bullion, half in fiduciary notes, which, with bullion, constitute our money, that the effect is divided between the two, both being attracted from out of the circulation. And that such is the case you will admit, because in most cases, when a raising of the rate attracts bullion, the note reserve generally also increases, and increases frequently without increase in bullion. According to my plan, however, there is no fixed fiduciary issue, and none at all at the normal rates, so that a rise in the rate of interest above them must concentrate its effect solely upon bullion. Take the case of interest of $2\frac{1}{2}$ per cent. or 3 per cent. as normal rates. A glance at the returns shows you that even at these low rates there are large amounts of fiduciary notes in circulation which come in with the bullion; whereas, according to my suggestions, there would be none in circulation, and consequently none to come in. So that if, under my plan, interest is $2\frac{1}{2}$ per cent., if by its rise to 5 per cent. we obtain the $1\frac{1}{4}$ proportion of bullion, the Bank, with its present system, must raise the rate to $7\frac{1}{2}$, so as to attract $2\frac{1}{2}$ of money, of which $1\frac{1}{4}$, the half, is bullion. The validity of the rule of doubling the increase, in accordance with the law of arbitrations of exchanges and the rules of supply and demand, thus remains undisturbed; but in the case of the present issue of the Bank of England, although I have spoken before of the necessity under which it labours to double the increase, I ought to have said then, but better say it now, that, in reality, the Bank must proceed at a quadruple ratio in order to attract bullion.

Again you may say: "but by your own plan you create a kind "of reserve." True, but the character of this reserve is quite different from that of the present one; it has no permanent existence, and does not lie like a dead weight upon the market. Its purpose and use can be distinctly appreciated as apart from the question of bullion. It is to meet local demands when local demands show themselves. But the purpose for which it serves principally is this: When the rate of discount rises, money is kept at home and brought in from abroad, and both flow into the Bank. When no fiduciary issue exists, all this money is gold, and upon the same principle enunciated before, one-half comes from the interior, say in sovereigns, one-half from abroad, say in bullion. Thus currency would be withdrawn from our inland intercourse for the sake of attracting bullion. *The reserve of notes to be created by my plan does nothing else than restore the equilibrium in the currency at home;* it has no immediate connection with foreign exchanges, and the effect of the rate of interest on foreign bullion remains the same. Do you appreciate the high importance of this action in connection with the whole system as I propose it?

It can be so appreciated without any direct reference to the principle involved in doubling the ratio of increase in the rate of discount, for it can be alleged that the country may not always require the whole replacement. Now, according to my plan, the Bank would *have the right* or power to make the issue, with the *increase* of interest, but it is not bound to do so; and although it would be obliged to reduce the issue with the reduction of the rate of interest, it is *not obliged* to *reduce* the rate of interest, and can maintain the power of the issue, and the issue itself, *within* the requirements. This marginal power of reserve (in which the discretionary part of the manager's action will find play) will serve to keep the rate of discount more steady, *i.e.*, it will leave a margin against immediate change; it will also produce, by a self-acting process, *the normal state and rate of interest.*

But, it may be said, at other times, the public may require more issue for home trade when the proportion of one-half is not enough. The signs by which this kind of demand is detected are simple enough. As soon as the state of exchanges indicates that we are either on a par with other nations, and that bullion is actually flowing in (the better observance of foreign exchanges is, therefore, necessary), we can relax at all events the forcible measures for its importation, and *must* do so in order to avoid surplus. The extra demand then becomes local, the whole allowance of the issue may then be made, and a further supply of means given by raising the rate, that is, by satisfying and at the same time checking the demand in the opposing proportions of one-half, vindicating a principle of insurance. The higher rate may also continue to attract bullion, but when the whole system has been in operation there will have arisen, before this, points of adjustment and compensation which will modify many necessities.

But what about speculation, that bugbear against which the Bank must guard, when its necessities go hand in hand with those for bullion? In that case, the whole force of a rise in discount must be brought to bear so as to effect both objects, that of checking speculation and that of attracting bullion. In this sense, I approve, for instance, of the action which the Bank has taken in October and November, 1872—when interest ruled at 6 and 7 per cent.—there being, evidently, not only strong local speculation which had absorbed the free money in the outer market—but when also an unfavourable state of exchanges existed. But, although I fully recognise that this fever of speculation is an element against which strong measures must be taken, I allege, at the same time, that it is fostered and nursed by the present habitual large reserve of notes, and if I start the proposition that if this nursing did not exist, would I be entitled to say that speculation would not be so strong? That, in order to deal fairly between the independent fault of the public and the fault of the Bank's fiduciary issue, speculation would only have half the force? If so, you will agree with me that speculation, if reduced to one-half, might, for the other half of its development, be checked on the way by more moderate rates, *i.e.*, rates not too low and not too high. And this might take place without involving so much foresight on the part of the directors as to the future effects of a present speculative tendency, for as we know, although all shake their heads at the future, yet the Bank directors keep the rate of interest low for long periods, as if no fear existed, until, as I said before, the gigantic spectre suddenly looms through the fog.

If you can believe that, through the abolition of the habitual reserve, interest will not fall so low as it has hitherto done, encouraging speculation, but that, so to speak, it will at all events halve it; that through the non-existence of this reserve we shall be able to obtain bullion in a more direct manner, without raising interest to so high a pitch; if you can believe that, through the better concurrence of mathematical truth and the more intelligent appreciation of the practical elements involved, we shall bring about a more regular state of things, you may deem it worth while to follow up the suggestions here made, of which, for want of time and space, I can only give the outlines.

It is not impossible, as we advance in the definition of the laws of supply and demand, that we may discover the paramount importance of the rules here laid down in all that relates to equilibrium between demand, supply, and price. In special cases its absoluteness may fail because other not visible influences, though in themselves depending upon the rule, intervene; but in large aggregates—and such an aggregate is represented by the millionfold movements of *ordinary* social and commercial intercourse, in which all factors have already, to some extent, exchanged compensation, until they come to the Bank of England—the rule will be found unfailing.

On this ground I uphold the rule of the one-half effect. You will agree with me generally, that proportions of three-fourths against one-fourth, or seven-eighths against one-eighth, whether they are made purposely and continuously, or by error of judgment spasmodically, cannot produce the equilibrium. The points of logic here arising I need not discuss, but I revert to such disproportions in order to bring out the capability of my system to meet special contingencies when wider questions arise, when, in contradistinction to the *ordinary* social and commercial intercourse (the term used in the last paragraph), *extraordinary* disturbances arise. Such extraordinary disturbances might be revolutions or long wars, requiring a considerable fiduciary issue. In such cases the rate of issue, instead of being at one-half of the increase in interest, might be raised to three-fourths or seven-eighths or more, and thereby assume, at all events, a clearly defined character far preferable to the more or less extravagant allowances, or the undefined loose issues, of which France, the United States, and other countries give us examples. The system is also capable of reduction by adopting measures below the one-half, say, to one-third or one-fourth, if we should ever reach such a state of stability.

The strongest confirmation that, in ordinary times of fair social and political life, the half-rate of which I speak is that which corresponds to the truth, can be gathered from the Bank returns themselves. For although, as I have stated, the majority of the instances show large and (but for the explanations I have given) *seemingly* inexplicable divergencies, there is, on the other hand, a not inconsiderable minority, where the rules applied upon normal rates of interest, are found in full operation. And this is especially the case when the reserve is all idle, and we stand, practically, on the bullion basis. I have here selected (see next page), as fair starting points, the two periods in 1852 and 1871, when the whole amount of the fiduciary issue was in reserve, *i.e.*, when we had the practical pure bullion basis. In 1852 interest was at 2 per cent., it rose to 4 per cent. on 3rd September, 1853, to 5 on the 22nd October, to 8 on 31st October, 1857, to 10 on 11th November; and, under the two columns "Fiduciary circulation" and "What it ought to be by "the half-rates," you will find how nearly they correspond, whilst, by the column "What it would be by the whole rates," the unsuitability of such a rate of increase is made manifest. Similar results appear from the reverse process of investigation between the year

1866-67 and 1871, when, in the latter year, interest stood at 2½ per cent.

[000's omitted.]

| Date. | *Circulation.* | Bullion. | Rate of Interest. | Fiduciary Circulation. | What it ought to be by the Half Rates. | What it would be by the Whole Rates. |
|---|---|---|---|---|---|---|
| 1852. | £ | £ | Per cnt. | £ | £ | £ |
| 21st June .... | 21,500, | 21,500, | 2 | Nil | Nil | Nil |
| 1853. | | | | | | |
| 3rd Sept..... | 22,400, | 16,100, | 4 | 6,300, | 8,000, | 16,000, |
| 22nd Oct. .... | 23,000, | 14,300, | 5 | 8,700, | 10,500, | 21,400, |
| 1857. | | | | | | |
| 31st Oct. .... | 20,300, | 8,100, | 8 | 12,200, | 12,150, | 24,300, |
| 11th Nov. .... | 20,100, | 6,600, | 10 | 13,500, | 13,200, | 26,400, |
| 1866. | | | | | | |
| 18th April.... | 22,100, | 13,000, | 6 | 9,100, | 9,100, | 18,200, |
| 30th May .... | 25,900, | 11,400, | 10 | 14,500, | 17,000, | 34,000, |
| 26th Sept..... | 23,000, | 15,600, | 5 | 7,400, | 7,800, | 15.600, |
| 1870. | | | | | | |
| 22nd June.... | 22,400, | 20,500, | 3 | 1,900, | 2,000, | 4,000, |
| 1871. | | | | | | |
| 31st May .... | 24,100, | 24,100, | 2½ | Nil | Nil | Nil |

I have selected these items almost at random, excepting that I started with the points of bullion basis alluded to, and, in the full general returns for the twenty-seven years you will find a large number of instances where similar results appear. I admit, however, that in the long periods when interest is exceptionally low, these instances are, if not mainly lost, at all events greatly diverging: these are the years of large idle reserves on one hand, and gradual enforced circulation and inflation, when the seeds of corruption are sown and manured, when the fiduciary issue is not required at all, and yet exists in all the glory of its misconception and misuse. There are also divergencies at times of pressure and crisis, when the fixed limit stops all further operation of the principles which I have elucidated. Note the accord between my rule and the state of things in November and December, 1857, when (less the 2 millions extra issue granted through the suspension of the Act) the fiduciary circulation stands at double that of the amount of bullion, interest at the Bank being 10 per cent., in the market 10 to 12½ per cent. My rule would have required 12½ per cent. in order to produce the same proportion, and if the Bank had had authority to increase the issue in this way at 12½ per cent., there would have been no need whatever for the suspension of the Act, whilst the effect on the import of bullion would have been enhanced. If, during the week of 18th March, 1857, when bullion stood at 6,100,000*l.*, and the fiduciary issue (including the 2 millions extra) at 15,300,000*l.*, the rate had been made $12\frac{1}{2}$ or 15 per cent., it would, by my rule, have produced that issue without violating the Act.

The following scale will serve as an easy means of testing the proportions between bullion and fiduciary circulation. If the normal rate of interest is taken at 2 per cent.—at which no fiduciary issue would seem necessary—the respective higher rates would authorise an issue in the following proportions on bullion:—

| | | | |
|---|---|---|---|
| 2 per cent. | Nil | $5\frac{1}{2}$ per cent. | $\frac{7}{8}$ |
| $2\frac{1}{2}$ ,, | $\frac{1}{8}$ | 6 ,, | $\frac{8}{8}$ |
| 3 ,, | $\frac{1}{4}$ | 7 ,, | $\frac{10}{8}$ |
| $3\frac{1}{2}$ ,, | $\frac{3}{8}$ | 8 ,, | $\frac{12}{8}$ |
| 4 ,, | $\frac{1}{2}$ | 9 ,, | $\frac{14}{8}$ |
| $4\frac{1}{2}$ ,, | $\frac{5}{8}$ | 10 ,, | $\frac{16}{8}$ |
| 5 ,, | $\frac{3}{4}$ | | |

But if $2\frac{1}{2}$ per cent. be taken as the normal rate, and it appears to me to be the more correct of the two, the allowable increase would be—

| | | | |
|---|---|---|---|
| 2 per cent. | Nil | $6\frac{1}{2}$ per cent. | $\frac{8}{10}$ |
| $2\frac{1}{2}$ ,, | ,, | 7 ,, | $\frac{9}{10}$ |
| 3 ,, | $\frac{1}{10}$ | $7\frac{1}{2}$ ,, | $\frac{10}{10}$ |
| $3\frac{1}{2}$ ,, | $\frac{2}{10}$ | 8 ,, | $\frac{11}{10}$ |
| 4 ,, | $\frac{3}{10}$ | 9 ,, | $\frac{13}{10}$ |
| $4\frac{1}{2}$ ,, | $\frac{4}{10}$ | 10 ,, | $\frac{15}{10}$ |
| 5 ,, | $\frac{5}{10}$ | 11 ,, | $\frac{17}{10}$ |
| $5\frac{1}{2}$ ,, | $\frac{6}{10}$ | 12 ,, | $\frac{19}{10}$ |
| 6 ,, | $\frac{7}{10}$ | $12\frac{1}{2}$ ,, | $\frac{20}{10}$ |

If the normal rate is taken at 3 per cent., the allowable increase over bullion would be—

| | | | |
|---|---|---|---|
| 2 per cent. | Nil | $5\frac{1}{2}$ per cent. | $\frac{5}{12}$ |
| $2\frac{1}{2}$ ,, | ,, | 6 ,, | $\frac{6}{12}$ |
| 3 ,, | ,, | $6\frac{1}{2}$ ,, | $\frac{7}{12}$ |
| $3\frac{1}{2}$ ,, | $\frac{1}{12}$ | 7 ,, | $\frac{8}{12}$ |
| 4 ,, | $\frac{2}{12}$ | 8 ,, | $\frac{10}{12}$ |
| $4\frac{1}{2}$ ,, | $\frac{3}{12}$ | 9 ,, | $\frac{12}{12}$ |
| 5 ,, | $\frac{4}{12}$ | 10 ,, | $\frac{14}{12}$ |

By either of these scales you may test the actual fiduciary circulation with bullion during the last twenty-seven years, in order to ascertain when the former was in excess, when it fell short of requirements, and when it agreed; in other words, when the rate of interest was too low or too high or normal. You will have to make certain allowances for half-yearly and quarterly dividend times, requirements for harvests and other regular matters during the course of the year.

In the table here following, I have noted down the respective changes in the rate of interest which have taken place during the twenty-seven years; and for the respective times or periods of each rate I have taken the average of bullion, together with the average of the amount of fiduciary issue out in circulation. This will be useful, in order to show again the great divergences at certain times in another form; but alongside of these columns I have placed others, viz., three principal columns, of which the first denotes the fiduciary issue which would have been allowable upon the bullion if the normal rate had been 2 per cent., with the excess actually issued and the excess which the rule would have allowed over the actual issue made. The second principal column (with its two side columns), gives the same thing at a supposed normal rate of 2½ per

TABLE I.—*Showing the Average Amount of Bullion during each Period of Change during the same Periods, together with the Issues which would have been allowed by Margins Over and Under the Allowances and the actual Fiduciary Circulation.*

[000's omitted.]

| To Date. | | Number of Weeks. | Average of Bullion. | Rate of Interest. | Average of Fiduciary Circulation actually made. | Normal Rate 2 per Cent. | | |
|---|---|---|---|---|---|---|---|---|
| | | | | | | What it ought to be. | Issued Over. | Issued Under. |
| | | | | Per cnt. | | | | |
| 1845 | 11th Oct. .... | 41 | 15,940, | 2½ | 5,576, | 1,880, | 3,696, | — |
| | 1st Nov. .... | 3 | 13,487, | 3 | 8,621, | 3,382, | 5,539, | — |
| | 27th Dec. .... | 8 | 12,756, | 3½ | 7,689, | 4,784, | 3,950, | — |
| 1846 | 22nd Aug. .... | 34 | 13,735, | 3½ | 6,451, | 5,151, | 1,300, | — |
| | 18th Dec. .... | 18 | 14,861, | 3 | 5,500, | 3,715, | 1,785, | — |
| 1347 | 9th Jan. .... | 2 | 13,905, | 3 | 6,529, | 3,476, | 3,053, | — |
| | 16th Jan. .... | 1 | 13,225, | 3½ | 7,454, | 4,959, | 2,495, | — |
| | 3rd April.... | 11 | 11,169, | 4 | 8,475, | 5,589, | 2,886, | — |
| | 31st July .... | 17 | 9,151, | 5 | 9,871, | 6,863, | 3,008, | — |
| | 11th Sept.... | 5 | 8,572, | 5½ | 9,811, | 7,500, | 3,311, | — |
| | 9th Oct. .... | 5 | 8,157, | 5 | 10,083, | 6,118, | 3,965, | — |
| | 23rd Oct. .... | 2 | 7,927, | 5½ | 11,911, | 6,936, | 4,957, | — |
| | 20th Nov. .... | 4 | 8,702, | 8 | 11,442, | 13,053, | — | 1,611, |
| | 27th Nov. .... | 1 | 9,956, | 7 | 9,013, | 12,445, | — | 3,432, |
| | 18th Dec. .... | 3 | 10,815, | 6 | 7,472, | 10,815, | — | 3,343, |
| | 25th Dec. .... | 1 | 11,609, | 5 | 6,213, | 8,707, | — | 2,494, |
| 1848 | 22nd Jan. .... | 4 | 12,068, | 5 | 6,554, | 9,051, | — | 2,497, |
| | 10th June .... | 20 | 13,386, | 4 | 4,839, | 6,693, | — | 1,854, |
| | 28th Oct. .... | 20 | 13,074, | 3½ | 4,061, | 4,903, | — | 842, |
| | 30th Dec. .... | 9 | 13,321, | 3 | 3,889, | 3,330, | 559, | — |
| 1849 | 17th Nov. .... | 46 | 14,102, | 3 | 4,355, | 3,525, | 870, | — |
| | 29th Dec. .... | 6 | 15,990, | 2½ | 1,999, | 1,999, | — | — |
| 1850 | 21st Dec. .... | 51 | 15,900, | 2½ | 3,440, | 1,987, | 1,453, | — |
| | 28th Lec. .... | 1 | 14,351, | 3 | 4,222, | 3,588, | 634, | — |
| 1851.... | 27th Dec. .... | 52 | 13,939, | 3 | 5,533, | 3,485, | 2,048, | — |

cent., and the third at 3 per cent. It is noticeable that the great over issues occur principally in the first years of the issue; in the latter years they are less, as if the Bank had unconsciously increased its base of interest (to use this term) from 2 to 3 per cent. Upon the whole, the rate of 2 per cent. would authorise an habitual excess of 2,124,000*l.* over the actual issue made; that of 3 per cent., exhibits an excess of 2,214,000*l.* of actual issue over allowance, so that the rate of 2½ per cent. would seem the mean rate. The rate of 2½ per cent. shows a continual allowance of 389,000*l.* over actual issue, but this seems in accord with what I propose, for so much allowance, or even more, could always be kept up in order to meet ordinary contingencies without raising the rate.

*of Rate of Discount, with the Average of Fiduciary Circulation (above Bullion) the system proposed at Normal Rates of 2, 2½, and 3 per Cent., and the respective*

[000's omitted.]

| Normal Rate 2½ per Cent. | | | Normal Rate 3 per Cent. | | | Number of Weeks. | To Date. | |
|---|---|---|---|---|---|---|---|---|
| What it ought to be. | Issued Over. | Issued Under. | What it ought to be. | Issued Over. | Issued Under. | | | |
| £ | £ | £ | £ | £ | £ | | | |
| Nil | 5,576, | — | Nil | 5,576, | — | 41 | 11th Oct. | 1845 |
| 1,348, | 7,273, | — | ,, | 8,626, | — | 3 | 1st Nov. | |
| 2,551, | 5,183, | — | 1,063, | 6,026, | — | 8 | 27th Dec. | |
| 2,757, | 3,694, | — | 1,144, | 5,337, | — | 34 | 22nd Aug. | 1846 |
| 1,486, | 4,014, | — | Nil | 5,500, | — | 18 | 18th Dec. | |
| 1,390, | 5,139, | — | Nil | 6,529, | — | 2 | 9th Jan. | 1847 |
| 2,645, | 4,709, | — | 1,102, | 6,352, | — | 1 | 16th Jan. | |
| 3,351, | 5,124, | — | 1,861, | 6,614, | — | 11 | 3rd April | |
| 4,575, | 5,296, | — | 3,050, | 6,821, | — | 17 | 31st July | |
| 5,143, | 4,668, | — | 3,571, | 6,240, | — | 5 | 11th Sept. | |
| 4,078, | 6,005, | — | 2,719, | 7,364, | — | 5 | 9th Oct. | |
| 4,756, | 7,155, | — | 3,302, | 8,609, | — | 2 | 23rd Oct. | |
| 9,572, | 1,870, | — | 1,251, | 10,191, | — | 4 | 20th Nov. | |
| 8,904, | 109, | — | 6,637, | 2,376, | — | 1 | 27th Nov. | |
| 7,570, | 89, | — | 5,407, | 2,065, | — | 3 | 18th Dec. | |
| 5,805, | 408, | — | 3,869, | 2,344, | — | 1 | 25th Dec. | |
| 6,034, | 520, | — | 4,022, | 2,532, | — | 4 | 22nd Jan. | 1848 |
| 4,016, | 823, | — | 2,231, | 2,608, | — | 20 | 10th June | |
| 2,615, | 1,446, | — | 1,006, | 3,055, | — | 20 | 28th Oct. | |
| 1,945, | 1,944, | — | Nil | 3,889, | — | 9 | 30th Dec. | |
| 1,410, | 2,945, | — | Nil | 4,355, | — | 46 | 17th Nov. | 1849 |
| Nil | 1,999, | — | ,, | 1,999, | — | 6 | 29th Dec. | |
| Nil | 3,440, | — | Nil | 3,440, | — | 51 | 21st Dec. | 1850 |
| 1,435, | 2,787, | — | ,, | 4,222, | — | 1 | 28th Dec. | |
| 1,394, | 4,139, | — | Nil | 5,533, | — | 52 | 27th Dec. .... | 1851 |

TABLE I.—*Showing the Average Amount of Bullion during each Period of*

[000's omitted.]

| To Date. | | Number of Weeks. | Average of Bullion. | Rate of Interest. | Average of Fiduciary Circulation actually made. | Normal Rate 2 per Cent. What it ought to be. | Issued Over. | Issued Under. |
|---|---|---|---|---|---|---|---|---|
| | | | £ | Per cnt. | £ | £ | £ | £ |
| 1852 | 3rd April.... | 14 | 18,286, | 2½ | 2,159, | 2,286, | — | 127, |
| | 24th Dec. .... | 38 | 20,875, | 2 | 1,636, | Nil | 1,636, | — |
| 1853 | 1st Jan. .... | 1 | 20,014, | 2 | 3,039, | Nil | 3,039, | — |
| | 15th Jan. .... | 2 | 18,918, | 2½ | 4,595, | 2,364, | 2,231, | — |
| | 28th May .... | 19 | 18,128, | 3 | 4,510, | 4,532, | — | 22, |
| | 27th Aug. .... | 13 | 17,515, | 3½ | 5,706, | 6,568, | — | 862, |
| | 10th Sept. .... | 2 | 16,015, | 4 | 6,317, | 8,007, | — | 1,090, |
| | 24th Sept. .... | 2 | 15,233, | 4½ | 6,946, | 9,520, | — | 2,574, |
| | 31st Dec. .... | 14 | 14,841, | 5 | 7,151, | 11,131, | — | 3,981, |
| 1854 | 6th May .... | 18 | 14,315, | 5 | 7,551, | 10,736, | — | 3,185, |
| | 29th July ... | 12 | 12,557, | 5½ | 7,853, | 10,987, | — | 3,436, |
| | 30th Dec. .... | 22 | 12,883, | 5 | 7,042, | 9,662, | — | 2,620, |
| 1855 | 31st Mar. .... | 13 | 12,652, | 5 | 6,800, | 9,489, | — | 2,689, |
| | 28th April.... | 4 | 14,477, | 4½ | 5,732, | 9,048, | — | 3,316, |
| | 9th June .... | 6 | 16,105, | 4 | 3,648, | 8,052, | — | 4,404, |
| | 1st Sept..... | 12 | 16,115, | 3½ | 4,224, | 6,043, | — | 1,819, |
| | 8th Sept. .... | 1 | 13,668, | 4 | 6,474, | 6,334, | 140, | — |
| | 22nd Sept..... | 2 | 12,902, | 4½ | 6,658, | 8,064, | — | 1,406, |
| | 29th Sept..... | 1 | 12,368, | 5 | 7,804, | 9,276, | — | 1,472, |
| | 29th Dec. .... | 13 | 10,707, | 5½ | 8,683, | 9,368, | — | 685, |
| 1856 | 17th May .... | 20 | 9,655, | 5½ | 9,580, | 8,448, | 1,132, | — |
| | 24th May .... | 1 | 9,939, | 6 | 9,393, | 9,939, | — | 546, |
| | 21st June .... | 4 | 9,003, | 5 | 8,166, | 6,752, | 1,414, | — |
| | 27th Sept..... | 14 | 11,737, | 4½ | 8,411, | 7,335, | 1,076, | — |
| | 4th Oct. .... | 1 | 10,226, | 5 | 10,699, | 7,669, | 3,030, | — |
| | 8th Nov. .... | 5 | 9,120, | 6½ | 11,428, | 10,260, | 1,168, | — |
| | 29th Nov. .... | 3 | 9,380, | 7 | 10,271, | 11,725, | — | 1,554, |
| | 13th Dec. .... | 2 | 9,951, | 6½ | 8,988, | 11,195, | — | 2,207, |
| | 27th Dec. .... | 2 | 9,763, | 6 | 8,815, | 9,763, | — | 948, |
| 1857 | 28th Mar. .... | 13 | 9,525, | 6 | 9,423, | 9,525, | — | 102, |
| | 13th June .... | 11 | 9,088, | 6½ | 10,268, | 10,224, | 44, | — |
| | 11th July .... | 4 | 10,736, | 6 | 8,608, | 10,736, | — | 2,128, |
| | 3rd Oct. .... | 12 | 10,685, | 5½ | 8,733, | 9,362, | — | 629, |
| | 10th Oct. .... | 1 | 9,540, | 6 | 10,451, | 9,540, | 911, | — |
| | 17th Oct. .... | 1 | 8,925, | 7 | 11,258, | 11,156, | 102, | — |
| | 4th Nov. .... | 3 | 8,273, | 8 | 11,842, | 12,409, | — | 757, |
| | 11th Nov. .... | 1 | 6,666, | 9 | 13,517, | 11,665, | 1,952, | — |
| | 23rd Dec. .... | 6 | 7,744, | 10 | 10,738, | 15,488, | — | 4,750, |
| | 30th Dec. .... | 1 | 10,906, | 8 | 8,410, | 16,359, | — | 7,949, |
| 1858 | 6th Jan. .... | 1 | 12,113, | 6 | 7,386, | 12,113, | — | 4,727, |
| | 20th Jan. .... | 2 | 13,492, | 5 | 6,605, | 10,119, | — | 3,514, |
| | 3rd Feb. .... | 2 | 14,789, | 4 | 5,080, | 7,394, | — | 2,314, |
| | 10th Feb. .... | 1 | 15,746, | 3½ | 3,858, | 5,905, | — | 2,047, |
| | 1st Dec. .... | 42 | 17,478, | 3 | 2,860, | 4,369, | — | 1,509, |
| | 29th Dec. .... | 4 | 18,409, | 2½ | 1,519, | 2,301, | — | 782, |

*Change of Rate of Discount, with the Average of Fiduciary Circulation—Contd.*

[000's omitted.]

| Normal Rate 2½ per Cent. | | | Normal Rate 3 per Cent. | | | Number of Weeks. | To Date. | |
|---|---|---|---|---|---|---|---|---|
| What it ought to be. | Issued Over. | Issued Under. | What it ought to be. | Issued Over. | Issued Under. | | | |
| £ | £ | £ | £ | £ | £ | | | |
| Nil | 2,159, | — | Nil | 2,159, | — | 14 | 3rd April | 1852 |
| „ | 1,636, | — | „ | 1,636, | — | 38 | 24th Dec. | |
| Nil | 3,039, | — | Nil | 3,039, | — | 1 | 1st Jan. | 1853 |
| „ | 4,595, | — | „ | 4,595, | — | 2 | 15th Jan. | |
| 1,813, | 2,697, | — | „ | 4,510, | — | 19 | 28th May | |
| 3,503, | 2,203, | — | 1,459, | 4,247, | — | 13 | 27th Aug. | |
| 4,803, | 1,514, | — | 2,669, | 3,648, | — | 2 | 10th Sept. | |
| 6,093, | 853, | — | 3,808, | 3,138, | — | 2 | 24th Sept. | |
| 7,901, | — | 270, | 4,947, | 2,204, | — | 14 | 31st Dec. | |
| 7,163, | 388, | — | 4,771, | 2,780, | — | 18 | 6th May | 1854 |
| 7,536, | 317, | — | 5,232, | 2,621, | — | 12 | 29th July | |
| 6,442, | 600, | — | 4,294, | 2,748, | — | 22 | 30th Dec. | |
| 6,326, | 474, | — | 4,217, | 2,583, | — | 13 | 31st Mar. | 1855 |
| 5,792, | — | 60, | 3,619, | 2,113, | — | 4 | 28th April | |
| 4,830, | — | 1,182, | 2,684, | 964, | — | 6 | 9th June | |
| 3,223, | — | 1,001, | 1,342, | 2,882, | — | 12 | 1st Sept. | |
| 4,100, | 2,574, | — | 2,278, | 4,196, | — | 1 | 8th Sept. | |
| 5,160, | 1,489, | — | 3,225, | 3,433, | — | 2 | 22nd Sept. | |
| 6,184, | 1,620, | — | 4,122, | 3,682, | — | 1 | 29th Sept. | |
| 6,450, | 2,233, | — | 4,461, | 4,222, | — | 13 | 29th Dec. | |
| 5,793, | 3,787, | — | 4,022, | 5,568, | — | 20 | 17th May | 1856 |
| 6,958, | 2,435, | — | 49,69, | 4,424, | — | 1 | 24th May | |
| 4,500, | 3,666, | — | 3,001, | 5,165, | — | 4 | 21st June | |
| 4,695, | 3,716, | — | 2,934, | 5,477, | — | 14 | 27th Sept. | |
| 5,113, | 5,566, | — | 3,408, | 7,291, | — | 1 | 4th Oct. | |
| 7,296, | 4,132, | — | 4,560, | 6,868, | — | 5 | 8th Nov. | |
| 8,442, | 1,829, | — | 6,253, | 4,018, | — | 3 | 29th Nov. | |
| 7,960, | 1,082, | — | 5,804, | 3,184, | — | 2 | 13th Dec. | |
| 6,834, | 1,981, | — | 4,881, | 3,934, | — | 2 | 27th Dec. | |
| 6,667, | 2,756, | — | 4,762, | 4,661, | — | 13 | 28th Mar. | 1857 |
| 7,272, | 2,996, | — | 5,301, | 4,967, | — | 11 | 13th June | |
| 7,511, | 1,097, | — | 5,368, | 3,240, | — | 4 | 11th July | |
| 6,412, | 2,321, | — | 4,452, | 4,281, | — | 12 | 3rd Oct. | |
| 6,678, | 3,773, | — | 4,770, | 5,681, | — | 1 | 10th Oct. | |
| 8,032, | 3,226, | — | 5,950, | 5,308, | — | 1 | 17th Oct. | |
| 9,100, | 2,742, | — | 6,894, | 4,948, | — | 3 | 4th Nov. | |
| 8,665, | 4,852, | — | 6,666, | 6,851, | — | 1 | 11th Nov. | |
| 11,616, | — | 878, | 9,034, | 1,704, | — | 6 | 23rd Dec. | |
| 11,990, | — | 3,508, | 9,088, | — | 678, | 1 | 30th Dec. | |
| 8,479, | — | 1,093, | 6,056, | 1,330, | — | 1 | 6th Jan. | 1858 |
| 6,746, | — | 141, | 4,497, | 2,108, | — | 2 | 20th Jan. | |
| 4,437, | 543, | — | 2,464, | 2,616, | — | 2 | 3rd Feb. | |
| 3,149, | 709, | — | 1,312, | 2,546, | — | 1 | 10th Feb. | |
| 1,748, | 1,112, | — | Nil | 2,860, | — | 42 | 1st Dec. | |
| Nil | 1,519, | — | „ | 1,519, | — | 4 | 29th Dec. | |

TABLE I.—*Showing the Average Amount of Bullion during each Period of*

[000's omitted.]

| To Date. | | Number of Weeks. | Average of Bullion. | Rate of Interest. | Average of Fiduciary Circulation actually made. | Normal Rate 2 per Cent. | | |
|---|---|---|---|---|---|---|---|---|
| | | | | | | What it ought to be. | Issued Over. | Issued Under. |
| | | | £ | Per cnt. | £ | £ | £ | £ |
| 1859 | 20th April.... | 16 | 18,580, | 2½ | 2,381, | 2,322, | 59, | — |
| | 27th April.... | 1 | 16,571, | 3½ | 4,978, | 6,214, | — | 1,263, |
| | 25th May .... | 4 | 16,683, | 4½ | 5,121, | 10,427, | — | 5,036, |
| | 1st June.... | 1 | 17,276, | 3½ | 3,996, | 6,478, | — | 2,582, |
| | 6th July .... | 5 | 17,499, | 3 | 3,557, | 4,375, | — | 881, |
| | 28th Dec. .... | 5 | 16,470, | 2½ | 5,121, | 2,059, | 3,062, | — |
| 1860 | 18th Jan. .... | 3 | 15,503, | 2½ | 15,503, | 1,938, | 4,451, | — |
| | 25th Jan. .... | 1 | 14,868, | 3 | 14,868, | 3,717, | 3,032, | — |
| | 28th Mar. .... | 9 | 14,466, | 4 | 14,466, | 7,233, | — | 715, |
| | 11th April.... | 2 | 14,063, | 4½ | 14,063, | 8,789, | — | 196, |
| | 9th May .... | 4 | 14,143, | 5 | 14,143, | 10,607, | — | 2,860, |
| | 23rd May .... | 2 | 14,923, | 4½ | 14,923, | 9,327, | — | 2,837, |
| | 31st Oct. .... | 23 | 14,987, | 4 | 14,987, | 7,493, | — | 1,090, |
| | 7th Nov. .... | 1 | 13,160, | 4½ | 13,160, | 8,225, | — | 180, |
| | 21st Nov. .... | 2 | 12,536, | 5½ | 12,536, | 10,969, | — | 2,970, |
| | 26th Dec. .... | 5 | 11,801, | 5 | 11,801, | 8,851, | — | 1,637, |
| 1861 | 2nd Jan. .... | 1 | 11,936, | 6 | 8,575, | 11,936, | — | 3,361, |
| | 3rd Feb. .... | 6 | 11,153, | 7 | 9,090, | 13,941, | — | 4,851, |
| | 20th Mar. .... | 5 | 11,217, | 8 | 7,866, | 16,825, | — | 8,959, |
| | 3rd April.... | 2 | 12,042, | 7 | 7,569, | 15,052, | — | 7,483, |
| | 10th April.... | 1 | 12,374, | 6 | 7,785, | 12,374, | — | 4,589, |
| | 15th May .... | 5 | 12,060, | 5 | 8,112, | 9,045, | — | 933, |
| | 3rd July .... | 7 | 11,287, | 6 | 8,264, | 11,287, | — | 3,023, |
| | 31st July .... | 4 | 10,926, | 6 | 9,335, | 10,926, | — | 1,591, |
| | 14th Aug. .... | 2 | 11,612, | 5 | 8,613, | 8,709, | — | 96, |
| | 28th Aug. .... | 2 | 12,116, | 4½ | 7,767, | 7,572, | 195, | — |
| | 18th Sept..... | 3 | 12,742, | 4 | 7,220, | 6,371, | 849, | — |
| | 6th Nov. .... | 7 | 13,340, | 3½ | 7,460, | 5,002, | 2,458, | — |
| | 24th Dec. .... | 7 | 14,248, | 3 | 5,715, | 3,562, | 2,153, | — |
| 1862 | 8th Jan. .... | 2 | 15,175, | 3 | 5,084, | 3,794, | 1,290, | — |
| | 21st May .... | 19 | 15,598, | 2½ | 5,068, | 1,949, | 3,119, | — |
| | 9th July .... | 7 | 15,035, | 3 | 5,911, | 3,759, | 2,152, | — |
| | 23rd July .... | 2 | 17,006, | 2½ | 5,274, | 2,126, | 3,148, | — |
| | 29th Oct. .... | 14 | 16,380, | 2 | 5,131, | Nil | 5,131, | — |
| | 31st Dec. .... | 9 | 14,186, | 3 | 5,748, | 3,546, | 2,202, | — |
| 1863 | 14th Jan. .... | 2 | 13,512, | 3 | 6,745, | 3,378, | 3,367, | — |
| | 18th Feb. .... | 3 | 12,846, | 4 | 6,525, | 6,423, | 102, | — |
| | 28th Jan. .... | 2 | 13,212, | 5 | 7,290, | 9,909, | — | 2,619, |
| | 22nd April.... | 9 | 14,103, | 4 | 5,969, | 7,051, | -- | 1,082, |
| | 29th April.... | 1 | 14,491, | 5½ | 6,377, | 5,435, | 832, | — |
| | 13th May .... | 2 | 14,012, | 3 | 6,694, | 3,503. | 3,191, | — |
| | 20th May .... | 1 | 13,695, | 3½ | 6,986, | 5,135, | 1,854, | — |
| | 28th Oct. .... | 23 | 14,111, | 4 | 7,042, | 7,055, | — | 13, |
| | 4th Nov. .... | 1 | 13,195, | 5 | 8,846, | 9,896, | — | 1,050, |
| | 25th Nov. .... | 3 | 12,729, | 6 | 8,280, | 12,729, | — | 4,449, |
| | 2nd Dec. .... | 1 | 12,434, | 7 | 8,588, | 15,542, | — | 6,954, |
| | 23rd Dec. .... | 3 | 12,899, | 8 | 6,984, | 19,348, | — | 12,364, |
| | 30th Dec. .... | 1 | 13,682, | 7 | 6,444, | 17,102, | — | 10,658, |

*Change of Rate of Discount, with the Average of Fiduciary Circulation—Contd.*

[000's omitted.]

| Normal Rate 2½ per Cent. | | | Normal Rate 3 per Cent. | | | Number of Weeks. | To Date. | |
|---|---|---|---|---|---|---|---|---|
| What it ought to be. | Issued Over. | Issued Under. | What it ought to be. | Issued Over. | Issued Under. | | | |
| £ | £ | £ | £ | £ | £ | | | |
| Nil | 2,381, | — | Nil | 2,381, | — | 16 | 20th April | |
| 3,314, | 1,664, | — | 1,380, | 3,598, | — | 1 | 27th April | |
| 6,673, | — | 1,552, | 4,170, | 951, | — | 4 | 25th May | |
| 3,456, | 540, | — | 1,439, | 2,557, | — | 1 | 1st June | 1859 |
| 1,750, | 1,807, | — | Nil | 3,557, | — | 5 | 6th July | |
| Nil | 5,121, | — | ,, | 5,121, | — | 5 | 28th Dec. | |
| Nil | 6,399, | — | Nil | 15,503, | — | 3 | 18th Jan. | |
| 1,486, | 5,263, | — | ,, | 14,868, | — | 1 | 25th Jan. | |
| 4,339, | 2,079, | — | 2,411, | 12,055, | — | 9 | 28th Mar. | |
| 5,264, | 2,969, | — | 3,513, | 10,550, | — | 2 | 11th April | |
| 7,072, | 675, | — | 4,714, | 9,429, | — | 4 | 9th May | |
| 5,769, | 721, | — | 3,730, | 11,193, | — | 2 | 23rd May | 1860 |
| 4,497, | 1,906, | — | 2,497, | 12,490, | — | 23 | 31st Oct. | |
| 5,264, | 2,781, | — | 3,290, | 9,870, | — | 1 | 7th Nov. | |
| 7,426, | 573, | — | 5,223, | 7,313, | — | 2 | 21st Nov. | |
| 5,905, | 1,309, | — | 3,933, | 7,868, | — | 5 | 26th Dec. | |
| 7,355, | 1,220, | — | 5,968, | 2,607, | — | 1 | 2nd Jan. | |
| 10,038, | — | 948, | 7,435, | 1,665, | — | 6 | 3rd Feb. | |
| 12,339, | — | 4,473, | 9,347, | — | 1,481, | 5 | 20th Mar. | |
| 10,838, | — | 3,269, | 8,028, | — | 459, | 2 | 3rd April | |
| 8,562, | — | 777, | 6,187, | 1,589, | — | 1 | 10th April | |
| 6,030, | 2,082, | — | 4,020, | 4,092, | — | 5 | 15th May | |
| 7,899, | 365, | — | 5,643, | 2,621, | — | 7 | 3rd July | 1861 |
| 7,648, | 1,687, | — | 5,463, | 3,872, | — | 4 | 31st July | |
| 5,806, | 2,807, | — | 3,870, | 4,743, | — | 2 | 14th Aug. | |
| 4,846, | 2,921, | — | 3,029, | 5,738, | — | 2 | 28th Aug. | |
| 3,713, | 3,487, | — | 2,123, | 5,097, | — | 3 | 18th Sept. | |
| 2,668, | 4,792, | — | 1,112, | 6,348, | — | 7 | 6th Nov. | |
| 1,425, | 4,290, | — | Nil | 5,715, | — | 7 | 24th Dec. | |
| 1,518, | 3,566, | — | Nil | 5,084, | — | 2 | 8th Jan. | |
| Nil | 5,068, | — | ,, | 5,068, | — | 19 | 21st May | |
| 1,506, | 4,405, | — | ,, | 5,911, | — | 7 | 9th July | |
| Nil | 5,274, | — | ,, | 5,274, | — | 2 | 23rd July | 1862 |
| ,, | 5,131, | — | ,, | 5,131, | — | 14 | 29th Oct. | |
| 1,419, | 4,329, | — | ,, | 5,748. | — | 9 | 31st Dec. | |
| 1,351, | 5,394, | — | Nil | 6,745, | — | 2 | 14th Jan. | |
| 3,855, | 2,670, | — | 2,141, | 4,381, | — | 3 | 18th Feb. | |
| 6,106, | 1,084, | — | 4,404, | 2,886, | — | 2 | 28th Jan. | |
| 4,231, | 1,738, | — | 2,350, | 3,619, | — | 9 | 22nd April | |
| 2,898, | 3,479, | — | 6,037, | 340, | — | 1 | 29th April | |
| 1,401, | 5,293, | — | Nil | 6,694, | — | 2 | 13th May | |
| 2,739, | 4,250, | — | 1,141, | 5,848, | — | 1 | 20th May | 1863 |
| 4,233, | 2,809, | — | 2,351, | 4,691, | — | 23 | 28th Oct. | |
| 6,598, | 2,248, | — | 4,398, | 4,448, | — | 1 | 4th Nov. | |
| 8,910, | — | 630, | 6,364, | 1,916, | — | 3 | 25th Nov. | |
| 11,190, | — | 2,602, | 8,289, | 299, | — | 1 | 2nd Dec. | |
| 14,190, | — | 7,306, | 10,749, | — | 3,765, | 3 | 23rd Dec. | |
| 12,313, | — | 5,869, | 9,121, | — | 2,677, | 1 | 30th Dec. | |

TABLE I.—*Showing the Average Amount of Bullion during each Period of*

[000's omitted.]

| Year | To Date. | Number of Weeks. | Average of Bullion. | Rate of Interest. | Average of Fiduciary Circulation actually made. | Normal Rate 2 per Cent. What it ought to be. | Issued Over. | Issued Under. |
|---|---|---|---|---|---|---|---|---|
| | | | £ | Per cnt. | £ | £ | £ | £ |
| 1864 | 20th Jan. | 3 | 12,955, | 7 | 7,816, | 16,194, | — | 8,378, |
| | 10th Feb. | 3 | 12,577, | 8 | 7,758, | 18,886, | — | 11,108, |
| | 24th Feb. | 2 | 12,958, | 7 | 6,953, | 16,197, | — | 9,244, |
| | 13th April | 7 | 13,145, | 6 | 7,232, | 13,145, | — | 5,913, |
| | 27th April | 2 | 11,942, | 7 | 9,107, | 14,927, | — | 5,820, |
| | 4th May | 1 | 11,778, | 8 | 9,706, | 17,667, | — | 7,961, |
| | 11th May | 1 | 12,059, | 9 | 8,900, | 21,103, | — | 12,203, |
| | 25th May | 2 | 12,821, | 8 | 7,797, | 19,231, | — | 11,434, |
| | 15th June | 3 | 13,441, | 7 | 6,988, | 16,801, | — | 9,813, |
| | 3rd Aug. | 7 | 12,909, | 6 | 8,399, | 12,909, | — | 4,510, |
| | 7th Sept. | 5 | 14,081, | 8 | 8,806, | 21,121, | — | 12,315, |
| | 9th Nov. | 9 | 12,400, | 9 | 8,390, | 21,700, | — | 13,310, |
| | 23rd Nov. | 2 | 13,260, | 8 | 6,619, | 19,890, | — | 13,271, |
| | 14th Dec. | 3 | 13,217, | 7 | 6,331, | 16,524, | — | 10,193, |
| | 28th Dec. | 2 | 13,455, | 5½ | 5,839, | 11,773, | — | 5,934, |
| 1865 | 11th Jan. | 2 | 13,364, | 5½ | 7,135, | 11,693, | — | 4,558, |
| | 1st Mar. | 7 | 13,720, | 5 | 6,450, | 10,290, | — | 3,840, |
| | 29th Mar. | 4 | 14,257, | 4½ | 5,493, | 8,910, | — | 3,417, |
| | 3rd May | 5 | 14,083, | 4 | 7,075, | 7,041, | 37, | — |
| | 24th May | 3 | 14,134, | 4½ | 7,000, | 8,834, | — | 1,834, |
| | 31st May | 1 | 14,919, | 4 | 5,991, | 7,459, | — | 1,468, |
| | 14th June | 2 | 14,491, | 3½ | 5,955, | 5,434, | 521, | — |
| | 26th July | 6 | 14,702, | 3 | 7,090, | 3,675, | 3,315, | — |
| | 2nd Aug. | 1 | 13,604, | 3½ | 8,993, | 5,101, | 3,892, | — |
| | 27th Sept. | 8 | 13,327, | 4 | 8,334, | 6,663, | 1,671, | — |
| | 4th Oct. | 1 | 12,440, | 4½ | 10,288, | 7,775, | 2,503, | — |
| | 11th Oct. | 1 | 11,956, | 5 | 10,356, | 8,967, | 1,389, | — |
| | 18th Oct. | 1 | 12,005, | 6 | 10,331, | 12,005, | — | 1,692, |
| | 22nd Nov. | 5 | 12,805, | 7 | 8,570, | 16,006, | — | 7,436, |
| | 27th Dec. | 5 | 13,201, | 6 | 7,270, | 13,201, | — | 5,913, |
| 1866 | 3rd Jan. | 1 | 12,380, | 7 | 9,397, | 15,475, | — | 6,078, |
| | 31st Jan. | 4 | 12,216, | 8 | 9,005, | 18,324, | — | 9,319, |
| | 21st Feb. | 3 | 12,548, | 8 | 8,466, | 18,822, | — | 10,356, |
| | 14th Mar. | 3 | 13,231, | 7 | 7,444, | 16,539, | — | 9,095, |
| | 2nd May | 7 | 13,236, | 6 | 8,758, | 13,236, | — | 4,478, |
| | 9th May | 1 | 12,295, | 7 | 10,050, | 15,369, | — | 5,319, |
| | 15th Aug. | 14 | 13,025, | 10 | 12,457, | 26,050, | — | 13,593, |
| | 22nd Aug. | 1 | 13,691, | 8 | 10,491, | 20,536, | — | 10,045, |
| | 29th Aug. | 1 | 14,732, | 7 | 9,166, | 18,415, | — | 9,249, |
| | 5th Sept. | 1 | 15,098, | 6 | 9,123, | 15,098, | — | 5,975, |
| | 26th Sept. | 3 | 15,229, | 5 | 8,050, | 11,422, | — | 3,372, |
| | 7th Nov. | 6 | 15,605, | 4½ | 8,309, | 9,753, | — | 1,444, |
| | 19th Dec. | 6 | 17,399, | 4 | 5,537, | 8,699, | — | 3,162, |
| | 26th Dec. | 1 | 18,308, | 3½ | 3,625, | 6,865, | — | 3,240, |
| 1867 | 6th Feb. | 6 | 18,176, | 3½ | 4,932, | 6,816, | — | 1,884, |
| | 29th May | 16 | 18,370, | 3 | 4,473, | 4,592, | — | 119, |
| | 24th July | 8 | 20,970, | 2½ | 2,589, | 2,621, | — | 32, |
| | 24th Dec. | 22 | 21,925, | 2 | 2,106, | Nil | 2,106, | — |

*Change of Rate of Discount, with the Average of Fiduciary Circulation—Contd.*

[000's omitted.]

| Normal Rate 2½ per Cent. | | | Normal Rate 3 per Cent. | | | Number of Weeks. | To Date. | |
|---|---|---|---|---|---|---|---|---|
| What it cught to be. | Issued Over. | Issued Under. | What it ought to be. | Issued Over. | Issued Under. | | | |
| £ | £ | £ | £ | £ | £ | | | |
| 11,695, | — | 3,879, | 8,652, | — | 834, | 3 | 20th Jan. | |
| 13,835, | — | 6,077, | 10,481, | — | 2,723, | 3 | 10th Feb. | |
| 11,663, | — | 4,710, | 8,650, | — | 1,597, | 2 | 24th Feb. | |
| 9,201, | — | 1,969, | 6,572, | 660 | — | 7 | 13th April | |
| 10,747, | — | 1,640, | 7,961, | 2,146, | — | 2 | 27th April | |
| 12,955, | — | 3,249, | 9,815, | — | 109, | 1 | 4th May | |
| 15,670, | — | 6,770, | 12,059, | — | 3,159, | 1 | 11th May | |
| 13,264, | — | 5,467, | 10,760, | — | 2,968, | 2 | 25th May | 1864 |
| 12,097, | — | 5,109, | 8,960, | — | 1,972, | 3 | 15th June | |
| 9,036, | — | 637, | 6,454, | 1,945, | — | 7 | 3rd Aug. | |
| 15,489, | — | 6,683, | 11,734, | — | 2,674, | 5 | 7th Sept. | |
| 16,120, | — | 7,730, | 12,400, | — | 4,010, | 9 | 9th Nov. | |
| 14,586, | — | 7,767, | 11,050, | — | 4,431, | 2 | 23rd Nov. | |
| 11,895, | — | 5,564, | 8,811, | — | 2,480, | 3 | 14th Dec. | |
| 8,073, | — | 2,134, | 5,767, | 72, | — | 2 | 28th Dec. | |
| 8,618, | — | 1,483, | 5,707, | 1,428, | — | 2 | 11th Jan. | |
| 6,860, | — | 410, | 4,573, | 1,877, | — | 7 | 1st Mar. | |
| 5,703, | — | 210, | 3,564, | 1,929, | — | 4 | 29th Mar. | |
| 4,225, | 2,843, | — | 2,347, | 4,728, | — | 5 | 3rd May | |
| 5,654, | 1,346, | — | 3,526, | 3,474, | — | 3 | 24th May | |
| 4,476, | 1,515, | — | 2,485, | 3,406, | — | 1 | 31st May | |
| 2,898, | 3,057, | — | 1,276, | 4,679, | — | 2 | 14th June | |
| 1,470, | 5,520, | — | Nil | 7,090, | — | 6 | 26th July | 1865 |
| 2,721, | 6,272, | — | 1,134, | 7,859, | — | 1 | 2nd Aug. | |
| 3,998, | 4,336, | — | 2,221, | 6,113, | — | 8 | 27th Sept. | |
| 4,976, | 5,312, | — | 3,110, | 7,178, | — | 1 | 4th Oct. | |
| 5,978, | 4,378, | — | 3,985, | 6,371, | — | 1 | 11th Oct. | |
| 8,404, | 1,909, | — | 6,002, | 4,311, | — | 1 | 18th Oct. | |
| 11,524, | — | 2,954, | 8,570, | — | — | 5 | 22nd Nov. | |
| 9,240, | — | 1,970, | 6,600, | 670, | — | 5 | 27th Dec. | |
| 11,142, | — | 1,745, | 8,254, | 1,143, | — | 1 | 3rd Jan. | |
| 13,437, | — | 4,432, | 10,180, | — | 1,175, | 4 | 31st Jan. | |
| 13,792, | — | 5,326, | 10,455, | — | 1,989, | 3 | 21st Feb. | |
| 11,907, | — | 3,463, | 8,820, | — | 1,376, | 3 | 14th Mar. | |
| 9,265, | — | 507, | 6,618, | 2,140, | — | 7 | 2nd May | |
| 11,065, | — | 1,015, | 8,198, | 1,825, | — | 1 | 9th May | |
| 19,526, | — | 7,069, | 15,196, | — | 2,739, | 14 | 15th Aug. | |
| 15,060, | — | 4,569, | 11,341, | — | 750, | 1 | 22nd Aug. | 1866 |
| 13,258, | — | 4,092, | 9,821, | — | 655, | 1 | 29th Aug. | |
| 10,568, | — | 1,445, | 7,549, | 1,674, | — | 1 | 5th Sept. | |
| 7,615, | 435, | — | 5,076, | 2,974, | — | 3 | 26th Sept. | |
| 6,242, | 2,067, | — | 3,901, | 4,408, | — | 6 | 7th Nov. | |
| 4,220, | 1,317, | — | 2,900, | 2,637, | — | 6 | 19th Dec. | |
| 3,662, | — | 87, | 1,526, | 1,099, | — | 1 | 26th Dec. | |
| 3,635, | 1,297, | — | 1,515, | 3,417, | — | 6 | 6th Feb. | |
| 1,837, | 2,636, | — | Nil | 4,473, | — | 16 | 29th May | |
| Nil | 2,589, | — | ,, | 2,589, | — | 8 | 24th July | 1867 |
| ,, | 2,106, | — | ,, | 2,106, | — | 22 | 24th Dec. | |

TABLE I.—*Showing the Average Amount of Bullion during each Period of*

[000's omitted.]

| To date. | | Number of Weeks. | Average of Bullion. | Rate of Interest. | Average of Fiduciary Circulation actually made. | Normal Rate 2 per Cent. | | |
|---|---|---|---|---|---|---|---|---|
| | | | | | | What it ought to be. | Issued Over. | Issued Under. |
| | | | £ | Per cnt. | £ | £ | £ | £ |
| 1868 | 18th Nov. .... | 47 | 20,003, | 2 | 4,034, | Nil | 4,034, | — |
| | 2nd Dec. .... | 2 | 17,072, | 2½ | 6,304, | 2,135, | 4,169, | — |
| | 30th Dec. .... | 4 | 17,031, | 3 | 6,065, | 4,258, | 1,807, | — |
| 1869 | 31st Mar. .... | 13 | 17,217, | 3 | 6,228, | 4,304, | 1,924, | — |
| | 5th May .... | 5 | 15,874, | 4 | 7,906, | 7,937, | — | 31, |
| | 9th June .... | 5 | 16,280, | 4½ | 7,114, | 1,017, | 6,097, | — |
| | 23rd June .... | 2 | 19,227, | 4 | 4,401, | 9,613, | — | 5,212, |
| | 14th July .... | 3 | 18,706, | 3½ | 5,061, | 7,105, | — | 2,044, |
| | 18th Aug. .... | 5 | 19,505, | 3 | 4,326, | 4,876, | — | 550, |
| | 3rd Nov. .... | 11 | 18,831, | 2½ | 4,831, | 2,354, | 2,477, | — |
| | 29th Dec. .... | 8 | 17,812, | 3 | 5,131, | 4,453, | 678, | — |
| 1870 | 20th July .... | 29 | 19,256, | 3 | 3,845, | 4,814, | — | 969, |
| | 27th July .... | 1 | 18,395, | 4 | 5,782, | 9,197, | — | 3,415, |
| | 3rd Aug. .... | 1 | 17,958, | 5 | 6,473, | 13,468, | — | 6,995, |
| | 10th Aug. .... | 1 | 18,230, | 6 | 5,550, | 18,230, | — | 12,680, |
| | 17th Aug. .... | 1 | 18,812, | 5½ | 4,720, | 16,460, | — | 11,740, |
| | 24th Aug. .... | 1 | 19,107, | 4½ | 4,139, | 11,942, | — | 7,803, |
| | 31st Aug. .... | 1 | 19,748, | 4 | 3,609, | 9,874, | — | 6,265, |
| | 14th Sept. .... | 2 | 20,421, | 3½ | 2,850, | 7,783, | — | 5,933, |
| | 24th Sept. .... | 2 | 21,245, | 3 | 1,940, | 5,311, | — | 3,371, |
| | 28th Dec. .... | 13 | 21,508, | 2½ | 2,154, | 2,689, | — | 535, |
| 1871 | 1st Mar. .... | 9 | 21,315, | 2½ | 2,381, | 2,664, | — | 283, |
| | 12th April .... | 6 | 21,321, | 3 | 2,314, | 5,330, | — | 3,016, |
| | 14th June .... | 9 | 23,391, | 2½ | 1,038, | 2,924, | — | 1,886, |
| | 12th July .... | 4 | 25,839, | 2½ | — | 1,615, | — | — |
| | 20th Sept. .... | 10 | 24,701, | 2 | 653, | Nil | 653, | — |
| | 27th Sept. .... | 1 | 20,303, | 3 | 4,710, | 5,076, | — | 366, |
| | 4th Oct. .... | 1 | 19,668, | 4 | 6,627, | 9,834, | — | 3,207, |
| | 15th Nov. .... | 6 | 21,087, | 5 | 4,454, | 15,815, | — | 11,361, |
| | 29th Nov. .... | 2 | 23,620, | 4 | 724, | 11,810, | — | 11,086, |
| | 13th Dec. .... | 2 | 23,860, | 3½ | 347, | 8,947, | — | 8,600, |
| | 27th Dec. .... | 2 | 24,320, | 3 | 29, | 6,080, | — | 6,051, |

The close study of this table, *i.e.*, the excesses over and below a regulated issue, can be brought into connection with many features in the commercial history of the country during the last twenty-seven years, showing the fruits of the Bank's liberality in the early years of the issue, the rapid development when money was too cheap, of speculative enterprise and "company-mongering," the times of "calls," of losses, disappointments, crisis—and it distinctly shows to what extent experience has guided; to what extent the system has failed to guide those who manage the use of the issue.

*Change of Rate of Discount, with the Average of Fiduciary Circulation—Contd.*

[000's omitted.]

| Normal Rate 2½ per Cent. | | | Normal Rate 3 per Cent. | | | Number of Weeks. | To Date. | |
|---|---|---|---|---|---|---|---|---|
| What it ought to be. | Issued Over. | Issued Under. | What it ought to be. | Issued Over. | Issued Under. | | | |
| £ | £ | £ | £ | £ | £ | | | |
| Nil | 4,034, | — | Nil | 4,034, | — | 47 | 18th Nov. | 1868 |
| ,, | 6,304, | — | ,, | 6,304, | — | 2 | 2nd Dec. | |
| 1,703, | 4,362, | — | ,, | 6,065, | — | 4 | 30th Dec. | |
| 1,722, | 4,506, | — | Nil | 6,228, | — | 13 | 31st Mar. | 1869 |
| 4,732, | 3,174, | — | 2,646, | 5,260, | — | 5 | 5th May | |
| 6,512, | 502, | — | 4,070, | 3,044, | — | 5 | 9th June | |
| 5,765, | — | 1,364, | 3,205, | 3,037, | — | 2 | 23rd June | |
| 3,741, | 1,320, | — | 1,559, | 3,502, | — | 3 | 14th July | |
| 1,951, | 2,375, | — | Nil | 4,326, | — | 5 | 18th Aug. | |
| Nil | 4,831, | — | ,, | 4,831, | — | 11 | 3rd Nov. | |
| 1,781, | 3,350, | — | ,, | 5,131, | — | 8 | 29th Dec. | |
| 1,926, | 1,919, | — | Nil | 3,845, | — | 29 | 20th July | 1870 |
| 5,518, | 264, | — | 3,066, | 2,716, | — | 1 | 27th July | |
| 8,979, | — | 2,506, | 5,986, | 487, | — | 1 | 3rd Aug. | |
| 12,761, | — | 7,211, | 9,115, | — | 3,560, | 1 | 10th Aug. | |
| 10,286, | — | 5,546, | 7,938, | — | 3,218, | 1 | 17th Aug. | |
| 7,643, | — | 3,504, | 4,777, | — | 538, | 1 | 24th Aug. | |
| 5,824, | — | 2,215, | 3,291, | — | 318, | 1 | 31st Aug. | |
| 4,084, | — | 1,234, | 1,701, | 1,149, | — | 2 | 14th Sept. | |
| 2,125, | — | 185, | Nil | 1,940, | — | 2 | 24th Sept. | |
| Nil | 2,154, | — | ,, | 2,154, | — | 13 | 28th Dec. | |
| Nil | 2,381, | — | Nil | 2,381, | — | 9 | 1st Mar. | 1871 |
| 2,182, | 182, | — | ,, | 2,314, | — | 6 | 12th April | |
| Nil | 1,038, | — | ,, | 1,038, | — | 9 | 14th June | |
| ,, | — | — | ,, | — | — | 4 | 12th July | |
| ,, | 653, | — | ,, | 653, | — | 10 | 20th Sept. | |
| 2,030, | 2,680, | — | ,, | 4,710, | — | 1 | 27th Sept. | |
| 5,900, | 727, | — | 3,278, | 3,349, | — | 1 | 4th Oct. | |
| 10,504, | — | 6,050, | 7,012, | — | 2,558, | 6 | 15th Nov. | |
| 7,086, | — | 7,362, | 3,936, | — | 3,212, | 2 | 29th Nov. | |
| 4,772, | — | 4,425, | Nil | 347, | — | 2 | 13th Dec. | |
| 2,432, | — | 2,403, | ,, | 29, | — | 2 | 27th Dec. | |

The following table arranges these items at the three respective rates, so that the eye may glance over them and see how the balances lie on the whole and during the respective years:—

TABLE J.—*Showing the Excesses of Fiduciary Issues, and the Excesses of Allowances over Actual Fiduciary Issues made at the respective Nominal Normal Rates of 2, 2½, and 3 per Cent.*

NORMAL RATE AT 2 PER CENT.

| Years | Millions Issued Over Normal Allowance. | | | | | | | | | | | | | | | | | Millions Issued Under Normal Allowance. | | | | | | | | | | | | | | | | |
|---|---|---|---|---|---|---|---|---|---|---|---|---|---|---|---|---|---|---|---|---|---|---|---|---|---|---|---|---|---|---|---|---|---|---|
| | ¼. | ½. | 1. | 2. | 3. | 4. | 5. | 6. | 7. | 8. | 9. | 10. | 11. | 12. | 13. | 14. | 15. | ¼. | Over ½. | 1. | 2. | 3. | 4. | 5. | 6. | 7. | 8. | 9. | 10. | 11. | 12. | 13. | 14. | 15. |
| 1845 | . | . | . | . | 2 | . | 1 | . | . | . | . | . | . | . | . | . | . | . | . | . | . | . | . | . | . | . | . | . | . | . | . | . | . | . |
| '46 | . | . | 2 | . | . | . | . | . | . | . | . | . | . | . | . | . | . | . | . | . | . | . | . | . | . | . | . | . | . | . | . | . | . | . |
| '47 | . | . | . | 3 | 3 | 1 | . | . | . | . | . | . | . | . | . | . | . | . | . | 1 | 1 | 2 | . | . | . | . | . | . | . | . | . | . | . | . |
| '48 | . | 1 | . | . | . | . | . | . | . | . | . | . | . | . | . | . | . | . | 1 | 1 | 1 | . | . | . | . | . | . | . | . | . | . | . | . | . |
| '49 | 1 | 1 | . | . | . | . | . | . | . | . | . | . | . | . | . | . | . | . | . | . | . | . | . | . | . | . | . | . | . | . | . | . | . | . |
| '50 | . | 1 | 1 | . | . | . | . | . | . | . | . | . | . | . | . | . | . | . | . | . | . | . | . | . | . | . | . | . | . | . | . | . | . | . |
| '51 | . | . | . | 1 | . | . | . | . | . | . | . | . | . | . | . | . | . | . | . | . | . | . | . | . | . | . | . | . | . | . | . | . | . | . |
| '52 | . | . | 1 | . | . | . | . | . | . | . | . | . | . | . | . | . | . | 1 | . | . | . | . | . | . | . | . | . | . | . | . | . | . | . | . |
| '53 | . | . | . | 1 | 1 | . | . | . | . | . | . | . | . | . | . | . | . | 1 | 1 | 1 | 1 | 1 | . | . | . | . | . | . | . | . | . | . | . | . |
| '54 | . | . | . | . | . | . | . | . | . | . | . | . | . | . | . | . | . | . | . | . | 1 | 2 | . | . | . | . | . | . | . | . | . | . | . | . |
| '55 | 1 | . | . | . | . | . | . | . | . | . | . | . | . | . | . | . | . | . | 1 | 3 | 1 | 1 | 1 | . | . | . | . | . | . | . | . | . | . | . |
| '56 | . | . | 4 | . | 1 | . | . | . | . | . | . | . | . | . | . | . | . | . | 2 | 1 | 1 | . | . | . | . | . | . | . | . | . | . | . | . | . |
| '57 | 2 | 1 | 1 | . | . | . | . | . | . | . | . | . | . | . | . | . | . | 1 | 2 | . | 1 | . | 1 | . | . | 1 | . | . | . | . | . | . | . | . |
| '58 | . | . | . | . | . | . | . | . | . | . | . | . | . | . | . | . | . | . | 1 | 1 | 2 | 1 | 1 | . | . | . | . | . | . | . | . | . | . | . |
| '59 | 1 | . | . | . | 1 | . | . | . | . | . | . | . | . | . | . | . | . | . | 1 | 1 | 1 | . | . | 1 | . | . | . | . | . | . | . | . | . | . |
| '60 | . | . | . | . | 1 | 1 | . | . | . | . | . | . | . | . | . | . | . | 2 | 1 | 2 | 3 | . | . | . | . | . | . | . | . | . | . | . | . | . |
| '61 | 1 | 1 | . | 2 | . | . | . | . | . | . | . | . | . | . | . | . | . | 1 | 1 | 1 | . | 2 | 2 | . | . | 1 | 1 | . | . | . | . | . | . | . |
| '62 | . | . | 1 | 2 | 2 | . | 1 | . | . | . | . | . | . | . | . | . | . | . | . | . | . | . | . | . | . | . | . | . | . | . | . | . | . | . |
| '63 | 1 | 1 | 1 | . | 2 | . | . | . | . | . | . | . | . | . | . | . | . | 1 | . | 2 | 1 | . | 1 | . | 1 | . | . | . | 1 | . | 1 | . | . | . |
| '64 | . | . | . | . | . | . | . | . | . | . | . | . | . | . | . | . | . | . | . | . | . | . | 1 | 3 | . | 1 | 1 | 2 | 1 | 2 | 2 | 2 | . | . |
| '65 | 1 | 1 | 2 | 1 | 2 | . | . | . | . | . | . | . | . | . | . | . | . | . | . | 3 | . | 2 | 1 | 1 | . | 1 | . | . | . | . | . | . | . | . |
| '66 | . | . | . | . | . | . | . | . | . | . | . | . | . | . | . | . | . | . | . | 1 | . | 3 | 1 | 2 | 1 | . | . | 3 | 2 | . | . | 1 | . | . |
| '67 | . | . | 1 | . | . | . | . | . | . | . | . | . | . | . | . | . | . | 2 | . | 1 | . | . | . | . | . | . | . | . | . | . | . | . | . | . |
| '68 | . | . | 1 | . | . | 2 | . | . | . | . | . | . | . | . | . | . | . | . | . | . | . | . | . | . | . | . | . | . | . | . | . | . | . | . |
| '69 | . | 1 | 1 | 1 | . | . | . | 1 | . | . | . | . | . | . | . | . | . | 1 | 1 | . | 1 | . | . | 1 | . | . | . | . | . | . | . | . | . | . |
| '70 | . | . | . | . | . | . | . | . | . | . | . | . | . | . | . | . | . | . | 2 | . | . | 2 | . | 1 | 2 | 1 | . | . | . | 1 | 1 | . | . | . |
| '71 | . | 1 | . | . | . | . | . | . | . | . | . | . | . | . | . | . | . | 2 | . | 1 | . | 2 | . | . | 1 | . | 1 | . | . | . | 2 | . | . | . |

NORMAL RATE AT 2½ PER CENT.

| Years | ¼. | ½. | 1. | 2. | 3. | 4. | 5. | 6. | 7. | 8. | 9. | 10. | 11. | 12. | 13. | 14. | 15. | ¼. | Over ½. | 1. | 2. | 3. | 4. | 5. | 6. | 7. | 8. | 9. | 10. | 11. | 12. | 13. | 14. | 15. |
|---|---|---|---|---|---|---|---|---|---|---|---|---|---|---|---|---|---|---|---|---|---|---|---|---|---|---|---|---|---|---|---|---|---|---|
| 1845 | . | . | . | . | . | . | 2 | . | 1 | . | . | . | . | . | . | . | . | . | . | . | . | . | . | . | . | . | . | . | . | . | . | . | . | . |
| '46 | . | . | . | . | 1 | 1 | . | . | . | . | . | . | . | . | . | . | . | . | . | . | . | . | . | . | . | . | . | . | . | . | . | . | . | . |
| '47 | 3 | . | 1 | . | . | 2 | 3 | 1 | 1 | . | . | . | . | . | . | . | . | . | . | . | . | . | . | . | . | . | . | . | . | . | . | . | . | . |
| '48 | . | 2 | 2 | . | . | . | . | . | . | . | . | . | . | . | . | . | . | . | . | . | . | . | . | . | . | . | . | . | . | . | . | . | . | . |
| '49 | . | . | 1 | 1 | . | . | . | . | . | . | . | . | . | . | . | . | . | . | . | . | . | . | . | . | . | . | . | . | . | . | . | . | . | . |
| '50 | . | . | . | 1 | 1 | . | . | . | . | . | . | . | . | . | . | . | . | . | . | . | . | . | . | . | . | . | . | . | . | . | . | . | . | . |
| '51 | . | . | . | . | . | 1 | . | . | . | . | . | . | . | . | . | . | . | . | . | . | . | . | . | . | . | . | . | . | . | . | . | . | . | . |
| '52 | . | . | 1 | 1 | . | . | . | . | . | . | . | . | . | . | . | . | . | . | . | . | . | . | . | . | . | . | . | . | . | . | . | . | . | . |
| '53 | . | 1 | 1 | 2 | 1 | 1 | . | . | . | . | . | . | . | . | . | . | . | 1 | . | . | . | . | . | . | . | . | . | . | . | . | . | . | . | . |
| '54 | 2 | 1 | . | . | . | . | . | . | . | . | . | . | . | . | . | . | . | . | . | . | . | . | . | . | . | . | . | . | . | . | . | . | . | . |
| '55 | 1 | . | 2 | 2 | . | . | . | . | . | . | . | . | . | . | . | . | . | 1 | . | 2 | . | . | . | . | . | . | . | . | . | . | . | . | . | . |
| '56 | . | . | 3 | 1 | 3 | 1 | 1 | . | . | . | . | . | . | . | . | . | . | . | . | . | . | . | . | . | . | . | . | . | . | . | . | . | . | . |
| '57 | . | . | 1 | 4 | 2 | 1 | . | . | . | . | . | . | . | . | . | . | . | . | 1 | . | . | 1 | . | . | . | . | . | . | . | . | . | . | . | . |
| '58 | . | 2 | 2 | . | . | . | . | . | . | . | . | . | . | . | . | . | . | 1 | . | 1 | . | . | . | . | . | . | . | . | . | . | . | . | . | . |
| '59 | . | 1 | 2 | 1 | . | . | 1 | . | . | . | . | . | . | . | . | . | . | . | . | 1 | . | . | . | . | . | . | . | . | . | . | . | . | . | . |
| '60 | . | 3 | 2 | 3 | . | . | 1 | 1 | . | . | . | . | . | . | . | . | . | . | . | . | . | . | . | . | . | . | . | . | . | . | . | . | . | . |
| '61 | 1 | . | 2 | 8 | 1 | 2 | . | . | . | . | . | . | . | . | . | . | . | . | 2 | . | . | 1 | 1 | . | . | . | . | . | . | . | . | . | . | . |
| '62 | . | . | . | . | 1 | 2 | 3 | . | . | . | . | . | . | . | . | . | . | . | . | . | . | . | . | . | . | . | . | . | . | . | . | . | . | . |
| '63 | . | . | 2 | 3 | 1 | 1 | 2 | . | . | . | . | . | . | . | . | . | . | . | 1 | . | 1 | . | . | 1 | . | 1 | . | . | . | . | . | . | . | . |
| '64 | . | . | . | . | . | . | . | . | . | . | . | . | . | . | . | . | . | . | 1 | 2 | 1 | 2 | 1 | 3 | 3 | 2 | . | . | . | . | . | . | . | . |
| '65 | . | . | 3 | 1 | 1 | 2 | 2 | 1 | . | . | . | . | . | . | . | . | . | 2 | . | 2 | 1 | . | . | . | . | . | . | . | . | . | . | . | . | . |
| '66 | 1 | . | 1 | 1 | . | . | . | . | . | . | . | . | . | . | . | . | . | 1 | 1 | 3 | . | 1 | 3 | 1 | . | 1 | . | . | . | . | . | . | . | . |
| '67 | . | . | 1 | 3 | . | . | . | . | . | . | . | . | . | . | . | . | . | . | . | . | . | . | . | . | . | . | . | . | . | . | . | . | . | . |
| '68 | . | . | . | . | . | 2 | . | 1 | . | . | . | . | . | . | . | . | . | . | . | . | . | . | . | . | . | . | . | . | . | . | . | . | . | . |
| '69 | . | 1 | 1 | 1 | 2 | 2 | . | . | . | . | . | . | . | . | . | . | . | . | . | 1 | . | . | . | . | . | . | . | . | . | . | . | . | . | . |
| '70 | 1 | . | 1 | 1 | . | . | . | . | . | . | . | . | . | . | . | . | . | 1 | . | 1 | 2 | 1 | . | 1 | . | 1 | . | . | . | . | . | . | . | . |
| '71 | . | 2 | 2 | 2 | . | . | . | . | . | . | . | . | . | . | . | . | . | . | . | . | 1 | . | 1 | . | 1 | 1 | . | . | . | . | . | . | . | . |

NORMAL RATE AT 3 PER CENT.

| Years | ¼. | ½. | 1. | 2. | 3. | 4. | 5. | 6. | 7. | 8. | 9. | 10. | 11. | 12. | 13. | 14. | 15. | ¼. | Over ½. | 1. | 2. | 3. | 4. | 5. | 6. | 7. | 8. | 9. | 10. | 11. | 12. | 13. | 14. | 15. |
|---|---|---|---|---|---|---|---|---|---|---|---|---|---|---|---|---|---|---|---|---|---|---|---|---|---|---|---|---|---|---|---|---|---|---|
| 1845 | . | . | . | . | . | . | 1 | 1 | . | 1 | . | . | . | . | . | . | . | . | . | . | . | . | . | . | . | . | . | . | . | . | . | . | . | . |
| '46 | . | . | . | . | . | . | 2 | . | . | . | . | . | . | . | . | . | . | . | . | . | . | . | . | . | . | . | . | . | . | . | . | . | . | . |
| '47 | . | . | 1 | 3 | . | . | . | 5 | 1 | 1 | . | . | . | . | . | . | . | . | . | . | . | . | . | . | . | . | . | . | . | . | . | . | . | . |
| '48 | . | . | . | 2 | 2 | . | . | . | . | . | . | . | . | . | . | . | . | . | . | . | . | . | . | . | . | . | . | . | . | . | . | . | . | 1 |
| '49 | . | . | 1 | . | . | 1 | . | . | . | . | . | . | . | . | . | . | . | . | . | . | . | . | . | . | . | . | . | . | . | . | . | . | . | . |
| '50 | . | . | . | . | 1 | 1 | . | . | . | . | . | . | . | . | . | . | . | . | . | . | . | . | . | . | . | . | . | . | . | . | . | . | . | . |
| '51 | . | . | . | . | . | . | 1 | . | . | . | . | . | . | . | . | . | . | . | . | . | . | . | . | . | . | . | . | . | . | . | . | . | . | . |
| '52 | . | . | 1 | 1 | . | . | . | . | . | . | . | . | . | . | . | . | . | . | . | . | . | . | . | . | . | . | . | . | . | . | . | . | . | . |
| '53 | . | . | . | 1 | 3 | 3 | . | . | . | . | . | . | . | . | . | . | . | . | . | . | . | . | . | . | . | . | . | . | . | . | . | . | . | . |
| '54 | . | . | . | 3 | . | . | . | . | . | . | . | . | . | . | . | . | . | . | . | . | . | . | . | . | . | . | . | . | . | . | . | . | . | . |
| '55 | . | 1 | . | 3 | 2 | 2 | . | . | . | . | . | . | . | . | . | . | . | . | . | . | . | . | . | . | . | . | . | . | . | . | . | . | . | . |
| '56 | . | . | . | . | 2 | 2 | 3 | 1 | 1 | . | . | . | . | . | . | . | . | . | . | . | . | . | . | . | . | . | . | . | . | . | . | . | . | . |
| '57 | . | . | 1 | . | 1 | 4 | 2 | 1 | . | . | . | . | . | . | . | . | . | . | 1 | . | . | . | . | . | . | . | . | . | . | . | . | . | . | . |
| '58 | . | . | 2 | 4 | . | . | . | . | . | . | . | . | . | . | . | . | . | . | . | . | . | . | . | . | . | . | . | . | . | . | . | . | . | . |
| '59 | . | 1 | . | 2 | 2 | . | 1 | . | . | . | . | . | . | . | . | . | . | . | . | . | . | . | . | . | . | . | . | . | . | . | . | . | . | . |
| '60 | . | . | . | . | . | . | . | . | 2 | . | 2 | 1 | 1 | 2 | . | 1 | 1 | . | . | . | . | . | . | . | . | . | . | . | . | . | . | . | . | . |
| '61 | . | . | 2 | 2 | 1 | 2 | 3 | 1 | . | . | . | . | . | . | . | . | . | 1 | . | 1 | . | . | . | . | . | . | . | . | . | . | . | . | . | . |
| '62 | . | . | . | . | . | . | 6 | . | . | . | . | . | . | . | . | . | . | . | . | . | . | . | . | . | . | . | . | . | . | . | . | . | . | . |
| '63 | 2 | . | 1 | 1 | 1 | 3 | 1 | 2 | . | . | . | . | . | . | . | . | . | . | . | . | 1 | 1 | . | . | . | . | . | . | . | . | . | . | . | . |
| '64 | 1 | 1 | 1 | 1 | . | . | . | . | . | . | . | . | . | . | . | . | . | 1 | 1 | 2 | 4 | 1 | 2 | . | . | . | . | . | . | . | . | . | . | . |
| '65 | 1 | 1 | 3 | . | 2 | 3 | . | 2 | 3 | . | . | . | . | . | . | . | . | . | . | . | . | . | . | . | . | . | . | . | . | . | . | . | . | . |
| '66 | . | . | . | . | . | 4 | 3 | . | 1 | . | . | . | . | . | . | . | . | . | 2 | 3 | 1 | . | . | . | . | . | . | . | . | . | . | . | . | . |
| '67 | . | . | . | . | . | . | 2 | 1 | 1 | . | . | . | . | . | . | . | . | . | . | . | . | . | . | . | . | . | . | . | . | . | . | . | . | . |
| '68 | . | . | . | . | . | . | . | . | 1 | . | 2 | . | . | . | . | . | . | . | . | . | . | . | . | . | . | . | . | . | . | . | . | . | . | . |
| '69 | . | . | . | . | . | . | . | 3 | 2 | 2 | 1 | . | . | . | . | . | . | . | . | . | . | . | . | . | . | . | . | . | . | . | . | . | . | . |
| '70 | 1 | . | 2 | 2 | 1 | . | . | . | . | . | . | . | . | . | . | . | . | 1 | 1 | . | . | 2 | . | . | . | . | . | . | . | . | . | . | . | . |
| '71 | 2 | 2 | 1 | 2 | 1 | 1 | . | . | . | . | . | . | . | . | . | . | . | . | . | . | 1 | 1 | . | . | . | . | . | . | . | . | . | . | . | . |

These tables will also be useful in leading to a clearer appreciation of what I have called "normal" rates of interest. My proposition implies, as a matter of course, that the fiduciary issue made should diminish as the rate of interest declines, until, when the latter reaches its normal state, the fiduciary part should altogether disappear. And here you will perceive what I mean by the self-acting process, which should determine this so-called normal rate. The Bank can allow the whole fiduciary issue to disappear without making a further decline in the rate of discount, and if it can maintain such a higher rate (than the present normal rate), or 3 per cent., on a pure bullion issue, such a rate becomes, *de facto*, the normal rate.

Such supposed higher rate, however, is subject to the checking power of competition in the market; for the Bank, as the central institution, is but the factor of the market, and under the arrangement, in its dependence upon the public, it would have no absolute power of its own in defiance of its constituents. If it held the rate too high, for the purpose of obtaining bullion, without issuing fiduciary notes, it would lose business which the market would take up. Hence the *necessary store of bullion would settle itself in a natural way by its competition with the sovereigns or bullion notes in the open market.* If the Bank held the rate too low, it would be overwhelmed with business. This same principle of competition would apply to all stages of interest and all stages of the issue, as in some measure it does now.

For the commencement of the new issue it would, however, be necessary to establish some starting point as the normal rate to begin with. It is of little importance whether this rate be 2 or 2½ or 3 per cent., for as after all, from the previous remarks, its influence is halved or quartered, there would be question only of this fractional effect upon proportions of increase of either one-eighth, or one-tenth, or one-twelfth. And whether the one or the other be adopted, or whether they were changed during the course of the experience made, any one of the three rates would afford a firm clear ground, without detracting from the definite and comprehensive character of the arrangement. Nevertheless, as, according to the figures shown, the choice lies between 2 as too low and 3 as too high (and for this reason normal rates of below 2 or above 3 are already out of the question), the proper figure would be 2½ per cent.; and this, as I have stated, gives the slight advantage in favour of issue which is desirable as a margin. So far, I think, we can follow the course of experience as a guide, for, when experience shows an infallible rule, it obtains the value of a principle.

If the arrangement be carried out, will it be simple in its control, or more complicated than now? The first thing which the managers of the Bank have to watch is bullion. They may maintain the rate of discount, without fiduciary issue, at any figure they like, until they have enough—or, rather, until the country has enough—for, if the Bank overdoes it, the competition of the market will check it. But, whether the bullion reserve be large or small, they can always observe the rates of exchange, and, independently of the market, protect their store of bullion whenever these exchanges, or their balance, appear against us. I do not know whether the close observance of the exchanges now forms part of the Bank's policy; I presume it does, but have no means of judging of the accuracy of the foundations. My impression is that there are very few people in this country who have more than a superficial knowledge of exchanges as a whole, and who can calculate to a point the results of shipments of bullion according to freight, charges, Mint and Bank regulations, stamps, and interest; yet upon such minute points do the exchanges turn; and the information is easily obtained and kept up. Our stock of bullion at the Bank is in immediate contact with exchanges, as the reservoir between our circulating coin and foreign trade; and nothing is more important than a close watch of all the channels through which it is supplied or exhausted. Any error, which might be avoided by quick appreciation and forestalled by a timely movement in the rate, may cause the loss of a million or more of bullion; and we all know how anxious we are when a few hundred thousands, or even 100,000*l.*, are withdrawn—*vide* the "money articles." You will agree with me that this matter of the stock of bullion stands on its own merits, and that less local prejudice, or rather, more cosmopolitan intelligence, may lead to a better appreciation of exchange matters. And when these are fully brought to bear, the operation of guiding the bullion store will become more automatic than it is at present—more rule will prevail and less discretion be required; and although the latter will still have its play, and most effectively if occasion calls for it, you may admit that, on the whole, the control over the bullion can be exercised with more certainty, therefore with more simplicity, upon my plan than under the present system.

The next thing the Bank would have to control is the fiduciary issue for satisfying the local demand. Finding the exchanges favourable, it can, without fear, make the issue; indeed, it must make it so as to prevent not only too large an accumulation of bullion, but also on account of the competition of the open market; and when it reduces the rate, and with it the issue, it just performs that beneficient and automatic action which marks the approach between two contending forces, and therefore enables the judgment to be formed at once, because the effect is brought about at once.

This more regulated proceeding does not, as I have said before, prevent the directors from giving to the country all the benefit of their wisdom and discretion, and they can exercise the latter with all the more immediately visible results just because certain main points are no longer subject to doubt.

And if, in thus meeting the discount market in either way, the directors were able to secure to themselves a regular supply of bills—that is, if the respective resources of the Bank, as well as the fiduciary issue, sought to meet the requirements regularly, without repelling them excessively at one time, and at other times spasmodically attracting them, if the "Discounted bills and temporary "advances" obtained anything like regularity (as they ought to do in every bank) the *Bank would supply an additional element of compensation* for regulating the market, viz., a reasonable absorption of the demand for money. How this element of compensation, which, as perhaps the most important of all, I must ask you now to add to the other elements spoken of as working in the same direction, for halving (so to speak) abrupt differences, has hitherto been treated, appears from the returns furnished.

The third subject which the directors must watch, is the ordinary one of general mercantile credit and that of individual credits. And here let me remark, that in spite of the high and, I may say, noble intention of those who rule the Bank, in spite of excellent machinery and powerful position, the Bank cannot control matters of general or special credit unless it is in regular and almost unbroken connection with the market, in continuous practical connection in which matters of fact and actual insight replace matters of hearsay. Through these means of regular connection only can the Bank retain its power and influence in the market, and it is not enough that it should merely have a hand in it, but as the richest and best institution it should be able to take the lead, so that it may be enabled to retain sufficient influence in general mercantile credit, the term "general" here being an element in the guidance of a policy. Without this general and continuous policy the Bank is liable to run an eccentric course, by which at certain times it encourages, at other times suddenly discourages a particular class of business, as the experience of bankers and discounters has shown. Further, when this practical share in the business of the country is gained, it will pay, and will bring with it a certain perfection of arrangements, which, with a broken course, remain ineffective for some time, in spite of every intelligent and high minded endeavour, as far as excellency of control is concerned. Many bankers and others may be able to appreciate these remarks and estimate them accordingly.

That this share of the Bank in the real business of the country can be recovered when the present misconceptions as to fiduciary issue are removed, and a better system is substituted, is not a matter of doubt in my mind. Is it not an astonishing fact, that whereas all other national banks have increased their business in accordance with the growth of the respective nation's trade and beyond (see Bank of France, Prussia, &c.); and whereas, our own joint stock banks have shown such splendid prosperity, whereas our trade has trebled since 1844, the Bank of England should alone have lagged behind, scarcely improving its position? It is true that during late years there have been larger deposits, the Bank has also more bullion; but this increase bears no sensible proportion to that of the general prosperity. And although the stock of bullion is larger, does it not appear as if this were consequent upon some change of policy in answering demands through the reserve—*i.e.*, in not acceding to them—does it not seem as if this slight improvement was rather due to some mysterious and painful effort? Then where lies the fault?

In my opinion, the Bank of England, with its gigantic capital and its superior management, ought to hold an amount of good bills largely in excess of that of any other bank or an aggregate of them, it ought to pay larger dividends than it does now, and thus, by making larger profits, be able to meet the public demands more fairly, and thereby bring into action another factor of compensation, through whom excesses of interest, excesses of import and export of bullion, excesses of speculation, with all their concurrent excrescences, may find amelioration for the mutual benefit of the Bank and all classes of the community, if not of the great system of commerce all over the world. If the idle note reserve were abolished, the deposits of the Bank, the real monetary power of the country, would enter again into their legitimate rights, and be better invested; it is now the deposits which rescue the Bank from the false position of the fiduciary issue; whereas the power of reserve contained in the proposal I make here would come to the assistance of the deposits. Under such altered circumstances, the question might even be mooted whether the Bank should not pay interest on certain classes of such deposits, as other Banks do.

The plan proposed by me demands, of course, a revision of the arrangement as to the share of profit which the State receives. The State is entitled to a share, not so much for the sake of State necessities, as in vindication of a principle. For the privilege and authority given to a bank to issue fiduciary notes resemble the loan of a capital; and if the Bank had this capital free of interest, the privilege would be too much, and become an odious monopoly. The fairest way of looking upon this matter is that of regarding the fiduciary issue as an interest-bearing deposit, upon the usual banking rules. Under the present Act the State receives 195,000*l.* per annum. I have already stated my objection to that, and propose that the State's profit should in future be in exact accordance with the actual issue made and the actual profit. If at any time an extra issue of, say, 10 millions were made, employed at 5 per cent., the gross profit would be 500,000*l.*; an issue of 5 millions, at 4 per cent., would give 200,000*l.*; an issue of 12 millions, at 8 per cent., would give 960,000*l.* At other times, there would be no issue and no profit. Referring now to what I have said before respecting the cost of bullion notes, I would propose that from the produce of the fiduciary issue there should first be deducted the expense attendant the issue. Among the items of this expenditure are several which may be reduced, viz., bankers' compensation (which expires at the expiration of the present issue); the expenses for the Bullion Office, &c., as not properly belonging to the fiduciary issue; other economies might be made; and in consideration of the fact that the Bank otherwise, through the same system, effects certain economies in its banking department, the Bank, or a bank, might be induced to accept the note contract as involving an annual expenditure of 120,000*l.* There would then remain upon the gross profits named above, balances of 380,000*l.*, 80,000*l.*, and 840,000*l.* At other times there would be a fiduciary issue below 5 millions, just covering or scarcely covering the expenditure; and there may be times when there is no necessity for any fiduciary issue at all. These times should be debited to the issue account; so that the whole arrangement stands on a pure, equitable basis, without the shadow of suspicion as to one-sidedness. The balances remaining should then be divided between the State and Bank, either by crediting the State with the interest at one-half or 1 per cent. below the Bank rate, or by allowing the Bank a proportionate share by way of *del credere*, the greater portion of the produce, of course, going to the State. But the Bank should suffer no loss whatever, as, according to my showing, it does now, and for the advantage gained, including the higher interest obtainable on its deposits, the Bank might be satisfied with but a small share on the net profits of the fiduciary issue.

It is quite true that in such a case the Chancellor of the Exchequer could no longer count on the regular annual income from the Bank of 195,000*l.* Instead of that he may sometimes go without, at other times receive much larger sums; and the more equitable operation of the whole may, after all, bring better results. I am of opinion that the actual working of the system would result in far more regular annual profits. Certain it is that, if we succeed in avoiding crises and their baneful consequences, there will be a considerable increase in the tax-bearing power of the country. Further, if the Bank Act requires amendment at all, such amendment must either be the total abolition of the issue, and with it that of the 195,000*l.*, or some more elastic plan in lieu of the present fixed limit, and to such elasticity the fixed payment to the State could not be reconciled. It is time altogether that our statesmen and financiers should open their eyes to the conflict between such an item in the Budget and the great diverse interests, the very foundation of it all, at stake in this instance; and that, instead of adhering tenaciously to such small tax, for the mere sake of the budget, they should gain the conception that, by abolishing it they might confer an incalculable benefit upon the public, the Bank, the State, *and* the budget.

It remains for me to state, that my proposal requires no essential alteration in the constitution of the Bank. The separation between the issue department and the banking department may be maintained as it is now, and there would, at one time, appear bullion on one side, notes on the other, without Government and other securities; at another time, certain sums in Government and other securities would appear in order to account for the increase of issue. These securities might be transferred from the banking department as the case may arise, to serve, as the State debt and other securities do now, as security for the issue. The proceeding is not new, for in 1857 the Bank transferred two millions of its Government securities from the banking department to the issue, a proceeding which, in the minds of some illogical financiers, was designated as the "safety valve" to the present system. You see how this resembles my plan, with this difference, that I require the safety valve to be in continuous operation for the regulation of the machinery, whereas these alchymists want to wait with its application until the machinery has whirled itself into partial destruction, and until the boiler is on the point of bursting.

For my part I consider the security and guarantee of the Bank itself perfect, and further, I think that in the case of issue "Other "securities," notably fair bills of exchange realisable, are the proper and legitimate guarantees. Other State banks think so too, but upon that point we need open no controversy; the British public looks to Government and other securities, and these can be furnished by the Bank, to stand as directly applicable to the issue, the interest on them belonging to the Bank. No change whatever would be required between the Bank and the public. The note system would go on as before, and nobody would be the wiser for the alteration but those who study the weekly accounts of the Bank, who would find that the large, inexplicable, and demoralising "reserves" of notes were no longer in the account, but they would also be aware that, in spite of the disappearance of this item money could be had at any time on fair principles of compensation, to meet contingencies.

I claim that the plan I have suggested will, when in operation, do the following:—

Firstly. It will, by a self-acting process, determine the amount of bullion which is suitable to the trade of this country, both as stock in the Bank, and as circulating coin in the country.

Secondly. It will check the export of bullion without disturbing the amount of currency at home, for the fiduciary power arising will replace the currency drawn in from the inland trade, and it will enable us to dispose of a surplus of bullion against profitable investment in a gradual and regular manner.

Thirdly. It will, by a self-acting process, determine a normal rate of interest, the departures from which will not be so violent or excessive as they are now, and thereby it will counteract undue speculation as well as ameliorate the severe effects of the results of speculation.

Fourthly. It will altogether put in force elements of compensation from which the commerce and prosperity of this country will derive advantages.

It remains for me only to notice other suggestions, which have been made from time to time in reference to an improved issue. One gentleman has lately proposed that the Bank of England, instead of holding English Government securities for the guarantee of the issue, should hold foreign securities, so that at any time they could be sent abroad to obtain the gold necessary for us. The suggestion is not suitable, if only for the question of buying-and-selling-price. Nor can the Bank of England hold foreign bills of which the full value may be realised. As a *quasi* national bank, the storehouse of the country's wealth, it has an implied degree of political importance which must be kept free of foreign securities of any kind. That our other banks and private bankers would do well to invest in foreign bills, so as to obtain a turn of exchange in our favour when necessary, I admit, and in the paper which I read before this Society in February, 1870, I advocated this policy. In order to carry it out, the science of exchanges and the considerations of credit connected with it must first be better understood in this country.

Other suggestions have been made, the most current one being that of the insufficiency of the 15 millions of fiduciary issue, as compared to the larger store of bullion, and the increase of the country's trade. So it has been suggested that this 15 millions should be increased to 20 or 25 millions. If you should agree with the evidence and the views I have here laid before you, you will admit that such an increase in the fixed fiduciary issue could only tend to increase the present gigantic evils from which we suffer.

The more reasonable of the reformers begin to perceive that the issue must be elastic, so as to admit of extension without neglecting the principle of concurrent limits. Several plans may be suggested for this purpose, but none has as yet been definitely proposed ; you will also admit that, in the main, the controlling and compensating factors should be found in the system itself, and not be dependent upon an outside assumption, just as little as any scientific subject, which, having the germ of vitality in itself, can be correctly and logically developed by dependence on any assumption or maxim outside its proper sphere. When such outside assumption carries an alchymistical semblance of being connected with financing, and is, falsely, taken as a guide, confusion becomes worse confounded. Such is the case with the idea of fixed issue, and the "stability" ensuing therefrom in our present arrangement, until some of our best thinkers have despaired of ever unravelling the mystery. Such would also be the case with so-called fixed sliding scales which assume a definite amount of bullion with definite rates of interest.

The question which those who peruse this paper must ask themselves is this: Does the proposal here made contain that great principle of prudence and conservatism which at all events is implied in the present fixed issue and its limitation? Let the proposal be tested by examples, *i.e.*, by calculation, and it will be found that, if anything, it is more prudent. If this point be gained, the most conservative supporters of the present issue, whose just conservatism is founded on the fear that any new proposal might lack this element of prudence, may be willing to admit that the plan here suggested combines this desirable characteristic with the element of productiveness.